本书旗帜鲜明地指出：有为政府与有效市场相融合，是成熟市场经济的基本标志；世界各国与各区域经济的增长，存在企业竞争和区域政府竞争的双重驱动力；竞争优势理论是破解"比较优势理论"困境，跨越"比较优势陷阱"，推动一个国家一个区域经济可持续增长的根本路径。

# Preface

Exploring the intrinsic sources of economic growth within a region or nation has consistently been a core topic of relentless inquiry among economists worldwide.

Classical economists such as Adam Smith, Malthus, and David Ricardo meticulously examined the relationship between the accumulation of social products, investment, and economic growth under the conditions of the Industrial Revolution. Neoclassical economists, represented by Marshall, believed that savings and investments could be regulated through interest rate changes to facilitate capital accumulation, and that full employment and accelerated economic growth could be promoted through price mechanisms and wage adjustments. Since the 1950s, economists like Tobin and Solow in the United States, Swan in Australia, and Meade in the United Kingdom have applied classical economic principles to propose a series of economic growth theories and models. The new economic growth theory, represented by economists such as Romer and Lucas, emphasizes the decisive role of knowledge accumulation and technological progress in economic growth. Douglas North and others have introduced institutional change and property rights arrangements into economic growth analysis, arguing that effectively incentivized economic organizations are key to economic growth.

In recent years, Professor Joseph Stiglitz, who won the Nobel Prize in Economics in 2001, has suggested that the best way to achieve sustained growth and long-term efficiency is to find an appropriate balance between government and the market, thereby steering the world economy back towards a more equitable and stable growth process. The research of Romer and Nordhaus, winners of the 2018 Nobel Prize in Economics, converges on the conclusion that knowledge, technology, and innovation are the endogenous drivers of economic growth, and that the relationship between carbon emissions, climate change, and sustainable economic growth should be studied.

Throughout this process, the theories of comparative advantage and competitive

# Theory of
# COMPETITIVE ADVANTAGE
Economic Growth Orientation

# 竞争优势论
经济增长导向说

陈云贤　徐雷　◎著

## 内 容 简 介

探寻一个区域或国家经济增长的内在源泉，成为世界各国经济学家不懈追溯的核心论题。本书倡导在探索一个区域或国家的经济增长路径、挖掘其经济增长源泉时，应高度重视区域政府在中观经济领域的市场主体作用。它与微观经济领域企业市场主体关联互动，形成市场竞争的双重驱动力，其理论能有效克服比较优势陷阱或单一企业竞争理论的缺陷，其实践能逐一破解为什么一些区域或国家富有而另一些区域或国家贫穷，为什么一些区域或国家能出现经济增长奇迹，以及世界各国对经济增长内在源泉与路径选择的迷茫。

**图书在版编目（CIP）数据**

竞争优势论：经济增长导向说 / 陈云贤，徐雷著. 北京：北京大学出版社，2025.3. -- ISBN 978-7-301-36046-0

Ⅰ．F114

中国国家版本馆 CIP 数据核字第 2025BZ2764 号

| | |
|---|---|
| 书　　名 | 竞争优势论：经济增长导向说<br>JINGZHENG YOUSHI LUN：JINGJI ZENGZHANG DAOXIANG SHUO |
| 著作责任者 | 陈云贤　徐　雷　著 |
| 策划编辑 | 王显超 |
| 责任编辑 | 陶鹏旭 |
| 标准书号 | ISBN 978-7-301-36046-0 |
| 出版发行 | 北京大学出版社 |
| 地　　址 | 北京市海淀区成府路 205 号　100871 |
| 网　　址 | http：//www.pup.cn　　新浪微博：@北京大学出版社 |
| 电子邮箱 | 编辑部 pup6@pup.cn　　总编室 zpup@pup.cn |
| 电　　话 | 邮购部 010-62752015　　发行部 010-62750672　　编辑部 010-62750667 |
| 印　刷　者 | 三河市北燕印装有限公司 |
| 经　销　者 | 新华书店 |
| | 787 毫米 x 1092 毫米　16 开本　23.5 印张　422 千字<br>2025 年 3 月第 1 版　2025 年 3 月第 1 次印刷 |
| 定　　价 | 168.00 元 |

未经许可，不得以任何方式复制或抄袭本书之部分或全部内容。

**版权所有，侵权必究**

举报电话：010-62752024　　电子邮箱：fd@pup.cn

图书如有印装质量问题，请与出版部联系，电话：010-62756370

advantage have emerged as frameworks for regions or countries to explore paths to economic growth. The essence of the comparative advantage theory is the theory of comparative cost trade, which posits that countries or regions should rely on their resource endowments,

# 序言

探寻一个区域或国家的经济增长内在源泉，历来都是世界各国经济学家不懈探索的核心课题。

古典经济学家亚当·斯密、马尔萨斯和大卫·李嘉图等悉心探究工业革命条件下社会产品的积累和投资与经济增长的关系。以马歇尔为代表的新古典经济学家认为可以通过利率变动调节储蓄和投资，从而进行资本积累，还可以借助价格机制和工资变动促进充分就业，加速经济增长。20世纪50年代以来，美国的托宾和索洛、澳大利亚的斯旺和英国的米德等应用古典经济学原理，提出一系列经济增长理论和模型。以罗默和卢卡斯等为代表的经济学家提出的新经济增长理论，强调知识积累、技术进步对经济增长的决定性作用。道格拉斯·诺思等把制度变迁和产权制度安排引入经济增长分析，认为有效激励的经济组织是经济增长的关键。

近年来，获得2001年诺贝尔经济学奖的约瑟夫·施蒂格利茨教授认为，获得持续增长和长期效率的最佳方法是找到政府与市场之间的适当平衡，使得世界经济回到一个更加公平、稳定的增长过程中。2018年诺贝尔经济学奖得主罗默和诺德豪斯的研究共同指向一个结论——知识、技术和创新是经济内生增长动力，应研究碳排放、气候变化与经济可持续增长的关系问题等。

在这一过程中，产生了一个区域或国家探寻经济增长路径的比较优势理论与竞争优势理论。比较优势理论的实质是比较成本贸易理论，该理论认为各国或各

concentrate on producing and exporting products with "comparative advantages", and importing products with "comparative disadvantages". The economies of various countries or regions form a continuous spectrum from low-income agricultural economies to high-income industrialized economies; with rational division of labor, resources can be fully utilized, and the total volume of import and export trade can be balanced. However, the competitive advantage theory suggests that a country's trade advantage is not simply determined by its natural resources, labor, interest rates, and exchange rates, as traditional international trade theory claims, but is largely dependent on its capacity for industrial innovation and upgrading. The formation and development of competitive advantages have increasingly played a significant role.

It should be said that, on the one hand, the explorations of economists throughout history into the intrinsic sources and paths of economic growth have made outstanding contributions to the economic development of countries worldwide. On the other hand, however, the author believes that their perspectives have primarily been confined to the realm of industrial economics and the market entity of microeconomic enterprises.

The core viewpoint of this book emphasizes that the economic development of a region or country is driven by the dual forces of enterprise competition and regional government competition. Among regional governments, there exists a competition framework consisting of "9-in-3", which persists throughout various growth stages dominated by industrial economic competition and cooperation, urban economic competition and cooperation, innovative economic competition and cooperation, as well as shared economic competition and cooperation. Regional economic competition and cooperation exhibit evolutionary characteristics of gradient shift and the formation of gradient equilibrium. The integration of an effective government with an efficient market is a fundamental indication of the maturity of a regional or national market economy. The competition and cooperation between these dual-entity of the market economy constitute the fundamental path to overcoming the pitfalls of comparative advantage or the deficiencies of the single-enterprise competition theory, thereby driving economic transformation, social transition, and sustainable high-quality economic growth in a region or country. From the perspective of economic growth, this provides answers to three fundamental questions that exist in reality: what are the intrinsic sources and paths of economic growth in various countries worldwide, why are some regions or countries wealthy while others are poor, and how to comprehend the economic growth miracles of certain regions or countries.

By this point, this book reveals the following points.

(1) Enterprises serve as market entity in the microeconomic realm, while regional governments serve as market entity in the mezzoeconomic realm. This breaks through the traditional economic approach of defining government economic behavior from a marginal market perspective.

区域应依靠资源禀赋，集中生产并出口其具有"比较优势"的产品，进口其具有"比较劣势"的产品。各国或各区域的经济是一条从低收入农业经济一直到高收入工业化经济的连续频谱，合理分工，资源就可以得到充分利用，进出口贸易总额就可以平衡。而竞争优势理论认为，一国的贸易优势并不像传统的国际贸易理论宣称的那样简单取决于一国的自然资源、劳动力、利率、汇率，而是在很大程度上取决于一国的产业创新和升级的能力，竞争优势的形成和发展已经日益发挥出重要作用。

应该说，一方面，历代经济学家对经济增长内在源泉和经济增长路径的探讨，为世界各国的经济发展做出了卓越贡献。但另一方面，笔者认为他们的视野仍然主要局限在产业经济这一领域和微观经济企业这一市场主体上。

本书的核心观点强调，一个区域或国家的经济发展存在企业竞争和区域政府竞争双重驱动力；区域政府之间存在"三类九要素"竞争，并且这一竞争贯穿于由产业经济竞争与合作主导的增长阶段、由城市经济竞争与合作主导的增长阶段、由创新经济竞争与合作主导的增长阶段，以及由共享经济竞争与合作主导的增长阶段；区域经济竞争与合作存在梯度推移与形成梯度均衡的演进特征。有为政府与有效市场的相互融合，是一个区域或国家市场经济成熟的基本表现；市场经济双重主体的竞争与合作，是克服比较优势陷阱或单一企业竞争理论缺陷，推动一个区域或国家经济转轨、社会转型和经济可持续高质量增长的根本路径。这从经济增长的角度，回答了世界各国经济增长的内在源泉与经济增长路径是什么，为什么一些区域或国家富有而另一些区域或国家贫穷，怎么理解一些区域或国家的经济增长奇迹这三个现实存在的基本问题。

至此，本书揭示出以下几点。

（1）企业是微观经济领域市场主体，区域政府是中观经济领域市场主体。它突破了传统经济学从市场边缘视角来界定政府经济行为的局限性。

(2) Economic behaviors of countries, regions, and enterprises exhibit correlation effects, with a ternary structure interacting to jointly promote economic development. This transcends the constraints of the traditional economic growth model based on a macro-micro binary structure.

(3) Regional governments engage in competition across "9-in-3", and the development of the market economy is driven by the dual forces of governments and enterprises. This challenges the assumption of a single market driver by enterprises within the framework of Western economics.

(4) Regional governments need to foresighted leading in the four stages of economic growth, constructing new engines of investment, innovation, and regulation. This moves beyond the traditional single "trade engine" path focused on the demand side of the industrial economy.

(5) The competitive advantage theory defines the competitive performance of regional governments across the "9-in-3", the dynamic competitive characteristics in the four stages of regional economic growth, and the formation of gradient structures and gradient equilibrium in regional economic competition. It effectively addresses the confusion surrounding the intrinsic sources and path choices of economic growth in theoretical and practical contexts worldwide.

We hereby seek guidance and learning from fellow economists, and hope that this book can make some exploratory contributions to the theory of economic growth!

2024.6.21.

（2）国家、区域、企业的经济行为存在关联效应，三元结构互动共推经济发展。它突破了传统经济学宏观与微观二元结构经济增长的束缚。

（3）区域政府存在"三类九要素"竞争，市场经济发展存在政府与企业双重驱动力。它突破了西方经济学架构中企业单一市场驱动力的假定。

（4）区域政府需要在经济增长的四个阶段进行超前引领，构建投资、创新、规则新引擎。它突破了传统经济学产业经济需求侧下的"贸易引擎"单一路径。

（5）竞争优势理论对区域政府"三类九要素"竞争表现、区域经济增长四个阶段的竞争动态特征，以及区域经济竞争的梯度结构和梯度均衡的形成这三个方面做出界定。它有效破解了世界各国在理论与实践中对经济增长内在源泉与路径选择的迷茫。

我们借此向各位经济学同人请教与学习，也愿此书能为经济增长理论做出一点探索与贡献！

2024.6.21.

# Contents

**Chapter 1  Limitations of the Comparative Advantage Development Strategy / 002**

Section1: Controversies of the Comparative Advantage Development Strategy / 002

　　I. The Comparative Advantage Development Strategy and Its Theoretical Development / 002

　　II. Academic Critiques of the Comparative Advantage Development Strategy / 004

Section 2: Comparative Advantage under Conditions of Large Country Demand, Economies of Scale, and Factor Mobility / 008

　　I. Basic Model Setup / 008

　　II. Large Country Demand and Comparative Advantage / 018

　　III. Economies of Scale and Comparative Advantage / 022

　　IV. Factor Mobility and Comparative Advantage / 032

Section 3: Scope of Application of Comparative Advantage Theory / 042

　　I. Scope of Application / 042

　　II. Beware of the "Comparative Advantage Trap" / 046

**Chapter 2  The Rise and Defects of Michael Porter's Competitive Advantage Theory / 050**

Section1: Michael Porter's Competitive Advantage Theory / 050

　　I. Michael Porter's Diamond Model of Competitive Advantage Theory / 050

　　II. Four Stages of National Competitive Advantage Development / 054

Section 2: Critique of Comparative Advantage Theory by Competitive Advantage Theory / 056

　　I. Views of Competitive Advantage Theory / 056

　　II. Industrial Export Data Fail to Support Comparative Advantage Theory / 058

Section 3: Limitations of Michael Porter's Competitive Advantage Theory / 064

　　I. Insufficient Understanding of the Role of Government / 064

　　II. Inadequate Explanation of How to Upgrade from Low to High Development Stages / 066

# 目录

## 第一章 比较优势发展战略的局限性 / 003

### 第一节 比较优势发展战略面临的争议 / 003
一、比较优势发展战略及其理论发展 / 003
二、学界对比较优势发展战略的质疑 / 005

### 第二节 大国需求、规模经济与要素可流动条件下的比较优势 / 009
一、基本模型设定 / 009
二、大国需求与比较优势 / 019
三、规模经济与比较优势 / 023
四、要素可流动与比较优势 / 033

### 第三节 比较优势理论的适用范围 / 043
一、适用范围 / 043
二、警惕"比较优势陷阱" / 047

## 第二章 迈克尔·波特竞争优势理论的兴起与缺陷 / 051

### 第一节 迈克尔·波特竞争优势理论 / 051
一、迈尔克·波特竞争优势理论的钻石模型 / 051
二、国家竞争优势发展的四个阶段 / 055

### 第二节 竞争优势理论对比较优势理论的批判 / 057
一、竞争优势理论的观点 / 057
二、产业出口数据难以佐证比较优势理论 / 059

### 第三节 迈克尔·波特竞争优势理论的局限 / 065
一、对政府作用的认识存在不足 / 065
二、对如何从低发展阶段向高发展阶段升级未做足够阐释 / 067

**Chapter 3  Mezzoeconomics and Its Competitive Advantage Theory / 070**

  Section 1: The Inheritance and Development of Mezzoeconomics to Existing Economic Theories / 070

  Section 2: Core Concepts of Mezzoeconomics / 076

   I. "Urban Resources" "Resource Generation", and "Generative Resources" / 076

   II. "Primary Resources" "Secondary Resources", and "Inverse Resources" / 084

   III. The "Efficient Markets" + "Effective Governments" Combination Model in Mezzoeconomics / 086

  Section 3: Dual Attributes of Regional Governments and Dual-entity Theory of Market Competition / 090

   I. "Quasi-micro" Attributes of Regional Governments / 090

   II. "Quasi-macro" Attributes of Regional Governments / 097

   III. Regional Competition under the Leadership of Regional Governments / 098

   IV. Dual-entity Theory of Market Competition / 100

  Section 4: Three Levels of Competitive Advantage Theory in Mezzoeconomics / 106

   I. "9-in-3" Competition of Regional Governments / 106

   II. Four Stages of Regional Economic Growth / 108

   III. Gradient Transference Model of Regional Economic Competition / 112

**Chapter 4  "9-in-3" Competitive Performance of Regional Governments / 116**

  Section 1: Characteristics of Regional Government Competition / 116

   I. Objectives of Regional Government Competition / 116

   II. Differences between Regional Government Competition and Enterprise Competition / 122

  Section 2: The Key to Aspects of Regional Government Competition / 128

   I. Concept Innovation / 130

   II. Institutional Innovation / 132

   III. Organizational Innovation / 133

   IV. Technological Innovation / 135

  Section 3: "9-in-3" Competition of Regional Governments / 136

   I. Level of Regional Economic Development / 140

   II. Regional Economic Policy Measures / 142

   III. Regional Economic Management Efficiency / 146

第三章　中观经济学及其竞争优势理论 / 071

　　第一节　中观经济学对现有经济学理论的继承与发展 / 071

　　第二节　中观经济学的核心概念 / 077

　　　　一、"城市资源""资源生成"与"生成性资源" / 077

　　　　二、"原生性资源""次生性资源"与"逆生性资源" / 085

　　　　三、中观经济学下的"有效市场"+"有为政府"组合模式 / 087

　　第三节　区域政府双重属性与市场竞争双重主体论 / 091

　　　　一、区域政府的"准微观"属性 / 091

　　　　二、区域政府的"准宏观"属性 / 097

　　　　三、区域政府引领下的区域竞争 / 099

　　　　四、市场竞争双重主体论 / 101

　　第四节　中观经济学竞争优势理论的三个层次 / 107

　　　　一、区域政府的"三类九要素"竞争 / 107

　　　　二、区域经济增长的四个阶段 / 109

　　　　三、区域经济竞争梯度推移模型 / 113


第四章　区域政府"三类九要素"竞争表现 / 117

　　第一节　区域政府竞争特点 / 117

　　　　一、区域政府竞争目标 / 117

　　　　二、区域政府竞争与企业竞争的区别 / 123

　　第二节　区域政府竞争的关键 / 129

　　　　一、理念创新 / 131

　　　　二、制度创新 / 133

　　　　三、组织创新 / 133

　　　　四、技术创新 / 135

　　第三节　区域政府"三类九要素"竞争 / 137

　　　　一、区域经济发展水平 / 141

　　　　二、区域经济政策措施 / 143

　　　　三、区域经济管理效率 / 147

Section 4: Determination Mechanism of Regional Government Competitiveness: DRP Model / 152
    I. Fiscal Surplus and "9-in-3" Determination Mechanism / 152
    II. Comprehensive Measurement and Objective Function / 160
    III. Government Performance Evaluation System / 164

## Chapter 5    Four Stages Competitive Dynamic Characteristics of Regional Economic Growth / 176

Section 1: Growth Stage Dominated by Industrial Economic Competition and Cooperation / 176
    I. Competition for Primary Resources / 176
    II. Regional Industrial Policy Matching in the Growth Stage Dominated by Industrial Economic Competition and Cooperation / 179
    III. Three Processes in the Growth Stage Dominated by Industrial Economic Competition and Cooperation / 180

Section 2: Growth Stage Dominated by Urban Economic Competition and Cooperation / 183
    I. The Process of Investment-driven Economic Growth Is the Development and Competition for Secondary Resources by Regional Governments / 184
    II. Regional Governments Supporting Policies in the Growth Stage Dominated by Urban Economic Competition and Cooperation / 186
    III. Dynamic Evolution of the Growth Stage Dominated by Urban Economic Competition and Cooperation / 188

Section 3: Growth Stage Dominated by Innovative Economic Competition and Cooperation / 191
    I. Concept Innovation of Regional Governments / 192
    II. Technological Innovation of Regional Governments / 194
    III. Organizational Innovation of Regional Governments / 194
    IV. Institutional Innovation of Regional Governments / 194

Section 4: Growth Stage Dominated by Shared Economic Competition and Cooperation / 196
    I. Characteristics of the Growth Stage Dominated by Shared Economic Competition and Cooperation / 198
    II. Four Basic Principles for Shared Products between Regional Governments / 202

第四节 区域政府竞争力决定机制：DRP 模型 / 153
　　一、财政盈余与"三类九要素"的决定机制 / 153
　　二、综合测度和目标函数 / 161
　　三、政府绩效评估体系 / 165

第五章　区域经济增长四阶段竞争动态特征 / 177
　第一节 由产业经济竞争与合作主导的增长阶段 / 177
　　一、对原生性资源的竞争 / 177
　　二、由产业经济竞争与合作主导的增长阶段的区域产业政策匹配 / 179
　　三、由产业经济竞争与合作主导的增长阶段的三个过程 / 181
　第二节 由城市经济竞争与合作主导的增长阶段 / 183
　　一、投资驱动经济增长的过程是区域政府对次生性资源的开发与争夺 / 185
　　二、由城市经济竞争与合作主导的增长阶段的区域政府配套政策 / 187
　　三、由城市经济竞争与合作主导的增长阶段的动态演进 / 189
　第三节 由创新经济竞争与合作主导的增长阶段 / 191
　　一、区域政府理念创新 / 193
　　二、区域政府技术创新 / 195
　　三、区域政府组织创新 / 195
　　四、区域政府制度创新 / 195
　第四节 由共享经济竞争与合作主导的增长阶段 / 197
　　一、由共享经济竞争与合作主导的增长阶段的特点 / 199
　　二、四种共享产品与区域政府间应遵循的基本原则 / 203

## Chapter 6　The Formation of Regional Economic Competition Gradient Structure and Gradient Equilibrium / 204

Section 1: Introduction to the Gradient Transference Model of Regional Economic / 204

Section 2: Four Supporting Economic Theories for the Gradient Transference Model of Regional Economic / 210

Section 3: Four Characteristics of the Gradient Transference Model of Regional Economic / 212

Section 4: Development Strategies for Livelihood Economy, Industrial Economy, and Urban Economy / 214

　　I. Safeguarding, Supporting, and Upgrading the Livelihood Economy / 214

　　II. Guiding, Adjusting, and Warning the Industrial Economy / 226

　　III. Allocating, Participating in, and Maintaining Order in Urban Economy / 244

Section 5: Building New Engines for Economic Growth / 264

　　I. Building a New Global Investment Engines / 264

　　II. Building a New Global Innovation Engine / 268

　　III. Building a New Global Regulation Engine / 272

## Chapter 7　Practical Experience of Competitive Economic Growth in Shenzhen / 276

Section 1: Growth Stage Dominated by Industrial Economic Competition and Cooperation / 276

　　I. Constraints of Land and Capital Factors / 278

　　II. Solutions by the Shenzhen Government / 280

　　III. Industrial Structure in the Early Stages of the Special Economic Zone / 282

Section 2: Growth Stage Dominated by Urban Economic Competition and Cooperation / 286

　　I. Loans for Infrastructure Construction / 286

　　II. Encouraging Social Capital Participation in Infrastructure Construction / 288

　　III. Development and Allocation of Secondary Resources in Shenzhen Metro Construction and Operation / 290

Section 3: Growth Stage Dominated by Innovative Economic Competition and Cooperation / 294

　　I. The Special Zone Is No Longer Special / 294

　　II. Construction of an Innovative City / 298

　　III. The "Focus Point" Effect of Daring to Be the First / 302

　　IV. Revisiting Shenzhen's Industrial Structure / 308

## 第六章 区域经济竞争梯度结构与梯度均衡的形成 / 205

第一节 区域经济竞争梯度推移模型介绍 / 205

第二节 区域经济竞争梯度推移模型的四种支持性经济学说 / 211

第三节 区域经济竞争梯度推移模型的四个特点 / 213

第四节 民生经济、产业经济与城市经济的发展战略 / 215

 一、保障、托底、提升民生经济 / 215

 二、导向、调节、预警产业经济 / 227

 三、调配、参与、维序城市经济 / 245

第五节 构建经济增长新引擎 / 265

 一、构建全球投资新引擎 / 265

 二、构建全球创新新引擎 / 269

 三、构建全球规则新引擎 / 273

## 第七章 深圳竞争型经济增长实践经验 / 277

第一节 由产业经济竞争与合作主导的增长阶段 / 277

 一、土地与资本要素约束 / 279

 二、深圳政府的破解 / 281

 三、经济特区建立初期的产业结构 / 283

第二节 由城市经济竞争与合作主导的增长阶段 / 287

 一、基础设施建设贷款 / 287

 二、鼓励社会资本参与基础设施建设 / 289

 三、深圳地铁建设和运营中对次生性资源的开发和配置 / 291

第三节 由创新经济竞争与合作主导的增长阶段 / 295

 一、特区不特 / 295

 二、创新型城市建设 / 299

 三、敢为人先的"聚点"效应 / 303

 四、再看深圳的产业结构 / 309

Section 4: Growth Stage Dominated by Shared Economic Competition and Cooperation / 312

    I. A Path for Higher Education Development Combining Self-Reliance and Introduction of Cooperation / 312

    II. Strategies for Building a Comprehensive Innovation Ecosystem that Integrates Resources Inside and Outside the Region to Enhance Innovation Capability / 316

Section 5: Cultivating Competitive Advantage Is the Fundamental Path to Promoting Regional Economic Growth / 324

    I. The Economic Growth Practices of Countries Worldwide Indicate the Existence of Dual-entity in Market Competition / 324

    II. Three Laws of Regional Competition / 328

    III. Cultivating Competitive Advantage Is the Fundamental Path to Promoting Regional Economic Growth / 336

**Afterword / 352**

第四节　由共享经济竞争与合作主导的增长阶段 / 313

　　一、自力更生与引进合作相结合的高等教育发展路径 / 313

　　二、整合区域内外资源提升创新能力的综合创新生态系统建设方略 / 317

第五节　培育竞争优势是推动区域经济增长的根本路径 / 325

　　一、世界各国的经济增长实践表明市场竞争存在双重主体 / 325

　　二、区域竞争三大定律 / 329

　　三、培育竞争优势是推动区域经济增长的根本路径 / 337


参考文献 / 340

后记 / 353

为什么世界上一些国家富有，一些国家贫穷？影响一国经济增长的因素是什么？怎么理解一些国家或区域出现的经济增长奇迹？本书阐述的竞争优势理论，不仅从自然禀赋和比较优势的角度，更从区域政府参与"三类九要素"竞争、竞争型经济增长贯穿经济发展的四个阶段、区域经济竞争呈现梯度推移发展和梯度结构均衡态势等三个层次内涵，指出了有为政府与有效市场相融合的经济发展模式，是推动一个区域乃至一个国家经济转轨、社会转型的根本路径。

Chapter 1

# Limitations of the Comparative Advantage Development Strategy

## Section1: Controversies of the Comparative Advantage Development Strategy

### I. The Comparative Advantage Development Strategy and Its Theoretical Development

The concept of comparative advantage was first proposed by Ricardo. The theory of comparative advantage explains why, even when two countries can produce the same two goods and both have access to the same factor of production (labor), with differing levels of production technology (productivity), each country can still enhance its welfare through trade by focusing on producing the good for which it has a comparative advantage. However, the theory does not explain whether comparative advantage still exists, and in what form, when one country is larger in scale, or when factors are freely mobile, or when there are economies of scale in production. This leaves the impression that the existence of comparative advantage seems to be "absolute".

New Structural Economics, developed based on comparative advantage theory, advocates developing local economies according to comparative advantages determined by factor endowments. It argues that the development strategy adopted by the government of a developing

第一章
# 比较优势发展战略的局限性

## 第一节 比较优势发展战略面临的争议

### 一、比较优势发展战略及其理论发展

比较优势的概念最早由李嘉图提出，比较优势理论解释了一个问题——两个国家在生产两种相同产品时，若都拥有一种相同的生产要素（劳动力），那么在生产技术（生产率）不同的情况下，为什么这两个国家专注于生产本国具有比较优势的产品时，可以通过贸易实现各自福利的提高。但该理论没有解释，当其中一个国家规模更大，或者要素可自由流动，或者生产存在规模经济性时，比较优势是否还存在，以什么样的形式存在。这就给人们留下一种印象，即比较优势的存在似乎是"绝对的"。

基于比较优势理论发展而来的新结构经济学主张依据由要素禀赋决定的比较优势发展地方经济，认为一个发展中国家的政府所采取的发展战略是决定该国收

country is an important factor in determining whether the country's income level can converge to high-income levels. More specifically, since an economy's industrial structure is endogenous to its factor endowment structure, only when the government of a developing country takes comparative advantage as the basic criterion for industrial development, can the economy have a well-functioning market, enterprises have sufficient self-sustaining capacity, and the factor endowment structure can be rapidly upgraded, thus promoting income convergence to high levels. In terms of specific strategy implementation, New Structural Economics proposed the Growth Identification and Facilitation Framework (GIFF) to identify a country's comparative advantages and formulate corresponding development strategies.

In recent years, comparative advantage theory has been continuously developed and refined.

Ju Jiandong et al. first constructed a growth model with infinite industries and proposed a theoretical mechanism of factor endowment-driven structural change.

Wang Yong et al. further introduced human capital, linking human capital with industrial structure, explaining theoretically and empirically the path of industrial structure evolving towards high-skilled labor-intensive direction.

Wang Yong et al. also linked industrial upgrading with income distribution, explaining how income inequality affects capital deepening within industries, and whether luxury industries with high income elasticity upgrade depends on demand, while whether necessity industries with low income elasticity upgrade depends on factor prices.

Lin Yifu et al. constructed a multi-industry theoretical model, depicting the mechanism of capital accumulation driving structural transformation through technology selection. Changes in endowment structure lead to changes in relative factor prices, causing micro-enterprises to upgrade production technology from labor-intensive to capital-intensive.

As the theoretical menu of New Structural Economics continues to expand, its influence in practical fields has also increased. However, this has not been able to conceal the academic community's questioning of this theory and the comparative advantage development strategy.

## II. Academic Critiques of the Comparative Advantage Development Strategy

Some scholars argue that following comparative advantage theory to formulate a comparative advantage development strategy may lead to a "comparative advantage trap". For example:Guo Xibao and Zhang Wei used world trade data from 161 countries under

入水平能否向高收入水平收敛的重要因素。更具体地说，由于一个经济体的产业结构内生于要素禀赋结构，所以只有当发展中国家的政府将比较优势作为产业发展的基本准则时，这个经济体才会有运行良好的市场，企业才能具备足够的自生能力，要素禀赋结构才能实现快速升级，从而推动收入水平向高收入水平收敛。①② 在具体的战略实施上，新结构经济学提出了增长甄别与因势利导框架（GIFF 框架），可以用来识别本国的比较优势，并制定相应的发展战略。③

近年来，比较优势理论不断得到发展和完善。

鞠建东等首次构建了一个具有无穷多个产业的增长模型，提出了要素禀赋驱动结构变迁的理论机制。

王勇等进一步引入人力资本，把人力资本和产业结构相联系，从理论和实证层面解释了产业结构不断朝着高技能劳动密集型方向发展的路径。

王勇等还将产业升级和收入分配联系在一起，阐述了收入不平等如何影响产业内的资本深化，高收入弹性的奢侈品产业是否升级取决于需求，低收入弹性的必需品产业是否升级取决于要素价格。

林毅夫等构建出多产业的理论模型，刻画了资本积累通过技术选择驱动结构转型的机制，禀赋结构的变化使得要素相对价格变动，导致微观企业的生产技术从劳动密集型向资本密集型升级。

随着新结构经济学理论菜单的不断丰富，其在实践领域中的影响力也不断提高，但这并未能掩盖学界对该理论和比较优势发展战略的质疑之声。

## 二、学界对比较优势发展战略的质疑

有学者认为遵循比较优势理论制定比较优势发展战略可能导致"比较优势

---

① 林毅夫：《新结构经济学——重构发展经济学的框架》，《经济学（季刊）》2011 年第 1 期。
② 林毅夫：《有为政府参与的中国市场发育之路》，《广东社会科学》2020 年第 1 期。
③ 林毅夫：《新结构经济学：反思发展与政策的理论框架》，苏剑译，北京大学出版社，2012，第 136-137 页。

the SITC regions code from 1987 to 2015, applying a multi-dimensional dynamic analysis method of the Markov chain model to prove the existence of the "comparative advantage trap". Liu Zaiqi and Wang Manli's empirical analysis based on the holistic network analysis method and country panel data shows that the "middle-income trap" is actually a "comparative advantage trap". Yang Wenshuang and Liu Xiaojing's research found that the biggest obstacle to industrial upgrading in Northeast China is that comparative advantages are solidified in traditional industries lacking innovation. If following the original path, it will fall deeply into the "comparative advantage trap". Lu Shanyong and Ye Ying pointed out that countries at various income levels may face an "income trap", and behind all "income traps" is actually a "comparative advantage trap". In this context, although the academic community is increasingly positive about industrial policies and actively promoting the theorization of China's successful practice of effective government, whether a country should follow its own comparative advantages to formulate a comparative advantage development strategy remains controversial.[①]

Some scholars have raised clear objections, Fang Xingqi pointed out that while the comparative advantage development strategy can have an "immediate effect" in small and medium-sized developing countries, it may not be effective in a large socialist developing country like China that is seizing the opportunities of the fourth industrial revolution. Yu Bin pointed out that the comparative advantage selection advocated by New Structural Economics not only fails to eliminate poverty but will also widen the income gap between developing and developed countries. Fan Gang established the concept of "development factors", pointing out that comparative advantage, late-development advantage, and local advantage are all elements of development, but the late-development advantage is more important than comparative advantage. Whether developing countries can ultimately achieve "convergence" with developed countries in industrial structure and income levels depends on whether they can fully leverage their late-development advantages, which have characteristics independent of comparative advantages. Luo Ying and Wang Yilin believe that in the context of globalization encountering headwinds

---

① The main arguments supporting industrial policies are as follows: industrial policies have positive externalities on economic development; industrial policies help improve coordination (or agglomeration) failures; industrial policies can provide more of the public inputs required for specific industrial activities.

陷阱",如郭熙保和张薇采用1987—2015年161个国家的SITC分类码下的世界贸易数据,运用马尔科夫链模型多维动态分析方法证明"比较优势陷阱"的确存在。刘再起和王曼莉基于整体网分析法和国别面板数据的实证分析结果表明,"中等收入陷阱"其实是"比较优势陷阱"。杨文爽和刘晓静的研究发现,我国东北地区产业升级遇到的最大障碍是比较优势固化在缺乏创新的传统产业中,按原路径走下去的话,会深深陷入"比较优势陷阱"。陆善勇和叶颖指出,处于各个收入水平的国家都有可能面临"收入陷阱",且所有"收入陷阱"的背后实际上都是"比较优势陷阱"。在这种情况下,尽管学界对产业政策的态度愈加积极,对中国有为政府成功实践的理论化工作也在积极推进,但一国是否应遵循自身的比较优势制定比较优势发展战略仍饱受争议。①

一些学者提出了明确的反对意见,如方兴起指出,虽然比较优势发展战略在中小发展中国家能起到"立竿见影"的作用,但在抢抓第四次工业革命机遇的中国这样一个大的社会主义发展中国家可能难以发挥作用。余斌指出,新结构经济学所主张的比较优势选择不仅无法消除贫困,还会扩大发展中国家与发达国家收入的差距。樊纲则建立了"发展要素"的概念,指出比较优势、后发优势和本土优势都属于发展的要素,但更重要的是后发优势而非比较优势,发展中国家最终能否实现与发达国家产业结构与收入水平"趋同",关键在于能否充分发挥后发优势,且后发优势与比较优势具有相互独立的特征。罗影和汪毅霖认为,在全球化遭遇逆流和中国已经成长为世界头号制造业大国的时代背景下,比较优势和后发优势等后发国家的传统优势已经无法支撑中国经济的高质量发展,中国经济未来的高质量发展系于新的国家竞争优势。

我们认为,比较优势发展战略有争议的根本原因是:涉及比较优势理论的几

---

① 支持产业政策的理由主要有三个方面:产业政策对经济发展具有正外部效应;产业政策有助于改善协调(或集聚)失效;产业政策能够提供更多的具体产业活动所需的公共投入。

advantage development strategy is that several basic issues related to comparative advantage theory have not been clarified, and existing academic debates have not been discussed within a consistent framework, leading to diverse understandings and definitions of relevant concepts and inconsistent theoretical logic.

The second section of this chapter will explore regional comparative advantages under conditions of large country demand, economies of scale, and factor mobility by constructing a mathematical model with two regions, two industries, and two sectors including consumers and enterprises. This breaks several important preconditions for the existence of comparative advantage but can better reflect China's current economic development environment. At the same time, this chapter will discuss the limitations of the comparative advantage development strategy under conditions of large country demand, economies of scale, and factor mobility.

# Section 2: Comparative Advantage under Conditions of Large Country Demand, Economies of Scale, and Factor Mobility

## I. Basic Model Setup

This section constructs a mathematical model with two regions, two industries, and two sectors including consumers and enterprises, to analyze how comparative advantage determines industrial division between regions.

### (i) Consumers

Consumer utility function:

$$U_i(x_{i1}, x_{i2}, R_i) = x_{i1} x_{i2} R_i \qquad (1\text{-}1)$$

Here, $i=A$ or $i=B$, representing two regions, A and B; $x_{i1}$ and $x_{i2}$ represent the consumption quantities of good 1 and good 2 by consumers in region $i$; $R_i$ represents the amount of leisure consumed by consumers in region $i$, referred to simply as leisure; the time endowment for consumers in both regions is $\bar{R}$, and the working time is $L_i$; leisure $R_i$ equals the time endowment $\bar{R}$ minus the working time $L_i$.

个基本问题未能得到厘清,且已有的学术争论未能在一个一致的框架下进行讨论,导致对相关概念的理解和界定见仁见智,理论逻辑也莫衷一是。

本章第二节将通过构建一个两地区、两产业,包含消费者和企业两部门的数理模型,探讨地区在大国需求、规模经济和要素可流动条件下的比较优势,这打破了比较优势存在的几项重要前置假设,但却能够更好地反映我国当前所处的经济发展环境。同时,本章将讨论在大国需求、规模经济和要素可流动条件下,比较优势发展战略的局限性。

## 第二节 大国需求、规模经济与要素可流动条件下的比较优势

### 一、基本模型设定

本部分将构建一个两地区、两产业,包含消费者和企业两部门的数理模型,用以分析比较优势如何决定地区间的产业分工。

#### (一)消费者

消费者效用函数:

$$U_i(x_{i1}, x_{i2}, R_i) = x_{i1} x_{i2} R_i \tag{1-1}$$

其中,$i$ = A 或 B,表示 A 和 B 两个地区;$x_{i1}$ 和 $x_{i2}$ 分别表示地区 $i$ 的消费者对商品 1 和商品 2 的消费数量;$R_i$ 表示地区 $i$ 的消费者对闲暇的消费数量,简称闲暇;两地区消费者的时间禀赋均为 $\bar{R}$,劳动时间为 $L_i$;闲暇 $R_i$ 等于时间禀赋 $\bar{R}$ 减去劳动时间 $L_i$。

The nominal wage rates in both regions are $w^{①}$. The total income $W_i$ of consumers comes from the wages earned through work:

$$W_i = wL_i = w(\bar{R} - R_i) \tag{1-2}$$

Therefore, the consumer's budget constraint is:

$$p_{i1}x_{i1} + p_{i2}x_{i2} = W_i = w(\bar{R} - R_i)$$

That is:

$$p_{i1}x_{i1} + p_{i2}x_{i2} + wR_i = w\bar{R} \tag{1-3}$$

Here, $p_{i1}$ and $p_{i2}$ represent the prices of goods 1 and 2 in region $i$.

Thus, the consumer's problem is to maximize their utility level under the budget constraint:

$$\begin{array}{c} \max\limits_{x_{i1},x_{i2},R_i} x_{i1}x_{i2}R_i \\ \text{s.t.} \quad p_{i1}x_{i1} + p_{i2}x_{i2} + wR_i = w\bar{R} \end{array} \tag{1-4}$$

Solving this problem, we can obtain the consumer's demands for goods 1, goods 2 and leisure respectively:

$$x_{i1} = \frac{w\bar{R}}{3p_{i1}}; \quad x_{i2} = \frac{w\bar{R}}{3p_{i2}}; \quad R_i = \frac{\bar{R}}{3} \tag{1-5}$$

(ii) Enterprises

The only input factor for enterprise production is labor. The production functions are:

$$\begin{array}{c} x_{i1} = f(L_{i1}) = \alpha_i L_{i1} \\ x_{i2} = g(L_{i2}) = \beta_i L_{i2} \\ L_{i1} + L_{i2} = L_i \end{array} \tag{1-6}$$

Here, $\alpha_i$ and $\beta_i$ represent the technological efficiency of labor in region $i$ producing the two goods; $L_{i1}$ and $L_{i2}$ represent the labor time used by region $i$ to produce goods 1 and goods 2 respectively, the sum of which is the total labor time $L_i$ of that labor.

Assuming there are no fixed costs in enterprise production, the costs of producing goods 1 and goods 2 for enterprises in the two regions are respectively:

$$\begin{array}{c} C_{i1} = wL_{i1} = \dfrac{w}{\alpha_i}x_{i1} \\ C_{i2} = wL_{i2} = \dfrac{w}{\beta_i}x_{i2} \end{array} \tag{1-7}$$

---

① This article does not separately construct the monetary market, so the value of currencies in the two regions cannot be compared. For the sake of simplicity in the model analysis, we assume that the nominal wage rates in both regions are the same, which will not affect the conclusions of the model.

两地区的名义工资率均为 $w$ [①]，消费者的全部收入 $W_i$ 来自工作得到的工资：

$$W_i = wL_i = w(\bar{R} - R_i) \tag{1-2}$$

因此，消费者的预算约束就是：

$$p_{i1}x_{i1} + p_{i2}x_{i2} = W_i = w(\bar{R} - R_i)$$

也即：

$$p_{i1}x_{i1} + p_{i2}x_{i2} + wR_i = w\bar{R} \tag{1-3}$$

其中，$p_{i1}$ 和 $p_{i2}$ 分别表示地区 $i$ 的商品1和商品2的价格。

由此，消费者的问题就是在预算约束下最大化其效用水平，即：

$$\max_{x_{i1},x_{i2},R_i} x_{i1}x_{i2}R_i$$
$$\text{s.t.} \quad p_{i1}x_{i1} + p_{i2}x_{i2} + wR_i = w\bar{R} \tag{1-4}$$

解这个问题，能够得到消费者对商品1、商品2和闲暇的需求分别为：

$$x_{i1} = \frac{w\bar{R}}{3p_{i1}}; \quad x_{i2} = \frac{w\bar{R}}{3p_{i2}}; \quad R_i = \frac{\bar{R}}{3} \tag{1-5}$$

## （二）企业

企业生产的唯一投入要素是劳动力。生产函数为：

$$\begin{aligned} x_{i1} &= f(L_{i1}) = \alpha_i L_{i1} \\ x_{i2} &= g(L_{i2}) = \beta_i L_{i2} \\ L_{i1} &+ L_{i2} = L_i \end{aligned} \tag{1-6}$$

其中，$\alpha_i$ 和 $\beta_i$ 分别表示地区 $i$ 劳动力生产两种商品的技术效率；$L_{i1}$ 和 $L_{i2}$ 分别表示地区 $i$ 的劳动力用于生产商品1和商品2的劳动时间，二者之和为该劳动力全部劳动时间 $L_i$。

假设企业生产没有固定成本，则两地区企业生产商品1和商品2的成本分别为：

$$\begin{aligned} C_{i1} &= wL_{i1} = \frac{w}{\alpha_i}x_{i1} \\ C_{i2} &= wL_{i2} = \frac{w}{\beta_i}x_{i2} \end{aligned} \tag{1-7}$$

---

[①] 本文并未对货币市场进行单独的构建，因此两地区的货币价值无法比较。为了模型分析的简洁，我们假设两地区的名义工资率相同，这并不会对模型结论产生影响。

Therefore, the profits of enterprises producing goods 1 and goods 2 are:

$$\pi_{i1} = p_{i1}x_{i1} - \frac{w}{\alpha_i}x_{i1} = p_{i1}\alpha_i L_{i1} - wL_{i1}$$
$$\pi_{i2} = p_{i2}x_{i2} - \frac{w}{\beta_i}x_{i2} = p_{i2}\beta_i L_{i2} - wL_{i2}$$
(1-8)

Solving the enterprise's profit maximization problem, we obtain the supply functions for goods 1 and goods 2, which also represent the demand for labor when region $i$ produces goods 1 and goods 2:

$$p_{i1} = \frac{w}{\alpha_i};\ p_{i2} = \frac{w}{\beta_i}$$
(1-9)

From equation (1-9), we can see that the technological efficiency (real wage) of labor producing two goods in region $i$ in the system is the nominal wage rate divided by the corresponding price, that is, the real wage of labor in region $i$ is equivalent to $\alpha_i$ units of goods 1 or $\beta_i$ units of goods 2.

### (iii) Equilibrium without trade

When there is no trade between regions, the equilibrium levels of various economic variables in region $i$ are:

$$x_{i1}^* = \frac{\alpha_i \overline{R}}{3};\ L_{i1}^* = \frac{\overline{R}}{3};\ x_{i2}^* = \frac{\beta_i \overline{R}}{3};\ L_{i2}^* = \frac{\overline{R}}{3};\ R_i^* = \frac{\overline{R}}{3}$$
(1-10)

At this time, the maximum utility level that consumers in region $i$ can achieve is:

$$U_{i,\max} = \frac{\alpha_i \beta_i \overline{R}^3}{27}$$
(1-11)

### (iv) Equilibrium with trade

When trade exists, we need to define the differences in production technology between the two regions to characterize the terms of trade. Assume:

$$\alpha_B = \mu\beta_B;\ \alpha_A = \sigma\beta_A;\ \alpha_A = \theta\alpha_B$$
(1-12)

From these relationships, we can obtain:

$$\alpha_B = \mu\beta_B;\ \beta_A = \frac{\theta\mu}{\sigma}\beta_B;\ \alpha_A = \theta\mu\beta_B$$
(1-13)

We assume there are no transportation costs for goods traded between the two regions. Then when trade exists, the total demand faced by each enterprise is the sum of the demands from the two regions, that is, the total demands for goods 1 and goods 2 are respectively:

因此，企业生产商品 1 和商品 2 的利润为：

$$\pi_{i1} = p_{i1}x_{i1} - \frac{w}{\alpha_i}x_{i1} = p_{i1}\alpha_i L_{i1} - wL_{i1}$$
$$\pi_{i2} = p_{i2}x_{i2} - \frac{w}{\beta_i}x_{i2} = p_{i2}\beta_i L_{i2} - wL_{i2}$$
（1-8）

求解企业的利润最大化问题，得到商品 1 和商品 2 的供给函数，该函数同时也表示地区 $i$ 生产商品 1 和商品 2 时对劳动力的需求：

$$p_{i1} = \frac{w}{\alpha_i}; \ p_{i2} = \frac{w}{\beta_i} \quad (1-9)$$

从式（1-9）可以看出，系统中地区 $i$ 的劳动力生产两种商品的技术效率（实际工资）就是名义工资率除以对应的价格，也即地区 $i$ 劳动力的实际工资相当于 $\alpha_i$ 单位的商品 1 或者是 $\beta_i$ 单位的商品 2。

### （三）不存在贸易时的均衡

当地区间不存在贸易时，地区 $i$ 各经济变量的均衡水平为：

$$x_{i1}^* = \frac{\alpha_i \bar{R}}{3}; \ L_{i1}^* = \frac{\bar{R}}{3}; \ x_{i2}^* = \frac{\beta_i \bar{R}}{3}; \ L_{i2}^* = \frac{\bar{R}}{3}; \ R_i^* = \frac{\bar{R}}{3} \quad (1-10)$$

此时，地区 $i$ 消费者能够达到的最大效用水平为：

$$U_{i,\max} = \frac{\alpha_i \beta_i \bar{R}^3}{27} \quad (1-11)$$

### （四）存在贸易时的均衡

当存在贸易时，我们需要定义两地区生产技术上的差异，从而对贸易条件进行刻画。假设：

$$\alpha_B = \mu\beta_B; \ \alpha_A = \sigma\beta_A; \ \alpha_A = \theta\alpha_B \quad (1-12)$$

从以上关系可得：

$$\alpha_B = \mu\beta_B; \ \beta_A = \frac{\theta\mu}{\sigma}\beta_B; \ \alpha_A = \theta\mu\beta_B \quad (1-13)$$

我们假设商品在两地区间的贸易不存在交通成本，那么在存在贸易时，每个企业面对的总需求是两个地区的需求之和，即商品 1 和商品 2 的总需求分别为：

$$x_1 = \frac{w\bar{R}}{3p_{A1}} + \frac{w\bar{R}}{3p_{B1}}$$
$$x_2 = \frac{w\bar{R}}{3p_{A2}} + \frac{w\bar{R}}{3p_{B2}}$$
(1–14)

The supply curves for the two goods in the two regions are respectively:

$$p_{A1} = \frac{w}{\alpha_A} = \frac{w}{\theta\mu\beta_B}; \quad p_{B1} = \frac{w}{\alpha_B} = \frac{w}{\mu\beta_B}$$
$$p_{A2} = \frac{w}{\beta_A} = \frac{\sigma w}{\theta\mu\beta_B}; \quad p_{B2} = \frac{w}{\beta_B}$$
(1–15)

Next, we will discuss the industrial division between the two regions under two situations: absolute advantage and comparative advantage.

1. Absolute advantage and industrial division

When $p_{A1} < p_{B1}$ and $p_{A2} > p_{B2}$, region A has an absolute advantage in the production of goods 1, while region B has an absolute advantage in the production of goods 2. At this time:

$$\frac{w}{\theta\mu\beta_B} < \frac{w}{\mu\beta_B} \text{ 且 } \frac{\sigma w}{\theta\mu\beta_B} > \frac{w}{\beta_B}$$
(1–16)

That is:

$$1 < \theta < \frac{\sigma}{\mu}$$
(1–17)

Assuming Bertrand competition in the goods market, region A will only produce goods 1, and region B will only produce goods 2. Thus, we have:

$$x_1^* = \frac{2\alpha_A \bar{R}}{3} > \frac{(\alpha_A + \alpha_B)\bar{R}}{3}$$
$$x_2^* = \frac{2\beta_B \bar{R}}{3} > \frac{(\beta_A + \beta_B)\bar{R}}{3}$$
(1–18)

Here, the total output of the two goods is greater than the sum of the equilibrium outputs of the two regions without trade given by equation (1-10), therefore, both regions focusing on producing goods in which they have absolute advantages can increase the total output level, thereby improving income levels through trade.

2. Comparative advantage and industrial division

When $p_{A1} < p_{B1}$ and $p_{A2} < p_{B2}$, region A has absolute advantages in the production of both goods, that is, relative to region A, region B is a less developed region. At this time: $\theta > 1$ and $\theta > \frac{\sigma}{\mu}$. When simultaneously:

$$\frac{1}{\sigma} = \frac{p_{A1}}{p_{A2}} < \frac{p_{B1}}{p_{B2}} = \frac{1}{\mu}$$
(1–19)

$$x_1 = \frac{w\bar{R}}{3p_{A1}} + \frac{w\bar{R}}{3p_{B1}}$$
$$x_2 = \frac{w\bar{R}}{3p_{A2}} + \frac{w\bar{R}}{3p_{B2}} \quad (1\text{-}14)$$

两个地区对两种商品的供给曲线分别为：

$$p_{A1} = \frac{w}{\alpha_A} = \frac{w}{\theta\mu\beta_B}; \quad p_{B1} = \frac{w}{\alpha_B} = \frac{w}{\mu\beta_B}$$
$$p_{A2} = \frac{w}{\beta_A} = \frac{\sigma w}{\theta\mu\beta_B}; \quad p_{B2} = \frac{w}{\beta_B} \quad (1\text{-}15)$$

下面，我们分别对绝对优势与比较优势两种情况下两地区间的产业分工进行讨论。

**1. 绝对优势与产业分工**

当 $p_{A1} < p_{B1}$ 且 $p_{A2} > p_{B2}$ 时，地区 A 在商品 1 的生产上具有绝对优势，而地区 B 在商品 2 的生产上具有绝对优势。此时有：

$$\frac{w}{\theta\mu\beta_B} < \frac{w}{\mu\beta_B} \text{ 且 } \frac{\sigma w}{\theta\mu\beta_B} > \frac{w}{\beta_B} \quad (1\text{-}16)$$

即：

$$1 < \theta < \frac{\sigma}{\mu} \quad (1\text{-}17)$$

假设商品市场进行伯川德竞争，那么地区 A 就将只生产商品 1，地区 B 就将只生产商品 2。于是，有：

$$x_1^* = \frac{2\alpha_A \bar{R}}{3} > \frac{(\alpha_A + \alpha_B)\bar{R}}{3}$$
$$x_2^* = \frac{2\beta_B \bar{R}}{3} > \frac{(\beta_A + \beta_B)\bar{R}}{3} \quad (1\text{-}18)$$

这里，两种商品的总产量大于由式（1-10）给出的不存在贸易时的两地区均衡产量之和，因此，两地区专注于生产各自具有绝对优势的商品能够提高总产量水平，进而通过贸易提升收入水平。

**2. 比较优势与产业分工**

当 $p_{A1} < p_{B1}$ 且 $p_{A2} < p_{B2}$ 时，地区 A 在两种商品的生产上都具有绝对优势，即相对于地区 A，地区 B 为欠发达地区，此时有：$\theta > 1$ 且 $\theta > \frac{\sigma}{\mu}$。当同时有：

$$\frac{1}{\sigma} = \frac{p_{A1}}{p_{A2}} < \frac{p_{B1}}{p_{B2}} = \frac{1}{\mu} \quad (1\text{-}19)$$

That is, when $\mu < \sigma$, region A has a comparative advantage in the production of goods 1, while region B has a comparative advantage in the production of goods 2. Conversely, region A has a comparative advantage in the production of goods 2, while region B has a comparative advantage in the production of goods 1. Below, we will discuss the first situation, that is, the case where region A has a comparative advantage in the production of goods 1, while region B has a comparative advantage in the production of goods 2.[①] At this time, if region A focuses on producing goods 1, and region B focuses on producing goods 2, then:

$$\begin{aligned} x_1^* = \frac{2\alpha_A \overline{R}}{3} > \frac{(\alpha_A + \alpha_B)\overline{R}}{3} \\ x_2^* = \frac{2\beta_B \overline{R}}{3} < \frac{(\beta_A + \beta_B)\overline{R}}{3} \end{aligned} \quad (1\text{-}20)$$

Without trade, the price of goods 2 in region A is $\sigma$ units of goods 1, and the price of goods 2 in region B is $\mu$ units of goods 1. Now, because $\mu < \sigma$, so under the condition of allowing trade, the price of goods 2 will be $\lambda$ ($\mu < \lambda < \sigma$) units of goods 1. Without trade, the consumption level of region A is $\left(\frac{\alpha_A \overline{R}}{3}, \frac{\beta_A \overline{R}}{3}\right)$, and the consumption level of region B is $\left(\frac{\alpha_B \overline{R}}{3}, \frac{\beta_B \overline{R}}{3}\right)$. Now, let region A retain $\frac{\alpha_A \overline{R}}{3}$ of goods 1 for local consumption, and use the other $\frac{\alpha_A \overline{R}}{3}$ goods 1 for trade; region B retains $\frac{\beta_B \overline{R}}{3}$ of goods 2 for local consumption, and uses the other $\frac{\beta_B \overline{R}}{3}$ goods 2 for trade.

For region B, without trade, $\frac{\beta_B \overline{R}}{3}$ quantity of goods 2 can be exchanged for $\frac{\mu \beta_B \overline{R}}{3} = \frac{\alpha_B \overline{R}}{3}$ units of goods 1. While for region A, without trade, $\frac{\beta_B \overline{R}}{3}$ of goods 2 can be exchanged for $\frac{\sigma \beta_B \overline{R}}{3} \left(> \frac{\mu \beta_B \overline{R}}{3} = \frac{\alpha_B \overline{R}}{3}\right)$ units of goods 1, therefore, region A is willing to exchange $\frac{\mu \beta_B \overline{R}}{3} = \frac{\alpha_B \overline{R}}{3}$ units of goods 1 with region B for $\frac{\beta_B \overline{R}}{3}$ units of goods 2.

After the trade is completed, the consumption level of region B is completely consistent with the consumption level under the condition of no trade. Region A consumes $\frac{2\alpha_A \overline{R}}{3} - \frac{\mu \beta_B \overline{R}}{3}$ units of goods 1 and $\frac{\beta_B \overline{R}}{3}$ units of goods 2. At this time, consumers in region

---

① The situation where region A has a comparative advantage in the production of goods 2, while region B has a comparative advantage in the production of goods 1 is similar. To save space in the article, these have been omitted in the main text. Readers who need this analysis can request it from the author.

即 $\mu<\sigma$ 时，地区 A 在商品 1 的生产上具有比较优势，而地区 B 在商品 2 的生产上具有比较优势。反之，则地区 A 在商品 2 的生产上具有比较优势，而地区 B 在商品 1 的生产上具有比较优势。下面，我们对第一种情况进行讨论，即地区 A 在商品 1 的生产上具有比较优势，而地区 B 在商品 2 的生产上具有比较优势的情况。[①] 此时，如果地区 A 专注生产商品 1，而地区 B 专注生产商品 2，则有：

$$\begin{aligned}x_1^* &= \frac{2\alpha_A \bar{R}}{3} > \frac{(\alpha_A+\alpha_B)\bar{R}}{3}\\ x_2^* &= \frac{2\beta_B \bar{R}}{3} < \frac{(\beta_A+\beta_B)\bar{R}}{3}\end{aligned} \qquad (1-20)$$

在不存在贸易的条件下，地区 A 商品 2 的价格是 $\sigma$ 个商品 1，地区 B 商品 2 的价格是 $\mu$ 个商品 1。现在，因为有 $\mu<\sigma$，所以，在允许贸易的条件下，商品 2 的价格将是 $\lambda$（$\mu<\lambda<\sigma$）个商品 1。在不存在贸易的条件下，地区 A 的消费水平为 $\left(\dfrac{\alpha_A \bar{R}}{3},\dfrac{\beta_A \bar{R}}{3}\right)$，地区 B 的消费水平为 $\left(\dfrac{\alpha_B \bar{R}}{3},\dfrac{\beta_B \bar{R}}{3}\right)$。现在，令地区 A 保留 $\dfrac{\alpha_A \bar{R}}{3}$ 的商品 1 用于本地区消费，另外的 $\dfrac{\alpha_A \bar{R}}{3}$ 商品 1 用于贸易；地区 B 保留 $\dfrac{\beta_B \bar{R}}{3}$ 的商品 2 用于本地区消费，另外的 $\dfrac{\beta_B \bar{R}}{3}$ 商品 2 用于贸易。

对于地区 B，在不存在贸易的条件下，$\dfrac{\beta_B \bar{R}}{3}$ 数量的商品 2 能够换得 $\dfrac{\mu\beta_B \bar{R}}{3}=\dfrac{\alpha_B \bar{R}}{3}$ 单位的商品 1。而对于地区 A，在不存在贸易的条件下，$\dfrac{\beta_B \bar{R}}{3}$ 的商品 2 能够换得 $\dfrac{\sigma\beta_B \bar{R}}{3}\left(>\dfrac{\mu\beta_B \bar{R}}{3}=\dfrac{\alpha_B \bar{R}}{3}\right)$ 单位的商品 1，因此，地区 A 愿意以 $\dfrac{\mu\beta_B \bar{R}}{3}=\dfrac{\alpha_B \bar{R}}{3}$ 单位的商品 1 与地区 B 交换 $\dfrac{\beta_B \bar{R}}{3}$ 单位的商品 2。

交易完成后，地区 B 的消费水平已经与不存在贸易的条件下的消费水平完全一致。而地区 A 则消费了 $\dfrac{2\alpha_A \bar{R}}{3}-\dfrac{\mu\beta_B \bar{R}}{3}$ 单位的商品 1 和 $\dfrac{\beta_B \bar{R}}{3}$ 单位的商品 2，此时，地区 A 的消费者比不存在贸易的条件下多消费了 $\dfrac{\alpha_A \bar{R}}{3}-\dfrac{\mu\beta_B \bar{R}}{3}$ 单位的商品 1，少消费了 $\dfrac{\beta_A \bar{R}}{3}-\dfrac{\beta_B \bar{R}}{3}$ 单位的商品 2。如果地

---

① 地区 A 在商品 2 的生产上具有比较优势，而地区 B 在商品 1 的生产上具有比较优势的情况与此类似，为了节省文章篇幅，本文在正文中进行了省略，如读者需要，可向笔者索取分析过程。

A consume $\frac{\alpha_A \bar{R}}{3} - \frac{\mu \beta_B \bar{R}}{3}$ more units of goods 1 and $\frac{\beta_A \bar{R}}{3} - \frac{\beta_B \bar{R}}{3}$ fewer units of goods 2 than under the condition of no trade. If region A uses the labor time to produce $\frac{\alpha_A \bar{R}}{3} - \frac{\mu \beta_B \bar{R}}{3}$ units of goods 1 to produce goods 2, it can produce $\frac{\theta-1}{\theta} \frac{\beta_A \bar{R}}{3}$ units of goods 2, and $\frac{\theta-1}{\theta} \frac{\beta_A \bar{R}}{3} > \frac{\beta_A \bar{R}}{3} - \frac{\beta_B \bar{R}}{3} = \frac{\theta \mu - \sigma}{\theta \mu} \frac{\beta_A \bar{R}}{3}$.

Therefore, through trade, while the overall utility level of consumers in region B remains unchanged, the overall utility level of consumers in region A will be improved. Of course, the increased welfare can be more reasonably distributed between regions A and B by changing the trade price. This shows that even if a region has absolute disadvantages in the production of both goods, it can still focus on producing goods in which it has a comparative advantage and improve economic welfare through trade with another region.

The simple model constructed in this section well illustrates that a region can gain greater benefits (economic welfare) by focusing on producing goods in which it has a comparative advantage. However, we need to be clear that this conclusion is based on several preconditions, including the following.

(1) The demand scales of the two regions are the same, which is mainly reflected in the fact that the time endowments of consumers in the two regions are consistent, both being $\bar{R}$.

(2) There are no economies of scale in enterprise production.

(3) Factors are immobile between regions.

From Ricardo's earliest construction of comparative advantage theory to the explanation of comparative advantage theory in modern economics textbooks, there is rarely any indication of what results would occur if these preconditions were broken. This has led to a lack of discussion on the applicability of comparative advantage theory in existing research, making the theory of comparative advantage "absolute".

This book will break these three preconditions one by one, use mathematical methods for logical deduction, and clearly point out the limitations of comparative advantage theory.

## II. Large Country Demand and Comparative Advantage

We still assume $p_{A1} < p_{B1}$ and $p_{A2} < p_{B2}$, that is, region A has absolute advantages in the production of both goods, and region B is a less developed region. However, at the same time, we distinguish the economic scales of the two regions, letting:

$$\bar{R}_B = k\bar{R}_A$$

区 A 将生产 $\dfrac{\alpha_A \bar{R}}{3} - \dfrac{\mu \beta_B \bar{R}}{3}$ 单位的商品 1 的劳动时间用于生产商品 2，则能够生产 $\dfrac{\theta - 1}{\theta} \dfrac{\beta_A \bar{R}}{3}$ 单位的商品 2，且 $\dfrac{\theta - 1}{\theta} \dfrac{\beta_A \bar{R}}{3} > \dfrac{\beta_A \bar{R}}{3} - \dfrac{\beta_B \bar{R}}{3} = \dfrac{\theta \mu - \sigma}{\theta \mu} \dfrac{\beta_A \bar{R}}{3}$。

因此，通过贸易，在地区 B 的消费者整体效用水平不变的情况下，地区 A 的消费者的整体效用水平将得到提升，当然也可以通过改变贸易价格使这部分福利增量在地区 A 与地区 B 之间进行更合理的分配。由此可见，尽管一个地区在两商品的生产上都具有绝对劣势，但它也可专注于生产其具有比较优势的商品，并通过与另一个地区的贸易提升经济福利。

本节构建的简单的模型很好地说明了一个地区能够通过专注于生产本地区具有比较优势的商品来获取更大的利益（经济福利）。但我们需要明确的是，这一结论是建立在几个前置假设之上的，包括以下几个。

（1）两地区的需求规模相同，这里主要表现为两地区消费者的时间禀赋是一致的，均为 $\bar{R}$。

（2）企业的生产不存在规模经济。

（3）要素在地区间是不可流动的。

从李嘉图最早构建的比较优势理论，到现代经济学教科书上对比较优势理论的阐述，都鲜少指明一旦打破这些前置假设会出现怎样的结果。这导致现有研究对比较优势理论的适用范围缺乏探讨，使比较优势理论变得"绝对化"。

本书将逐一打破这三个前置假设，运用数理方法进行逻辑推演，对比较优势理论的局限性进行明确。

## 二、大国需求与比较优势

我们仍假设 $p_{A1} < p_{B1}$ 且 $p_{A2} < p_{B2}$，即地区 A 在两种商品的生产上都具有绝对优势，地区 B 为欠发达地区。但同时，我们对两地区经济规模做出区分，令：

$$\bar{R}_B = k\bar{R}_A$$

At this time, the population size of region B $\bar{R}_B$ is $k$ times that of region A $\bar{R}_A$, where $k>1$, that is, relative to region A, region B is a large country. We take the example of region B having a comparative advantage in the production of goods 2 to explore whether this comparative advantage will lead region B to focus on the production of goods 2, at this time, $1<\dfrac{\sigma}{\mu}<\theta$.

If region A focuses on producing goods 1 and region B focuses on producing goods 2, then the total output of goods 1 is:

$$x_1^T = \frac{2\alpha_A \bar{R}_A}{3} = \frac{2\theta \alpha_B \bar{R}_A}{3} \tag{1-21}$$

While in the case of no trade and independence between the two regions, the total output of goods 1 is:

$$x_1^N = \frac{\alpha_A \bar{R}_A + \alpha_B \bar{R}_B}{3} = \frac{\theta \alpha_B \bar{R}_A + \alpha_B k \bar{R}_A}{3} = \frac{(\theta + k)\alpha_B \bar{R}_A}{3} \tag{1-22}$$

Obviously, when $k > \theta$, $x_1^T < x_1^N$, that is, when region A focuses on producing goods 1, the total output of goods 1 is less than the total output without trade.

Similarly, if region A focuses on producing goods 1 and region B focuses on producing goods 2, then the total output of goods 2 is:

$$x_2^T = \frac{2\beta_B \bar{R}_B}{3} = \frac{2k\beta_B \bar{R}_A}{3} \tag{1-23}$$

While in the case of no trade and independence between the two regions, the total output of goods 2 is:

$$x_2^N = \frac{\beta_A \bar{R}_A + \beta_B \bar{R}_B}{3} = \frac{\dfrac{\theta\mu}{\sigma}\beta_B \bar{R}_A + k\beta_B \bar{R}_A}{3} = \frac{\left(\dfrac{\theta\mu}{\sigma} + k\right)\beta_B \bar{R}_A}{3} \tag{1-24}$$

Obviously, when $\dfrac{\theta\mu}{\sigma} < k$, $x_2^T > x_2^N$, that is, when region B focuses on producing goods 2, the total output of goods 2 is greater than the total output without trade. Because $\sigma > \mu$, therefore $\dfrac{\mu}{\sigma}<1$. Therefore, we assume $k > \theta$, at this time $\dfrac{\theta\mu}{\sigma} < k$ is naturally satisfied.

Under the condition of no trade, the quantity of goods 1 produced and consumed by region B is $\dfrac{\alpha_B \bar{R}_B}{3} = \dfrac{\dfrac{k}{\theta}\alpha_A \bar{R}_A}{3}$. However, in the case of trade, region A can only provide $\dfrac{\alpha_A \bar{R}_A}{3}$. To exchange for these goods 1, region B needs at least $\dfrac{\mu\alpha_A \bar{R}_A}{3}$ units of goods 2. After the transaction, the quantity of goods 1 consumed by region B is $\dfrac{\alpha_A \bar{R}_A}{3}$, and the quantity of goods 2 consumed is $\dfrac{2\beta_B \bar{R}_B}{3} - \dfrac{\mu\alpha_A \bar{R}_A}{3}$. At this time, the utility level realized by region B is:

此时，地区 B 人口规模 $\bar{R}_B$ 是地区 A 人口规模 $\bar{R}_A$ 的 $k$ 倍，这里有 $k>1$，也即相对于地区 A 而言，地区 B 是一个大国。我们以地区 B 在商品 2 的生产上具有比较优势为例探讨这种比较优势是否会导致地区 B 专注于商品 2 的生产，此时有 $1<\dfrac{\sigma}{\mu}<\theta$。

如果地区 A 专注生产商品 1，而地区 B 专注生产商品 2，则商品 1 的总产量为：

$$x_1^T = \frac{2\alpha_A \bar{R}_A}{3} = \frac{2\theta \alpha_B \bar{R}_A}{3} \qquad (1-21)$$

而在没有贸易，两地区相互独立的情况下，商品 1 的总产量为：

$$x_1^N = \frac{\alpha_A \bar{R}_A + \alpha_B \bar{R}_B}{3} = \frac{\theta \alpha_B \bar{R}_A + \alpha_B k \bar{R}_A}{3} = \frac{(\theta+k)\alpha_B \bar{R}_A}{3} \qquad (1-22)$$

显然，当 $k>\theta$ 时，有 $x_1^T < x_1^N$，也即地区 A 专注生产商品 1 时商品 1 的总产量小于没有贸易时的总产量。

同理，如果地区 A 专注生产商品 1，而地区 B 专注生产商品 2，则商品 2 的总产量为：

$$x_2^T = \frac{2\beta_B \bar{R}_B}{3} = \frac{2k\beta_B \bar{R}_A}{3} \qquad (1-23)$$

而在没有贸易，两地区相互独立的情况下，商品 2 的总产量为：

$$x_2^N = \frac{\beta_A \bar{R}_A + \beta_B \bar{R}_B}{3} = \frac{\dfrac{\theta\mu}{\sigma}\beta_B \bar{R}_A + k\beta_B \bar{R}_A}{3} = \frac{\left(\dfrac{\theta\mu}{\sigma}+k\right)\beta_B \bar{R}_A}{3} \qquad (1-24)$$

显然，当 $\dfrac{\theta\mu}{\sigma}<k$ 时，$x_2^T > x_2^N$，也即地区 B 专注生产商品 2 时商品 2 的总产量大于没有贸易时的总产量。因为 $\sigma>\mu$，所以 $\dfrac{\mu}{\sigma}<1$。因此，我们假设 $k>\theta$，此时 $\dfrac{\theta\mu}{\sigma}<k$ 自然得到满足。

在不存在贸易的条件下，地区 B 生产和消费的商品 1 的数量为 $\dfrac{\alpha_B \bar{R}_B}{3} = \dfrac{k}{\theta}\dfrac{\alpha_A \bar{R}_A}{3}$。但是在存在贸易的情况下，地区 A 仅能提供 $\dfrac{\alpha_A \bar{R}_A}{3}$，为了换取这些商品 1，地区 B 至少需要 $\dfrac{\mu\alpha_A \bar{R}_A}{3}$ 单位的商品 2。交易后，地区 B 消费商品 1 的数量为 $\dfrac{\alpha_A \bar{R}_A}{3}$，消费商品 2 的数量为 $\dfrac{2\beta_B \bar{R}_B}{3} - \dfrac{\mu\alpha_A \bar{R}_A}{3}$。则此时，地区 B 实现的效用水平为：

$$U_B = \left[\left(2-\frac{1}{k}\theta\mu^2\right)\frac{\theta}{k}\right]\frac{\alpha_B\beta_B\overline{R}_B^3}{27} \tag{1-25}$$

While in the case of no trade and independence between the two regions, the maximum utility level that region B can achieve is:

$$U_{B,max} = \frac{\alpha_B\beta_B\overline{R}_B^3}{27} \tag{1-26}$$

If $U_B < U_{B,max}$, that is $\left(2-\frac{1}{k}\theta\mu^2\right)\frac{\theta}{k} < 1$, then the less developed region B focusing on producing goods 2 and then trading for goods 1 will lead to an overall decline in welfare. At this time, we can derive:

$$k > \frac{2\theta + \sqrt{4\theta^2 - 4\theta^2\mu^2}}{2} = \frac{2\theta + 2\theta\sqrt{1-\mu^2}}{2} = \theta\left(1+\sqrt{1-\mu^2}\right) \tag{1-27}$$

or ($k > \theta$):

$$\mu^2 > \frac{2\theta k - k^2}{\theta^2} > \frac{2\theta^2 - \theta^2}{\theta^2} = 1 \tag{1-28}$$

In other words, when the demand scale of the less developed region B is large enough, that is, when it satisfies $k > \theta\left(1+\sqrt{1-\mu^2}\right)$, or when the technological efficiency of region B in producing goods 1 is higher than that in producing goods 2 ($\mu > 1$), although region B has a comparative advantage in the production of goods 2, focusing on the production of goods 2 is disadvantageous to it.

From the above analysis, it can be seen that for large countries with a larger scale of local market demand, if they must follow a comparative advantage development strategy, they may lose industrial development opportunities that should belong to their own country, thereby leading to a decline in their income levels. Therefore, industrial development should not be confined to the principle of comparative advantage. If the international market cannot meet domestic demand, even industries in which the country does not have a comparative advantage should be developed.

## III. Economies of Scale and Comparative Advantage

Economies of scale have a circular cumulative causal characteristic. When a region develops economies of scale in a certain industry, it gains a competitive advantage. This competitive advantage further drives industrial upgrading, reinforcing the economies of scale and competitive advantage. Therefore, when production exhibits economies of scale, whether comparative advantage is still the determining factor in regional industrial selection requires careful discussion. Based on the basic model, this section introduces capital as an input factor in the production function (only considering fixed costs here) to construct economies of scale

$$U_\text{B} = \left[\left(2 - \frac{1}{k}\theta\mu^2\right)\frac{\theta}{k}\right]\frac{\alpha_\text{B}\beta_\text{B}\bar{R}_\text{B}^3}{27} \quad (1\text{-}25)$$

而在没有贸易，两地区相互独立的情况下，地区 B 能够实现的最大效用水平为：

$$U_{\text{B,max}} = \frac{\alpha_\text{B}\beta_\text{B}\bar{R}_\text{B}^3}{27} \quad (1\text{-}26)$$

如果有 $U_\text{B} < U_\text{B,max}$，即 $\left(2 - \frac{1}{k}\theta\mu^2\right)\frac{\theta}{k} < 1$，那么，欠发达地区 B 专注于生产商品 2，之后再交易商品 1，会导致整体福利下降。此时，我们能够解得：

$$k > \frac{2\theta + \sqrt{4\theta^2 - 4\theta^2\mu^2}}{2} = \frac{2\theta + 2\theta\sqrt{1-\mu^2}}{2} = \theta\left(1 + \sqrt{1-\mu^2}\right) \quad (1\text{-}27)$$

或（$k > \theta$ 时）：

$$\mu^2 > \frac{2\theta k - k^2}{\theta^2} > \frac{2\theta^2 - \theta^2}{\theta^2} = 1 \quad (1\text{-}28)$$

也就是说，当欠发达地区 B 的需求规模足够大，即满足 $k > \theta\left(1 + \sqrt{1-\mu^2}\right)$ 时，或地区 B 生产商品 1 的技术效率高于生产商品 2 的技术效率时（$\mu > 1$），尽管地区 B 在商品 2 的生产上具有比较优势，但专注于商品 2 的生产却是对其不利的。

由以上分析可知，对于拥有较大规模本地市场需求的大国来说，如果一定要遵循比较优势发展战略，则可能会失去本应属于本国的产业发展机会，并由此导致本国收入水平下降。因此，产业的发展不应囿于比较优势原则，如果国际市场难以满足本国需求，那么即使是本国不具有比较优势的产业，也应得到发展。

## 三、规模经济与比较优势

规模经济具有循环累积的因果特征，当一个地区在某种产业上形成了规模经济后，该地区也就具有了竞争优势，这种竞争优势会进一步引导产业升级，使规模经济和竞争优势得到进一步强化。因此，当生产具有规模经济特性时，比较优势是否还是地区产业选择的决定力量是需要认真讨论的。下文在基本模

and examine its relationship with comparative advantage.

## (i) Supply and Demand of Goods and Factors

We add a fixed amount of capital $\bar{K}$ to the production function, representing the fixed costs of enterprises. At this time:

$$\begin{aligned} x_{i2} &= g(K_{i2}, L_{i2}) = \beta_i \bar{K} L_{i2} \\ x_{i1} &= f(K_{i1}, L_{i1}) = \alpha_i \bar{K} L_{i1} \\ L_{i1} + L_{i2} &= L_i \end{aligned} \quad (1\text{--}29)$$

Let the nominal price of capital be $r$, then the costs for enterprises to produce goods 1 and 2 are:

$$\begin{aligned} C_{i1} &= r\bar{K} + w L_{i1} \\ C_{i2} &= r\bar{K} + w L_{i2} \end{aligned} \quad (1\text{--}30)$$

Given the output, solve for the solution that minimizes the enterprises' costs:

$$\min_{L_{i1}} r\bar{K} + w L_{i1} \\ \text{s.t. } \alpha_i \bar{K} L_{i1} = x_{i1} \quad (1\text{--}31)$$

From this, we can derive:

$$L_{i1} = \frac{x_{i1}}{\alpha_i \bar{K}} \quad (1\text{--}32)$$

Therefore, the total cost function, marginal cost function and average cost function for enterprises producing good 1 in region $i$ are respectively:

$$C_{i1}(x_{i1}) = r\bar{K} + \frac{w}{\alpha_i \bar{K}} x_{i1}; \quad MC_{i1} = \frac{w}{\alpha_i \bar{K}}; \quad AC_{i1} = \frac{r\bar{K}}{x_{i1}} + \frac{w}{\alpha_i \bar{K}} \quad (1\text{--}33)$$

Similarly, the total cost function, marginal cost function and average cost function for enterprises producing good 2 in region $i$ are:

$$C_{i2}(x_{i2}) = r\bar{K} + \frac{w}{\beta_i \bar{K}} x_{i2}; \quad MC_{i2} = \frac{w}{\beta_i \bar{K}}; \quad AC_{i2} = \frac{r\bar{K}}{x_{i2}} + \frac{w}{\beta_i \bar{K}} \quad (1\text{--}34)$$

The above cost functions show that as enterprise output increases, average costs decrease, indicating that enterprise production exhibits economies of scale.

From enterprise profit maximization, we can derive the goods supply function as:

$$p_{i1} = \frac{w}{\alpha_i \bar{K}}; \quad p_{i2} = \frac{w}{\beta_i \bar{K}} \quad (1\text{--}35)$$

Also from enterprise profit maximization, we can derive the labor demand function as:

$$w = p_{i1} \alpha_i \bar{K}; \quad w = p_{i2} \beta_i \bar{K} \quad (1\text{--}36)$$

Since the consumer utility function and budget constraint remain unchanged, the demand for goods and leisure is still given by equation (1-5).

型的基础上，在生产函数中引入资本这一投入要素（在此只考虑固定成本），以此构建规模经济并考查它与比较优势的关系。

## （一）商品和要素的供给与需求

我们在生产函数中加入一个固定的资本量$\bar{K}$，即企业的固定成本，此时有：

$$
\begin{aligned}
x_{i2} &= g(K_{i2}, L_{i2}) = \beta_i \bar{K} L_{i2} \\
x_{i1} &= f(K_{i1}, L_{i1}) = \alpha_i \bar{K} L_{i1} \\
L_{i1} &+ L_{i2} = L_i
\end{aligned}
\tag{1-29}
$$

令资本的名义价格为$r$，则企业生产商品1和商品2的成本为：

$$
\begin{aligned}
C_{i1} &= r\bar{K} + wL_{i1} \\
C_{i2} &= r\bar{K} + wL_{i2}
\end{aligned}
\tag{1-30}
$$

给定产出，求使企业的成本最小化的解，即：

$$
\begin{aligned}
&\min_{L_{i1}} r\bar{K} + wL_{i1} \\
&\text{s.t. } \alpha_i \bar{K} L_{i1} = x_{i1}
\end{aligned}
\tag{1-31}
$$

由此，可解得：

$$
L_{i1} = \frac{x_{i1}}{\alpha_i \bar{K}}
\tag{1-32}
$$

因此，地区$i$商品1的生产企业的总成本函数、边际成本函数和平均成本函数分别为：

$$
C_{i1}(x_{i1}) = r\bar{K} + \frac{w}{\alpha_i \bar{K}} x_{i1}; \quad MC_{i1} = \frac{w}{\alpha_i \bar{K}}; \quad AC_{i1} = \frac{r\bar{K}}{x_{i1}} + \frac{w}{\alpha_i \bar{K}}
\tag{1-33}
$$

同理可得地区$i$商品2的生产企业的总成本函数、边际成本函数和平均成本函数为：

$$
C_{i2}(x_{i2}) = r\bar{K} + \frac{w}{\beta_i \bar{K}} x_{i2}; \quad MC_{i2} = \frac{w}{\beta_i \bar{K}}; \quad AC_{i2} = \frac{r\bar{K}}{x_{i2}} + \frac{w}{\beta_i \bar{K}}
\tag{1-34}
$$

上述成本函数表明，随着企业产量的增加，平均成本是下降的，因此企业生产具有规模经济特性。

由企业的利润最大化，可推导出商品供给函数为：

$$
p_{i1} = \frac{w}{\alpha_i \bar{K}}; \quad p_{i2} = \frac{w}{\beta_i \bar{K}}
\tag{1-35}
$$

仍由企业利润最大化，可推导得出劳动力需求函数为：

$$
w = p_{i1} \alpha_i \bar{K}; \quad w = p_{i2} \beta_i \bar{K}
\tag{1-36}
$$

由于消费者效用函数和预算约束未发生改变，因此商品需求和闲暇需求仍由式（1-5）给出。

### (ii) No-Trade Equilibrium

Under the above model settings, we can obtain the equilibrium output of goods 1 in region $i$ without trade as:

$$x_{i1}^* = \frac{w\bar{R}}{3p_{i1}} = \frac{p_{i1}\alpha_i \bar{K}\bar{R}}{3p_{i1}} = \frac{\alpha_i \bar{K}\bar{R}}{3} \tag{1-37}$$

The equilibrium output of goods 2 in region $i$ is:

$$x_{i2}^* = \frac{w\bar{R}}{3p_{i2}} = \frac{p_{i2}\beta_i \bar{K}\bar{R}}{3p_{i2}} = \frac{\beta_i \bar{K}\bar{R}}{3} \tag{1-38}$$

The optimal leisure level is:

$$R_i^* = \frac{\bar{R}}{3} \tag{1-39}$$

At this time, the maximum utility level that consumers in both regions can achieve is:

$$U_{i,\max} = x_{i1}^* x_{i2}^* R_i^* = \frac{\alpha_i \bar{K}\bar{R}}{3} \frac{\beta_i \bar{K}\bar{R}}{3} \frac{\bar{R}}{3} = \frac{\alpha_i \beta_i \bar{K}^2 \bar{R}^3}{27} \tag{1-40}$$

At this time, the actual profit of enterprises is negative:

$$\pi = \pi_{i1} + \pi_{i2} = -r(\bar{K} + \bar{K}) = -2r\bar{K} \tag{1-41}$$

Therefore, the total social welfare of region $i$ is:

$$TW_i^N = U_{i,\max} + \pi = \frac{\alpha_i \beta_i \bar{K}^2 \bar{R}^3}{27} - 2r\bar{K} \tag{1-42}$$

The total social welfare of both regions without trade is:

$$TW^N = TW_A^N + TW_B^N = \frac{\alpha_A \beta_A \bar{K}^2 \bar{R}^3}{27} + \frac{\alpha_B \beta_B \bar{K}^2 \bar{R}^3}{27} - 4r\bar{K} \tag{1-43}$$

### (iii) Comparative Advantage under Economies of Scale

When $MC_{A1} < MC_{B1}$ and $MC_{A2} < MC_{B2}$, region A has absolute advantage in producing both goods. This requires:

$$MC_{A1} = \frac{w}{\alpha_A \bar{K}} < \frac{w}{\alpha_B \bar{K}} = MC_{B1}; \quad MC_{A2} = \frac{w}{\beta_A \bar{K}} < \frac{w}{\beta_B \bar{K}} = MC_{B2} \tag{1-44}$$

That is, it requires $\alpha_A > \alpha_B$ and $\beta_A > \beta_B$. Because $\alpha_A = \theta \alpha_B$, $\beta_A = \frac{\theta \mu}{\sigma} \beta_B$, it is equivalent to requiring $\theta > 1$ and $\theta > \frac{\sigma}{\mu}$. At this time, if:

$$\frac{1}{\sigma} = \frac{MC_{A1}}{MC_{A2}} < \frac{MC_{B1}}{MC_{B2}} = \frac{1}{\mu} \tag{1-45}$$

That is, $\mu < \sigma$, then region A has a comparative advantage in producing goods 1, while region

## （二）无贸易均衡

在以上模型设定下，我们可以得到不存在贸易的条件下地区 $i$ 商品 1 的均衡产量为：

$$x_{i1}^* = \frac{w\bar{R}}{3p_{i1}} = \frac{p_{i1}\alpha_i \bar{K}\bar{R}}{3p_{i1}} = \frac{\alpha_i \bar{K}\bar{R}}{3} \quad (1-37)$$

地区 $i$ 商品 2 的均衡产量为：

$$x_{i2}^* = \frac{w\bar{R}}{3p_{i2}} = \frac{p_{i2}\beta_i \bar{K}\bar{R}}{3p_{i2}} = \frac{\beta_i \bar{K}\bar{R}}{3} \quad (1-38)$$

最优闲暇水平为：

$$R_i^* = \frac{\bar{R}}{3} \quad (1-39)$$

此时，两地区消费者能够达到的最大效用水平为：

$$U_{i,\max} = x_{i1}^* x_{i2}^* R_i^* = \frac{\alpha_i \bar{K}\bar{R}}{3} \frac{\beta_i \bar{K}\bar{R}}{3} \frac{\bar{R}}{3} = \frac{\alpha_i \beta_i \bar{K}^2 \bar{R}^3}{27} \quad (1-40)$$

此时，企业的实际利润为负：

$$\pi = \pi_{i1} + \pi_{i2} = -r(\bar{K} + \bar{K}) = -2r\bar{K} \quad (1-41)$$

因此，地区 $i$ 的社会总福利为：

$$TW_i^N = U_{i,\max} + \pi = \frac{\alpha_i \beta_i \bar{K}^2 \bar{R}^3}{27} - 2r\bar{K} \quad (1-42)$$

无贸易时两地区的社会总福利为：

$$TW^N = TW_A^N + TW_B^N = \frac{\alpha_A \beta_A \bar{K}^2 \bar{R}^3}{27} + \frac{\alpha_B \beta_B \bar{K}^2 \bar{R}^3}{27} - 4r\bar{K} \quad (1-43)$$

## （三）规模经济下的比较优势

当 $MC_{A1} < MC_{B1}$ 且 $MC_{A2} < MC_{B2}$ 时，地区 A 在两种商品的生产上都具有绝对优势，此时要求：

$$MC_{A1} = \frac{w}{\alpha_A \bar{K}} < \frac{w}{\alpha_B \bar{K}} = MC_{B1}; \quad MC_{A2} = \frac{w}{\beta_A \bar{K}} < \frac{w}{\beta_B \bar{K}} = MC_{B2} \quad (1-44)$$

即要求 $\alpha_A > \alpha_B$ 和 $\beta_A > \beta_B$，因为 $\alpha_A = \theta \alpha_B$，$\beta_A = \frac{\theta \mu}{\sigma}\beta_B$，所以等价于要求 $\theta > 1$ 且 $\theta > \frac{\sigma}{\mu}$。此时，如果有：

$$\frac{1}{\sigma} = \frac{MC_{A1}}{MC_{A2}} < \frac{MC_{B1}}{MC_{B2}} = \frac{1}{\mu} \quad (1-45)$$

即 $\mu < \sigma$，则地区 A 在商品 1 的生产上具有比较优势，而地区 B 在商品 2 的生产

B has a comparative advantage in producing goods 2. Conversely, region A has a comparative advantage in producing goods 2, while region B has a comparative advantage in producing goods 1. Then, under conditions of economies of scale, if a region focuses on producing products in which it does not have a comparative advantage, can it improve welfare levels?

When region A focuses on producing goods 2 in which it does not have a comparative advantage, the market demand it faces is:

$$x_2 = \frac{w\overline{R}}{3p_2} + \frac{w\overline{R}}{3p_2} = \frac{2w\overline{R}}{3p_2} \tag{1-46}$$

The market supply is:

$$p_2 = \frac{w}{\beta_A \overline{K}} \tag{1-47}$$

Therefore, the total market output of goods 2 is:

$$x_2^* = \frac{2w\overline{R}}{3\dfrac{w}{\beta_A \overline{K}}} = \frac{2\beta_A \overline{K}}{3} \overline{R} \tag{1-48}$$

When region B focuses on producing goods 1, which it does not have a comparative advantage in, the market demand it faces is:

$$x_1 = \frac{w\overline{R}}{3p_1} + \frac{w\overline{R}}{3p_1} = \frac{2w\overline{R}}{3p_1} \tag{1-49}$$

The market supply is:

$$p_1 = \frac{w}{\alpha_B \overline{K}} \tag{1-50}$$

Thus, the total market output of goods 1 is:

$$x_1^* = \frac{2w\overline{R}}{3\dfrac{w}{\alpha_B \overline{K}}} = \frac{2\alpha_B \overline{K}}{3} \overline{R} \tag{1-51}$$

Now, let's assume that both regions trade their own produced $\frac{1}{2}$ goods for $\frac{1}{2}$ goods produced by the other region, at this point, the quantities of goods 1 and goods 2 consumed by region A are:

$$x_{A1} = \frac{\alpha_B \overline{K}}{3} \overline{R}; \quad x_{A2} = \frac{\beta_A \overline{K}}{3} \overline{R} \tag{1-52}$$

The quantities of goods 1 and goods 2 consumed by region B are:

$$x_{B1} = \frac{\alpha_B \overline{K}}{3} \overline{R}; \quad x_{B2} = \frac{\beta_A \overline{K}}{3} \overline{R} \tag{1-53}$$

Therefore, the total social welfare of region A is:

$$TW_A^T = U_{i,\max} + \pi = \frac{\alpha_B \overline{K}}{3}\overline{R} \frac{\beta_A \overline{K}}{3}\overline{R}\frac{\overline{R}}{3} - r\overline{K} = \frac{\alpha_B \beta_A \overline{K}^2 \overline{R}^3}{27} - r\overline{K} \tag{1-54}$$

上具有比较优势。反之，则地区 A 在商品 2 的生产上具有比较优势，而地区 B 在商品 1 的生产上具有比较优势。那么，在存在规模经济的条件下，如果一个地区专注于生产它不具有比较优势的产品，是否能够提升福利水平呢？

当地区 A 专注于生产不具有比较优势的商品 2 时，其面对的市场需求为：

$$x_2 = \frac{w\bar{R}}{3p_2} + \frac{w\bar{R}}{3p_2} = \frac{2w\bar{R}}{3p_2} \quad (1\text{-}46)$$

市场供给为：

$$p_2 = \frac{w}{\beta_A \bar{K}} \quad (1\text{-}47)$$

因此，商品 2 的市场总产出为：

$$x_2^* = \frac{2w\bar{R}}{3\frac{w}{\beta_A \bar{K}}} = \frac{2\beta_A \bar{K}}{3}\bar{R} \quad (1\text{-}48)$$

当地区 B 专注于生产不具有比较优势的商品 1 时，其面对的市场需求为：

$$x_1 = \frac{w\bar{R}}{3p_1} + \frac{w\bar{R}}{3p_1} = \frac{2w\bar{R}}{3p_1} \quad (1\text{-}49)$$

市场供给为：

$$p_1 = \frac{w}{\alpha_B \bar{K}} \quad (1\text{-}50)$$

因此，商品 1 的市场总产出为：

$$x_1^* = \frac{2w\bar{R}}{3\frac{w}{\alpha_B \bar{K}}} = \frac{2\alpha_B \bar{K}}{3}\bar{R} \quad (1\text{-}51)$$

现在，我们假设两个地区均以自己生产商品的 $\frac{1}{2}$ 交易另一地区生产商品的 $\frac{1}{2}$，此时，地区 A 消费的商品 1 和商品 2 的数量分别为：

$$x_{A1} = \frac{\alpha_B \bar{K}}{3}\bar{R}; \quad x_{A2} = \frac{\beta_A \bar{K}}{3}\bar{R} \quad (1\text{-}52)$$

地区 B 消费的商品 1 和商品 2 的数量分别为：

$$x_{B1} = \frac{\alpha_B \bar{K}}{3}\bar{R}; \quad x_{B2} = \frac{\beta_A \bar{K}}{3}\bar{R} \quad (1\text{-}53)$$

因此，地区 A 的社会总福利为：

$$TW_A^T = U_{i,\max} + \pi = \frac{\alpha_B \bar{K}}{3}\bar{R}\frac{\beta_A \bar{K}}{3}\bar{R}\frac{\bar{R}}{3} - r\bar{K} = \frac{\alpha_B \beta_A \bar{K}^2 \bar{R}^3}{27} - r\bar{K} \quad (1\text{-}54)$$

The total social welfare of region B is:

$$TW_B^T = U_{i,\max} + \pi = \frac{\alpha_B \bar{K}}{3}\bar{R}\frac{\beta_A \bar{K}}{3}\bar{R}\frac{\bar{R}}{3} - r\bar{K} = \frac{\alpha_B \beta_A \bar{K}^2 \bar{R}^3}{27} - r\bar{K} \quad (1-55)$$

Therefore, under the condition of trade, the total social welfare of the two regions is:

$$TW^T = TW_A^T + TW_B^T = \frac{\alpha_B \beta_A \bar{K}^2 \bar{R}^3}{27} - r\bar{K} + \frac{\alpha_B \beta_A \bar{K}^2 \bar{R}^3}{27} - r\bar{K}$$
$$= \frac{2\alpha_B \beta_A \bar{K}^2 \bar{R}^3}{27} - 2r\bar{K} \quad (1-56)$$

So, there is:

$$TW^T - TW^N = \frac{2\alpha_B \beta_A \bar{K}^2 \bar{R}^3}{27} - 2r\bar{K} - \left(\frac{\alpha_A \beta_A \bar{K}^2 \bar{R}^3}{27} - 2r\bar{K} + \frac{\alpha_B \beta_B \bar{K}^2 \bar{R}^3}{27} - 2r\bar{K}\right)$$
$$= (2\alpha_B \beta_A - \alpha_A \beta_A - \alpha_B \beta_B)\frac{\bar{R}^3 \bar{K}^2}{27} + 2r\bar{K} \quad (1-57)$$

If $TW^T - TW^N > 0$, which requires:

$$(2\alpha_B \beta_A - \alpha_A \beta_A - \alpha_B \beta_B)\frac{\bar{R}^3 \bar{K}^2}{27} + 2r\bar{K} > 0 \quad (1-58)$$

Thus:

$$\bar{K} > \frac{54r}{(\alpha_A \beta_A + \alpha_B \beta_B - 2\alpha_B \beta_A)\bar{R}^3} \quad (1-59)$$

Therefore, if capital exists in production along with the resulting fixed costs, leading to economies of scale in production, then as long as a region focuses on producing one type of good, even if that good is not one in which it has a comparative advantage, it may still improve the region's total social welfare level.

In fact, in the development of economic theory, the importance of economies of scale has been continuously increasing. Krugman's new trade theory based on economies of scale attempts to go beyond the analytical paradigm of comparative advantage, making the theory more aligned with developments in trade practice. This new trade theory based on economies of scale provides a more powerful explanation for issues such as division of labor, specialization, and economic growth. At the same time, research on economic growth has developed to the stage of endogenous growth theory, which also views economies of scale as a basic assumption and driver of growth. However, scholars advocating comparative advantage theory persist in promoting comparative advantage development strategies based on factor endowments, ignoring the impact of economies of scale on regional specialization. This not only contradicts the direction of theoretical development but may also provide incorrect guidance for practice.

地区 B 的社会总福利为：

$$TW_B^T = U_{i,\max} + \pi = \frac{\alpha_B \bar{K}}{3}\bar{R}\frac{\beta_A \bar{K}}{3}\bar{R}\frac{\bar{R}}{3} - r\bar{K} = \frac{\alpha_B \beta_A \bar{K}^2 \bar{R}^3}{27} - r\bar{K} \quad (1-55)$$

因此，在存在贸易的条件下，两地区社会总福利为：

$$TW^T = TW_A^T + TW_B^T = \frac{\alpha_B \beta_A \bar{K}^2 \bar{R}^3}{27} - r\bar{K} + \frac{\alpha_B \beta_A \bar{K}^2 \bar{R}^3}{27} - r\bar{K}$$
$$= \frac{2\alpha_B \beta_A \bar{K}^2 \bar{R}^3}{27} - 2r\bar{K} \quad (1-56)$$

所以，有：

$$TW^T - TW^N = \frac{2\alpha_B \beta_A \bar{K}^2 \bar{R}^3}{27} - 2r\bar{K} - \left(\frac{\alpha_A \beta_A \bar{K}^2 \bar{R}^3}{27} - 2r\bar{K} + \frac{\alpha_B \beta_B \bar{K}^2 \bar{R}^3}{27} - 2r\bar{K}\right)$$
$$= \left(2\alpha_B \beta_A - \alpha_A \beta_A - \alpha_B \beta_B\right)\frac{\bar{R}^3 \bar{K}^2}{27} + 2r\bar{K} \quad (1-57)$$

如果 $TW^T - TW^N > 0$，即要求：

$$\left(2\alpha_B \beta_A - \alpha_A \beta_A - \alpha_B \beta_B\right)\frac{\bar{R}^3 \bar{K}^2}{27} + 2r\bar{K} > 0 \quad (1-58)$$

即：

$$\bar{K} > \frac{54r}{\left(\alpha_A \beta_A + \alpha_B \beta_B - 2\alpha_B \beta_A\right)\bar{R}^3} \quad (1-59)$$

因此，如果生产中存在资本以及由此产生的固定成本，从而导致生产是规模经济的，那么一个地区只要专注于生产一种商品，即使该商品不是其具有比较优势的商品，也可能会提升地区社会总福利水平。

实际上，在经济理论的发展中，规模经济的重要性是不断提升的。克鲁格曼基于规模经济建立的新贸易理论便试图超越比较优势的分析范式，使理论更加契合于贸易实践的发展。这种基于规模经济的新贸易理论，在对分工、专业化和经济增长等问题的解释上更加有力。与此同时，对经济增长的研究发展到了内生增长理论阶段，该理论也将规模经济视为一项基本假设和增长动力。但鼓吹比较优势理论的学者，却坚持倡导基于要素禀赋的比较优势发展战略，忽视了规模经济对地区专业化的影响，这不仅与理论发展方向相悖，也可能对实践形成错误的指导。

## IV. Factor Mobility and Comparative Advantage

Another important prerequisite for the validity of comparative advantage theory is that factors are immobile between regions. As Samuelson stated: "Ricardo's trade theory traditionally assumes a 0% possibility of factor mobility, while the possibility of goods flowing between countries or regions is 100%." Once factors become mobile, when there are differences in factor endowments between regions, factors will flow to regions with higher marginal returns, ultimately eliminating differences in factor endowments between regions and thus eliminating comparative advantage. This section makes slight modifications to the basic model, allowing for factor mobility, and studies comparative advantage under these conditions.

### (i) Supply and Demand of Goods and Factors

Since the consumer utility function and budget constraint remain unchanged, the demand for goods and leisure is still given by equation (1-5).

Labor remains the only input factor for enterprise production, with the production function adjusted to:

$$\begin{aligned} x_{i1} &= f(L_{i1}) = \alpha_i L_{i1}^{\gamma} \\ x_{i2} &= g(L_{i2}) = \beta_i L_{i2}^{\gamma} \\ L_{i1} + L_{i2} &= L_i \end{aligned} \quad (1\text{-}60)$$

Here, the parameter $\gamma < 1$. Assuming there are no fixed costs for enterprise production, the costs for enterprises in the two regions to produce goods 1 and 2 are:

$$\begin{aligned} C_{i1} &= wL_{i1} = w\left(\frac{x_{i1}}{\alpha_i}\right)^{\frac{1}{\gamma}} \\ C_{i2} &= wL_{i2} = w\left(\frac{x_{i2}}{\beta_i}\right)^{\frac{1}{\gamma}} \end{aligned} \quad (1\text{-}61)$$

Therefore, the profits for enterprises producing goods 1 and 2 are:

$$\begin{aligned} \pi_{i1} &= p_{i1}x_{i1} - w\left(\frac{x_{i1}}{\alpha_i}\right)^{\frac{1}{\gamma}} = p_{i1}\alpha_i L_{i1}^{\gamma} - wL_{i1} \\ \pi_{i2} &= p_{i2}x_{i2} - w\left(\frac{x_{i2}}{\beta_i}\right)^{\frac{1}{\gamma}} = p_{i2}\beta_i L_{i2}^{\gamma} - wL_{i2} \end{aligned} \quad (1\text{-}62)$$

## 四、要素可流动与比较优势

比较优势理论成立的另一个重要前置假设是要素在地区间不可流动，正如萨缪尔森所言："李嘉图的贸易理论传统上假设要素流动的可能性为0%，而商品在国家或地区间流动的可能性为100%。"而一旦要素可流动，当地区之间存在要素禀赋的差异时，要素就会流向边际回报更高的地区，最终抹平地区间的要素禀赋差异，也就消除了比较优势。本节对基本模型稍作改动，同时允许要素流动，在此种情况下对比较优势进行研究。

### （一）商品与要素的供给与需求

由于消费者效用函数和预算约束未发生改变，所以商品需求和闲暇需求仍由式（1-5）给出。

企业生产的唯一投入要素仍是劳动力，生产函数调整为：

$$\begin{aligned} x_{i1} &= f(L_{i1}) = \alpha_i L_{i1}^{\gamma} \\ x_{i2} &= g(L_{i2}) = \beta_i L_{i2}^{\gamma} \\ L_{i1} &+ L_{i2} = L_i \end{aligned} \quad (1\text{-}60)$$

这里的参数$\gamma<1$。假设企业生产没有固定成本，则两地区企业生产商品1和商品2的成本为：

$$\begin{aligned} C_{i1} &= wL_{i1} = w\left(\frac{x_{i1}}{\alpha_i}\right)^{\frac{1}{\gamma}} \\ C_{i2} &= wL_{i2} = w\left(\frac{x_{i2}}{\beta_i}\right)^{\frac{1}{\gamma}} \end{aligned} \quad (1\text{-}61)$$

因此，企业生产商品1和商品2的利润为：

$$\begin{aligned} \pi_{i1} &= p_{i1}x_{i1} - w\left(\frac{x_{i1}}{\alpha_i}\right)^{\frac{1}{\gamma}} = p_{i1}\alpha_i L_{i1}^{\gamma} - wL_{i1} \\ \pi_{i2} &= p_{i2}x_{i2} - w\left(\frac{x_{i2}}{\beta_i}\right)^{\frac{1}{\gamma}} = p_{i2}\beta_i L_{i2}^{\gamma} - wL_{i2} \end{aligned} \quad (1\text{-}62)$$

Solving the enterprise's profit maximization problem gives the supply functions for goods 1 and 2:

$$p_{i1} = \frac{w}{\gamma} \frac{1}{\alpha_i} \left(\frac{x_{i1}}{\alpha_i}\right)^{\frac{1}{\gamma}-1} = \frac{w}{\gamma \alpha_i^{\frac{1}{\gamma}}} x_{i1}^{\frac{1-\gamma}{\gamma}}$$

$$p_{i2} = \frac{w}{\gamma} \frac{1}{\beta_i} \left(\frac{x_{i2}}{\beta_i}\right)^{\frac{1}{\gamma}-1} = \frac{w}{\gamma \beta_i^{\frac{1}{\gamma}}} x_{i2}^{\frac{1-\gamma}{\gamma}}$$

(1-63)

And the labor demand function:

$$w = \gamma p_{i1} \alpha_i L_{i1}^{\gamma-1}$$
$$w = \gamma p_{i2} \beta_i L_{i2}^{\gamma-1}$$

(1-64)

### (ii) Model Equilibrium

From the goods demand given by equation (1-5) and the goods supply given by equation (1-63), we can calculate the goods market equilibrium as:

$$x_{i1} = \left(\frac{\gamma \alpha_i^{\frac{1}{\gamma}} \overline{R}_i}{3}\right)^{\gamma} ; \quad x_{i2} = \left(\frac{\gamma \beta_i^{\frac{1}{\gamma}} \overline{R}_i}{3}\right)^{\gamma}$$

(1-65)

The labor demand function for region $i$ is given by equation (1-64), and the equilibrium real wage is:

$$\frac{w}{p_{i1}} = \gamma \alpha_i L_{i1}^{\gamma-1}$$
$$\frac{w}{p_{i2}} = \gamma \beta_i L_{i2}^{\gamma-1}$$

(1-66)

As can be seen, the real wage is equal to the marginal product of labor.

Because the real wage of labor within a region should be the same, i.e.:

$$\gamma \alpha_i L_{i1}^{\gamma-1} = \gamma \beta_i L_{i2}^{\gamma-1}$$

(1-67)

Thus, we have:

$$\frac{L_{i1}^{\gamma-1}}{L_{i2}^{\gamma-1}} = \frac{\beta_i}{\alpha_i}$$

(1-68)

That is:

$$\frac{L_{i1}}{L_{i2}} = \left(\frac{\beta_i}{\alpha_i}\right)^{\frac{1}{\gamma-1}}$$

(1-69)

Namely:

$$L_{i1} = \left(\frac{\beta_i}{\alpha_i}\right)^{\frac{1}{\gamma-1}} L_{i2}$$

(1-70)

求解企业的利润最大化问题,得到商品 1 和商品 2 的供给函数:

$$p_{i1} = \frac{w}{\gamma}\frac{1}{\alpha_i}\left(\frac{x_{i1}}{\alpha_i}\right)^{\frac{1}{\gamma}-1} = \frac{w}{\gamma \alpha_i^{\frac{1}{\gamma}}} x_{i1}^{\frac{1-\gamma}{\gamma}}$$

$$p_{i2} = \frac{w}{\gamma}\frac{1}{\beta_i}\left(\frac{x_{i2}}{\beta_i}\right)^{\frac{1}{\gamma}-1} = \frac{w}{\gamma \beta_i^{\frac{1}{\gamma}}} x_{i2}^{\frac{1-\gamma}{\gamma}}$$

(1-63)

以及劳动力的需求函数:

$$w = \gamma p_{i1}\alpha_i L_{i1}^{\gamma-1}$$
$$w = \gamma p_{i2}\beta_i L_{i2}^{\gamma-1}$$

(1-64)

### (二)模型均衡

由式(1-5)给出的商品需求和式(1-63)给出的商品供给,可计算得到商品市场均衡为:

$$x_{i1} = \left(\frac{\gamma \alpha_i^{\frac{1}{\gamma}} \overline{R}_i}{3}\right)^{\gamma} \; ; \; x_{i2} = \left(\frac{\gamma \beta_i^{\frac{1}{\gamma}} \overline{R}_i}{3}\right)^{\gamma}$$

(1-65)

地区 $i$ 的劳动力需求函数由式(1-64)给出,均衡的实际工资为:

$$\frac{w}{p_{i1}} = \gamma \alpha_i L_{i1}^{\gamma-1}$$
$$\frac{w}{p_{i2}} = \gamma \beta_i L_{i2}^{\gamma-1}$$

(1-66)

可以看出,实际工资就是劳动力的边际产出。

因为一个地区内劳动力的实际工资应是相同的,即:

$$\gamma \alpha_i L_{i1}^{\gamma-1} = \gamma \beta_i L_{i2}^{\gamma-1}$$

(1-67)

于是,有:

$$\frac{L_{i1}^{\gamma-1}}{L_{i2}^{\gamma-1}} = \frac{\beta_i}{\alpha_i}$$

(1-68)

即有:

$$\frac{L_{i1}}{L_{i2}} = \left(\frac{\beta_i}{\alpha_i}\right)^{\frac{1}{\gamma-1}}$$

(1-69)

即:

$$L_{i1} = \left(\frac{\beta_i}{\alpha_i}\right)^{\frac{1}{\gamma-1}} L_{i2}$$

(1-70)

The labor supply in region $i$ is:

$$L_i = L_{i1} + L_{i2} = \bar{R}_i - R_i = \bar{R}_i - \frac{\bar{R}_i}{3} = \frac{2}{3}\bar{R}_i \tag{1-71}$$

So:

$$\left(\frac{\beta_i}{\alpha_i}\right)^{\frac{1}{\gamma-1}} L_{i2} + L_{i2} = \frac{2}{3}\bar{R}_i \tag{1-72}$$

That is:

$$\left[1+\left(\frac{\beta_i}{\alpha_i}\right)^{\frac{1}{\gamma-1}}\right] L_{i2} = \frac{2}{3}\bar{R}_i \tag{1-73}$$

Therefore, we have:

$$
\begin{aligned}
L_{i2} &= \frac{\frac{2}{3}\bar{R}_i}{1+\left(\frac{\beta_i}{\alpha_i}\right)^{\frac{1}{\gamma-1}}} = \frac{\frac{2}{3}\bar{R}_i}{\frac{\alpha_i^{\frac{1}{\gamma-1}}+\beta_i^{\frac{1}{\gamma-1}}}{\alpha_i^{\frac{1}{\gamma-1}}}} \\
&= \frac{\frac{2}{3}\bar{R}_i}{\frac{\alpha_i^{\frac{1}{\gamma-1}}+\beta_i^{\frac{1}{\gamma-1}}}{\alpha_i^{\frac{1}{\gamma-1}}}} = \frac{\left(\frac{2}{3}\alpha_i^{\frac{1}{\gamma-1}}\right)\bar{R}_i}{\alpha_i^{\frac{1}{\gamma-1}}+\beta_i^{\frac{1}{\gamma-1}}}
\end{aligned}
\tag{1-74}
$$

$$
\begin{aligned}
L_{i1} &= \frac{2}{3}\bar{R}_i - L_{i2} = \frac{2}{3}\bar{R}_i - \frac{\left(\frac{2}{3}\alpha_i^{\frac{1}{\gamma-1}}\right)\bar{R}_i}{\alpha_i^{\frac{1}{\gamma-1}}+\beta_i^{\frac{1}{\gamma-1}}} \\
&= \frac{2}{3}\bar{R}_i\left(1-\frac{\alpha_i^{\frac{1}{\gamma-1}}}{\alpha_i^{\frac{1}{\gamma-1}}+\beta_i^{\frac{1}{\gamma-1}}}\right) = \frac{\left(\frac{2}{3}\beta_i^{\frac{1}{\gamma-1}}\right)\bar{R}_i}{\alpha_i^{\frac{1}{\gamma-1}}+\beta_i^{\frac{1}{\gamma-1}}}
\end{aligned}
$$

Thus:

$$\frac{w}{p_{i1}} = \gamma\alpha_i L_{i1}^{\gamma-1} = \gamma\alpha_i\left[\frac{\left(\frac{2}{3}\beta_i^{\frac{1}{\gamma-1}}\right)\bar{R}_i}{\alpha_i^{\frac{1}{\gamma-1}}+\beta_i^{\frac{1}{\gamma-1}}}\right]^{\gamma-1} = \gamma\alpha_i\beta_i\left(\frac{\frac{2}{3}\bar{R}_i}{\alpha_i^{\frac{1}{\gamma-1}}+\beta_i^{\frac{1}{\gamma-1}}}\right)^{\gamma-1} = \frac{w}{p_{i2}} \tag{1-75}$$

Let:

$$\varpi_i = \frac{w}{p_{i1}} = \frac{w}{p_{i2}} \tag{1-76}$$

地区 $i$ 的劳动力供给为：

$$L_i = L_{i1} + L_{i2} = \bar{R}_i - R_i = \bar{R}_i - \frac{\bar{R}_i}{3} = \frac{2}{3}\bar{R}_i \tag{1-71}$$

所以：

$$\left(\frac{\beta_i}{\alpha_i}\right)^{\frac{1}{\gamma-1}} L_{i2} + L_{i2} = \frac{2}{3}\bar{R}_i \tag{1-72}$$

即：

$$\left[1 + \left(\frac{\beta_i}{\alpha_i}\right)^{\frac{1}{\gamma-1}}\right] L_{i2} = \frac{2}{3}\bar{R}_i \tag{1-73}$$

因此，有：

$$\begin{aligned}
L_{i2} &= \frac{\frac{2}{3}\bar{R}_i}{1 + \left(\frac{\beta_i}{\alpha_i}\right)^{\frac{1}{\gamma-1}}} = \frac{\frac{2}{3}\bar{R}_i}{\frac{\alpha_i^{\frac{1}{\gamma-1}} + \beta_i^{\frac{1}{\gamma-1}}}{\alpha_i^{\frac{1}{\gamma-1}}}} \\
&= \frac{\frac{2}{3}\bar{R}_i}{\frac{\alpha_i^{\frac{1}{\gamma-1}} + \beta_i^{\frac{1}{\gamma-1}}}{\alpha_i^{\frac{1}{\gamma-1}}}} = \frac{\left(\frac{2}{3}\alpha_i^{\frac{1}{\gamma-1}}\right)\bar{R}_i}{\alpha_i^{\frac{1}{\gamma-1}} + \beta_i^{\frac{1}{\gamma-1}}}
\end{aligned} \tag{1-74}$$

$$\begin{aligned}
L_{i1} &= \frac{2}{3}\bar{R}_i - L_{i2} = \frac{2}{3}\bar{R}_i - \frac{\left(\frac{2}{3}\alpha_i^{\frac{1}{\gamma-1}}\right)\bar{R}_i}{\alpha_i^{\frac{1}{\gamma-1}} + \beta_i^{\frac{1}{\gamma-1}}} \\
&= \frac{2}{3}\bar{R}_i\left(1 - \frac{\alpha_i^{\frac{1}{\gamma-1}}}{\alpha_i^{\frac{1}{\gamma-1}} + \beta_i^{\frac{1}{\gamma-1}}}\right) = \frac{\left(\frac{2}{3}\beta_i^{\frac{1}{\gamma-1}}\right)\bar{R}_i}{\alpha_i^{\frac{1}{\gamma-1}} + \beta_i^{\frac{1}{\gamma-1}}}
\end{aligned}$$

于是：

$$\frac{w}{p_{i1}} = \gamma\alpha_i L_{i1}^{\gamma-1} = \gamma\alpha_i\left[\frac{\left(\frac{2}{3}\beta_i^{\frac{1}{\gamma-1}}\right)\bar{R}_i}{\alpha_i^{\frac{1}{\gamma-1}} + \beta_i^{\frac{1}{\gamma-1}}}\right]^{\gamma-1} = \gamma\alpha_i\beta_i\left(\frac{\frac{2}{3}\bar{R}_i}{\alpha_i^{\frac{1}{\gamma-1}} + \beta_i^{\frac{1}{\gamma-1}}}\right)^{\gamma-1} = \frac{w}{p_{i2}} \tag{1-75}$$

令：

$$\varpi_i = \frac{w}{p_{i1}} = \frac{w}{p_{i2}} \tag{1-76}$$

So:

$$\varpi_A = \gamma \alpha_A \beta_A \left( \frac{\frac{2}{3}\bar{R}_A}{\alpha_A^{\frac{1}{\gamma-1}} + \beta_A^{\frac{1}{\gamma-1}}} \right)^{\gamma-1}$$

$$\varpi_B = \gamma \alpha_B \beta_B \left( \frac{\frac{2}{3}\bar{R}_B}{\alpha_B^{\frac{1}{\gamma-1}} + \beta_B^{\frac{1}{\gamma-1}}} \right)^{\gamma-1}$$

(1-77)

The real wage is actually the marginal product. So we have:

$$\varpi_A - \varpi_B = \left(\frac{2}{3}\right)^{\gamma-1} \gamma \left[ \alpha_A \beta_A \left( \frac{\bar{R}_A}{\alpha_A^{\frac{1}{\gamma-1}} + \beta_A^{\frac{1}{\gamma-1}}} \right)^{\gamma-1} - \alpha_B \beta_B \left( \frac{\bar{R}_B}{\alpha_B^{\frac{1}{\gamma-1}} + \beta_B^{\frac{1}{\gamma-1}}} \right)^{\gamma-1} \right] \quad (1\text{-}78)$$

When $\varpi_A - \varpi_B > 0$, it indicates that the real wage in region A is higher than in region B, which will lead to labor migration from region B to region A, manifested as an increase in $\bar{R}_A$ and a decrease in $\bar{R}_B$; conversely, $\bar{R}_A$ decreases and $\bar{R}_B$ increases. When $\varpi_A = \varpi_B$, the system will reach a stable state, labor will no longer migrate, and $\bar{R}_A$ and $\bar{R}_B$ will no longer change. At this time, the marginal product levels of labor in the two regions are completely consistent. We then have:

$$\varpi_A = \frac{w}{p_{A1}} = \frac{w}{p_{A2}} = \frac{w}{p_{B1}} = \frac{w}{p_{B2}} = \varpi_B \quad (1\text{-}79)$$

Therefore, we have:

$$\frac{p_{A1}}{p_{B1}} = \frac{w}{w} = \frac{p_{A2}}{p_{B2}} \quad (1\text{-}80)$$

That is:

$$p_{A1} = p_{B1}; \quad p_{A2} = p_{B2} \quad (1\text{-}81)$$

This indicates that the prices of the same goods between the two regions are consistent, and thus there will be no trade between the two regions. Therefore, the immobility of factors is a basic assumption for comparative advantage to hold. If factors are mobile, it will weaken the factor endowments of regions and cause the relative prices of different goods to converge.

Next, we will use an example with specific numerical values to illustrate this process intuitively.

### (iii) Numerical Analysis

For equation (1-78), we assign values to each parameter, letting $\bar{R}_A + \bar{R}_B = 1$, $\gamma = 0.6$, $\beta_A = \beta_B = 1$. Below, we will discuss two scenarios: $\sigma = 1$ and $\mu = 1$.

则：

$$\varpi_A = \gamma \alpha_A \beta_A \left( \frac{\frac{2}{3}\bar{R}_A}{\alpha_A^{\frac{1}{\gamma-1}} + \beta_A^{\frac{1}{\gamma-1}}} \right)^{\gamma-1} \tag{1-77}$$

$$\varpi_B = \gamma \alpha_B \beta_B \left( \frac{\frac{2}{3}\bar{R}_B}{\alpha_B^{\frac{1}{\gamma-1}} + \beta_B^{\frac{1}{\gamma-1}}} \right)^{\gamma-1}$$

实际工资其实就是边际产出。于是，有：

$$\varpi_A - \varpi_B = \left(\frac{2}{3}\right)^{\gamma-1} \gamma \left[ \alpha_A \beta_A \left( \frac{\bar{R}_A}{\alpha_A^{\frac{1}{\gamma-1}} + \beta_A^{\frac{1}{\gamma-1}}} \right)^{\gamma-1} - \alpha_B \beta_B \left( \frac{\bar{R}_B}{\alpha_B^{\frac{1}{\gamma-1}} + \beta_B^{\frac{1}{\gamma-1}}} \right)^{\gamma-1} \right] \tag{1-78}$$

当 $\varpi_A - \varpi_B > 0$ 时，表明地区 A 的实际工资高于地区 B，这将导致地区 B 的劳动力向地区 A 迁移，表现为 $\bar{R}_A$ 提高和 $\bar{R}_B$ 下降；反之，则是 $\bar{R}_A$ 下降和 $\bar{R}_B$ 提高。当 $\varpi_A = \varpi_B$ 时，系统将达到稳定状态，劳动力不再迁移，$\bar{R}_A$ 和 $\bar{R}_B$ 不再变化。此时，两地区劳动力的边际产出水平完全一致。这时有：

$$\varpi_A = \frac{w}{p_{A1}} = \frac{w}{p_{A2}} = \frac{w}{p_{B1}} = \frac{w}{p_{B2}} = \varpi_B \tag{1-79}$$

因此，有：

$$\frac{p_{A1}}{p_{B1}} = \frac{w}{w} = \frac{p_{A2}}{p_{B2}} \tag{1-80}$$

也即：

$$p_{A1} = p_{B1}; \quad p_{A2} = p_{B2} \tag{1-81}$$

这表明，两地区之间相同商品的价格是一致的，从而两地区之间将不会有交易发生。因此，要素的不可流动性是比较优势得以成立的基本假设，如果要素可流动，就会弱化地区的要素禀赋，使不同商品的相对价格趋于一致。

下面，我们将以一个有具体数值的例子对此过程进行直观的展示。

### （三）数值分析

对式（1-78），我们为各参数进行赋值，令 $\bar{R}_A + \bar{R}_B = 1$，$\gamma = 0.6$，$\beta_A = \beta_B = 1$。下面，我们再分 $\sigma = 1$ 和 $\mu = 1$ 两种情况进行讨论。

## 1. The case of $\sigma = 1$

From $\beta_A = \beta_B = 1$, when $\sigma = 1$, we have $\alpha_A = 1$. We take $\mu$ values as 1, 1.8, and 3.2, then the corresponding $\alpha_B$ values are 1, 1.8, and 3.2, and the corresponding $\theta$ values are 1, 0.5556, and 0.3125. Since $\alpha_B = \mu \beta_B$, larger $\mu$ values represent higher efficiency in producing goods 1 in region B. Below, we plot the graph of $\varpi_A - \varpi_B$. In Figure 1-1, the vertical axis represents $\varpi_A - \varpi_B$, and the horizontal axis represents $\bar{R}_A$. As can be seen, as the $\mu$ value increases, the $\bar{R}_A$ of the system's stable state becomes smaller, meaning the population size of region A becomes smaller. In the stable state, the marginal products of the two goods in both regions are consistent, prices are equal, comparative advantage dissipates between regions, and trade stops.

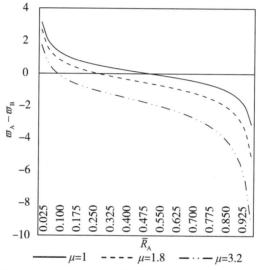

Figure 1-1  Inter-regions Distribution of Labor when $\sigma = 1$

## 2. The case of $\mu = 1$

From $\beta_A = \beta_B = 1$, when $\mu = 1$, we have $\alpha_B = 1$. We take $\sigma$ values as 1, 1.8, and 3.2, then the corresponding $\alpha_A$ values are 1, 1.8, and 3.2, and the corresponding $\theta$ values are 1, 1.8, and 3.2. Since $\alpha_A = \sigma \beta_A$, larger $\sigma$ values represent higher efficiency in producing goods 1 in region A. Below, we plot the graph of $\varpi_A - \varpi_B$. In Figure 1-2, the vertical axis represents $\varpi_A - \varpi_B$, and the horizontal axis represents $\bar{R}_A$. As can be seen, as the $\sigma$ value increases, the $\bar{R}_A$ of the system's stable state becomes larger, meaning the population size of region A becomes larger. In the stable state, the marginal products of the two goods in both regions are consistent, prices are equal, comparative advantage dissipates between regions, and trade stops.

**1. $\sigma=1$ 的情况**

由 $\beta_A=\beta_B=1$，当 $\sigma=1$ 时，有 $\alpha_A=1$。我们分别取 $\mu$ 值为 1、1.8 和 3.2，则对应的 $\alpha_B$ 值分别为 1、1.8 和 3.2，对应的 $\theta$ 值分别为 1、0.5556 和 0.3125。由于 $\alpha_B=\mu\beta_B$，因此越大的 $\mu$ 值代表地区 B 生产商品 1 的效率越高。下面，我们绘制出 $\varpi_A-\varpi_B$ 的图像。图 1-1 中纵轴表示 $\varpi_A-\varpi_B$，横轴表示 $\bar{R}_A$。可以看出，随着 $\mu$ 值的提高，系统的稳定状态的 $\bar{R}_A$ 越来越小，也即地区 A 的人口规模越来越小。在稳定状态下，两地区两种商品的边际产出是一致的，价格相等，比较优势在地区间消散，贸易停止。

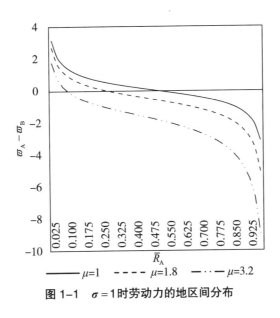

图 1-1 $\sigma=1$ 时劳动力的地区间分布

**2. $\mu=1$ 的情况**

由 $\beta_A=\beta_B=1$，当 $\mu=1$ 时，有 $\alpha_B=1$。我们分别取 $\sigma$ 值为 1、1.8 和 3.2，则对应的 $\alpha_A$ 值分别为 1、1.8 和 3.2，对应的 $\theta$ 值分别为 1、1.8 和 3.2。由于 $\alpha_A=\sigma\beta_A$，所以越大的 $\sigma$ 值代表地区 A 生产商品 1 的效率越高。下面，我们绘制出 $\varpi_A-\varpi_B$ 的图像。图 1-2 中纵轴表示 $\varpi_A-\varpi_B$，横轴表示 $\bar{R}_A$。可以看出，随着 $\sigma$ 值的增大，系统的稳定状态的 $\bar{R}_A$ 越来越大，也即地区 A 的人口规模越来越大。在稳定状态下，两地区两种商品的边际产出是一致的，价格相等，比较优势在地区间消散，贸易停止。

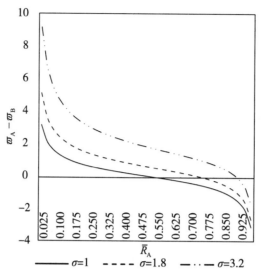

Figure 1-2　Inter-regions Distribution of Labor when $\mu = 1$

The above analysis shows that if production factors can flow between regions, they will move towards regions with higher marginal returns. Due to diminishing marginal returns, this transfer will continue until the marginal returns of factors in the two regions are consistent. At this point, the prices of goods in the two regions will be the same, and comparative advantage will no longer exist. Therefore, under conditions of factor mobility, comparative advantage is not suitable as a basis for formulating regional development strategies.

# Section 3: Scope of Application of Comparative Advantage Theory

### I. Scope of Application

From the analysis in Section 2, we can see that comparative advantage theory is not applicable to large countries, and it also excludes factor mobility between countries and economies of scale. Based on this, we can make a comprehensive discussion on the scope of application of comparative advantage theory.

First, for large countries like China, comparative advantage theory is not applicable. This is because large countries have a sufficient population, and even in the early stages of

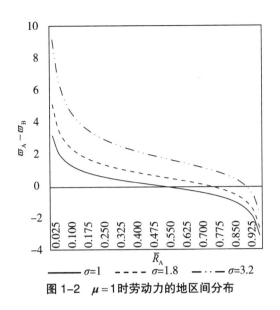

**图 1-2　$\mu=1$ 时劳动力的地区间分布**

以上分析表明，如果生产要素可以在地区间流动，那么它就将向要素边际报酬更高的地区转移，由于边际报酬递减，这种转移将持续到两地区要素边际报酬一致的时候。此时，两地区的商品价格将相同，比较优势不复存在。因此，在要素可流动的条件下，比较优势并不适合作为制定地区发展战略的依据。

# 第三节　比较优势理论的适用范围

## 一、适用范围

由第二节的分析可知，比较优势理论是不适用于大国的，另外它还排斥要素在国家间的流动和规模经济。由此，我们可以对比较优势理论的适用范围做一个总结性探讨。

第一，对于中国这样的大国而言，比较优势理论是不适用的。这是因为，大国拥有充足的人口数量，即使处在工业化初期，对各类产品也都具有较大规模的需求。又由于资本可在国家间流动，因此即使在工业化初期，大国也是资本稀缺的，也能够吸引外部投资来生产资本密集型产品。同时，在规模经济的作用下，

industrialization, they have a large-scale demand for various products. Also, since capital can flow between countries, even in the early stages of industrialization, large countries are capital-scarce and can attract external investment to produce capital-intensive products. At the same time, under the effect of economies of scale, various factors continuously aggregate, forming central areas of industrial agglomeration and promoting economic growth. In addition, high-end industries that surpass the country's resource endowment conditions often have a relatively obvious driving effect on other industries, that is, these high-end industries tend to have positive externalities. For large countries, their enormous economic scale and complete industrial categories are sufficient to internalize the benefits of these positive externalities, which is an advantage that small countries cannot possess. It can be seen that for large countries, when factors can flow between countries and production has economies of scale characteristics, even industrial sectors without comparative advantage can develop well and have sufficient self-sustaining capabilities.

Second, even for small countries, comparative advantage theory is not fully applicable. Take Singapore as an example, it is one of the three major free trade ports in the world. In Singapore, capital can flow freely, and the government does not control foreign exchange. No income tax is levied on the repatriation of corporate profits, and there are no other administrative restrictions. Enterprises have a high degree of freedom in setting up accounts, with accounts in Singapore dollars, US dollars, euros, Australian dollars, etc. all available, and enterprises have the right to decide the settlement currency. Enterprises conducting import and export trade in Singapore are also very free, requiring no government approval, only needing to register with the Accounting and Corporate Regulatory Authority of Singapore. Singapore does not set industry restrictions on foreign investment entry, with almost all industries open to foreign investment, except for some special industries such as finance, insurance, and securities, where foreign investment entry requires prior filing with the competent authorities. Due to the complete opening of the capital market, Singapore's relative prices of capital and labor will synchronize with the global market. Economies with a high degree of factor market openness similar to Singapore have strong similarities in factor endowment structure. Therefore, the formation and development of their industrial structure are determined by the global market's demand for the products and services they can provide, that is, determined by their scale advantages and competitive advantages in specific industries. Although history cannot be assumed, if Singapore had developed its industries based on comparative advantage development strategies, its current industrial structure and development level would probably not significantly surpass its Southeast Asian neighbors. Obviously, comparative advantage theory lacks explanatory power for the industrial development of such fully open economies.

Excluding the above two situations, comparative advantage theory may only have some explanatory power for the industrial development of small and medium-sized economies where

各类要素不断积聚，可以形成产业集聚的中心区，促进经济增长。另外，超越本国资源禀赋条件的高端产业对其他产业往往具有比较明显的拉动作用，也就是说，这类高端产业会具有正外部性。对于大国而言，其庞大的经济体量和完整的产业门类足以使这种正外部性收益内部化，这是小国无法拥有的优势。可见，对于大国而言，当要素可在国家间流动，生产具有规模经济特性时，即使是不具备比较优势的产业部门，也能够得到很好的发展，具备足够的自生能力。

第二，即使对于小国，比较优势理论也不能完全适用。以新加坡为例，它是全球三大自贸港之一。在新加坡，资金可以自由流动，政府没有对外汇进行管制。对于企业利润汇出不征收所得税，也没有其他行政性限制。企业在设立账户方面拥有很高的自由度，新加坡元、美元、欧元、澳大利亚元等账户均可设立，企业拥有决定结算货币种类的权利。企业在新加坡开展进出口贸易也是非常自由的，不需要政府审批，只需在新加坡会计与企业管制局进行注册即可。新加坡对外资进入也没有设置行业限制，几乎是全行业对外资开放，只是在金融、保险和证券等一些较为特殊的行业中，外资进入时需要事先在主管部门进行备案。由于资本市场的完全放开，新加坡的资本与劳动的相对价格将与全球市场同步，与新加坡类似的要素市场开放度较高的经济体在要素禀赋结构上具有很强的相似性，因此其产业结构的形成和发展就是由全球市场对其所能提供的产品和服务的需求所决定的，即由它在特定产业所具有的规模优势和竞争优势所决定的。尽管历史不能假设，但如果新加坡依据比较优势发展战略发展自身产业，它现在的产业结构和发展水平应该不会大幅度超越它的东南亚邻国。显然，比较优势理论对这类完全开放的经济体的产业发展也是缺乏解释力的。

排除了以上两种情况，那么比较优势理论仅可能对商品可自由贸易、要素不能自由流动的中小经济体的产业发展具有一定的解释力。然而，当我们去观察此

goods can be freely traded but factors cannot freely flow. However, when we observe the development trajectories of such economies, we find that economies with these characteristics often fall into the "comparative advantage trap" of economic stagnation.

## II. Beware of the "Comparative Advantage Trap"

As mentioned earlier, comparative advantage theory only has some explanatory power for the industrial development of small and medium-sized economies where goods can be freely traded but factors cannot freely flow, and they are also more likely to fall into the "comparative advantage trap".

There are two main reasons for the formation of the "comparative advantage trap".

First, so-called comparative advantage is a comparison between industries within an economy. However, even for industries with comparative advantage in their own country, it is uncertain whether their goods have sufficient competitiveness in the international market. In addition to price factors, factors such as product quality, performance, brand, and consumer loyalty also need to be considered. Therefore, the competitiveness of a product in the international market depends not only on the cost and price advantages brought by resource endowment conditions but also on whether the product can bring differentiated satisfaction to consumers. This ability may come from the raw materials and production processes of the product, or directly from the place of origin itself. The stronger the degree of product differentiation, the stronger its market power and the higher its degree of market monopoly. Because developed countries have newer and better production technologies, although their product prices are higher, the degree of differentiation in product quality and performance is also stronger, leading to a stronger ability to obtain high prices in the international market. For small developing countries, due to their small domestic market size and restricted factor mobility, it is difficult to utilize foreign direct investment to achieve industrial and technological upgrades. With poor domestic R&D capabilities and difficulty in realizing economies of scale advantages, they have to compress profit margins to maintain survival in the international market. Although such economies can obtain certain benefits from international division of labor, they are easily trapped in the "comparative advantage trap" due to difficulties in achieving industrial upgrading.

Second, generally speaking, developed countries are at the high end of the industrial chain and value chain, continuously obtaining high added value and high income in this field.

类经济体的发展轨迹时却发现，具备这种特征的经济体往往会陷入经济停滞的"比较优势陷阱"。

## 二、警惕"比较优势陷阱"

如前文所讲到的，比较优势理论仅对那些商品可自由贸易而要素不能自由流动的中小经济体的产业发展具有一定的解释力，而它们也更容易陷入"比较优势陷阱"。

"比较优势陷阱"形成的主要原因有以下两点。

第一，所谓比较优势，是一个经济体内部产业间的比较。然而，即使是在本国具有比较优势的产业，其商品在国际市场中是否具有足够的竞争力也是不能确定的。除了价格因素，还要看商品的质量、性能、品牌和消费者忠诚度等诸多因素。因此，一种商品在国际市场的竞争力，不仅取决于由资源禀赋条件带来的成本和价格优势，还要看这种商品能否给消费者带来差异化的满足，这种能力既可能来自商品的原材料和生产工艺，也可能直接来自产地自身。商品的差异化程度越强，其市场势力也就越强，对市场的垄断程度也就越高。由于发达国家拥有更新、更好的生产技术，所以尽管其产品价格偏高，但产品质量、性能等方面的差异化程度也更强，导致其在国际市场中获取高价的能力也更强。而对于小的发展中国家而言，本国市场规模小、要素流动受到限制，所以难以利用外商直接投资实现产业和技术的升级；而本国研发能力差、规模经济优势难以实现，所以不得不压缩利润率以在国际市场中保持生存状态。这样的经济体虽然能够在国际分工中获取一定的收益，但由于难以实现产业升级，很容易陷入"比较优势陷阱"。

第二，一般来讲，发达国家会处于产业链和价值链的高端，在这一领域里持续获取高附加值和高收入。而发展中国家一般处于产业链和价值链的中低端，产

Developing countries are generally at the mid to low end of the industrial chain and value chain, with low product added value and low income. As Lewis said: "If the engines of growth are exports of industrial products from more developed countries and primary products from less developed countries, then the engines of more developed countries turn slightly faster than those of less developed countries." In addition to limitations in domestic demand scale, economies of scale, and factor mobility, the artificial barriers set by developed countries for other countries in industrial upgrading are also an important reason that cannot be ignored for falling into the "comparative advantage trap". This makes it more difficult for economies that develop their domestic industries following comparative advantage development strategies to achieve industrial structure upgrading as envisioned by comparative advantage development strategies as their factor endowment structure upgrades.

From the above analysis and related empirical facts, it is highly questionable whether relying on comparative advantage theory to formulate comparative advantage development strategies can enable developing countries to achieve industrial structure upgrading and thus make their income levels converge towards those of developed countries. In fact, it is difficult to clearly draw a picture of industrial structure changes upgrading according to comparative advantage for countries like Japan and the Republic of Korea that have successfully entered the high-income ranks. Instead, we should pay more attention to their simultaneous development of light and heavy industries and their high emphasis on technological innovation. Therefore, the changes in their industrial structure reflect more of changes in demand, economies of scale, and technological upgrades, rather than changes in their domestic factor endowment structure. Therefore, developing countries must adjust their economic development strategies and break through the constraints of comparative advantage development strategies. As Professor Chen Yunxian pointed out, the keynote of economic growth in countries around the world is competitive economic growth.

品附加值低,收入也低。正如刘易斯所说:"如果增长的引擎是较发达的国家的工业产品和欠发达的国家的初级产品的出口,那么较发达国家的引擎就比欠发达国家的引擎转动得略微快一些。"除了本国需求规模、规模经济和要素流动等方面的限制,发达国家对其他国家在产业升级上设置的人为阻碍也是陷入"比较优势陷阱"不可忽略的一个重要原因。这导致遵循比较优势发展战略发展本国产业的经济体,更难以像比较优势发展战略所设想的那样随着要素禀赋结构的升级而实现产业结构升级。

从以上分析和相关的经验事实可以看出,依赖比较优势理论制定比较优势发展战略是否能使发展中国家实现产业结构升级,进而使收入水平向发达国家的收入水平收敛是存在很大疑问的。实际上,像日本、韩国等成功跨入高收入行列的国家,其经济发展历程也很难清晰地绘制出一幅依比较优势升级的产业结构变迁图谱。反而,我们更应关注的是其轻重工业的同步发展以及对技术创新的高度重视,因此,其产业结构的变化更多反映的是需求变化、规模经济和技术升级,而不是本国要素禀赋结构的变化。因此,发展中国家必须要调整自己的经济发展战略,突破比较优势发展战略的束缚。正如陈云贤教授所指出的,世界各国的经济增长的基调都是竞争型经济增长。①

---

① 陈云贤:《市场竞争双重主体论——兼谈中观经济学的创立与发展》,北京大学出版社,2020,第129页。

Chapter 2
# The Rise and Defects of Michael Porter's Competitive Advantage Theory

## Section1: Michael Porter's Competitive Advantage Theory

### I. Michael Porter's Diamond Model of Competitive Advantage Theory

Professor Michael Porter's Diamond Model, which is used to explain national competitiveness, has already been widely disseminated globally. This book will provide a brief introduction to it once again.

First, in the Diamond Model, the factors (core factors) that play a supporting role in a country's industrial development are divided into four categories, namely factor conditions, demand conditions, related and supporting industries, and firm strategy, structure and rivalry.

(1) Factor conditions mainly include human capital, natural resources, geographical conditions, climate, physical capital, knowledge and technology, and modern infrastructure, etc. They are further divided into basic factors, such as natural resources, geographical conditions, climate, etc.; and advanced factors, such as modern infrastructure, human capital, knowledge and technology, etc.

(2) Demand conditions refer to the domestic market demand for a certain product or service in a country. The importance of the domestic market lies in that it is the driving force for industrial development.

第二章

# 迈克尔·波特竞争优势理论的兴起与缺陷

## 第一节 迈克尔·波特竞争优势理论

### 一、迈尔克·波特竞争优势理论的钻石模型

迈克尔·波特教授用于解释国家竞争力的钻石模型早已在全球广泛传播，这里本书再对其进行一个简单的介绍。

第一，在钻石模型中，对一国产业发展发挥支撑作用的因素（核心因素）分为四类，即生产要素，需求条件，相关和支持性产业及企业战略、结构和同业竞争。

（1）生产要素主要包括人力资本、自然资源、地理条件、气候、物质资本、知识与技术以及现代化基础设施等。它又被分为初级生产要素，如自然资源、地理条件、气候等；高级生产要素，如现代化基础设施、人力资本、知识与技术等。

（2）需求条件指的是一国的国内市场对某一产品或服务的需求。国内市场的重要意义在于它是产业发展的动力。

(3) Related and supporting industries mainly refer to the upstream industries and supporting industries of a certain industry. The performance and capabilities of related and supporting industries will naturally drive innovation and internationalization of the entire industrial chain, thereby enhancing the competitiveness of the entire industry and the country.

(4) Firm strategy, structure, and rivalry among competitors refer to the ways in which businesses are created, organized, and managed, as well as the state of competitors. The goals, strategies, organizational structures, and management styles of enterprises vary from country to country. The ability to form a national competitive advantage lies in whether these differing conditions can achieve an optimal combination to enhance the international competitiveness of enterprises.

Secondly, apart from the aforementioned four core factors, Professor Porter believes that chance and government also have significant impacts on industrial competitive advantages (see Figure 2-1).

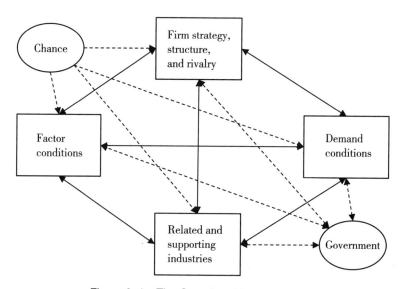

Figure 2-1　The Complete Diamond Model

Chance refers to unforeseen events that significantly influence business operations but cannot be controlled by human intervention, such as major breakthroughs in basic research leading to technological revolutions, energy crises, wars, epidemics, etc. Chance can bring about significant disruptions to the current industrial ecosystem, breaking the existing competitive landscape.

The government influences national competitiveness through its impact on the four core factors. Porter points out: "The relationship between government and other key elements is neither positive nor negative……Government can either be an enabler or an obstacle to

（3）相关和支持性产业主要是指某一产业的上游产业和配套产业。相关和支持性产业的表现与能力，自然会带动整个产业链的创新和国际化，从而提升整个产业和国家的竞争力。

（4）企业战略、结构和同业竞争指的是创立、组织和管理企业的方式，以及竞争对手的状态。各国的企业目标、战略、组织结构和管理方式等都有所不同，国家竞争优势能否形成就取决于这些差异条件能否实现最优组合以提高企业的国际竞争力。

第二，除了上述四个核心因素，波特教授认为机遇和政府也会对产业竞争优势产生重要影响（图2-1）。

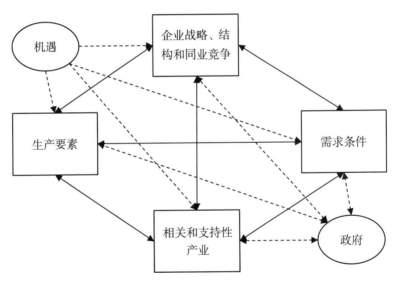

图2-1 完整的钻石模型

资料来源：迈克尔·波特：《国家竞争优势》，李明轩、邱如美译，华夏出版社，2002，第119页。

机遇是指那些无法进行人为控制的对企业经营具有重要影响的突发事件，如基础研究上的重大突破所带来的技术革命、能源危机、战争、疫病等。机遇能够给当前的产业生态带来重大冲击，打破原有竞争格局。

政府通过影响四个核心因素作用于国家竞争力，波特指出："政府与其他关键要素之间的关系既非正面，也非负面……政府既可能是产业发展的助力，也可

industry development." Therefore, the examination of the effectiveness of government actions should focus on how they affect the four core factors.

The Diamond Model tells us that in the modern global economy, a country can choose whether to move towards prosperity: if the policies and laws implemented by a country and the institutional environment established are conducive to productivity improvement, then this country has chosen the path to prosperity; conversely, if a country's policies have a destructive and hindering effect on the development of productivity, or its policies can only benefit a small number of interest groups, then the country has chosen the path to poverty. Therefore, the establishment of a country's competitive advantage is not determined by its innate resource endowment conditions, but is the result of the government leading the people's efforts in building it.

## II. Four Stages of National Competitive Advantage Development

Professor Porter proposed four stages of national competitive advantage development, namely the factor-driven stage, investment-driven stage, innovation-driven stage, and wealth-driven stage (Figure 2-2), and pointed out that in this stage division, the first three stages are the rising period of national competitive advantage development, which usually brings economic prosperity. The fourth stage is a turning point, where economic development may enter a downward trend.

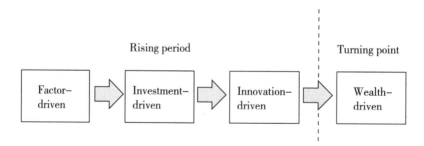

Figure 2-2  Four Stages of National Competitive Advantage Development

In the factor-driven stage, the successful development of a country's industries depends on basic production factors, including abundant natural resources and cheap labor, while the knowledge, technology, and physical capital needed for production mainly rely on foreign inputs.

能是障碍。"① 因此,对于政府作用效果的考查,要看其对四个核心因素产生了什么样的影响。

钻石模型告诉我们,在现代全球经济下,一国可以自己选择是否走向繁荣:如果一国所实施的政策和法律,所建立的制度环境是有利于生产率提高的,这个国家就选择了繁荣之路;反之,如果一国所实施的政策对生产力的发展产生了破坏和阻碍作用,或其政策仅能使得少部分利益团体获利,则该国就选择了通往贫穷的道路。因此,一国竞争优势的建立不是由其先天资源禀赋条件决定的,而是这个国家的政府带领人民后天努力的结果。

## 二、国家竞争优势发展的四个阶段

波特教授提出了国家竞争优势发展的四个阶段,即要素驱动(Factor-driven)阶段、投资驱动(Investment-driven)阶段、创新驱动(Innovation-driven)阶段和财富驱动(Wealth-driven)阶段(图2-2),并指出在这种阶段划分中,前三个阶段是国家竞争优势发展的上升期,通常会带来经济上的繁荣。第四个阶段则是一个转折点,经济发展可能会在此阶段进入下行趋势。

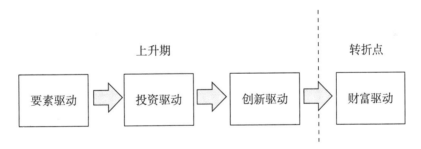

图2-2 国家竞争优势发展的四个阶段

资料来源:迈克尔·波特:《国家竞争优势》,李明轩、邱如美译,华夏出版社,2002,第530页。

在要素驱动阶段,一国产业能否实现成功发展依赖于基本生产要素,包括丰富的自然资源和廉价的劳动力,而生产所需的知识和技术、物质资本则主要依赖于国外输入,此阶段国家竞争优势的主要来源就是钻石模型中的生产要素因素。

---

① 迈克尔·波特:《国家竞争优势》,李明轩、邱如美译,华夏出版社,2002,第118页。

At this stage, the main source of national competitive advantage is the factor conditions in the Diamond Model. In the investment-driven stage, enterprises engage in frequent investment activities, aiming to improve the sophistication and competitiveness of various industrial links. The key determining factor for enterprises to advance from the factor-driven stage to the investment-driven stage is their ability to introduce, absorb, and re-innovate production technologies.

In the investment-driven stage, the main sources of a country's competitive advantage cover three aspects of the Diamond Model: factor conditions; demand conditions; firm strategy, structure, and rivalry.

In the innovation-driven stage, enterprises can not only improve foreign production technologies and methods but also cultivate their independent innovation capabilities. At this stage, the sources of national competitive advantage have covered all four core factors in the Diamond Model.

In the wealth-driven stage, due to the decline of domestic competitive activities, the shift of business strategies from active to conservative, the decreased willingness of enterprises to reinvest, and large enterprises influencing government protection policies to isolate themselves from competitors, enterprises begin to lose their competitive advantages internationally.

# Section 2: Critique of Comparative Advantage Theory by Competitive Advantage Theory

### I. Views of Competitive Advantage Theory

Despite the long-standing dominance of comparative advantage theory in analyzing and explaining international trade, Professor Porter candidly points out that comparative advantage theory generally considers a country's competitiveness to primarily stem from material endowments such as labor, natural resources, and financial capital. However, he believes the role of these input factors is diminishing in today's rapidly globalizing world. A country's competitiveness cannot be determined by the size of its territory or the strength of its military, as these factors are not directly related to productivity. Instead, countries should create a favorable business environment and supportive institutions to ensure input factors can be efficiently used and upgraded.

在投资驱动阶段，企业进行频繁的投资活动，其目的在于提高各产业环节的精密性和竞争力。企业能否从要素驱动阶段晋升到投资驱动阶段的关键决定因素是其对生产技术的引进、消化、再创新的能力。

在投资驱动阶段，一国竞争优势的主要来源涵盖了钻石模型中的生产要素，需求条件以及企业战略、结构和同业竞争三个方面。

在创新驱动阶段，企业不仅能够改善国外的生产技术和生产方式，还培育了自主创新的能力。在此阶段，国家竞争优势的来源已经覆盖到钻石模型中的四个核心因素。

在财富驱动阶段，由于国内竞争活动衰退、经营战略由积极转趋保守、企业再投资的意愿降低、大企业左右政府保护政策使自己与竞争者隔离，所以企业开始丧失它们在国际上的竞争优势。

# 第二节 竞争优势理论对比较优势理论的批判

## 一、竞争优势理论的观点

尽管比较优势理论已经在对国际贸易的分析和解释中占据了长期的主导地位，但波特教授却毫不掩饰地指出，比较优势理论一般认为一国的竞争力主要来源于劳动力、自然资源、金融资本等物质禀赋的投入，而他认为这些投入要素在全球化快速发展的今天，作用日趋减少。一国的竞争力不可能由其国土的大小和军队的强弱来决定，因为这些因素与生产率没有直接的关系。取而代之的是，国家应该创造一个良好的经营环境和支持性制度，以确保投入要素能够得到高效的使用和升级换代。[1]

---

[1] 迈克尔·波特：《国家竞争优势》，李明轩、邱如美译，华夏出版社，2002，第2页。

Porter believes that although there is a synergistic relationship between productivity and competitiveness from a macro perspective, an industrial development strategy that blindly pursues productivity may come at the cost of future competitiveness. For example, under the influence of comparative advantage theory, governments, whether right or wrong, have proposed a series of policies to improve the comparative advantage of production factors. The most obvious examples are governments lowering interest rates, suppressing wages, depreciating currencies, providing subsidies, granting special depreciation for certain equipment, and offering financing for specific export projects. In specific times and spaces, these policy tools each have certain effects. However, developing countries can easily fall into this trap. They almost unanimously compete on production costs and prices, basing their development plans on cost-oriented new industries, unable to break free from the constraints of production costs. As a result, these countries are constantly under threat of losing competitiveness, facing wage and capital turnover issues year after year. Their limited profits are entirely dependent on international economic fluctuations.

In fact, as early as the 1950s, Nobel Prize winner in Economics Leontief proposed the so-called "Leontief Paradox" in response to the resource endowment theory. This paradox points out that as a country with advantages in capital and technological factors, the United States should have exported capital-intensive products and imported labor-intensive products, but the actual situation was exactly the opposite. The Republic of Korea, at the end of the Korean War, was severely lacking in capital, yet established export-oriented capital-intensive industries such as steel, shipbuilding, and automobiles.

## II. Industrial Export Data Fail to Support Comparative Advantage Theory

Below, we select several representative industries to examine whether comparative advantage has played a role based on the export data of these industries.

In terms of agricultural product exports, comparative advantage theory can indeed provide a better explanation, as agricultural product exports strictly depend on a country's natural resources. As shown in Figure 2-3, as the world's largest exporter of agricultural products, the

United States' agricultural product exports accounted for over 10% of its total exports in most years from 2014 to 2022, far higher than China and the global average.

波特认为，尽管从宏观的角度上看，生产率和竞争力之间存在着协同关系，但片面地追求生产率的产业发展战略可能是以牺牲未来的竞争力为代价的。[①] 例如，在比较优势理论的影响下，各国政府不论对错地提出一连串改善生产要素比较优势的政策。最明显的例子就是政府降低利率、压低工资、使货币贬值、给予补贴、特许某些设备折旧、针对特定出口项目提供融资等。在特定的时空中，这些政策工具各有其一定的效果。[②] 然而，发展中国家很容易掉入这种陷阱。它们几乎一窝蜂地在生产成本与价格上竞争，其开发计划便是以成本导向的新产业为基础，无法摆脱生产成本的限制。因此，这类国家时时处在失去竞争力的威胁中，年复一年面临薪水与资本周转的问题。它们有限的利润完全仰仗于国际经济波动。[③]

实际上，早在 20 世纪 50 年代，诺贝尔经济学奖得主里昂惕夫就针对资源禀赋说提出了所谓的"里昂惕夫悖论（Leontief Paradox）"。该悖论指出，作为在资本和科技要素上具有优势的国家，美国本应出口资本密集型产品、进口劳动密集型产品，但实际的情况却恰好与此相反。而朝鲜战争结束时的韩国，资本奇缺，却建立了出口导向的钢铁、造船、汽车等资本密集型产业。

## 二、产业出口数据难以佐证比较优势理论

下面，我们选择几个代表性的产业，从这些产业的出口数据考查比较优势是否发挥了作用。

在农产品的出口上，比较优势理论确实能够做出较好的解释，因为农产品的出口严格依赖于一国的自然资源。如图 2-3 所示，作为全球最大的农产品出口国，美国 2014—2022 年的农产品出口额占其出口总额的比例大部分年份都超过了 10%，远高于中国和全球平均水平。

---

① 张金昌：《波特的国家竞争优势理论剖析》，《中国工业经济》2001 年第 9 期。
② 迈克尔·波特：《国家竞争优势》，李明轩、邱如美译，华夏出版社，2002，第 11 页。
③ 迈克尔·波特：《国家竞争优势》，李明轩、邱如美译，华夏出版社，2002，第 14-15 页。

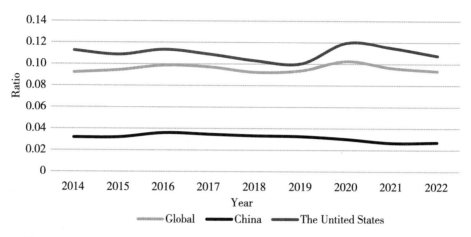

Figure 2-3　Proportion of Agricultural Product Exports to Total Exports for China, the United States, and Global from 2014 to 2022

Data Source: Compiled based on statistics from the World Trade Organization (WTO).

Taking the capital-intensive steel industry as an example, Figure 2-4 shows that from 2014 to 2022, the proportion of China's steel product exports in its total exports was much higher than that of the United States and, for most years, was also higher than the global average. However, China is not a country abundant in capital, nor does it have an advantageous reserve of iron ore. The reason China has been able to develop a large-scale steel industry is that the massive demand for steel products during its industrialization process has driven the development of the steel industry. Supported by economies of scale, this has led to the formation of a competitive advantage.

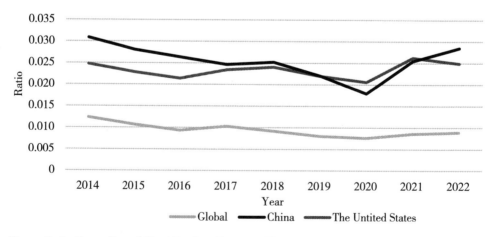

Figure 2-4　Proportion of Steel Product Export to Total Exports for China, the United States, and Global From 2014 to 2022

Data Source: Compiled based on statistics from the World Trade Organization (WTO).

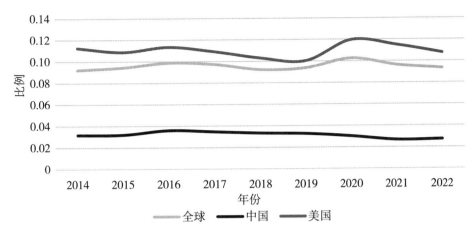

**图 2-3　2014—2022 年中国、美国和全球农产品出口额占出口总额比例**

数据来源：根据世界贸易组织统计数据整理。

再以资本密集型的钢铁产业为例，图 2-4 显示出，2014—2022 年，中国的钢铁产品出口额占出口总额的比例远高于美国，大部分年份也高于全球平均水平。然而，中国并不是一个资本丰裕国，铁矿石储量也并没有优势。中国之所以能够发展出巨大规模的钢铁产业，是因为本国工业化进程中对钢铁产品形成的巨大需求推动了钢铁产业的发展，并在规模经济的支撑下，形成了竞争优势。

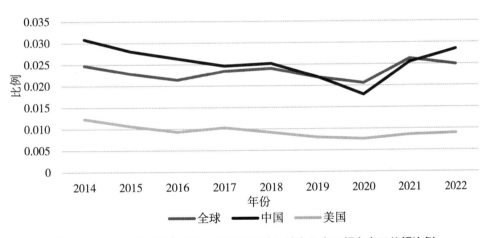

**图 2-4　2014—2022 年中国、美国和全球钢铁产品出口额占出口总额比例**

数据来源：根据世界贸易组织统计数据整理。

Taking the technology-intensive electronic data processing and office equipment industry as another example. Figure 2-5 shows that from 2014 to 2022, China's proportion of electronic data processing and office equipment exports to total exports was far higher than that of the United States and the global average. Of course, this industry may indeed have certain labor-intensive industry characteristics, but its development in China was not based on comparative advantage: first, without the introduction of capital and technology, this industry could not have developed in China; second, without the support of China's ultra-large-scale demand market, this industry would have struggled to achieve extreme economies of scale and thus realize globally leading competitive advantages.

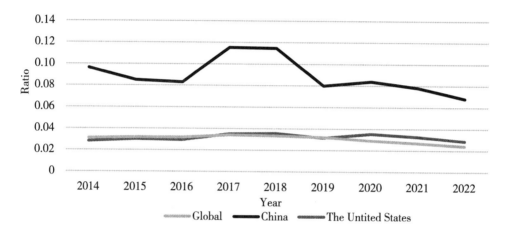

Figure 2-5 Proportion of Electronic Data Processing and Office Equipment Exports to Total Exports for China, the United States, and Globall from 2014 to 2022

Data Source: Compiled based on statistics from the World Trade Organization (WTO).

It can be seen that in the current regional industry development and international trade pattern, comparative advantage no longer constitutes the dominant force. So what is the dominant force? Porter attributes it to national competitive advantage, that is, whether a country can create a good business environment and supportive system for enterprises to ensure that input factors can be efficiently used and upgraded. To better explain national competitive advantage, Porter proposed the famous Diamond Model.

再以技术密集型的电子数据处理和办公设备产业为例。图 2-5 显示出，2014—2022 年，中国电子数据处理和办公设备出口额占出口总额的比例远高于美国和全球平均水平。当然，也许该产业确实存在一定的劳动密集型产业的属性特征，但该产业在中国却并不是基于比较优势得以发展的：第一，如果没有资本和技术的引进，该产业就无法在中国得到发展；第二，如果没有中国超大规模需求市场的支撑，该产业也难以达到极端的规模经济效应从而实现全球领先的竞争优势。

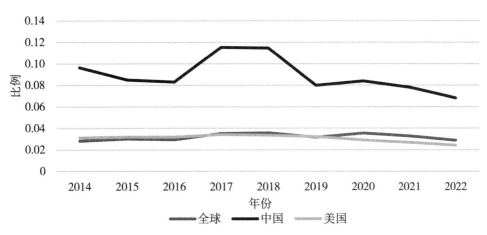

图 2-5  2014—2022 年中国、美国和全球电子数据处理和办公设备出口额占出口总额比例
数据来源：根据世界贸易组织统计数据整理。

由此可见，在当前的区域产业发展和国际贸易格局中，比较优势已不再构成主导力量，那主导力量又是什么呢？波特将其归结为国家竞争优势，也即国家能否为企业创造一个良好的经营环境和支持性制度，以确保投入要素能够被高效地使用和升级换代。为更好地对国家竞争优势进行解释，波特提出了著名的钻石模型。

# Section 3: Limitations of Michael Porter's Competitive Advantage Theory

## I. Insufficient Understanding of the Role of Government

In the Diamond Model of competitive advantage theory, the government can influence any of the four core factors of the Diamond Model through its own activities, thereby achieving the purpose of influencing enterprise competitive advantage. However, Porter believes that the role of the four core factors is irreplaceable, and without the existence and coordination of the four core factors, the influence of government alone would not enable enterprises to gain competitive advantage. This is because "the government's influence is optimistic", but "the government itself cannot help enterprises create competitive advantage". It can be seen that Porter's understanding of the government's role still has certain limitations.

For example, he believes that in some aspects (such as trade barriers, pricing, etc.), the government should intervene in the market as little as possible, while in other aspects (such as ensuring strong competition, providing high-quality education and training), it should play an active role. The government should not be a component of the four core factors of the Diamond Model, but the government will have more or less influence on each factor of the Diamond Model, and this influence is the best way to understand the relationship between government and competition.

He also believes that although the government plays an important role in creating and maintaining national advantages, its effect is one-sided. If an industry lacks a basic, competitive environment, even the best policies are in vain. The government cannot control national competitive advantage; what it can do is influence competitive advantage through subtle, conceptual policies.

It can be seen that in Porter's national competitive advantage framework, the government's role is not independent, but based on the four core factors of the Diamond Model (main channels of government policy in this theory are shown in Table 2-1). This explanation is actually a weakening

# 第三节 迈克尔·波特竞争优势理论的局限

## 一、对政府作用的认识存在不足

在竞争优势理论的钻石模型中，政府可以通过自己的活动来影响钻石模型四种核心因素中的任何一种，从而达到影响企业竞争优势的目的。但是，波特认为，四种核心因素的作用是不可替代的，如果没有四种核心因素的存在和相互配合，单纯政府的影响并不会使企业取得竞争优势。这是因为，"政府的影响虽然乐观"，但"政府本身并不能帮助企业创造竞争优势"。[①] 由此可见，波特对政府作用的理解还存在一定局限。

又如，他认为，政府在有些方面（比如贸易壁垒、定价等）应该尽量不干预市场，而在另外一些方面（诸如确保强有力的竞争，提供高质量的教育和培训）则要扮演积极的角色。政府不应该是钻石模型四种核心因素的一个组成部分，但政府对钻石模型的每一个因素都会产生或多或少的影响，这种影响是理解政府与竞争之间关系的最佳方式。[②]

他还认为，虽然政府在创造和保持国家优势上扮演重要角色，但它的效果却是片面的。一个产业如果缺少基本的、具有竞争优势的环境，政策再好也是枉然。政府并不能控制国家竞争优势，它所能做的就是通过微妙的、观念性的政策影响竞争优势。[③]

可见，在波特的国家竞争优势框架里，政府的作用并不是独立的，而是建立在钻石模型四种核心因素基础上的（该理论中政府政策的主要作用渠道见表2-1）。这种解释实际上是对政府职能的一种弱化，未能全面展示政府作用。一些成功的发展中国家的经验告诉我们，很多时候，政府是钻石模型中四种核

---

[①] 迈克尔·波特：《国家竞争优势》，李明轩、邱如美译，华夏出版社，2002，第118-120页。
[②] 迈克尔·波特：《国家竞争优势》，李明轩、邱如美译，华夏出版社，2002，第3页。
[③] 迈克尔·波特：《国家竞争优势》，李明轩、邱如美译，华夏出版社，2002，第602页。

of government functions and fails to fully demonstrate the role of government. The experience of some successful developing countries tells us that in many cases, the government is the creator of the four core factors in the Diamond Model, and its role is played before these four core factors, which is the "foresighted leading" mentioned in mezzoeconomics.

Table 2-1  Main Channels of Government Policy Influence in Porter's Competitive Advantage Theory

| Channels of Influence | Government Policies |
| --- | --- |
| Factor Conditions | Creation and enhancement of factor conditions; emphasis on education and training; proactive development of key technologies; infrastructure development; opening up capital channels; fostering information integration capabilities; tax reduction and subsidies; effective monetary policies and factor conditions |
| Demand Conditions | Government procurement policies; standardization of products and processes; encouragement of refined demand; setting technical standards; expansion of domestic market |
| Related and Supporting Industries | Active media policy; promote the development of industrial clusters; set up a regional development plan |
| Firm strategy, Structure, and Rivalry | Promotion of internationalization; setting clear development goals; maintaining intensity of domestic competition; lowering industry entry barriers to encourage new business entries; proactive trade policies; encouragement of foreign investment |

## II. Inadequate Explanation of How to Upgrade from Low to High Development Stages

As mentioned earlier, Porter proposed four stages of national competitive advantage development, pointing out the dominant driving forces at each stage. However, Porter did not provide a sufficient explanation on how a country can upgrade from a low development stage to a high development stage. Porter only emphasized in his work that a country does not necessarily go through each development stage in sequence, and the development process can be leapfrogging. He believed that Italy directly leapt from the factor-driven stage to the innovation-driven stage without going through the investment-driven stage. At the same time, Porter also pointed out that a country's economic development is not entirely linear progress, and situations of stagnation or even regression may occur.

So why is there insufficient discussion in Professor Porter's competitive advantage theory on how to achieve the upgrade of development stages? This book believes that this is closely related to Professor Porter's cognitive limitations on government functions. After a country enters a development stage, it is difficult for the four core factors of the Diamond Model to achieve a self-generated upgrade process. At this time, an external shock force is needed to help the entire model achieve an upgrade, and this exogenous shock force is the role of

心因素的创造者，其作用的发挥是先于这四种核心因素的，也即中观经济学所说的"超前引领"。

表 2-1 波特竞争优势理论中政府政策的主要作用渠道

| 作用渠道 | 政府政策 |
| --- | --- |
| 生产要素 | 创造生产要素和提升生产要素水平；重视教育和培训；主动研发重要科技；发展基础设施；开放资本渠道；培养信息整合能力；减税与补贴；有效的生产要素和货币政策 |
| 需求条件 | 政府采购政策；规范产品和制程标准；鼓励精制型需求；设定技术标准；延伸国内市场 |
| 相关和支持性产业 | 积极的媒体政策；促进产业集群发展；设定区域发展计划 |
| 企业战略、结构和同业竞争 | 推动国家化；设定明确的发展目标；保持国内竞争强度；降低行业准入门槛，鼓励新企业进入；积极的贸易政策；鼓励外商投资 |

资料来源：迈克尔·波特：《国家竞争优势》，李明轩、邱如美译，华夏出版社，2002，第610-654页。

## 二、对如何从低发展阶段向高发展阶段升级未做足够阐释

如前所述，波特提出了国家竞争优势发展的四个阶段，指出了每个阶段的主导驱动力量。然而，对于一国如何从低发展阶段向高发展阶段升级，波特却并未给出充分的解释。波特仅在其著作中强调，一国不是必然地逐一经历每个发展阶段，发展过程可能是跨越式的，并认为意大利就在没有经过投资驱动阶段的情况下，直接从要素驱动阶段跨越到创新驱动阶段。同时，波特也指出，一国的经济发展也并非完全的直线前行，停滞甚至倒退的情况也是可能出现的。

那么，波特教授的竞争优势理论对如何实现发展阶段的升级为什么讨论不足呢？本书认为，这与波特教授对政府职能的认知局限是紧密联系在一起的。一国进入一个发展阶段后，钻石模型的四个核心因素很难实现自生性的升级过程，这时就需要一个外在的冲击力量帮助整个模型实现升级，而这个外生的冲

government. However, it is precisely due to the insufficient understanding of the government's role that Professor Porter only focused on the state that the four core factors should possess at each development stage, but failed to explore in depth how to promote the four core factors to reach the state level required for upgrading the development stage. It has to be said that this is a major defect and regret in Porter's competitive advantage theory.

击力量就是政府作用。然而，正是由于对政府作用的认识不足，波特教授才仅关注到在每个发展阶段四个核心因素所应具备的状态，但却没能深入探讨如何推动四个核心因素达到发展阶段升级所要求的状态水平，不得不说这是波特竞争优势理论的一个重大缺陷和遗憾。

# Chapter 3
# Mezzoeconomics and Its Competitive Advantage Theory

## Section 1: The Inheritance and Development of Mezzoeconomics to Existing Economic Theories

Mezzoeconomics, with regional governments as its main research object, provides a breakthrough answer to the relationship between market and government. It emerged in the process of exploring how to leverage the roles of "Efficient Markets" and "Effective Governments" to compensate for market failures and government failures.

Government failure refers to the situation where the government intervenes in the market through legislation, administrative management, and various economic policy measures to correct and compensate for the functional defects of the market mechanism, but the intervention results go against the expected goals: not only failing to effectively correct market failures, but also hindering and limiting the normal functioning of the market, distorting the normal market operation order under government intervention, leading to market chaos and failure of the price mechanism. Government failure damages the resource allocation function of the market, resulting in ineffective government intervention in the market and loss of social welfare.

Under the framework of general equilibrium in economics, when the required prerequisite assumptions can be met, a free competitive market economy can achieve a Pareto optimal equilibrium solution. However, idealized assumptions cannot always be satisfied, and in

# 第三章
# 中观经济学及其竞争优势理论

## 第一节 中观经济学对现有经济学理论的继承与发展

中观经济学以区域政府为主要研究对象，对市场和政府关系做出了突破性回答，是在探索如何发挥"有效市场"和"有为政府"作用，以弥补市场失灵和政府失灵的过程中产生的。

政府失灵是指政府为了纠正和弥补市场机制的功能缺陷而采取立法、行政管理以及各种经济政策手段干预了市场，但干预结果却与预期目标背道而驰：不但对于市场失灵未能进行有效纠正，还对市场功能的正常发挥造成了阻碍和限制，使得正常的市场运行秩序在政府干预下被扭曲，导致了市场的混乱和价格机制的失效。政府失灵会损害市场的资源配置功能，造成政府干预市场的效率低下和社会福利损失。

在经济学一般均衡的框架下，在所要求的前提假设条件能够得到满足时，自由竞争的市场经济就能够得到一个帕累托最优的均衡解。但是，理想化的假设条件并不是总能得到满足的，现实中存在垄断、外部性、不完全信息等情况，这时

reality, there are situations such as monopolies, externalities, and incomplete information. In these cases, relying solely on market forces cannot achieve Pareto optimal resource allocation results. This is the realm of market failure, where government intervention is needed to improve resource allocation efficiency.

Therefore, mezzoeconomics believes: "The modern market economy operates on the basis of market mechanisms and is an economic model that integrates 'Effective Governments' and 'Efficient Markets'. The market is a natural law that we should recognize and understand more, while the government has more initiative. While giving play to the 'decisive role' of the market in resource allocation, we should better leverage the role of government. We should accurately position the government in the modern market economy, scientifically handle the relationship between government and market, government and society, and rationally delineate the boundaries between government and market, government and society. We should construct the two wheels of the modern market economy——'Efficient Markets' and 'Effective Governments'——to complement and support each other, achieving a 'dual-wheel driven' modern market economy system." It can be seen that based on the insufficient research on the relationship between market and government in existing literature, mezzoeconomics explores a new theory of economic growth driven by the dual wheels of "Efficient Markets" + "Effective Governments" based on China's great practice of reform and opening-up, which is an important breakthrough in economic theory.

Mezzoeconomics overlaps with regional economics, urban economics, and industrial economics or structural economics that are closely related to regional development in terms of research scope. It is natural to view regional economy, urban economy, and industrial economy as mezzoeconomy, but it may not be accurate to directly view regional economics, urban economics, and industrial economics as mezzoeconomics. These three disciplines still belong to applied economics, which is different from mezzoeconomics as theoretical economics. Additionally, in terms of research methods, besides microeconomics and macroeconomics, mezzoeconomics also draws on theoretical tools and research methods from disciplines such as public finance and public administration. Based on the integration of multiple disciplines, it has constructed the research framework and theoretical system of mezzoeconomics, providing a feasible solution for establishing socialist economic theory with Chinese characteristics.

The mezzoeconomics founded by Professor Chen Yunxian mainly studies regional government competition. Although it also involves issues of regional economics and industrial economics, they appear as the objects of regional government competition, not as the objects to be studied by this theory. The theoretical basis of Chen Yunxian's mezzoeconomics lies

仅依靠市场的力量就无法实现帕累托最优的资源配置结果,这就是市场失灵的领域,此时需要政府干预以提升资源配置效率。

因此,中观经济学认为:"现代市场经济是建立在市场机制基础上运行的,是'有为政府'和'有效市场'相融合的经济模式。市场作为一种自然规律,我们更多的是认识它、理解它,政府拥有更多的主动权,在发挥市场在资源配置中'决定性作用'的同时,要更好地发挥政府的作用。找准政府在现代市场经济中的位置,科学处理政府与市场、政府与社会的关系,合理划分政府与市场、政府与社会的边界。构筑'有效市场'和'有为政府'这两个现代市场经济的轮子,使其相互补充,相互支撑,实现'双轮驱动'的现代市场经济体制。"① 可见,中观经济学基于现有文献对市场与政府关系研究不足这一情况,以中国改革开放伟大实践为基础,探索"有效市场"+"有为政府"双轮驱动经济增长的崭新理论,这是对经济学理论的重要突破。

中观经济学在研究范畴上与区域经济学、城市经济学,以及与区域发展紧密联系的产业经济学或结构经济学有交叉,把区域经济、城市经济和产业经济视为中观经济自然是可以的,但是,把区域经济学、城市经济学和产业经济学直接视为中观经济学则未必确切,这三门学科仍属于应用经济学,与作为理论经济学的中观经济学不同。② 另外,在研究方法上,除微观经济学和宏观经济学外,中观经济学也借鉴了财政学、公共管理等学科的理论工具和研究方法,在多学科交叉融合的基础上,构建了中观经济学的研究框架和理论体系,为建立中国特色社会主义经济理论提供了可行方案。

陈云贤教授所创立的中观经济学以区域政府竞争为主要研究对象,尽管也涉及区域经济和产业经济的问题,但它们是作为区域政府竞争的标的物出现的,而不是该理论所要研究的对象。陈云贤中观经济学的理论基础在于对"城市资源"

---

① 陈云贤、顾文静:《中观经济学》(第二版),北京大学出版社,2019,第9-10页。
② 陈云贤、顾文静:《中观经济学》(第二版),北京大学出版社,2019,第17页。

in the pioneering definition of "urban resources" and the related "resource generation" and "generative resources".

Firstly, from the perspective of urban resources, there is a distinction between broad and narrow senses. "Urban resources in the broad sense include industrial resources, livelihood resources, and infrastructure/public works resources…… Urban resources in the narrow sense include investment and construction of infrastructure hardware and software, as well as the development and operation of smart cities in the further modernization process." Urban resources exist as an important generative resource.

Secondly, resource generation refers to "things that already exist or appear due to objective needs as time progresses, moving from static to dynamic until they possess economic and productive characteristics".

Thirdly, generative resources refer to a type of resource derived from resource generation, "which, like industrial resources, belong to economic resources and possess three major characteristics: dynamism, economic nature, and productivity".

After defining these basic concepts, Professor Chen Yunxian points out that in the modern market economic system, enterprises are the resource allocation subjects of the industrial economy, mainly competing for and allocating the so-called "scarce resources" in traditional economics; regional governments are the resource allocation subjects of the urban economy, mainly competing for and allocating "generative resources". Therefore, enterprises and governments together constitute the dual driving forces of modern market economic development (Figure 3-1). This theory further points out that urban infrastructure is an important generative resource, which is a public works facility providing public services for social production and residents' lives. As a public goods system, the role of urban infrastructure is to ensure the normal operation of national and regional industrial economies and people's livelihoods. This kind of urban resource has obvious public goods attributes and positive externalities, thus requiring government provision, and the efficiency of regional governments in providing such urban resources reflects their competitiveness. Chen Yunxian's mezzoeconomics, through the definition of concepts such as "urban resources" "resource generation", and "generative resources", clarifies the competitive scope of regional governments, delineates a resource allocation field that is distinctly different from traditional economic theories, and thus forms the theoretical idea of government "foresighted leading".

以及与其相关联的"资源生成"和"生成性资源"所做的开创性的定义。

第一,从城市资源来看,它有广义与狭义之分,"广义的城市资源包括了产业资源、民生资源和基础设施/公共工程资源……狭义的城市资源包括基础设施硬件、软件的投资建设,以及更进一步的现代化进程中智能城市的开发和运作"[①]。城市资源是作为一种重要的生成性资源而存在的。

第二,所谓资源生成是指"原已存在或随着时代进程的客观需要而出现的事物,它由静态进入动态,直至具备经济性和生产性"[②]。

第三,所谓生成性资源是指由资源生成派生的一种资源,"与产业资源一样同属于经济资源,它具备三大特性:动态性、经济性、生产性"[③]。

在定义了这些基础性概念之后,陈云贤教授指出,在现代市场经济体系中,企业是产业经济的资源配置主体,主要是对传统经济学中所谓的"稀缺性资源"进行竞争与配置;区域政府是城市经济的资源配置主体,主要是对"生成性资源"进行竞争与配置。因此,企业和政府共同构成了现代市场经济发展的双重驱动力(图3-1)。该理论进而指出城市基础设施是一种重要的生成性资源,它是为社会生产和居民生活提供公共服务的公共工程设施。作为一种公共物品系统,城市基础设施的作用在于保证国家和区域的产业经济和民生经济得以正常运转。这种城市资源具有明显的公共物品属性和正的外部性,因此需要由政府提供,而区域政府对这种城市资源的提供效率则体现了它的竞争力。陈云贤中观经济学通过对"城市资源""资源生成"和"生成性资源"等概念的定义,明确了区域政府的竞争范围,圈定了一个与传统经济学理论截然不同的资源配置领域,进而形成了政府"超前引领"的理论思想。

---

[①] 陈云贤:《市场竞争双重主体论——兼谈中观经济学的创立与发展》,北京大学出版社,2020,第56—57页。
[②] 陈云贤:《市场竞争双重主体论——兼谈中观经济学的创立与发展》,北京大学出版社,2020,第56页。
[③] 陈云贤:《市场竞争双重主体论——兼谈中观经济学的创立与发展》,北京大学出版社,2020,第56页。

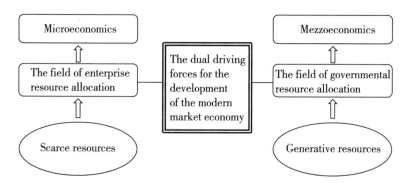

Figure 3-1  The Dual Driving Forces of Modern Market Economic Development under Chen Yunxian's Mezzoeconomic Framework

It can be seen that Professor Chen Yunxian's mezzoeconomics has achieved breakthroughs in traditional economics in various aspects of its theoretical framework, including research objects, research methods, research content, and policy propositions. Moreover, Chen Yunxian's mezzoeconomics has pioneered a new paradigm for studying government behavior. It is not confined to the realm of market failure under the traditional economic framework, emphasizing the government's leading and regulatory role in the behavior of market microeconomic entities, thus promoting the upgrading of industrial structures, economic growth, and income growth, all of which contribute to the improvement of macroeconomic performance. The research content in the fields of micro, mezzo, and macro levels is shown in Figure 3-2.

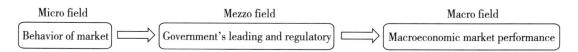

Figure 3-2  The research content in the fields of micro, mezzo, and macro levels

## Section 2: Core Concepts of Mezzoeconomics

### I. "Urban Resources" "Resource Generation", and "Generative Resources"

(i) Urban Resources

Mezzoeconomics innovatively defines the concept of "urban resources" and points out that urban resources can be distinguished between broad and narrow senses.

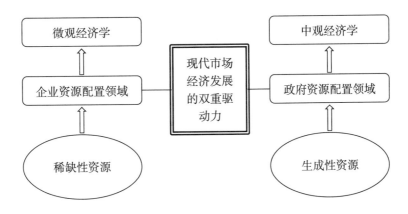

图 3-1 陈云贤中观经济学框架下的现代市场经济发展的双重驱动力

由此可见,陈云贤教授的中观经济学在研究对象、研究方法、研究内容以及政策主张等理论架构的各个方面都实现了对传统经济学的突破。不仅如此,陈云贤的中观经济学还开创了对政府行为进行研究的新范式,它不囿于传统经济学框架下的市场失灵领域,强调政府对市场微观主体行为的引领和调节,从而推进产业结构升级、经济和收入增长等宏观市场运行绩效的提升,微观、中观和宏观领域的研究内容见图 3-2。

图 3-2 微观、中观和宏观领域的研究内容

## 第二节 中观经济学的核心概念

### 一、"城市资源""资源生成"与"生成性资源"

#### (一)城市资源

中观经济学创新性地定义了"城市资源"的概念,并指出城市资源有广义与狭义之分。

Urban resources in the broad sense include industrial resources, livelihood resources, and infrastructure/public works resources.

Among them, industrial resources, also known as operative resources, refer to the primary, secondary, and tertiary industry sectors. The main bodies allocating these resources are generally enterprises, thus they are operational.

Livelihood resources, also known as non-operative resources, are mainly social welfare products and public goods in various regions, including economy (security), history, geography, image, spirit, ideas, emergency, safety, assistance, and other social needs of the region. Because these resources have public goods attributes, their allocation bodies are generally governments, so they are non-operative resources.

Infrastructure/public works resources correspond to urban construction, also known as quasi-operative resources, mainly including public service systems that ensure the normal operation of national or regional socio-economic activities, as well as hardware and software infrastructure that provide public services for social production and residents' lives, such as transportation, postal and telecommunications, power and water supply, environmental protection, education, science and technology, culture, health, sports, and other urban public works facilities and public life service facilities. Generally speaking, these resources have certain public goods attributes, so they should also be provided by the government. However, with the development of technology and institutional innovation, many of these resources can now be provided by the market. Both government and market have the functional attributes to allocate these resources, hence they are called quasi-operative resources.

Urban resources in the narrow sense refer to infrastructure/public works resources as quasi-operative resources. For the allocation of such resources, regional governments should determine whether to develop and allocate them as operative resources or operate and manage them as public welfare undertakings based on factors such as regional development direction, fiscal status, capital flow, enterprise demands, and the acceptance level and affordability of society and the public. The deep insights into the laws of resource allocation in this field, especially the comprehensive explanation of competition and cooperation among regional governments in this resource allocation field, are outstanding contributions made by mezzoeconomics.

广义的城市资源包括了产业资源、民生资源和基础设施/公共工程资源。①

其中，产业资源也称可经营性资源，也即第一、第二和第三产业部门，这类资源配置的主体一般是企业，因此它是可经营的。

民生资源也称非经营性资源，它以各区域的社会公益产品、公共物品为主，包括经济（保障）、历史、地理、形象、精神、理念、应急、安全、救助，以及区域的其他社会需求。②因为这类资源具有公共物品属性，其配置主体一般为政府，所以是非经营性资源。

基础设施/公共工程资源与城市建设相对应，也称准经营性资源，主要包括保证国家或区域的社会经济活动正常进行的公共服务系统，以及为社会生产、居民生活提供公共服务的软硬件基础设施，如交通、邮电、供电供水、环境保护、教育、科技、文化、卫生、体育事业等城市公共工程设施和公共生活服务设施等。③一般来讲，此类资源具有一定的公共物品属性，因此也应由政府提供。但随着技术的发展、制度的创新，此类资源中有很多已经能够交给市场来提供，政府和市场都具有对此类资源进行配置的功能属性，因此称其为准经营性资源。

狭义的城市资源是指作为准经营性资源的基础设施/公共工程资源，对于此类资源的配置，各区域政府应根据区域发展方向、财政状况、资金流量、企业需求和社会民众的接受程度与承受力等因素，来确定其是按可经营性资源来开发调配，还是按公益性事业来运行管理。对这一领域资源配置规律所做出的深入洞察，尤其是对区域政府在这一资源配置领域中的竞争与合作的全面解释，是中观经济学所做出的突出贡献。

---

① 陈云贤：《经济新引擎——兼论有为政府与有效市场》，钟礼荣译，外语教学与研究出版社，2019，第57页。
② 陈云贤：《市场竞争双重主体论——兼谈中观经济学的创立与发展》，北京大学出版社，2020，第59页。
③ 陈云贤：《市场竞争双重主体论——兼谈中观经济学的创立与发展》，北京大学出版社，2020，第59页。

## (ii) Resource Generation

When traditional economics discusses resource allocation, its premise is the scarcity of resources. Mankiw's definition of economics is: economics is the study of how to allocate scarce resources, and scarcity refers to the limitedness of social resources. Mezzoeconomics does not deny the importance of effectively allocating scarce resources, but it also focuses on the issue of "resource generation". Mezzoeconomics points out that resource generation is not the result of government planning, but refers to "things that already exist or appear due to objective needs as time progresses, moving from static to dynamic until they possess economic and productive characteristics". In modern society, the hardware and software infrastructure needed for economic and social development, and even the series of projects in the development and construction process of smart cities further on, are all important generative resources. The construction of these modern infrastructures forms an important pulling and supporting role for a country's economic growth, thus the issue of "resource generation" arises. This new resource generation field is the urban resource field, which is different from the nature and allocation method of traditional industrial resources, playing a positive role in promoting economic growth through another channel.

## (iii) Generative Resources

Generative resources refer to a type of resource derived from resource generation, "which, like industrial resources, belong to economic resources and possess three major characteristics: dynamism, economic nature, and productivity". In fact, natural resources such as land, minerals, water, forests, and grasslands become operational industrial resources after dynamic development, which is the simplest example of generative resources. The urban hardware and software infrastructure in modern economic construction mentioned above is also a type of generative resource, but unlike the operability of industrial resources, it belongs to quasi-operative resources. While these resources have obvious characteristics of dynamism, economic nature, and productivity, they also have high risks, especially large-scale urban hardware and software infrastructure, most of which are capital-intensive construction projects with the following characteristics.

First, large initial investment.

Second, long construction period.

## （二）资源生成

传统经济学在论及资源配置时，其前提条件即资源的稀缺性。曼昆对经济学的定义就是：经济学是一门研究如何对稀缺性资源进行配置的学问，而所谓稀缺性则是指社会资源的有限性。中观经济学并不否认对稀缺性资源进行有效配置的重要性，但与此同时还重点关注了"资源生成"问题。中观经济学指出，资源生成不是政府计划的结果，而是指"原已存在或随着时代进程的客观需要而出现的事物，它由静态进入动态，直至具备经济性和生产性"。[①] 在现代社会里，经济社会发展所需的软硬件基础设施，乃至更进一步的智能城市开发与建设过程中的系列工程，都是重要的生成性资源。这些对现代化基础设施的建设对一国经济增长形成了重要的拉动和支撑作用，这样，"资源生成"问题就产生了。而这个新的资源生成领域就是城市资源领域，它有别于传统产业资源的性质和配置方式，从另一途径发挥着促进经济增长的积极作用。

## （三）生成性资源

所谓生成性资源是指由资源生成派生的一种资源，"与产业资源一样同属于经济资源，它具备三大特性：动态性、经济性、生产性"。[②] 实际上，土地、矿产、水、森林、草原等自然资源在经过动态开发后就成为可经营性的产业资源，这是生成性资源最简单的例子。上面提到的现代经济建设中的城市软硬件基础设施，也是一种生成性资源，但与产业资源的可经营性不同，它属于准经营性资源。这类资源在具有明显的动态性、经济性和生产性特征的同时，还具有高风险性，特别是大型的城市软硬件基础设施，大多属于资本密集型的建设项目，具有如下特点：

第一，前期投资大；

第二，建设周期长；

---

① 陈云贤：《市场竞争双重主体论——兼谈中观经济学的创立与发展》，北京大学出版社，2020，第55-56页。

② 陈云贤：《经济新引擎——兼论有为政府与有效市场》，钟礼荣译，外语教学与研究出版社，2019，第56页。

Third, high cost.

Fourth, potential investment failure.

Fifth, difficult to control unexpected events, and so on.

Therefore, the conversion of quasi-operative resources to operative resources is accompanied by unique investment risks, operational risks, and management risks, and also faces many limitations.

First, non-government investment is carried out by enterprises or individuals with independent legal status, pursuing micro-level profitability, which is its primary characteristic.

Second, the funds for non-government investment mainly come from personal accumulation or social financing, with the investment scale being greatly limited.

Third, enterprises or individuals are confined to a single industry, making it difficult to take care of non-economic social undertakings.

Therefore, even if some quasi-operative resources can possess exclusivity and competitiveness through some modern technologies, it is economically unfeasible to operate them as operative resources due to high costs and high risks. At this time, for such quasi-operative resources, the government will still develop them according to the standards of non-operative resources and make investment decisions based on the policy objectives of government provision of public goods. Thus, in this field, how regional governments should effectively allocate quasi-operative resources to implement foresighted leading regional economies is the research scope of mezzoeconomics. Figure 3-3 shows mezzoeconomics' expansion of the research field of traditional economics.

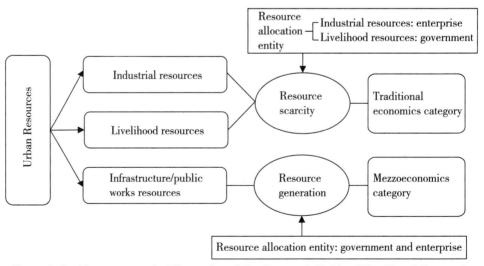

Figure 3–3  Mezzoeconomics' Expansion of the Research Fields of Traditional Economics

第三，成本高；

第四，投资可能失败；

第五，突发事件难以控制；等等。

因此，准经营性资源向可经营性资源转换时伴随着特有的投资风险、运营风险和管理风险，而且还面临诸多限制：

第一，非政府投资是由具有独立法人资格的企业或个人从事的投资，要追求微观上的盈利，这是其首要特征；

第二，非政府投资的资金主要来自个人的积累或社会融资，投资规模受到很大限制；

第三，企业或个人囿于一行一业，难以顾及非经济的社会事业。

因此，即使通过一些现代技术的加持能够使一些准经营性资源同样具有排他性和竞争性，但因为成本太高，风险太大，所以将其按照可经营性资源去运作在经济上是不可行的。此时，对这类准经营性资源，政府仍然会按照非经营性资源的标准去开发，并根据政府提供公共物品的政策目标做出投资决策。因此，在这一领域中，区域政府应如何对准经营性资源进行有效调配，从而对区域经济实施超前引领是中观经济学的研究范畴。中观经济学对传统经济学研究领域的拓展见图3-3。

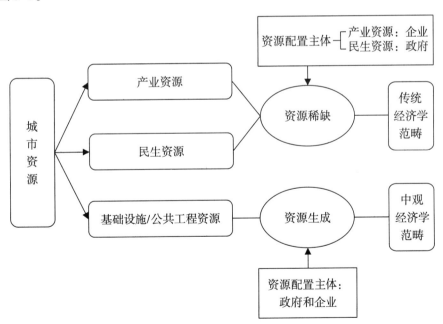

图3-3 中观经济学对传统经济学研究领域的拓展

To specifically analyze how the government allocates quasi-operative resources such as urban hardware and software infrastructure, mezzoeconomics innovatively distinguishes the dual attributes of regional governments: on one hand, regional governments also have "quasi-macro" attributes like central governments, undertaking the function of coordinating individual economic entities' behaviors; on the other hand, regional governments themselves are economic entities with their own interests, possessing "quasi-micro" attributes.

Due to the dual attributes of regional governments, they implement "basic bottom line, fairness and justice, effective improvement" policies in the livelihood economy; "planning, guidance; support, regulation; supervision, management" policies in the industrial economy; and "participation in competition, allocation and supervision" policies in the urban economy. At the same time, regional governments appear as competitive subjects in nine areas of competition, including project competition, industrial chain supporting competition, import and export competition, infrastructure competition, talent and technology competition, fiscal and financial competition, environmental system competition, policy system competition, and management efficiency competition. In the fierce competition for urban resources, regional governments continuously explore new economic growth points and achieve sustainable regional economic growth by vigorously promoting new investment engines, innovation engines, and rule engines centered on infrastructure development and construction.

## II. "Primary Resources" "Secondary Resources", and "Inverse Resources"

After defining generative resources, mezzoeconomics further points out that generative resources include at least three levels of resources: primary resources, secondary resources, and inverse resources.

First, primary resources. For example, for space resources, deep-sea resources, polar resources, and deep earth exploration resources, if these resources are not developed, they are static natural resources. If investment is made to develop these resources, their dynamism, economic nature, and productivity transform them into primary resources in the resource generation field. Primary resources are characterized by large investment scale, long development cycle, and many uncertain factors, i.e., high risk. Therefore, countries and regional governments must become the first investors in primary resources to gain advantages in world regional economic competition.

为了对政府如何配置城市软硬件基础设施这种准经营资源进行具体分析，中观经济学创新性地区分了区域政府的双重属性：一方面，区域政府也具有中央政府一样的"准宏观"属性，它承担着协调个体经济主体行为的职能；另一方面，区域政府本身也是一个经济行为主体，它拥有自身的利益诉求，具有"准微观"属性。

由于区域政府拥有这样的双重属性，因此，它才在民生经济中实施"基本托底、公平公正、有效提升"政策；在产业经济中实施"规划、引导；扶持、调节；监督、管理"政策；在城市经济中实施"参与竞争、调配监督"政策。同时，区域政府是以竞争主体的身份出现在九个领域的竞争中的，包括项目竞争、产业链配套竞争、进出口竞争、基础设施竞争、人才科技竞争、财政金融竞争、环境体系竞争、政策体系竞争和管理效率竞争。区域政府在对城市资源的激烈竞争中，通过全力推动以基础设施开发建设为主体的投资新引擎、创新新引擎和规则新引擎，不断开拓新的经济增长点，实现区域经济的可持续增长。

## 二、"原生性资源""次生性资源"与"逆生性资源"

中观经济学在定义了生成性资源后，进一步指出，生成性资源至少包含三个层面的资源，即原生性资源、次生性资源和逆生性资源。[①]

第一，原生性资源。例如，对于太空资源、深海资源、极地资源以及地球深探资源等来说，如果不去开发这类资源，它们就是静态的自然资源。如果投资开发这类资源，其动态性、经济性和生产性又使这类资源转换为资源生成领域中的原生性资源。原生性资源具有投资规模大、开发周期长、不确定因素多等特点，即具有高风险性，因此各国、各区域政府为了在世界区域经济竞争中使本国、本区域获得优势，必须成为原生性资源的第一投资人。

---

① 陈云贤：《市场竞争双重主体论——兼谈中观经济学的创立与发展》，北京大学出版社，2020，第97页。

Second, secondary resources. Taking urban hardware and software infrastructure as an example, it is originally a quasi-operational resource, but when it becomes an operational resource through the application of some modern technologies and the implementation of relevant policies, it becomes a secondary resource in the resource generation field. The investment and development of such resources also have four major characteristics: dynamism, economic nature, productivity, and high risk. Therefore, national and regional governments must also act as the first investors for this type of resource.

Third, inverse resources. This type of resource did not exist originally. It is a unique type of generative resource formed inversely by the external spillover effects in regional economic development, such as carbon emission trading resources. In the development and regulation of inverse resources[1], the government must be the primary responsible entity.

## III. The "Efficient Markets" + "Effective Governments" Combination Model in Mezzoeconomics

Mezzoeconomics further points out that only the combination of "Strong Effective Governments" and "Strong Efficient Markets" constitutes a mature market economy. Mezzoeconomics delineates six subsystems of the modern market vertical system[2], and based on how these six subsystems function, divides the efficient markets into three levels: "Weak Efficient Markets" "Semi-strong Efficient Markets", and "Strong Efficient Markets". For a "Weak Efficient Market", only the market elements system and market organization system exist within it, allowing the market to maintain basic operations. Building on this, if the region forms a relatively sound market legal system and market supervision system, and these systems can be well implemented, then this market becomes a "Semi-strong Efficient Market".

---

[1] Apart from carbon emission trading resources being inverse resources, waste can also be considered an inverse resource. This is because waste originally has no value, but with the continuous advancement of waste management technology and the establishment and implementation of waste sorting systems, waste gradually transforms from a mere discard into a resource, thus making it an inverse resource.

[2] In mezzoeconomics, the six subsystems of the modern market vertical system refer to: the market elements system, the market organization system, the market legal system, the market supervision system, the market environment system, and the market infrastructure.

Further, if the market environment system and market infrastructure can be established and improved, such a market becomes a "Strong Efficient Market".

Similar to the efficient markets, effective governments can also be divided into three types: "Weak Effective Governments" "Semi-strong Effective Governments", and "Strong Effective Governments". The basis for this division is whether the regional government has

第二，次生性资源。以城市软硬件基础设施为例，它本是一种准经营性资源，但若通过一些现代技术的加持和相关政策的实施，这种准经营性资源变为了可经营性资源，它就成为资源生成领域中的次生性资源。此类资源的投资开发同样具有动态性、经济性、生产性和高风险性四大特征，因此各国、各区域政府也必须充当该类资源的第一投资人。

第三，逆生性资源。这一类资源本来并不存在，它是由区域经济发展中的外部溢出效应逆向形成的一类独特的生成性资源，比如碳排放交易资源等。在对逆生性资源①的开发与管制方面，政府必定是第一责任主体。

## 三、中观经济学下的"有效市场"+"有为政府"组合模式

中观经济学进一步指出，只有"强式有为政府"与"强式有效市场"的组合才是成熟市场经济。中观经济学刻画了现代市场纵向体系的六大子系统②，并按这六大子系统发挥作用的情况将有效市场划分为"弱式有效市场""半强式有效市场"和"强式有效市场"三个层次。对于"弱式有效市场"，只有市场要素体系和市场组织体系存在其中，市场能够维持基本的运行；在此基础上，如果该区域形成了比较健全的市场法治体系和市场监管体系，并且这些制度能够得到很好的执行，那么这种市场就成为"半强式有效市场"；在此基础上，如果市场环境体系与市场基础设施能够得到建立和完善，那么这样的市场就成为"强式有效市场"。

与有效市场类似的，有为政府也可划分为"弱式有为政府""半强式有为政

---

① 除了碳排放交易资源是逆生性资源，垃圾也可视为一种逆生性资源。这是因为：垃圾本没有价值，但随着垃圾处理技术的不断进步，以及垃圾分类这项制度的制定和实施，垃圾逐渐由一种废弃物变为了资源，因此是逆生性资源。

② 在中观经济学中，现代市场纵向体系的六大子系统是指：市场要素体系、市场组织体系、市场法治体系、市场监管体系、市场环境体系和市场基础设施。

relevant policies for allocating livelihood resources, industrial resources, and infrastructure/public works resources. A government that only focuses on livelihood resources, i.e., only plays a role in allocating non-operative resources, is a "Weak Effective Government". In fact, this type of government is the "limited government" advocated by scholars adhering to traditional economic theories. Building on the "Weak Effective Government", if the regional government also focuses on industrial resources, i.e., optimizing and guiding the allocation of operative resources, then this government is a "Semi-strong Effective Government". Further, if the regional government adopts active supporting policies for the allocation of infrastructure/public works resources, i.e., quasi-operative resources, actively participates in the allocation and competition of these resources, and provides strong support and guarantee for industrial economic development, then such a government that becomes one of the driving forces of economic development is a "Strong Effective Government".

The organic combination of three types of efficient markets and three types of effective governments constitutes nine combination models of "Efficient Markets" + "Effective Governments" (Figure 3-4). Among these nine models, the combination of "Strong Efficient Markets" + "Strong Effective Governments" is naturally the development goal of a mature market economy. In this combination model, a strong effective government has the ability to foresighted leading regional economic development, while a strong efficient market can ensure the optimal allocation of various resources. The organic combination of the two can both ensure the scientific nature of enterprise decision-making, enabling enterprises to gain competitive advantages in the allocation and competition of industrial resources, and better play out the advantages of regional governments in the allocation and competition of urban resources, further enhancing enterprise competitiveness through the overall support of regional competitiveness under government support.

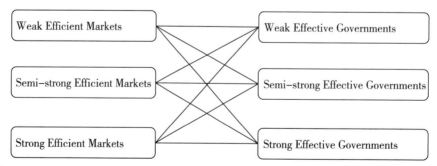

Figure 3-4　Nine Combination Models of "Efficient Markets" + "Effective Governments"

府"和"强式有为政府"三种类型,其划分依据在于区域政府是否具有对民生资源、产业资源和基础设施/公共工程资源进行调配的相关政策。只关注民生资源,即仅对非经营性资源的调配发挥作用的政府属于"弱式有为政府",实际上,这种政府也就是坚持传统经济学理论的学者所倡导的"有限政府";在"弱式有为政府"基础上,如果区域政府还关注产业资源,即对可经营性资源配置的优化和引导,则这种政府属于"半强式有为政府";在此基础上,如果区域政府对基础设施/公共工程资源,即准经营性资源的配置采取积极的配套政策,主动参与到这种资源的配置和竞争当中,为产业经济发展提供有力的支撑与保障,则成为经济发展驱动力之一的政府就成为"强式有为政府"。

三种类型的有效市场与三种类型的有为政府的有机结合构成了"有效市场"+"有为政府"的九种组合模式(图3-4)。在这九种模式中,能够作为成熟市场经济发展目标的模式自然是"强式有效市场"+"强式有为政府"的组合。在这样的组合模式中,强式有为政府具有超前引领区域经济发展的能力,强式有效市场则能够保证各类资源的优化配置。二者的有机结合既能够保证企业决策的科学性,使企业在产业资源的配置与竞争中取得竞争优势,又能够更好地发挥区域政府在城市资源的配置与竞争中的优势,通过政府支持下区域竞争力的整体支撑,进一步增强企业竞争力。

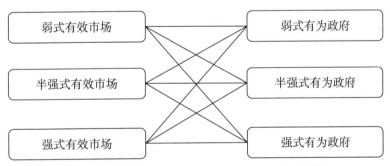

**图3-4 "有效市场"+"有为政府"的九种组合模式**

资料来源:陈云贤:《市场竞争双重主体论——兼谈中观经济学的创立与发展》,北京大学出版社,2020,第266页。

# Section 3: Dual Attributes of Regional Governments and Dual-entity Theory of Market Competition

In the mezzoeconomics system, regional governments possess dual attributes——"quasi-micro" attributes and "quasi-macro" attributes. The dialectical unity of these two attributes determines the different characteristics of regional governments in handling the relationship between market and government.

## I. "Quasi–micro" Attributes of Regional Governments

### (i) The Connotation of Regional Governments' "Quasi–micro" Attributes

"Micro" attributes refer to the characteristics possessed by microeconomic entities participating in market economic activities, including two specific attributes: having a clear objective function and individuals having complete rationality. The economic behavior of microeconomic entities is determined by these two specific attributes. Mezzoeconomics believes that the role of regional governments is multidimensional: they are both agents of higher-level governments and representatives of the interests of non-governmental entities in the region; they are both managers of the jurisdiction and providers of public goods, as well as economic organizations pursuing profit maximization. Therefore, regional governments also possess the basic attributes of microeconomic entities.

"Quasi" implies not belonging to a certain category, but to some extent undertaking or possessing certain functions or attributes identical to that category. Regional governments' planning, guidance, and support for operative resources, as well as their investment, operation, and participation in quasi-operative resources, i.e., urban infrastructure, make them concentrated agents of microeconomic entities in the regional economy.

Therefore, the so-called "quasi-micro" attributes of regional governments refer to regional governments not being microeconomic entities, but possessing behavioral characteristics of microeconomic entities to a certain extent. The specific connotations are as follows.

## 第三节　区域政府双重属性与市场竞争双重主体论

在中观经济学的体系里，区域政府具有双重属性——"准微观"属性和"准宏观"属性，这两种属性的辩证统一关系决定了区域政府在处理市场和政府之间关系方面的不同特点。

### 一、区域政府的"准微观"属性

#### （一）区域政府"准微观"属性的内涵

"微观"属性是指参与市场经济活动的微观主体所具备的属性，包括具有明确的目标函数和个体具有完全理性这两种具体属性，微观主体的经济行为即由这两种具体属性决定。中观经济学认为，区域政府的角色是多维度的：既是上级政府的代理，又是区域非政府主体的利益代表；既是辖区的管理者和公共物品的提供者，又是一个追求利益最大化的经济组织。因此，区域政府也具有微观主体的基本属性。

"准"意味着不属于某个范畴，却在一定程度上承担或具备某种与该范畴相同的职能或属性。区域政府对可经营性资源的规划、引导、扶持，以及对准经营性资源，即城市基础设施的投资、运营与参与，使它成为区域经济中微观主体的集中代理。

因此，所谓区域政府的"准微观"属性是指，区域政府不是微观主体，但又具有一定程度上的微观主体行为特征，其具体内涵表述如下。[①]

---

① 陈云贤、顾文静：《中观经济学》（第二版），北京大学出版社，2019，第43页。

First, in terms of internal organization and management, regional governments can fully absorb and draw upon rich theoretical models and excellent practical experiences from enterprise management to establish an efficiently operating internal management model, becoming an important force for institutional innovation, organizational innovation, technological innovation, and conceptual innovation.

Second, regional governments have strong economic independence, aiming to maximize the economic interests of their regions. They have strong motivation to carry out institutional innovation and technological innovation. Regional leaders should cultivate reform courage and forward-thinking in competition and should possess distinct "political entrepreneurship".

Third, the behavior of regional governments should fully respect the dominant position of the market as a means of resource allocation, adhere to exercising management functions according to market laws, strengthen the market adaptability of regional government behavior, and engage in benign competition among regional governments, with the efficiency of regional market operation and the realized economic and social benefits as the main assessment targets of competition. Regional governments thus achieve a role transformation from power institutions far from market competition to "quasi-micro" institutions participating in market competition and improving management performance.

## (ii) Basis for Regional Governments' "Quasi-micro" Attributes

Mezzoeconomics provides the basis for regional governments' "quasi-micro" attributes from two aspects: the differences and connections between the attributes possessed by regional governments and enterprises. The specific explanations are as follows.

### 1. Differences between Attributes Possessed by Regional Governments and Enterprises

Although regional governments possess certain "micro" attributes, we need to be clear that there are still important logical differences between the economic behaviors of regional governments and enterprises, mainly including the following points.

(1) Different purposes. From the perspective of their mission, the purpose of regional government behavior is mainly to provide non-profit products or services to their constituents, maximizing social welfare. Regional governments are not profit-oriented, have obvious public welfare nature, and belong to the non-market category. Enterprises, on the other hand, are mainly centered on the price mechanism, realizing maximum corporate profits through a series

of behaviors such as production and sales, with profit as their purpose.

(2) Different survival modes. Regional government management is non-profit, and the products or services provided are usually free or symbolically charged. Their survival cannot rely on selling products or services, but mainly depends on the authorization of legislative

第一,区域政府内部的组织管理,可以充分吸收借鉴企业管理中丰富的理论模型和优秀的实践经验,建立高效运转的内部管理模式,成为制度创新、组织创新、技术创新和理念创新的重要力量。

第二,区域政府拥有较强的经济独立性,以实现本区域经济利益最大化为目标,自身具有强烈的开展制度创新和技术创新等的动力,区域执政者应在竞争中培养改革魄力和超前思维,应具有鲜明的"政治企业家精神"。

第三,区域政府的行为应充分尊重市场作为资源配置手段的主导地位,坚持按照市场规律发挥管理职能,强化区域政府行为的市场适应性,展开区域政府之间的良性竞争,以各区域市场运转的效率、实现的经济和社会收益作为竞争的主要考核目标。区域政府因而实现从远离市场竞争的权力机构到参与市场竞争、提高管理绩效的"准微观"机构的角色转换。

## (二)区域政府"准微观"属性的依据

中观经济学从区域政府与企业所具有属性的差异和联系两个方面为区域政府的"准微观"属性提供了依据,具体阐述如下。①

### 1. 区域政府与企业所具有属性的差异

尽管区域政府具有一定的"微观"属性,但我们需要明确的是,区域政府与企业的经济行为仍存在重要的逻辑差异,这主要包含以下几点。

(1)目的不同。从存在的使命来看,区域政府行为的目的主要是给所属民众提供非营利性的产品或服务,实现社会福利的最大化。区域政府不以盈利为目的,具有明显的公益性质,属于非市场范畴。而企业主要是以价格机制为核心,通过生产、销售等一系列行为实现企业利润最大化,以盈利为目的。

(2)生存方式不同。区域政府管理是非营利性的,所提供的产品或服务通常是免费或象征性收费的,其生存不能靠销售产品或服务来维持,而主要依赖立

---

① 陈云贤、顾文静:《中观经济学》(第二版),北京大学出版社,2019,第43-45页。

institutions. Their main source of funds is taxation, and budget expenditures belong to public finance expenditures, which cannot be arbitrarily disposed of by government managers but must be made public and subject to taxpayer supervision. In contrast, enterprise management is profit-oriented, and the various material resources needed mainly come from investment returns and profits obtained. Therefore, the use of funds by enterprises is an "internal affair" of the enterprise, which others have no right to interfere with, and budget expenditures are mainly determined based on their own profitability. Enterprises are autonomous, and the material resources needed for their management are also autonomous and do not need to be made public. For this reason, regional government management decisions often need to reflect the inclinations of the public or legislative departments, while enterprise management decisions are largely influenced by market factors, i.e., consumer demand.

(3) Different management limiting factors. From the perspective of management limiting factors, the entire process of regional government management is restricted by law, that is, the legislative body will clearly stipulate its management authority, organizational form, activity method, basic responsibilities, and legal responsibilities in the form of articles, which can make regional government management operate strictly within the procedures and scope prescribed by law. Enterprise management is different; the law is merely an external constraining factor in its activities. Enterprise management is mainly carried out in the economic field, managed according to the requirements of the market mechanism. As long as market demand exists and enterprise behavior is not illegal, enterprise management must revolve around the goal of maximizing corporate profits.

(4) Different performance evaluation standards. From the perspective of performance evaluation standards, the legality of behavior, the quality of public opinion, the degree of reduction in various conflicts, the implementation effect of public projects, the quantity and consumption of public goods, etc., are the main indicators for evaluating the effectiveness of regional government management. In enterprise management, sales volume, net profit rate, net return on capital, production scale, market share, etc., are the main performance evaluation standards, the main indicators of management level and effect, and also the markers of managers' performance. Obviously, the performance evaluation standards of regional government management emphasize social benefits, while those of enterprise management emphasize economic benefits.

## 2. Connections between Attributes Possessed by Regional Governments and Enterprises

(1) Analysis based on the essential attributes of enterprises shows that enterprises possess an internal resource allocation mechanism similar to the market resource allocation mechanism. Internal enterprise management is the allocation of resources owned by the

法机构的授权；其资金来源主要是税收，经费预算属于公共财政支出，不能任意由政府管理人员支配，而必须公开化，接受纳税人的监督。相反，企业管理以盈利为目的，所需要的各种物质资源主要来自投资的回报，来自所获取的利润。因此，企业的资金使用状况属于企业的"内部事务"，其他人无权干涉，经费预算也主要依据自身盈利状况而定。企业是自主的，其管理所需的物质资源也是自主的，不需要公开化。正因为如此，区域政府管理的决策常常要反映公众或立法部门的倾向性，而企业管理的决策在很大程度上受市场因素，即消费者需求的影响。

（3）管理限制因素不同。从管理限制因素来看，区域政府管理的整个过程都受法律的限制，即立法机构会对其管理权限、组织形式、活动方式、基本职责和法律责任等以条文形式予以明确规定，这可以使区域政府管理严格地在法律规定的程序和范围内运行。而企业管理则不同，法律在其活动中仅仅是一种外部制约因素。企业管理主要是在经济领域进行，按照市场机制的要求去管理。只要市场需求存在，企业行为又不违法，企业管理就必须围绕实现企业利润最大化这一目标而运转。

（4）绩效评估标准不同。从绩效评估标准看，行为的合法性、公众舆论的好坏、各种冲突减少的程度、公共项目的实施效果、公共物品的数量及其消耗程度等，是评估区域政府管理成效的主要指标。在企业管理中，销售额、净收益率、资本的净收益、生产规模、市场占有率等是主要的绩效评估标准，是企业管理水平和管理效果的主要显示器，也是管理人员绩效的标志。显然，区域政府管理的绩效评估标准偏重于社会收益，企业管理的绩效评估标准则强调经济效益。

**2. 区域政府与企业所具有属性的联系**

（1）根据企业的本质属性分析可以看出，企业拥有一种和市场资源调配机制相似的企业内部资源调配机制。企业内部管理就是通过计划、组织、人事管理、

enterprise according to the principle of profit maximization through a series of means such as planning, organization, personnel management, and budgeting. Regional governments also possess certain public resources, and allocating and utilizing these public resources to stimulate maximum output efficiency is an important responsibility of regional governments. Regional governments also possess means of resource allocation such as planning, organization, personnel management, and budgeting. Therefore, like enterprises, regional governments have the function of resource allocation, only differing in scope, purpose, and other aspects.

(2) Competition mechanisms always exist between regional governments and between enterprises, and are the driving force for the development of both. Competition between enterprises is endowed by the market mechanism. Whether in perfectly competitive markets, monopolistically competitive markets, or oligopolistic markets, enterprises must compete with rivals for survival and development. Even in monopolistic markets, enterprises must continuously compete to prevent potential competitors from entering. Competition between regional governments also exists in reality, and can even be extremely intense. From a global perspective, national governments are also regional governments, and competition in national strength between countries has been ongoing.

(3) The behaviors of both regional governments and enterprises are carried out on the premise of respecting the market mechanism. Under market economy conditions, enterprises can only achieve survival and development by respecting market laws, receiving market price signals, and adapting to market demand. The economic behavior of regional governments must also be based on respecting and conforming to market laws. Regional government interventions that violate market laws will distort resource allocation and reduce efficiency.

(4) Both regional governments and enterprises must fulfill general internal management functions. To maintain the normal operation of an organization, micro-management of the organization's internal affairs is necessary. There are many similarities between the internal management of regional governments and enterprises. For example, both regional governments and enterprises have human resource management, project management, financial management, technology management, information management, equipment management, process management, cultural management, and other contents. In terms of management levels, they can both be divided into decision-making management, business management, execution management, and other levels.

## II. "Quasi–macro" Attributes of Regional Governments

The "quasi-macro" attributes of regional governments emphasize that regional governments possess certain characteristics of the state in structure and function, namely,

预算等一系列手段对企业拥有的资源按照利润最大化原则进行配置。区域政府也拥有一定的公共资源，配置和利用这些公共资源以激发最大的产出效率，是区域政府的重要职责，区域政府也同样拥有计划、组织、人事管理、预算等进行资源调配的手段。所以，区域政府与企业一样，具有进行资源调配的功能，只是在范围、目的等方面存在差异。

（2）竞争机制在区域政府之间与企业之间始终存在，并且是二者发展的原动力。企业之间的竞争是市场机制所赋予的。不论在完全竞争市场、垄断竞争市场还是寡头市场，企业都要为了生存和发展与对手展开竞争。即使在垄断市场，企业也要为了阻止潜在竞争者的进入而不断展开竞争。区域政府之间的竞争也是现实存在的，甚至异常激烈。而从全球的视角考察，国家政府也是区域政府，国家政府在国力上的竞争更是一直在持续地进行着。

（3）区域政府和企业的行为都是在尊重市场机制的前提下展开的。在市场经济条件下，企业只有尊重市场规律，接收市场价格信号，适应市场需求，才能实现生存和发展。区域政府的经济行为也要建立在尊重和顺应市场规律的基础之上，违背市场规律的区域政府干预会扭曲资源配置，降低效率。

（4）区域政府和企业都必须履行一般的内部管理职能。要维护一个组织的正常运转，就需要对组织内部进行微观管理。区域政府和企业的内部管理有很多异曲同工之处，例如，区域政府和企业都有人力资源管理、项目管理、资金管理、技术管理、信息管理、设备管理、流程管理、文化管理等内容；在管理层次上也都可以分为决策管理、业务管理、执行管理等多个层次。

## 二、区域政府的"准宏观"属性

区域政府的"准宏观"属性强调的是区域政府在结构上、职能上具备国家的

regional governments' planning, guidance, support, regulation, supervision, and management of operative resources; as well as their basic bottom-line, fairness and justice, and effective improvement of non-operative resources, i.e., public goods or social welfare products, making them representatives of the state within their regions.

In a country, the national government can use its public nature and coercive power to influence the establishment and maintenance of market order in that country. Similarly, in a region, regional governments can act as agents of the national government, using the public nature and coercive power granted by state power to promote the establishment and maintenance of market order in their regions. This is where the "quasi-macro" attributes of regional governments lie.

Reflected in the economic behavior of regional governments, their "quasi-macro" attributes are manifested in: regional governments possess the macro-control functions of general governments and can judiciously use means such as fiscal policy based on the state of economic operation, thereby affecting region's aggregate demand and income, achieving region's national income balance. Similarly, regional governments also undertake macro-economic functions such as promoting regional economic growth, reducing unemployment rates, and maintaining price stability, and can use corresponding fiscal policies and other means to regulate economic operation.

## III. Regional Competition under the Leadership of Regional Governments

The practice of regional management in various countries worldwide and the successful experience of China's reform and opening-up have told us that, on the basis of ensuring "basic bottom-line, fairness and justice, and effective improvement" in the supply of social welfare products and public goods in their regions, to prevent issues such as idle waste of urban resources (especially urban infrastructure) or inefficient operation of urban construction, and disorderly urban management, governments will use market mechanisms to hand over part or most of the urban infrastructure to society for investment, development, and management. In this process of quasi-operative resources transforming into operative resources, the determination of urban infrastructure investment vehicles, i.e., the equity structure and nature of urban infrastructure investment enterprises (such as government sole proprietorship, joint ventures, cooperation, joint-stock system, or even state-owned private enterprises), must comply with market rules. The capital operation of urban infrastructure investment——whether through Build-Operate-Transfer,

某些特征,即区域政府对可经营性资源的规划、引导、扶持、调节、监督、管理;以及对非经营性资源,即公共物品或社会公益产品的基本托底、公平公正、有效提升,使它成为本区域内的国家代表。[①]

在一个国家中,国家政府可以利用其公共性和强制力影响该国市场秩序的建立和维持。同样,在一个区域中,区域政府可以代理国家政府,利用国家政权授予的公共性和强制力,促进本区域市场秩序的建立和维持,这就是区域政府"准宏观"属性之所在。

反映在区域政府的经济行为上,其"准宏观"属性体现在:区域政府具备一般政府的宏观调控职能,可以依据经济运行状态对财政政策等手段进行斟酌使用,从而影响区域总需求和总收入,实现区域国民收入均衡。同样地,区域政府也承担着推动本区域经济增长、降低失业率、保持物价稳定等宏观经济职能,可以运用相应的财政政策等手段对经济运行进行调控。

## 三、区域政府引领下的区域竞争

世界各国区域管理的实践和中国改革开放的成功经验都已经告诉我们,在确保对本区域社会公益产品和公共物品供给"基本托底、公平公正、有效提升"的基础上,为防范城市资源尤其是城市基础设施闲置浪费或城市建设低效运作、城市管理无序进行等问题,政府都会通过市场机制,把部分或大部分城市基础设施交给社会去投资、开发和管理。在这一准经营性资源向可经营性资源转变的过程中,城市基础设施投资载体的确定,即城市基础设施投资企业的股权结构及其性质(如政府独资、合资、合作、股份制甚至国有民营等),必须符合市场规则;

---

① 陈云贤:《市场竞争双重主体论——兼谈中观经济学的创立与发展》,北京大学出版社,2020,第76页。

public utility privatization, and other franchise methods, or through issuing bonds, stocks, and other means——must pass the test of market competition.

Therefore, we can say that the supply level of urban infrastructure has a significant impact on urban competitiveness, while the economic returns of urban infrastructure construction projects have a significant impact on the supply level of urban infrastructure. Hence, an important manifestation of competition between regional governments is how to improve the economic returns of region's urban infrastructure construction projects to attract more investors, thereby enhancing the region's urban infrastructure supply level and increasing region's carrying capacity.

As a result, the modern market system has formed dual economic entities: enterprises and regional governments. Enterprise competition mainly occurs in the industrial economy, while regional government competition mainly occurs in the urban economy. There is no competitive relationship between enterprises and regional governments in the industrial economy. The competition of regional governments is mainly concentrated in the field of region's infrastructure construction. Its essence is the competition for various tangible or intangible resources in regional economic development. Its purpose is mainly to optimize the allocation of urban resources in the region, improve the efficiency and economic return rate of the urban economy in the region. Regional governments mainly develop supporting policies and measures around the leading advantages and sustainable development goals of their region's urban economies. The regional government competition and enterprise competition occurring in different fields jointly constitute the dual-layer market competition system in the modern market system. Regional governments and enterprises, as dual-entity of market competition, form a complementary relationship.

## IV. Dual-entity Theory of Market Competition

Mezzoeconomics reveals the "quasi-micro" attributes possessed by regional governments, thus discovering the dual-entity in the modern market system, namely, the enterprise subject in the industrial economy competition field and the regional government entity in the urban economy competition field.

Regional governments and enterprises belong to two different subject categories. Enterprises are microeconomic entities, while regional governments are mezzoeconomic entities. There are clear distinctions between regional governments and enterprises——their purposes, survival modes, management limiting factors, and performance evaluation standards

城市基础设施投资的资本运营——不管是通过建设—经营—移交、公用事业民营化等特许经营方式，还是通过发行债券、股票等方式——必须通过市场竞争的检验。

因此，我们可以这样讲，城市基础设施的供给水平对城市竞争力产生重要影响，而城市基础设施建设项目的经济回报又对城市基础设施的供给水平产生重要影响。由此，区域政府之间竞争的一个重要体现就在于如何提高区域的城市基础设施建设项目的经济回报以吸引更多的投资者，从而提升区域的城市基础设施供给水平，提高区域承载力。

所以，现代市场体系就形成了二元经济主体，即企业和区域政府。企业竞争主要发生在产业经济中，区域政府竞争主要发生在城市经济中，企业与区域政府在产业经济中不存在竞争关系。区域政府的竞争主要集中在区域基础设施建设领域，其实质是对区域经济发展中各种有形或无形资源的竞争，其目的主要在于优化本区域城市资源配置，提高本区域城市经济效率和经济回报率，区域政府主要围绕本区域城市经济的领先优势和可持续发展目标来配套政策措施。在不同领域发生的区域政府竞争和企业竞争共同构成现代市场体系中的双层市场竞争体系，区域政府和企业作为市场竞争双重主体，形成了相辅相成的关系。

## 四、市场竞争双重主体论

中观经济学揭示了区域政府所具有的"准微观"属性，从而发现了现代市场体系中的双重主体，即产业经济竞争领域中的企业主体和城市经济竞争领域中的区域政府主体。

区域政府和企业属于两个不同的主体范畴。企业是微观经济主体，区域政府则是中观经济主体。区域政府和企业有明显的区别——目的、生存方式、管理限

are different, but the behaviors of regional governments and enterprises also have similarities.

This mainly includes the following points.

First, both regional governments and enterprises are subjects of resource allocation.

Second, competition mechanisms always exist between regional governments and between enterprises, and are the driving force for regional economic development.

Third, both regional governments and enterprises must operate on the premise of respecting market rules.

Fourth, both regional governments and enterprises allocate resources with the initial goal of maximizing benefits.

Mezzoeconomics further elucidates the relationship between the dual-entity of market competition. The enterprise competition system and the regional government competition system are dual-loop operating systems, which are both independent and interrelated, jointly constituting the dual competition system in the market economy.

The enterprise competition system only operates between enterprises in the microeconomy. Any regional government function is only a factor supplier, environment provider, and market supplier for enterprise competition, ensuring open, fair, and just competition among enterprises from policy, system, and environmental aspects, while interacting with micro-enterprises in terms of factors, environment, and market supply. Regional governments should not become microeconomic entities like enterprises, participating in enterprise competition activities, nor do they have the right to directly intervene in enterprises' microeconomic affairs.

The competition between regional governments also only occurs between regional governments. Regional governments are equal competitive market entities in the mezzoeconomic field, competing in terms of regional resource allocation, regional economic efficiency, and effectiveness from the supply-side "three-horse carriage". Competition between regional governments is premised on respecting enterprises' market competition and does not incorporate enterprise competition into the level of regional government competition.

At the same time, the regional government competition system relies on the enterprise competition system and plays a guiding, coordinating, and supervisory role for the enterprise competition system. Enterprise competition is the fundamental attribute of the market economy and an important factor in invigorating the market economy. An economy without enterprise

制因素和绩效评估标准都不同，但区域政府行为与企业行为又有相似性。①

这主要包括以下几点。

第一，区域政府与企业都是资源调配的主体。

第二，竞争机制在区域政府之间与企业之间始终存在并且是区域经济发展的原动力。

第三，区域政府和企业都必须在尊重市场规则的前提下活动。

第四，区域政府和企业都以利益最大化为最初目标调配资源。

中观经济学还进一步阐明了市场竞争双重主体之间的关系。企业竞争体系和区域政府竞争体系是双环运作体系，二者既相互独立又相互联系，共同构成市场经济中的双重竞争系统。

企业竞争体系只作用于微观经济中的企业之间，任何区域政府职能只是企业竞争的要素供给者、环境供给者和市场供给者，既从政策、制度和环境上确保企业开展公开、公平、公正的竞争，又从要素、环境、市场供给三个方面与微观企业运行关联互动。区域政府不应和企业一样成为微观经济的主体，参与到企业竞争活动中去，也无权对企业的微观经济事务进行直接干预。

而区域政府间的竞争也只是在区域政府之间展开，各区域政府是中观经济领域平等竞争的市场主体，它们从供给侧"三驾马车"就区域资源的调配、区域经济效率及效益等方面展开竞争。区域政府之间的竞争以尊重企业的市场竞争为前提，不将企业竞争纳入区域政府竞争的层面。

同时，区域政府竞争体系又以企业竞争体系为依托，并对企业竞争体系发挥引导、协调和监督作用。企业竞争是市场经济的根本属性，是市场经济焕发生机和活力的重要因素，没有企业竞争的经济不是市场经济，企业层面的竞争是市场

---

① 陈云贤:《市场竞争双重主体论——兼谈中观经济学的创立与发展》，北京大学出版社，2020，第230–232页。

the foundation of a market economy, competition between regional governments would evolve into administrative power disputes. Therefore, in the modern market system, there exists competition at the enterprise level, which in turn drives competition between regional governments. It can be said that the establishment of dual-entity of market competition originates from the improvement and perfection of the modern market system and mechanism. Regional government competition is mainly reflected in the implementation of major projects, improvement of industrial chains, import and export facilitation, and competition in talent, technology, capital, policy, environment, efficiency, and other supporting aspects in specific practical work. It plays a foresighted leading role in enterprise competition.

The core of enterprise competition is the optimal allocation of resources under resource scarcity conditions, while the core of regional government competition is the optimal allocation of resources based on resource generation.

Research on enterprise competitive behavior and its consequences is actually a study of the optimal allocation of resources under resource scarcity conditions in microeconomic operations. The focus of the research is on the main economic variables in enterprise competition, namely the price determination mechanism. The content of the research extends to form price theory, consumer choice theory, production factor price determination theory, industrial organization theory, etc.

Research on regional government competitive behavior and its consequences is actually a study of the optimal allocation of resources based on resource generation in mezzoeconomic operations. The focus of the research is on the main economic variables affecting regional government competition, namely the determination mechanism of regional fiscal revenue and expenditure. The content of the research extends to form resource generation theory, dual attribute theory of regional governments, dual-entity theory of market competition, government foresighted leading theory, new engine theory of economic development, and dual-strong mechanism theory of mature market economy.

The driving force of the modern market economy comes not only from enterprise competition in the microeconomic field but also from regional government competition in the mezzoeconomic field. They are the dual-entity in the modern market system, constituting the dual driving forces for the development of the modern market economy, promoting sustainable development of the region's economy.

竞争的基础；而区域政府竞争是基于区域内的企业竞争，围绕着企业竞争的要素条件、环境、政策、效率和空间等展开的。没有企业竞争等同于缺乏市场经济的基础，区域政府间的竞争就会演化为行政权纷争。因此，在现代市场体系中，存在企业层面的竞争，而企业层面的竞争又带动了区域政府间的竞争，可以说，市场竞争双重主体的确立源于现代市场体系和机制的健全与完善。区域政府竞争在具体的实践工作中主要体现在重大项目落地，产业链完善，进出口便利和人才、科技、资金、政策、环境、效率等配套的竞争上，它对企业竞争发挥着超前引领的作用。

企业竞争的核心是在资源稀缺条件下的资源优化配置问题，区域政府竞争的核心是在资源生成基础上的资源优化配置问题。

对企业的竞争行为及其后果的研究其实是在微观经济运行中对资源稀缺条件下资源优化配置问题的研究，研究的焦点是企业竞争中的主要经济变量，即价格决定机制，研究的内容延伸形成了价格理论、消费者选择理论、生产要素价格决定理论、产业组织理论等。

而对区域政府的竞争行为及其后果的研究其实是在中观经济运行中对资源生成基础上的资源优化配置问题的研究，研究的焦点是影响区域政府竞争的主要经济变量，即区域财政收入与支出的决定机制，研究的内容延伸形成了资源生成理论、区域政府双重属性理论、市场竞争双重主体论、政府超前引领理论、经济发展新引擎理论和成熟市场经济的双强机制理论等。

现代市场经济的驱动力，不仅来自微观经济领域的企业竞争，而且来自中观经济领域的区域政府竞争，它们是现代市场体系中的双重主体，构成现代市场经济发展的双动力，推动着区域经济的可持续发展。

# Section 4: Three Levels of Competitive Advantage Theory in Mezzoeconomics

Porter's competitive advantage theory broke through the traditional comparative advantage theory, providing theoretical basis for countries worldwide to participate in international competition at a higher level from the perspective of competitive advantage, and offering methods and ideas for a country to cultivate national competitive advantage and achieve competitive stage transformation from a dynamic development perspective. However, Porter's competitive advantage theory does not fully recognize the role of government, merely viewing the government factor as a variable, excluding it from the core factors forming national competitive advantage. In fact, governments of some countries, especially those of developing countries, can even bypass the four core factors, directly invest in certain industries and form competitive advantages, thereby supporting and leading a country's economy to achieve a leap in economic development stages. Particularly, in today's reality of increasingly large global economic volume, significantly improved urbanization levels, and deeply adjusted economic structures, the importance of regional governments in regional economic development is growing day by day. To this end, mezzoeconomics especially emphasizes the importance of regional governments forming competitive advantages in the field of resource generation, and proposes a systematic competitive economic growth theory, complementing and developing existing comparative advantage theory and competitive advantage theory.

The competitive economic growth theory of mezzoeconomics covers content at three levels: first, the "9-in-3" competitive performance of regional governments; second, the Four Stages competitive dynamic characteristics of regional economic growth; third, the formation process of regional economic competitive gradient structure and gradient equilibrium.

## I. "9–in–3" Competition of Regional Governments[①]

Mezzoeconomics believes that a country's economic growth is driven by dual forces,

---

① This section provides only an initial introduction to the "9-in-3" competition of regional governments. For detailed content, refer to Chapter 4 of this book——"9-in-3" competitive performance of regional governments.

with both enterprises and regional governments being subjects driving economic growth——enterprise competition plays an important role in promoting industrial economic development, while regional government competition plays an important role in promoting urban economic

## 第四节　中观经济学竞争优势理论的三个层次

　　波特的竞争优势理论对传统的比较优势理论进行了突破，从竞争优势的角度，为世界各国在更高层次上参与国际竞争提供了理论依据，并从动态发展的角度，为一国培育国家竞争优势、实现竞争阶段的转换提供了方法和思路。然而，波特的竞争优势理论对政府作用的认识还不够全面，仅将政府因素视为一个变数，排除在形成国家竞争优势的核心因素之外。但事实上，一些国家的政府，尤其是发展中国家的政府，甚至能够跨越四大核心因素，直接投资某些产业并形成竞争优势，从而支撑和引领一国经济实现经济发展阶段的跃升。特别地，在当今全球经济总量日益庞大、城市化水平大幅提高、经济结构深度调整的现实背景下，区域政府在区域经济发展中的重要性与日俱增。为此，中观经济学尤其强调区域政府在资源生成领域形成竞争优势的重要性，并提出了系统的竞争型经济增长理论，对现有的比较优势理论和竞争优势理论进行了补充和发展。

　　中观经济学的竞争型经济增长理论涵盖三个层次的内容：一是区域政府的"三类九要素"竞争表现；二是区域经济增长的四阶段竞争动态特征；三是区域经济竞争梯度结构和梯度均衡的形成过程。

### 一、区域政府的"三类九要素"竞争[①]

　　中观经济学认为，一国的经济增长是由双动力驱动的，企业和区域政府都是推动经济增长的主体——企业竞争对促进产业经济发展具有重要作用，区域政府

---

[①] 本部分仅对区域政府的"三类九要素"竞争作初步介绍，详细内容，参看本书第四章——区域政府"三类九要素"竞争表现。

growth. Among these, regional government competition is manifested through effective allocation of region's resource factors. In a broad sense, regional government competition is reflected in the full-factor competition of allocating "operative resources" "quasi-operative resources", and "non-operative resources". In a narrow sense, regional government competition focuses on the structural adjustment and effective allocation of "quasi-operative resources".

Furthermore, mezzoeconomics uses the "9-in-3" theory to summarize the main manifestations of regional government competition: regional government competition is concentrated in three categories of regional economic development level, regional economic policy measures, and regional economic management efficiency. Each category includes three elements, thus forming project competition, industrial chain competition, and import-export competition related to regional economic development level; infrastructure investment policy competition, talent and technology support policy competition, and fiscal and financial support policy competition related to regional economic policy measures; policy system efficiency competition, environmental system efficiency competition, and management system efficiency competition related to regional economic management efficiency.

## II. Four Stages of Regional Economic Growth

Mezzoeconomics believes that the keynote of economic growth in all countries worldwide is competitive economic growth. However, the theoretical discussions on economic growth in economics to date are still mainly limited to the field of industrial economics, considering enterprises as the main driving force of economic growth, with the power of economic growth being the increase in factor inputs and the progress of production technology. As for another important driving force of economic growth——urban economy and its subject, i.e., the role of regional governments, traditional economic theories either ignore or express this point vaguely. But the actual situation in the real world is that a country's economic growth is driven by dual forces, with both enterprises and regional governments being subjects driving economic growth. Economic growth comes not only from the enhancement of enterprise competitiveness but also from the manifestation of regional government competitive advantages. Therefore, in mezzoeconomics, economic growth is competitive economic growth driven by the competitiveness of enterprises and regional governments. The major breakthrough of mezzoeconomics over traditional economic theories

竞争对促进城市经济增长具有重要作用。其中,区域政府竞争通过对区域资源要素的有效配置来体现。广义的区域政府竞争体现在对"可经营性资源""准经营性资源""非经营性资源"三类资源进行配置的全要素竞争,狭义的区域政府竞争则侧重体现在对"准经营性资源"的结构调整与有效配置上。①

进一步,中观经济学使用"三类九要素"理论概括区域政府竞争的主要表现:区域政府竞争集中体现在区域经济发展水平、区域经济政策措施、区域经济管理效率三大类别上,每个类别又包括三个要素,由此形成与区域经济发展水平相关的项目竞争、产业链竞争和进出口竞争;与区域经济政策措施相关的基础设施投资政策竞争,人才、科技扶持政策竞争和财政、金融支持政策竞争;与区域经济管理效率相关的政策体系效率竞争、环境体系效率竞争和管理体系效率竞争。

## 二、区域经济增长的四个阶段②

中观经济学认为,世界各国经济增长的基调都是竞争型经济增长,但经济学发展至今对经济增长的理论探讨,仍主要局限在产业经济领域,认为推动经济增长的主体是企业,经济增长的动力是要素投入的增加和生产技术的进步;对于经济增长的另一重要动力——城市经济及其主体,即区域政府的作用,传统经济学理论或忽略,或表述模糊。但现实世界的实际情况是,一国的经济增长是由双动力驱动的,企业和区域政府都是推动经济增长的主体,经济增长不仅来自于企业竞争力的提升,也是区域政府竞争优势的体现。因此,在中观经济学中,经济增长是企业和区域政府竞争力驱动的竞争型经济增长,而中观经济学对传统经济学

---

① 陈云贤、顾文静:《中观经济学》(第二版),北京大学出版社,2019,第149页。
② 陈云贤:《市场竞争双重主体论——兼谈中观经济学的创立与发展》,北京大学出版社,2020,128-151页。

lies in taking regional government competitiveness as another fulcrum of regional economic growth and systematically deconstructing it.

From the perspective of regional government economic development worldwide, the resource allocation path of regional governments has mainly gone through four stages: factor-driven stage, investment-driven stage, innovation-driven stage, and wealth-driven stage. In the dynamic changes of regional government resource allocation paths, there are differences in the core driving forces of regional economic growth, thus forming four stages of regional economic growth, namely: growth stage dominated by industrial economic competition and cooperation, growth stage dominated by urban economic competition and cooperation, growth stage dominated by innovative economic competition and cooperation, and growth stage dominated by sharing economic competition and cooperation.①

First, the growth stage dominated by industrial economic competition and cooperation refers to the development stage that mainly relies on factor and industrial economic competition to drive economic growth. For regional governments, industrial economic competition and cooperation mainly dominate in the initial stage of regional economic growth, i.e., the factor-driven stage, mainly manifested in the competition of regional industrial chain supporting and industrial cluster development degree and regional industrial policies. Its essence is the competition of regional governments in regional production factor allocation, a kind of allocation and competition for primary resources by regional governments.

Second, the growth stage dominated by urban economic competition and cooperation refers to the development stage that mainly relies on investment and urban economic competition and cooperation to drive economic growth. For regional governments, urban economic competition and cooperation mainly dominate in the second stage of regional economic growth, i.e., the investment-driven stage, mainly manifested in the development and construction of urban infrastructure and even smart cities, as well as the competition of supporting policies and measures. Its essence is that the region has broken through the limitations of factor-driven economic growth and moved towards the process of investment-driven economic growth, which is the development and competition for secondary resources by regional governments.

---

① This book will provide a more detailed introduction to the four stages of regional economic growth in Chapter 5.

Third, the growth stage dominated by innovative economic competition and cooperation refers to the development stage that mainly relies on science and technology and innovative economic competition and cooperation to drive economic growth. For regional governments, innovative economic competition and cooperation mainly dominate in the third stage of regional economic growth, i.e., the innovation-driven stage, mainly manifested in the

理论的重大突破就在于将区域政府竞争力作为区域经济增长的另一个支点,并对其进行了系统的解构。

从世界各国区域政府的经济发展来看,区域政府的资源配置路径主要经历了要素驱动阶段、投资驱动阶段、创新驱动阶段、财富驱动阶段四个阶段。在区域政府资源配置路径的动态变化中,区域经济增长的核心驱动力存在差异,由此形成了区域经济增长的四个阶段,分别是:由产业经济竞争与合作主导的增长阶段,由城市经济竞争与合作主导的增长阶段,由创新经济竞争与合作主导的增长阶段,以及由共享经济竞争与合作主导的增长阶段。[①]

第一,由产业经济竞争与合作主导的增长阶段,是指主要依靠要素和产业经济竞争驱动经济增长的发展阶段。对于区域政府来说,产业经济竞争与合作主要是在区域经济增长的初始阶段,即要素驱动阶段占据主导地位,主要表现为区域产业链配套与产业集群发展程度和区域产业政策的竞争,其实质是区域政府在区域生产要素配置方面的竞争,是区域政府对原生性资源的一种调配与争夺。

第二,由城市经济竞争与合作主导的增长阶段,是指主要依靠投资和城市经济竞争与合作驱动经济增长的发展阶段。对于区域政府来说,城市经济竞争与合作主要是在区域经济增长的第二阶段,即投资驱动阶段占据主导地位,主要表现为城市基础设施乃至智能城市的开发建设,以及与之配套的政策措施的竞争。其实质是区域突破了由要素驱动经济增长的局限,迈向由投资驱动经济增长的过程,是区域政府对次生性资源的开发与争夺。

第三,由创新经济竞争与合作主导的增长阶段,是指主要依靠科技和创新经济竞争与合作驱动经济增长的发展阶段。对于区域政府来说,创新经济竞争与合

---

① 本书将在第五章对区域经济增长的四个阶段进行更详细的介绍。

competition of policy measures promoting concept, technology, management, and institutional innovation by regional governments. Its main characteristic is a kind of regulation and control of inverse resources.

Fourth, the growth stage dominated by sharing economic competition and cooperation refers to the development stage that mainly relies on competition and cooperation as well as win-win cooperation in the sharing economy to drive economic growth. For regional governments, competition and cooperation as well as win-win cooperation mainly dominate in the fourth stage of regional economic growth, i.e., the wealth-driven stage, mainly manifested in a kind of competition and sharing by regional governments of four types of public goods: ideological public goods, material public goods, organizational public goods, and institutional public goods.

## III. Gradient Transference Model of Regional Economic Competition

Mezzoeconomics uses the gradient transference model of regional economic competition to explain the dynamic change characteristics of regional economic development and the focus of resource allocation by regional governments during this process. The schematic diagram of the gradient transference model of regional economic competition is shown in Figure 3-5, where A to I represent different regions, and 1 to 4 represent the four stages of regional economic growth.[①]

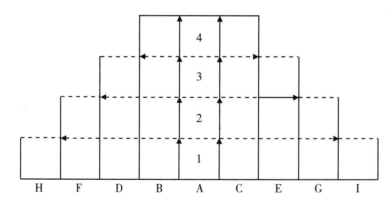

Figure 3-5  The Schematic Diagram of the Gradient Transference Model of Regional Economic Competition

---

[①] This book will provide a more detailed introduction to the model of regional economic competition gradient shift in Chapter 6.

作主要是在区域经济增长的第三阶段,即创新驱动阶段占据主导地位,主要表现为区域政府促进理念、技术、管理以及制度创新的政策措施的竞争,主要特征是对逆生性资源的一种调控与遏制。

第四,由共享经济竞争与合作主导的增长阶段,是指主要依靠竞争与合作以及合作共赢的共享经济驱动经济增长的发展阶段。对于区域政府来说,竞争与合作以及合作共赢主要是在区域经济增长的第四阶段,即财富驱动阶段占据主导地位,主要表现为区域政府对思想性公共物品、物质性公共物品、组织性公共物品、制度性公共物品等四类公共物品的一种争夺与共享。

### 三、区域经济竞争梯度推移模型①

中观经济学使用区域经济竞争梯度推移模型来阐释区域经济发展的动态变化特质,以及其过程中区域政府进行资源配置的侧重点。区域经济竞争梯度推移模型的示意图如图3-5所示,其中,A至I表示不同的区域,1至4表示区域经济增长的四个阶段。②

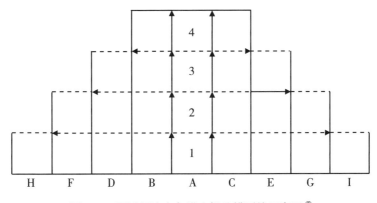

图3-5 区域经济竞争梯度推移模型的示意图③

---

① 陈云贤:《市场竞争双重主体论——兼谈中观经济学的创立与发展》,北京大学出版社,2020,第152-153页。
② 本书将在第六章对区域经济竞争梯度推移模型进行更详细的介绍。
③ 陈云贤:《市场竞争双重主体论——兼谈中观经济学的创立与发展》,北京大学出版社,2020,第152页。

The growth stage dominated by industrial economic competition and cooperation is the first stage, belonging to the initial stage of regional economic development. At this stage, the technological level is low, capital accumulation is limited, and regions rely more on simple expansion in the quantity of production factors such as labor and natural resources to form growth momentum. Therefore, it shows factor-driven characteristics, and its economic growth mode has fundamental and universal applicability. This is the first level of regional government competition.

The growth stage dominated by urban economic competition and cooperation is the second stage, belonging to the expansion stage of regional economic development. This stage starts with large investments in urban hardware infrastructure, proceeds through large investments in urban software infrastructure and urban-rural integrated hardware and software facilities, and ends with the development and improvement of smart cities. Regional economic growth thus experiences one climax after another, showing investment-driven characteristics. The traces of government participation are evident in this economic growth mode, which is the second level of regional government competition.

The growth stage dominated by innovative economic competition and cooperation is the third stage, belonging to the high-quality stage of regional economic development. At this stage, technological innovation, as the dominant force, leads comprehensive innovation in concepts, organizations, and institutions, thus constantly updating the economic growth model and achieving all-round improvement in the quality of economic development. This stage shows innovation-driven characteristics, pushing regional economic competition towards high-end development. This is the third level of regional government competition.

Finally, regional economic development will move towards the fourth stage, namely the advanced stage of shared economic development integrating competition and cooperation. At this stage, regional economies will advance along the trajectory of "competition-dominated → coexistence of competition and cooperation → cooperation and win-win dominated", showing sharing-driven characteristics. At this time, the ideological, material, organizational, and institutional public goods formed in regional economic competition will become the universally shared results of economic growth among regions, promoting the common progress of regional economies and societies.

由产业经济竞争与合作主导的增长阶段为第一阶段，属于区域经济发展的初始阶段。在此阶段，技术水平较低，资本积累较少，区域更多是依靠劳动力、自然资源等生产要素在数量上的简单扩张来形成增长动力，因此呈现出要素驱动的特征，其经济增长方式具有基础性和普适性。这是区域政府竞争的第一个层次。

由城市经济竞争与合作主导的增长阶段是第二阶段，属于区域经济发展的扩张阶段。此阶段以对城市硬件基础设施的大量投资为起点，以对城市软件基础设施和城乡一体化的软硬件设施的大量投资为过程，以对智能城市的开发和完善为终结。区域经济增长由此出现一个又一个高潮，呈现出投资驱动的特征。其经济增长方式中政府参与的痕迹明显，这是区域政府竞争的第二个层次。

由创新经济竞争与合作主导的增长阶段是第三阶段，属于区域经济发展的高质量阶段。在此阶段，技术创新作为主导力量，引领着理念、组织和制度等全面创新，从而使经济增长模式不断推陈出新，使经济发展的质量获得全方位提升。此阶段呈现出创新驱动的特征，推动着区域经济竞争向高端化发展，这是区域政府竞争的第三个层次。

最终，区域经济发展将迈向第四阶段，即竞争与合作相融合的共享经济发展的高级阶段。在此阶段，区域经济将沿着"竞争为主→竞争与合作共存→合作共赢为主"的轨迹前行，表现出共享驱动的特征。此时，在区域经济竞争中形成的思想性、物质性、组织性和制度性公共物品，将成为区域间普惠共享的经济增长成果，推动各区域经济社会的共同进步。

Chapter 4
# "9-in-3" Competitive Performance of Regional Governments

## Section 1: Characteristics of Regional Government Competition

Within the framework of mezzoeconomics, regional competitiveness refers to the force that can support the sustained survival and development of a region. It is the attractiveness, the ability to compete for, possess, control and transform resources, as well as the ability to compete for, possess and control markets that a region has compared to other regions in the process of competition and development. In short, it is the ability to optimize resource allocation needed for its own development. In other words, regional competitiveness is the attractiveness to resources and the competitiveness for markets needed for a region's development. Mezzoeconomics points out that the economic behavior of regional governments has an important impact on regional competitiveness. Regional governments formulating fiscal policies, expanding the scale of fiscal revenue, and optimizing the structure of fiscal expenditure will play an important role in the development strategy and policy objectives of regional economy within a certain period, as well as the sustainable development of regional economy.[①]

### I. Objectives of Regional Government Competition

Although regional governments are multi-task subjects, from the perspective of regional economic competitiveness, the objective function of regional government competition can be set as the fiscal revenue determination mechanism.

# 第四章
# 区域政府"三类九要素"竞争表现

## 第一节 区域政府竞争特点

在中观经济学的框架下,区域竞争力是指能支撑一个区域持久生存和发展的力量,即一个区域在竞争和发展的过程中,与其他区域相比较所具有的吸引力,争夺、占有、调控和转化资源的能力,以及争夺、占有和调控市场的能力,也就是其自身发展所需的优化资源配置的能力。简言之,区域竞争力是一个区域发展所需的对资源的吸引力和对市场的争夺力。中观经济学指出,区域政府的经济行为对区域竞争力具有重要影响,区域政府制定财政政策、扩大财政收入规模、优化财政支出结构,将对一定时期内区域经济的发展战略和政策目标,以及区域经济的可持续发展,发挥重要的作用。[①]

### 一、区域政府竞争目标

尽管区域政府是多元任务主体,但从区域经济竞争力的视角出发,可将区域政府竞争的目标函数设定为财政收入决定机制。

---

[①] 陈云贤:《市场竞争双重主体论——兼谈中观经济学的创立与发展》,北京大学出版社,2020,第96页。

Fiscal revenue refers to the sum of all funds raised by regional governments to fulfill their functions of implementing public policies and providing public goods and services. It is manifested as the total monetary income obtained by regional governments within a certain period (usually a fiscal year). Fiscal revenue is an important indicator to measure the financial strength of regional governments. The scope and quantity of public goods and services provided by regional governments in socio-economic activities largely depend on the fiscal revenue situation.

The internationally accepted classification of fiscal revenue is related to the form in which governments obtain fiscal revenue. According to the form of government obtaining fiscal revenue, fiscal revenue can be divided into tax revenue, state-owned asset income, government bond income, fee income, and other income.

Among them, tax revenue is a form of fiscal revenue that regional governments obtain forcibly and without compensation, based on their political power and according to specific standards, to realize their functions. It is the most important form of income and the main source of income in modern fiscal revenue.

State-owned asset income refers to the general term for profits, rents, dividends, bonuses, and fund usage fees obtained by regional governments based on the ownership of state-owned assets.

Government bond income mostly refers to the compensatory income obtained by regional governments through credit means.

Fee income refers to the form of income where regional governments charge certain usage fees and regulatory fees to beneficiaries when providing public services, implementing administrative management, or providing specific public facilities.

So, why does mezzoeconomics consider the fiscal revenue determination mechanism as the objective function of regional government competition? The reasons are explained below.

First, the functions of regional governments are continuously expanding, and their economic regulation functions are increasing, requiring support from the scale of fiscal revenue. In the economic development practice of countries worldwide, the functions of governments have undergone a transformation from few to many. Regional governments have gradually transformed from the role of "night watchman" that only maintains the effective operation of region's political power, maintains social stability, defends against foreign invasion, and maintains judicial justice, to a regulatory, intervention, and management system adapted to modern market economy and socialized mass production. An important way for regional governments to regulate, intervene, and manage is to expand fiscal expenditure.

财政收入是指区域政府为履行实施公共政策、提供公共物品与服务等职能而筹集的一切资金的总和,表现为区域政府在一定时期(一般为一个财政年度)内所取得的货币收入总和。财政收入是衡量区域政府财力的重要指标,区域政府在社会经济活动中提供公共物品和服务的范围与数量,在很大程度上取决于财政收入状况。

国际通行的对财政收入的分类与政府取得财政收入的形式有关。按政府取得财政收入的形式,财政收入可分为税收收入、国有资产收益、政府债券收入、收费收入以及其他收入等。

其中,税收收入是区域政府为实现其职能,凭借其政治权力,按照特定的标准,强制、无偿地取得财政收入的一种形式,它是现代财政收入中最重要的收入形式和最主要的收入来源。

国有资产收益是指区域政府凭借国有资产所有权获得的利润、租金、股息、红利、资金使用费等收入的总称。

政府债券收入多指区域政府通过信用方式取得的有偿性收入。

收费收入是指区域政府在提供公共服务、实施行政管理或提供特定公共设施时,向受益人收取一定使用费和规费的收入形式。

那么,中观经济学为何认为财政收入决定机制是区域政府竞争的目标函数?下面对其原因进行阐述。[①]

第一,区域政府职能不断扩张,其经济调控功能增加,需要财政收入规模做支撑。在世界各国的经济发展实践中,各国政府的职能经历了由少到多的转变,区域政府从只维持区域政权有效运转、维护社会稳定、防御外来入侵、维护司法公正等的"守夜人"角色,逐步转变为与现代市场经济和社会化大生产相适应的调控、干预和管理系统。区域政府进行调控、干预和管理的一个重要方式就是扩大财政支出。因此,随着区域政府职能的不断扩张和财政支出规模

---

① 陈云贤:《市场竞争双重主体论——兼谈中观经济学的创立与发展》,北京大学出版社,2020,第102–104页。

Therefore, with the continuous expansion of regional government functions and fiscal expenditure scale, the scale of regional fiscal revenue also needs to grow continuously.

Second, the continuous growth of region's population and the increase in the total demand for region's public services by the people require support from the scale of fiscal revenue. The growth of region's population objectively poses many requirements for regional governments, such as the need to improve education, medical and health care, culture and sports, employment training, clothing, food, housing and transportation, as well as social environment and regional management. Moreover, the enhancement of population mobility and the development of region's population aging will also affect the structure and scale of regional government fiscal expenditure. The changes in the quantity and structure of region's population bring about changes in demand, therefore the scale of region's fiscal revenue also needs to grow correspondingly to provide support.

Third, the continuous expansion of region's urban scale and the continuous growth of social public investment require support from the scale of fiscal revenue. The city is a dynamic concept. With the construction of urban hardware infrastructure, the improvement of urban software infrastructure, the development of smart cities, the acceleration of urban-rural integration process, the expansion of existing cities and the increase of emerging cities, a large number of municipal engineering construction needs have appeared in the region, requiring a large amount of investment. This objectively also requires the continuous growth of region's fiscal revenue scale to provide guarantees.

Fourth, the continuous improvement of regional scientific and technological level promotes regional governments to constantly explore new scientific and technological fields and production fields, which also requires support from the scale of fiscal revenue. For example, primary resources in the field of resource generation——resources explored through space exploration, marine development, base exploration and research, etc., as well as inverse resources in the field of resource generation——such as carbon emission trading resources, all require regional governments to increase investment to build leading human, financial and material systems for high-tech industries. These also need to be supported by the growth of regional fiscal revenue scale.

Fifth, the development of region's social welfare undertakings requires support from the scale of fiscal revenue. On one hand, regional governments should continuously narrow the gap between the rich and the poor, resolve the problem of polarization in region's social distribution, so as to alleviate the contradiction between the rich and the poor as much as possible and resolve region's instability factors. On the other hand, with economic development and the improvement of income levels, regional governments need to continuously improve people's labor capacity, cultural level and health level to promote the improvement of region's total factor productivity, which also requires support from the growth of regional fiscal revenue scale.

的不断扩大，区域财政收入规模也需要不断增长。

第二，区域人口不断增长，民众对区域公共服务的需求总量增加，需要财政收入规模做支撑。区域人口的增长在客观上对区域政府提出诸多要求，如教育、医疗卫生、文化体育、就业培训、衣食住行，以及社会环境、区域管理等都需要提升。而且人口流动性的增强和区域人口老龄化的发展，也将对区域政府财政支出的结构和规模产生影响。区域人口数量和结构的变化带来了需求的变化，因此区域财政收入规模也要相应增长，为其提供支撑。

第三，区域城市规模不断扩大，社会公共投资不断增长，需要财政收入规模做支撑。城市是个动态的概念，随着城市硬件基础设施的建设、城市软件基础设施的提升、智能城市的发展、城乡一体化进程的加快、原有城市的扩展和新兴城市的增加等，区域中出现了大量的市政工程建设需求，需要大量的投资，这在客观上也需要区域财政收入规模不断增长，为其提供保障。

第四，区域科技水平不断提高，推动区域政府不断开拓新的科技领域和生产领域，这也需要财政收入规模做支撑。比如资源生成领域中的原生性资源——通过空间探索、海洋开发、基地探研等发掘的资源，又如资源生成领域中的逆生性资源——碳排放交易资源等，都需要区域政府加大投资力度，为高科技行业建设领先的人财物体系，这些也需要区域财政收入规模的增长来支撑。

第五，区域社会福利事业的发展，需要财政收入规模做支撑。一方面，区域政府应不断缩小贫富差距，化解区域社会分配中的两极分化问题，从而尽可能缓和贫富矛盾，化解区域不安定因素；另一方面，随着经济发展和收入水平的提高，区域政府需要不断提升民众的劳动能力、文化水平和健康水平，以促进区域全要素生产率的提高，这也需要区域财政收入规模的增长做支撑。

This series of factors become important reasons for regional governments to take the fiscal revenue determination mechanism as the objective function of regional government competition.

## II. Differences between Regional Government Competition and Enterprise Competition

In the theoretical system of mezzoeconomics, there are several significant differences between regional government competition and enterprise competition.

First, the objective functions of competition are different. The objective function of regional government competition is the fiscal revenue determination mechanism; the objective function of enterprise competition is the price determination mechanism. Within their own jurisdictions, regional governments' support and subsidies for the industrial economy, investment and promotion of the urban economy, and provision of public goods and services in the livelihood economy largely depend on the regional fiscal revenue situation. Regional fiscal revenue thus becomes an important indicator to measure the ability of regional governments to carry out various socio-economic activities. Under the given conditions of government bond income and state-owned asset income, it mainly depends on tax revenue and fee income, which in turn mainly depend on the level of regional economic development, economic policy measures and economic management efficiency. Therefore, focusing on region's project construction, industrial chain supporting, cluster development and domestic and overseas market expansion, regional governments can promote investment attraction under the goal of maximizing fiscal revenue by optimizing policies and facilitating measures. This is different from enterprise competition, which revolves around microeconomic factors that determine commodity prices such as cost, quality, supply, and demand.

Second, the means to achieve goals are different. Regional governments first strive to improve total factor productivity as an important means to promote sustainable economic growth; enterprises first influence commodity costs, supply and demand, etc., by improving labor productivity. This is because regional governments promote economic development around the goal of increasing fiscal revenue, and their measures optimize the structure of regional fiscal expenditure firstly, such as achieving the best ratio of investment expenditure, consumption expenditure and transfer expenditure to obtain the maximum economic and social benefits. Usually, after simple expansion of tangible factors such as land, projects, and

这一系列因素成为区域政府将财政收入决定机制作为区域政府竞争目标函数的重要原因。

## 二、区域政府竞争与企业竞争的区别

在中观经济学的理论体系中，区域政府竞争与企业竞争之间存在着以下几点显著的区别。[①]

第一，竞争的目标函数不同。区域政府竞争的目标函数是财政收入决定机制；企业竞争的目标函数是价格决定机制。区域政府在自己管辖的范围内，对产业经济的扶持与补贴，对城市经济的投资与推动，对民生经济中公共物品和公共服务的提供，其力度在很大程度上取决于区域财政收入状况。区域财政收入因此成为衡量区域政府开展社会经济各项活动的能力大小的一个重要指标。而在政府债券收入和国有资产收益既定的情况下，它主要取决于税收收入和收费收入，税收收入和收费收入又主要取决于区域的经济发展水平、经济政策措施和经济管理效率。因此，围绕区域的项目建设、产业链配套、集群发展以及海内外市场开拓等，区域政府可以在财政收入最大化这一目标牵引下，以优化政策、便利措施等来推动招商引资。这与企业竞争围绕着成本、质量、供给、需求等决定商品价格的微观因素来运转是不一样的。

第二，达成目标的手段不同。区域政府首先将努力提高全要素生产率作为促进经济可持续增长的重要手段；企业则首先通过提高劳动生产率来影响商品的成本、供求等。这是因为，区域政府围绕着提高财政收入这一目标来推动经济发展，其措施首先是优化区域财政支出结构，如使投资性支出、消费性支出与转移性支出达到最佳比例，以获取最大的经济和社会收益。通常来讲，在经过拼土

---

[①] 陈云贤：《市场竞争双重主体论——兼谈中观经济学的创立与发展》，北京大学出版社，2020，第104-107页。

capital, the bottleneck of diminishing returns to capital makes extensive economic growth difficult to continue. So when the input of relevant tangible factors remains unchanged, regional governments will focus on the input, increase and improvement of intangible factors, allocating resources and adjusting structures around technological progress with innovation at its core, providing support in terms of organization, policy, regulations, environment, etc. The optimization of regional fiscal expenditure structure will bring about a series of changes in the regional policy environment, which will become a new driving force for regional economic development and urban construction.

Third, the paths to achieve goals are different. Regional government performance is dominated by fair and efficient growth, while enterprise performance is dominated by input-type profit growth. From the development practices of regional governments worldwide, their economic growth paths generally go through factor-driven stage, investment-driven stage, innovation-driven stage and wealth-driven stage. Regional governments drive and guide the whole society to invest funds by optimizing the combination of tangible and intangible resource factors, promoting regional economic fair and efficient growth. The continuous improvement of enterprise performance comes from the continuous input of production factors by enterprises, including capital, labor, land, technology, talent and management. The investment strategy of enterprises is mainly quantity-based extensive expansion in the initial stage, gradually developing to the quality improvement stage, and then to the expansion-type management stage. Continuous and effective input is the key to profitability.

Fourth, investment and financing mechanisms are different. Regional government investment and financing need to balance fairness and efficiency, mainly to solve market failure problems; enterprise investment and financing are based on profitability and efficiency principles, mainly to better engage in competition. In terms of investment, in addition to ensuring social equity through non-reimbursable grants, regional governments are increasingly adopting diversified investment methods combining direct and indirect investments such as compensatory loans, public-private partnerships, and share cooperation. In terms of financing, in addition to adopting monetary financing when necessary, regional governments are more likely to use debt financing to expand investment scale and promote regional economic development.

Fifth, the price determination mechanisms are different. The prices of quasi-public goods are mostly based on market economic rules and determined by regional governments through regulated pricing; enterprise commodity pricing is entirely determined by market competition. Regional governments usually weigh the pros and cons among average cost pricing method, two-part pricing method and load pricing method, choose one to apply or apply in combination, and then led by regional governments with social participation, promote

地、拼项目、拼资本等有形要素的简单扩张后，资本报酬递减这一瓶颈会使粗犷式经济增长难以为继，所以在相关有形要素投入量保持不变时，区域政府会将重心放在无形要素的投入、增加和改善上，围绕以创新为内核的技术进步去调配资源、调整结构，提供组织、政策、法规、环境等方面的支持。区域财政支出结构的优化会带来区域政策环境的系列变化，这将会成为区域经济发展和城市建设的新的驱动力。

第三，实现目标的路径不同。区域政府绩效以公平与效率型增长为主导，企业绩效以投入型盈利增长为主导。从世界各国区域政府的发展实践来看，其经济增长路径一般会经历要素驱动阶段、投资驱动阶段、创新驱动阶段和财富驱动阶段。区域政府通过优化组合有形与无形的资源要素，带动并引导全社会进行资金投入，促进区域经济实现公平与效率型增长。而企业绩效的持续提高则来自企业不断投入的生产要素，包括资本、劳动、土地、技术以及人才与管理等。企业投入的策略是，初期以数量型外延扩张为主，逐渐发展到质量型提升阶段，再到拓展型管理阶段，持续和有效的投入是获取盈利的关键。

第四，投融资机制不同。区域政府的投融资要兼顾公平与效率，主要是为了解决市场失灵问题；企业投融资则以营利性和效率为原则，主要是为了更好地展开竞争。投资方面，除以无偿拨款方式保障社会公平外，区域政府也越来越多地采用了有偿贷款、公私合营、股份合作等直接与间接投资相结合的多元化投资方式。融资方面，除了在必要时采取货币融资方式，区域政府更多会以债务化融资方式来扩大投资规模，推动区域经济发展。

第五，价格决定机制不同。准公共物品的价格大多以市场经济规则为基础，由区域政府以管制定价的方式来决定；企业的商品定价则完全由市场竞争来决定。区域政府通常在平均成本定价法、二部定价法和负荷定价法之间权衡利弊，选择其一应用或融合应用，再由区域政府牵头、社会参与，推动准公共物品项目

the investment, development and construction of quasi-public goods projects. Government participation in the investment, development, and construction of quasi-public goods in the field of resource generation, and regulating the initial pricing of quasi-public goods, has become a regular practice in countries worldwide. The price determination mechanism in this field can hardly be the same as the commodity price determination mechanism of enterprises.

Sixth, the competition orientations are different. Regional government competition is supply optimization-oriented; enterprise competition is demand satisfaction-oriented. Effectively allocating the supply of tangible resource factors such as land, capital, and talent, effectively regulating the supply of intangible resource factors such as planning, investment, consumption, price, tax, interest rate, exchange rate, and law, and promoting supply-side structural reform through means such as concept innovation, institutional innovation, organizational innovation, and technological innovation, is the necessary path for regional governments to develop the economy, build cities, and improve social welfare. Enterprise competition, on the other hand, starts from market demand, from demand quantity, demand structure to enterprise strategy and tactics, whether they can adapt to market demand becomes the key to enterprise success or failure.

Seventh, the competition fields are different. Regional government competition is mainly manifested in the competition for urban economy and urban resource allocation; enterprise competition focuses on the competition for industrial economy and industrial resource allocation. The two are relatively independent, with the two systems complementing each other. Regional governments are the research subjects of mezzoeconomics, and their competition with each other is mainly in the field of urban economy. Regional governments, firstly, need to grasp the quantity, quality, structure, and layout of urban resources; secondly, they need to regulate the allocation of urban resources within the region and attract resource factors from outside the region through establishing systems and policies, thereby optimizing resource allocation and improving regional competitiveness. The competition of regional governments in the mezzoeconomic market affects the competition of enterprises in the microeconomic market. Enterprises are the research subjects of microeconomics, and enterprise competition is mainly in the industrial economic market, focusing on the allocation of industrial resources in the industrial economy. The market equilibrium theory based on firms is the dominant theory of traditional classical economics. With the pursuit of profit maximization as the premise, supply, demand, market equilibrium price, market structure types, and different competitive strategies under different market structure types are the main influencing factors of competition among enterprises. Enterprise competition is the premise and foundation of regional government competition.

Eighth, the competition roles are different. Regional governments are mezzoeconomic entities, playing dual roles of quasi-macro and quasi-micro in regional economic development;

的投资、开发、建设。政府参与资源生成领域的准公共物品投资、开发、建设，管制准公共物品的初始定价，已在世界各国成为一种常规做法。这一领域的价格决定机制很难与企业的商品价格决定机制一样。

第六，竞争导向不同。区域政府竞争以优化供给为导向；企业竞争以满足需求为导向。有效配置土地、资本、人才等有形资源要素的供给，有效调节规划、投资、消费、价格、税收、利率、汇率、法律等无形资源要素的供给，并通过理念创新、制度创新、组织创新、技术创新等手段促进供给侧结构性改革，是区域政府发展经济、建设城市、提升社会福利的必由之路。而企业竞争则从市场需求出发，从需求量、需求结构到企业战略战术，它们能否适应市场需求成为企业成败的关键。

第七，竞争领域不同。区域政府竞争主要表现在对城市经济、城市资源配置方面的争夺上；企业竞争则侧重对产业经济、产业资源配置方面的争夺。二者之间相对独立，两个体系相辅相成。区域政府是中观经济（学）的研究主体，其相互之间的竞争主要是在城市经济领域的竞争。区域政府一是要掌握城市资源的数量、质量、结构、布局；二是要通过制定制度和政策来调控区域内城市资源的配置，吸引区域外资源要素，从而优化资源配置，提高区域竞争力。区域政府在中观经济市场的竞争影响着企业在微观经济市场的竞争。而企业是微观经济（学）的研究主体，企业竞争主要是在产业经济市场中的竞争，以产业经济中的产业资源配置为主。以厂商为主体的市场均衡理论是传统古典经济学的主导理论。企业以追求利润最大化为前提，供给、需求、市场均衡价格、市场结构类型及不同市场结构类型下的不同竞争策略等，是企业之间竞争的主要影响因素。企业竞争是区域政府竞争的前提和基础。

第八，竞争角色不同。区域政府是中观经济主体，在区域经济发展中扮演准

enterprises belong to the microeconomic field, playing the role of micro entities in the market economy. On the one hand, regional governments' planning, guidance, and support for operative resources and investment, development, and operation of quasi-operative resources make them the concentrated agents of regional economic micro-interest entities, with their behavior showing quasi-micro attributes. On the other hand, regional governments' regulation, supervision, and management of operative resources and supply of non-operative resources make them the representatives of the state in regional economic society, with their behavior showing quasi-macro attributes. The dual attributes of regional governments give them dual roles of competition and cooperation in regional economic development, which is different from the purely competitive role of enterprises in the microeconomic field.

Ninth, the management models are different. Regional governments mainly adopt the District Resource Planning (DRP) system, while enterprises mainly adopt the Enterprise Resource Planning (ERP) system. Through the ERP system, enterprises can effectively manage resources such as materials, funds, information, and customers in an integrated manner. The ERP system can help enterprises achieve effective coordination and allocation across regions, departments, and industries in terms of logistics, human resources, finance, and information flow, thereby effectively integrating resources, exerting rapid adjustment functions, improving production efficiency, and ultimately effectively enhancing enterprise competitiveness with market orientation. Regional governments can effectively allocate various resource factors within the region, including land, population, finance, environment, technology, and policies, through the DRP system. According to the layout of regional planning and strategy, they can judge market changes, allocate regional resources, and improve regional competitiveness with systematic management ideas and means. The establishment of the DRP management model helps to improve regional total factor productivity, thereby promoting sustainable development of regional economy and society.

## Section 2: The Key to Aspects of Regional Government Competition

The key to competition among regional governments is innovation. Innovation is the original driving force, innovation is competitiveness, and continuous innovation is the source for regions to maintain lasting competitiveness.

宏观和准微观的双重角色；企业则属于微观经济领域，在市场经济中发挥微观主体作用。一方面，区域政府对可经营性资源的规划、引导、扶持和对准经营性资源的投资、开发、运营，使其成为区域经济微观利益主体的集中代理，其行为呈现准微观属性；另一方面，区域政府对可经营性资源的调节、监督、管理和对非经营性资源的供给，使其成为区域经济社会中的国家代表，其行为呈现准宏观属性。区域政府的双重属性使其在区域经济发展中具有竞争与合作的双重角色，这有别于企业在微观经济领域的纯竞争性角色。

第九，管理模式不同。区域政府主要采用区域资源规划（District Resource Planning，DRP）系统，企业则主要采用企业资源规划（Enterprise Resource Planning，ERP）系统。通过ERP系统，企业可以对物质、资金、信息、客户等资源进行有效的一体化管理。ERP系统可以帮助企业在物流、人流、财流和信息流等方面实现跨地区、跨部门、跨行业的有效协调与配置，从而以市场为导向，有效集成资源，发挥快速调剂功能，提高生产效率，最终有效提升企业竞争力。区域政府则可通过DRP系统，有效调配区域内包括土地、人口、财政、环境、技术、政策等在内的各种资源要素，按照区域规划和战略的布局，以系统化的管理思想和手段，判断市场变化，调配区域资源，提高区域竞争力。DRP管理模式的确立有助于区域全要素生产率的提高，从而有助于推动区域经济社会的可持续发展。

## 第二节 区域政府竞争的关键

区域政府之间竞争的关键是创新，创新是原动力，创新是竞争力，持续的创新是区域保持持久竞争力的源泉。

## I. Concept Innovation

Concept innovation refers to new ideas and thoughts that both conform to objective reality and can develop new paths. It means being down-to-earth while also having a broad perspective. If one follows old ways, remains closed off, and has a lazy attitude, they will fall behind the pace of the times. Competition requires innovation, and innovation first requires concept innovation. Advanced concepts, service concepts, competition concepts, responsibility concepts, etc., all need a process of continuous improvement.

Regional governments need advanced concepts. Being advanced means breaking through conventional thinking, breaking through the status quo and oneself, daring to be pioneers and challengers, fully exerting the economic orientation, regulation, and early warning functions of regional governments, relying on market rules, leveraging market forces, and effectively allocating resources through means such as investment, pricing, taxation, and law, and methods like organizational innovation, institutional innovation, and technological innovation, to form leading advantages and promote scientific and sustainable development of the regional economy.

Regional governments need service concepts. They should transform administrative concepts and management concepts into service concepts, serving the market, enterprises, and society. Service concepts include: first, all market participants and social public within the region are service objects; second, government behavior mainly focuses on support services, regulatory services, development services, and innovative services; third, service satisfaction is the core standard for measuring service levels; fourth, services change according to the needs of service objects. In this process, regional governments are providers of public goods and services, while people, enterprises, and institutions within the region are demanders of public goods and services.

Regional governments need competition concepts. Traditional economic theories always thought that competition exists only between enterprises, not between governments, but in reality, as long as resources are limited, competition exists between regional governments. Regional governments, especially leadership teams, must have a sense of competition, a spirit of strength, and the courage to strive. From eastern to central to western China, the economic gap between regional governments shows a gradient, and the reason for this gap, besides differences in resource endowments, is more importantly the difference in competition concepts and competitiveness. From east to central to west, the sense of competition among regional governments also shows a decreasing gradient.

## 一、理念创新

理念创新就是既符合客观实际，又能开拓发展的新观念、新思想；既能脚踏实地，又能高屋建瓴。若因循守旧，闭关自守，作风懒散，则会跟不上时代发展的步伐。竞争需要创新，创新首先需要的是理念创新。超前理念、服务理念、竞争理念、责任理念等都需要有一个不断提升的过程。

区域政府需要超前理念。超前就是要打破思维定式，突破现状、突破自我，敢为人先、敢于挑战，充分发挥区域政府的经济导向、调节、预警作用，依靠市场规则，借助市场力量，通过投资、价格、税收、法律等手段和组织创新、制度创新、技术创新等方式，有效配置资源，形成领先优势，促进区域经济科学发展、可持续发展。

区域政府需要服务理念。要将行政理念、管理理念转变为服务理念，服务市场、服务企业、服务社会。服务理念包括：第一，所有区域内的市场参与者和社会民众都是服务对象；第二，政府行为以扶持服务、监管服务、开拓服务、创新服务为主；第三，服务满意度是衡量服务水平的核心标准；第四，服务以服务对象的需求为转移。在这个过程中，区域政府是公共物品和公共服务的提供者，区域范围内的民众、企业和机构是公共物品和公共服务的需求者。

区域政府需要竞争理念。传统经济学理论总以为竞争是企业之间的竞争，而不存在政府之间的竞争，但实际上，只要资源有限，区域政府与区域政府之间的竞争就存在。区域政府特别是领导团队一定要有竞争意识，要有强者精神和敢于拼搏的勇气。中国区域政府从东部到中部再到西部，经济差距具有阶梯性，产生这种差距的原因除了资源禀赋的差异，更重要的是竞争理念和竞争力的差异，从东部到中部再到西部，区域政府间的竞争意识也呈现梯度递减状况。

Regional governments need responsibility concepts. Regional governments need to strengthen the concept of responsibility based on responsibility and aimed at ensuring the interests of service objects to compete with other regional governments. Among responsibility, power, and benefits, "responsibility" comes first, "benefits" last, and "power" in the middle. Adhering to the concept of responsibility first requires a responsible subject; any matter, behavior, or consequence must have a responsible subject. Second, there must be responsibility evaluation, using an evaluation system to assess the results of responsibility fulfillment. Finally, there must be responsibility supervision mechanisms and responsibility reward and punishment mechanisms. Regional governments should truly become subjects that bear responsibility, accept evaluation, and endure supervision and punishment.

## II. Institutional Innovation

Institutional innovation is the foundation and guarantee of regional government innovation and the concentrated manifestation of regional government competition. Institutional innovation implements concept innovation at the operational level, making it possible for concepts to guide practice. Without institutional innovation, other innovations can hardly exist continuously.

For regional governments, if institutions are provided as public goods, institutional innovation should include innovation in public service systems, public safety systems, social welfare systems, housing systems, healthcare service systems, social employment systems, education and training systems, income distribution systems, infrastructure construction systems, public environmental protection systems, etc.

However, when we mainly discuss innovation around specific systems of regional government market competition, these systems are actually the integration and sum of specific policies, measures, and methods at the level of the aforementioned basic systems. Relative to the micro-subjects in the market——enterprises and individuals, the macro innovation costs of regional governments may be far lower than the sum of micro innovation costs of enterprises and individuals. The lower this cost and the greater the benefits, the more obvious the competitive advantage of regional institutional innovation will be.

## III. Organizational Innovation

Regional government organizational innovation is the optimization of regional

区域政府需要责任理念。区域政府需要强化以责任为基础、以保证服务对象的利益为归属来与其他区域政府进行竞争的责任理念。在责、权、利中,"责"在前,"利"在后,"权"在中。坚持责任理念首先要有责任主体,任何事务、任何行为、任何后果都要有责任主体;其次要有责任评价,要用评价体系来评价责任承担结果;最后要有责任监督机制和责任奖惩机制,区域政府应真正成为承担责任、接受评价、承受监督和惩罚的主体。

## 二、制度创新

制度创新是区域政府创新的基础和保障,是区域政府竞争的集中表现。制度创新将理念创新落实到操作层面上,使理念指导实践成为可能。没有制度创新,其他创新也难以持续存在。

对于区域政府而言,如果把制度当作公共物品来提供的话,制度创新就应当包括对公共服务制度、公共安全制度、社会福利制度、住房制度、医疗卫生服务制度、社会就业制度、教育培训制度、收入分配制度、基础设施建设制度、公共环境保护制度等的创新。

但是,当我们主要围绕着区域政府市场竞争的具体制度来讨论创新时,这些制度实际上就是前述基本制度层面的具体政策、措施和方法的集成与总和。相对于市场中的微观主体——企业和个人而言,区域政府的宏观创新成本可能要远远低于企业和个人的微观创新成本之和。此成本越低,收益越大,那么构成的区域制度创新竞争优势就越明显。

## 三、组织创新

区域政府组织创新是对区域政府组织管理的优化,特别是对组织管理结构

government organizational management, especially the optimization of organizational management structure and mechanisms. It includes both the optimization of organizational management at the regional government level and within internal departments. As a competitive means, organizational innovation forms advantages through comparing the organizational management efficiency of different regional governments. Efficiency has been the goal pursued by government operations from the beginning. With the development of times and advancement of technology, new organizational management structures constantly emerge. The appearance of these new organizational management structures is undoubtedly to provide new diversified operational modes for public goods and services. For example, flat management is a type of organizational innovation. It means reducing management levels in regional governments, moderately expanding the management scope of institutions, and delegating authority and responsibility downwards. The province-directly-managing-county reform implemented in China is such a case. Structurally, this reform reduced one level in the vertical hierarchy of organization, transforming the three-level administrative management system of province-city-county into a two-level system of province-city (county).

Take Israel as another example. Israel's science and technology system belongs to a loose multi-headed management type. More than ten departments including the Ministry of Science and Technology, Ministry of Industry and Trade, Ministry of Defense, Ministry of Agriculture, Ministry of Health, Ministry of Communications, Ministry of Education, Ministry of Environment, Ministry of National Infrastructure, as well as institutions like the Academy of Sciences and Humanities jointly form the national science and technology decision-making system, coordinating national science and technology work. Meanwhile, Israel adopts a chief scientist responsibility system, with major government departments all having chief scientist offices. The Israeli government has also established a Chief Scientists Forum, chaired by the Minister of Science and Technology, to discuss major issues of science and technology policy, thus avoiding duplication or omission of science and technology projects. This organizational arrangement has promoted the enhancement of Israel's science and technology competitiveness.

## IV. Technological Innovation

Regional government technological innovation competition is mainly manifested in four aspects: first, technologically transforming regional governments to enhance their administrative capabilities; second, providing advanced technological environments within the

与组织管理机制的优化,既包括区域政府层面的组织管理优化,也包括区域政府内部机构的组织管理优化。组织创新作为一种竞争手段,就是通过对不同的区域政府的组织管理效率进行比较而形成的优势。效率从一开始就是政府运作所要追求的目标,随着时代的发展和科技的进步,新的组织管理结构不断出现。这些新的组织管理结构的出现无疑是为了给公共物品和公共服务提供多元化的新的运作方式。例如,扁平化管理是一种组织创新。即区域政府管理层次减少,适度扩大机构管理幅度,将权责下沉。中国实施的省直管县改革就是这种情况。从结构上讲,这一改革在组织纵向的等级上减少了一个层次,也就是将省—市—县三级行政管理体制转变为省—市(县)二级行政管理体制。

再以以色列为例。以色列的科技体制属松散的多头管理型,由科技部、工贸部、国防部、农业部、卫生部、通信部、教育部、环境部、国家基础设施部等十余个部门以及科学与人文科学院等机构共同组成了国家的科技决策体系,协调全国的科技工作。同时,以色列采用首席科学家负责制,主要政府部门都设有首席科学家办公室。以色列政府还成立了首席科学家论坛,由科技部部长担任论坛主席,以商讨科技政策的重大问题,从而避免了科技项目的重复投入或遗漏,这种组织上的安排促进了以色列科技竞争力的提升。

## 四、技术创新

区域政府技术创新竞争主要表现在四个方面:一是对区域政府进行技术性改造,从技术上提升区域政府的行政能力;二是在区域内提供先进技术环境,通过优化技术环境来提高区域的吸引力;三是那些区域内技术创新条件要求高、资金流量

region to increase region's attractiveness through optimizing the technological environment; third, organizing technological innovation for projects that require high technological innovation conditions, large capital flow, numerous personnel, and long time within the region, which other market innovation subjects are unable or incapable of undertaking; fourth, regional governments help other market innovation subjects (enterprises, research institutions or individuals) within the region to carry out technological innovation by increasing financial support. Technological innovation is essentially the innovation of regional governments in formulating science and technology progress policies and selecting policy tools.

Again, taking Israel as an example, to help develop incubators, the Tel Aviv-Yafo municipal government established a very detailed database of various enterprises' development situations, including enterprises' scale, number of employees, location, product market, development stage, production scale, main financing forms, current main problems, etc. The government refers to this constantly updated database and uses professional financial analysis tools to analyze the optimal financing modes and scales for various enterprises, reducing fiscal burden and making capital allocation more effective and reasonable. Although most financing is left to the market, the Tel Aviv-Yafo municipal government still holds various entrepreneurship competitions, selecting the best teams and providing support. After injecting capital, the government completely transfers its ownership and use rights to enterprises and teams. If enterprises and teams fail, they do not need to return the capital; if successful, they need to return the capital year by year. It can be seen that regional governments establish various big data centers, information centers, coordination centers, etc., to technologically transform the regional environment, thereby gaining technological competitive advantages in market competition.

# Section 3: "9-in-3" Competition of Regional Governments

As mentioned earlier, the objective function of regional government competition is the fiscal revenue determination mechanism. Given fixed state-owned asset income and government bond income, the scale of regional fiscal revenue depends on the scale of tax revenue and fee income. At a certain stage of economic development, the scale of regional tax revenue and fee income mainly depends on the level of regional economic development, regional economic policy measures to promote economic development, and regional economic management efficiency.

The level of regional economic development is constrained by projects, industrial chains, and import-export; regional economic policy measures to promote economic development are

大、人员多、时间长，其他市场创新主体无力或无法承担的项目，由区域政府来组织进行技术创新；四是区域政府通过加大财政支持力度，帮助区域内其他市场创新主体（企业、科研院所或个人）进行技术创新。技术创新实质上又是区域政府对科技进步政策制定及政策工具选择的创新。

再以以色列为例，以色列特拉维夫－雅法市政府为了帮助孵化器发展，建立了非常详细的各类企业的发展情况数据库，包括企业的规模、人数、区位、产品市场、发展阶段、生产规模、主要融资形式、当前的主要问题等。政府通过参考这一不断更新的数据库，并运用专业的金融分析工具，分析各类企业的最优融资模式和规模，减轻了财政负担，也使得资本配置更加有效与合理。虽然大部分融资交给了市场，但特拉维夫－雅法市政府依然举办各种创业竞赛，选出最优秀的团队，给予支持。政府将资本注入之后，就将其所有权和使用权彻底交给企业、团队。企业、团队如果失败，则无须返回资本；如果成功，则须逐年返回资本。可见，区域政府建立各种大数据中心、信息中心、协同中心等，是为了对区域环境进行技术化改造，从而在市场竞争中获得技术竞争优势。

## 第三节　区域政府"三类九要素"竞争

如前所述，区域政府竞争的目标函数是财政收入决定机制。在国有资产收益和政府债券收入既定的情况下，区域财政收入规模取决于税收收入和收费收入规模。在经济发展的一定阶段，区域税收收入和收费收入规模主要取决于区域经济发展水平、推动经济发展的区域经济政策措施以及区域经济管理效率等。

区域的经济发展水平受制于项目、产业链和进出口；推动经济发展的区域经

manifested in regional governments' infrastructure investment policies, talent and technology support policies, and fiscal and financial support policies; regional economic management efficiency is reflected in the efficiency of regional policy systems, environmental systems, and management systems. These three aspects and nine elements directly or indirectly determine the size of regional fiscal revenue and the level of regional competitiveness. Therefore, regional government competition is mainly manifested as "9-in-3" competition, as shown in Figure 4-1.

Mezzoeconomics calls this theory the "9-in-3 Competition Theory" or "Ram's Horn Competition Theory" (as the shape resembles a ram's horn) of regional governments. The left horn is formed by the objective function of regional government competition——fiscal revenue determination mechanism, and the right horn is formed by the indicator function of regional government competition——regional competitiveness determination mechanism. The core influencing factors of the objective function and indicator function of regional government competition are the level of regional economic development, which includes three elements——projects, industrial chains, and import-export; key supporting conditions are regional economic policy measures and regional economic management efficiency, the former including infrastructure investment policies, talent and technology support policies, and fiscal and financial support policies, the latter including the efficiency of policy system, the efficiency of environmental system, and the efficiency of management system. We will elaborate on the "9-in-3 Competition Theory" or "Ram's Horn Competition Theory" as follows.

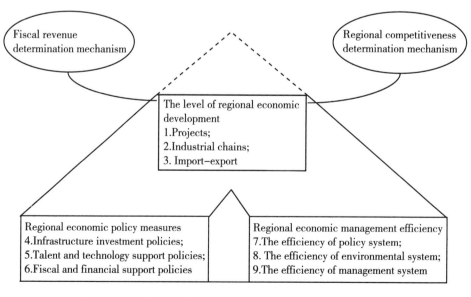

Figure 4-1　"9-in-3" Competition of Regional Governments

济政策措施表现为区域政府的基础设施投资政策,人才、科技扶持政策以及财政、金融支持政策;区域经济管理效率则体现为区域的政策体系效率、环境体系效率和管理体系效率。这三大方面九个要素直接或间接地决定了区域财政收入规模的大小和区域竞争力的高低。因此,区域政府竞争主要表现为"三类九要素"竞争,如图4-1所示。

中观经济学称这一理论为区域政府的"三类九要素竞争理论"或"羊角竞争理论"(图形似羊角)。左角由区域政府竞争的目标函数——财政收入决定机制构成,右角由区域政府竞争的指标函数——区域竞争力决定机制构成。区域政府竞争的目标函数和指标函数的核心影响因素是区域经济发展水平,其包含三个要素——项目、产业链和进出口;关键支持条件是区域经济政策措施和区域经济管理效率,前者包括基础设施投资政策,人才、科技扶持政策和财政、金融支持政策,后者包括政策体系效率、环境体系效率和管理体系效率。我们将"三类九要素竞争理论"或"羊角竞争理论"具体阐述如下。[①]

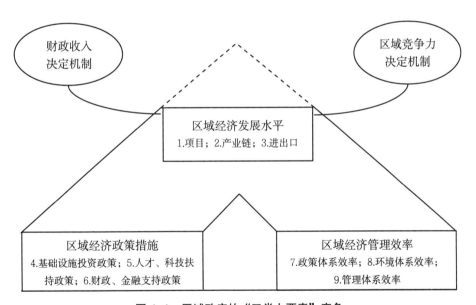

**图 4-1 区域政府的"三类九要素"竞争**

资料来源:陈云贤:《市场竞争双重主体论——兼谈中观经济学的创立与发展》,北京大学出版社,2020,第109页。

---

① 陈云贤:《市场竞争双重主体论——兼谈中观经济学的创立与发展》,北京大学出版社,2020,第109-115页。

## I. Level of Regional Economic Development

Competition related to level of regional economic development includes project competition, industrial chain competition, and import-export competition.

First, project competition. It mainly includes the following three categories. One is major national projects, including national major special projects, major projects of national science and technology support plans, national major science and technology infrastructure construction projects, major engineering projects and industrialization projects funded by national finance; two is social investment projects, such as investment projects in high-tech industries, emerging industries, equipment manufacturing industries, raw material industries, and services industries like finance and logistics; three is foreign investment projects, such as investment projects in areas like intelligent manufacturing, cloud computing and big data, Internet of Things, and smart city construction. Regional governments compete for projects, firstly to directly introduce capital, talent, and industries; secondly to effectively solve region's fundraising, financing, and land acquisition issues based on the legitimacy of project policies and the rationality of public services; thirdly to guide region's land development, urban facility construction, expand investment attraction, drive industrial development, optimize resource allocation, and enhance policy capabilities through project implementation, ultimately promoting sustainable development of regional society and economy. Therefore, project competition has become a competitive focus for various regional governments. Enhancing project awareness, development awareness, efficiency awareness, advantage awareness, condition awareness, policy awareness, and risk awareness has become an inevitable requirement for the marketization of competition among regional governments.

Second, industrial chain competition. Generally speaking, each region has its own industrial foundation and characteristics——mostly determined by the natural resource endowments within the region. As for how to maintain and optimize the endowed resources within the region and gather high-end resources from outside the region, industrial structure optimization and effective allocation of industrial chains are key, while developing towards the high-end of industries, forming industrial agglomeration, and leading industrial clusters are breakthrough points. Regional governments' industrial chain competition mainly unfolds in two aspects. One is in production factors. Low-end or primary production factors cannot form stable and lasting competitiveness; only by introducing and investing in high-end production factors, such as industrial technology, modern information technology, network resources, transportation facilities, professional talents, think tank research and development, etc., can strong and competitive industries be established. The other is in industrial clusters

# 一、区域经济发展水平

区域经济发展水平的竞争包括项目竞争、产业链竞争和进出口竞争。

第一，项目竞争。主要包括以下三类：一是国家重大项目，包括国家重大专项、国家科技支撑计划重大项目、国家重大科技基础设施建设项目、国家财政资助的重大工程项目和产业化项目；二是社会投资项目，比如高技术产业、新兴产业、装备制造业、原材料产业及金融、物流等服务业的投资项目；三是外资引进项目，比如智能制造、云计算与大数据、物联网、智能城市建设等领域的投资项目。区域政府之间展开项目的争夺，一则可以直接引进资金、人才和产业；二则可以凭借项目政策的合法性、公共服务的合理性来有效解决区域内筹资、融资和征地等问题；三则可通过项目落地，引导开发区域土地、建设城市设施、扩大招商引资、带动产业发展、优化资源配置、提升政策能力，最终促进区域社会经济的可持续发展。因此，项目竞争成为各区域政府的竞争重点。提高项目意识、发展意识、效率意识、优势意识、条件意识、政策意识和风险意识，成为各区域政府竞争市场化的必然要求。

第二，产业链竞争。一般来说，每个区域都有自己的产业基础和特色——多数取决于本区域内的自然资源禀赋。就如何保持和优化区域内的禀赋资源并汇聚区域外的高端资源来说，产业结构优化、产业链有效配置是关键，向产业高端发展、形成产业集聚、引领产业集群是突破点。区域政府的产业链竞争主要从两个方面展开。一是生产要素方面。低端或初级生产要素无法形成稳定持久的竞争力，只有引进并投资于高端生产要素，比如工业技术、现代信息技术、网络资源、交通设施、专业人才、智库研发等，才能建立起强大且具有竞争优势的产

and industrial supporting systems. Regional competitiveness theory tells us that establishing effective industrial supporting systems led by existing industrial foundations within the region can reduce enterprise transaction costs and increase enterprise profitability. The industrial smile curve tells us that the most valuable places are concentrated at both ends of the industrial chain——research and development, as well as market. Cultivating advantageous industries, complemented by complete industrial chains, and attracting investment in a targeted manner according to industrial structure is an important path for sustainable regional development.

Third, import-export competition. In an open international economic system, import-export competition among various regions of the world has become an important link affecting regional competitiveness. Regional governments' import-export competition is mainly reflected in four aspects: first, in the development of processing trade and general trade, regional governments strive to reduce the proportion of processing trade and increase the proportion of general trade to enhance the driving force of regional commodity and service trade; second, in foreign investment, regional governments strive to promote enterprises' overseas layout and compete for overseas projects to extend the region's interest layout and market value chain overseas; third, in capital export, regional governments strive to advance capital project exchange, that is, under the condition of international current account investment facilitation, adopt various measures to promote capital circulation and currency free exchange facilitation; fourth, in imports, especially in the introduction of high-tech products, industries, and projects, regional governments comprehensively adopt preferential policies and measures to attract and support them, even at great expense to assist their investment, deployment, and production. The effectiveness of import-export competition is one of the important factors affecting economic growth in various regions of the world.

## II. Regional Economic Policy Measures

Regional economic policy measures mainly include infrastructure investment policies competition, talent and technology support policies competition, and fiscal and financial support policies competition.

First, infrastructure investment policies competition includes a series of investment policies competitions such as the hardware and software construction of urban infrastructure and even the development of modern smart cities. Urban infrastructure hardware includes transportation facilities such as highways, railways, ports, and aviation, energy facilities such as electricity and natural gas, information platform facilities such as optical cables and

业。二是产业集群、产业配套方面。区域竞争力理论告诉我们，建立以区域内现有产业基础为主导的产业有效配套，能减少企业交易成本，提高企业盈利水平。产业微笑曲线告诉我们，价值最丰厚的地方集中在产业链的两端——研发和市场。培植优势产业，配以完整的产业链，按照产业结构有的放矢地招商引资，是区域可持续发展的重要路径。

第三，进出口竞争。在开放型的国际经济体系中，世界各区域的进出口竞争成为影响区域竞争力的一个重要环节。区域政府的进出口竞争主要体现在四个层面：一是在加工贸易与一般贸易的发展中，区域政府力图降低加工贸易占比，提高一般贸易占比，以增强区域商品和服务贸易的原动力；二是在对外投资上，区域政府力图推动企业海外布局，竞争海外项目，以促使本区域的利益布局和市场价值链条延伸至海外；三是在资本输出上，区域政府力图推进资本项目兑换，即在国际经常项目投资便利化的情况下，采取各项措施促进货币资本流通、货币自由兑换便利化等；四是在进口方面，尤其是对高科技产品、产业、项目的引进方面，区域政府全面采取优惠政策措施，予以吸引、扶持，甚至不惜重金辅助其投入、布点和生产。进出口竞争的成效是影响世界各区域经济增长的重要因素之一。

## 二、区域经济政策措施

区域经济政策措施，主要包括基础设施投资政策竞争，人才、科技扶持政策竞争，财政、金融支持政策竞争。

第一，基础设施投资政策竞争，包括城市基础设施的软硬件建设乃至现代化智能城市的开发等一系列投资政策竞争。城市基础设施硬件包括高速公路、铁路、港口、航空等交通设施，电力、天然气等能源设施，光缆、网络等信息化平台设施，以及科技园区、工业园区、创业孵化园区、创意产业园区等工程性基础

networks, and engineering infrastructure such as science and technology parks, industrial parks, entrepreneurship incubation parks, and creative industry parks; urban infrastructure software includes social infrastructure such as education, science and technology, healthcare, sports, culture, and social welfare; the development of modern smart cities includes the construction of intelligent technology platforms such as big data, cloud computing, and the Internet of Things. A region's infrastructure system supports the social and economic development of that region, mainly including three types: forward-looking, adaptive, and lagging. If the supply of region's infrastructure can be moderately forward-looking, it will not only increase the region's direct benefits but also enhance regional competitiveness, create high-quality urban structures, facility scales, spatial layouts, provide quality services, thereby reducing costs for enterprises in market competition, improving their production efficiency, and thus promoting industrial development. The degree of improvement in region's infrastructure will directly affect the current status and future of regional economic development.

Second, talent and technology support policies competition. The most fundamental aspect of competition in this field is establishing the concept that talent resources are the primary resource and science and technology are the primary productive force; the most basic is to improve the local talent cultivation system, increase investment in local talent cultivation and scientific and technological innovation; the most crucial is to create conditions to attract, introduce, cultivate, and apply talents. The main indicators for measuring talent and technology competitiveness include the regional science and technology talent resource index, the number of people engaged in scientific and technological activities per 10,000 people, the number of scientists and engineers per 10,000 people, the number of students in ordinary higher education institutions per 10,000 people, the total expenditure on scientific and technological activities, the proportion of scientific and technological expenditure in regional GDP, per capita research and development expenditure, the percentage of science and technology appropriations in regional fiscal expenditure, per capita fiscal education expenditure, total regional fiscal education expenditure, the number of full-time teachers in higher education institutions, etc. Regional governments should strive to improve and enhance related indicators to increase local talent and technology competitiveness.

Third, fiscal and financial support policies competition. Regional fiscal competition includes fiscal revenue competition and fiscal expenditure competition. As mentioned earlier, the growth of regional fiscal revenue mainly relies on economic growth, increased tax revenue and fee income; while fiscal expenditure is the key to competition, including social consumption expenditure, transfer expenditure and investment expenditure, among which the most important fiscal expenditure competition occurs in the field of investment expenditure, including government infrastructure investment, scientific and technological research and development investment, policy-based financial investment (supporting industries in urgent

设施；城市基础设施软件包括教育、科技、医疗卫生、体育、文化、社会福利等社会性基础设施；现代化智能城市的开发包括对大数据、云计算、物联网等智能科技平台的建设。一个区域的基础设施体系支撑着该区域社会经济的发展，其主要包括三种类型：超前型、适应型和滞后型。区域基础设施的供给如能适度超前，不但会增加区域自身的直接利益，而且会增强区域竞争力，创造优质的城市结构、设施规模、空间布局，提供优质服务，从而减少企业在市场竞争中的成本，提高其生产效益，进而促进产业发展。区域基础设施的完善程度将直接影响区域经济发展的现状和未来。

第二，人才、科技扶持政策竞争。这一领域的竞争，最根本的是确立人才资源是第一资源，科技是第一生产力的理念；最基础的是完善本土人才培养体系，加大本土人才培养投入和科技创新投入；最关键的是创造条件吸引人才、引进人才、培养人才、应用人才。衡量人才、科技竞争力的主要指标包括区域科技人才资源指数、每万人中从事科技活动的人数、每万人中科学家和工程师人数、每万人中普通高校在校学生数、科技活动经营支出总额、科技经费支出占区域生产总值比重、人均科研经费、科技拨款占区域财政支出百分比、人均财政性教育经费支出、区域财政教育支出总额、高校专任教师数等。各区域政府应通过努力改善、提高相关指标来提高本土的人才和科技竞争力。

第三，财政、金融支持政策竞争。区域财政竞争包括财政收入竞争和财政支出竞争。如前所述，区域财政收入的增长主要依靠经济增长、税收收入和收费收入增加；而财政支出是竞争的关键，其包括社会消费性支出、转移性支出和投资性支出，其中最主要的财政支出竞争发生在投资性支出领域，包括政府的基础设施投资、科技研发投资、政策性金融投资（支持急需发展的产业）等。投资性支出是经济增长的重要驱动力。在财政收支总体规模有限的条件下，各区域政府积

need of development), etc. Investment expenditure is an important driving force for economic growth. Under the condition of limited overall scale of fiscal revenue and expenditure, various regional governments actively set up various investment and financing platforms to mobilize and attract funds, talents, information and other resources from financial institutions within and outside the region to the maximum extent, serving region's industrial development, urban construction, and social livelihood. Regional governments also compete in various preferential policies, such as the focus of fiscal expenditure and financial means of absorbing funds.

## III. Regional Economic Management Efficiency

Regional economic management efficiency includes policy system efficiency competition, environmental system efficiency competition and management system efficiency competition.

First, policy system efficiency competition. The policy system is divided into two levels: one is the policies issued by regional governments externally; the other is a series of policies issued by regional governments internally. It's the same between countries. Since policies themselves are public goods, characterized by non-exclusivity and easy imitation, a competitive good policy system must include the following characteristics: first, practicality, that is, conforming to reality and meeting the requirements of economic and social development; second, advancement, that is, having foresight, forward-looking nature, and innovativeness; third, operability, that is, policies are clear, targeted and implementable; fourth, organization, that is, having special institutions and personnel responsible for and executing; fifth, effect orientation, that is, having inspection, supervision, assessment, and evaluation mechanisms, including playing the role of third parties, to effectively achieve policy objectives. The efficiency of policy systems in various regions of the world also has a great impact on regional competitiveness.

Second, environmental system efficiency competition. The environment here mainly refers to the ecological environment, cultural environment, policy environment, social credit system environment, etc. Harmonizing development investment with ecological protection, matching investment attraction with policy services, aligning wealth pursuit with social

极搭建各类投融资平台，最大限度地动员和吸引区域内、区域外各类金融机构的资金、人才、信息等资源，为本区域产业发展、城市建设、社会民生服务。区域政府在各种优惠政策上也开展竞争，如财政支出的侧重、吸纳资金的金融手段等。

### 三、区域经济管理效率

区域经济管理效率，包括政策体系效率竞争、环境体系效率竞争和管理体系效率竞争。

第一，政策体系效率竞争。政策体系分为两个层次：一是区域政府对外出台的政策；二是区域政府对内出台的系列政策。国家与国家之间也是一样。由于政策本身是公共物品，具有非排他性和易效仿性的特点，因此，有竞争性的好的政策体系一定包含以下特征：一是求实性，即符合实际，符合经济、社会发展要求；二是先进性，即有预见性、超前性、创新性；三是操作性，即政策是清晰的、有针对性和可实施的；四是组织性，即有专门机构和人员负责和执行；五是效果导向性，即有检查、监督、考核、评价机制，包括发挥第三方作用，有效实现政策目标。世界各区域政策体系的效率对区域竞争力的影响也极大。

第二，环境体系效率竞争。此处的环境主要指生态环境、人文环境、政策环境和社会信用体系环境等。发展投资与保护生态相和谐，吸引投资与政策服务相配套，追逐财富与回报社会相契合，法治监督与社会信用相支撑，等等，均是区域政府竞争必需、必备的发展环境。良好的环境体系建设成为区域政府招商引资、开发项目、促进经济持续发展的成功秘诀，这已被海内外区域成功发展的经验所证明。

Third, management system efficiency competition. The efficiency of regional governments' management systems is an overall reflection of their economic management vitality, speed, quality, and effectiveness. It includes four categories: macro efficiency, micro efficiency, organizational efficiency, and individual efficiency. In terms of administrative compliance, regional governments should follow legality standards, benefit standards, and quality standards in management system efficiency competition; in terms of administrative efficiency, regional government management should conform to quantity standards, time standards, speed standards, and budget standards. The essence of regional government's management system efficiency competition is the competition of organizational systems, subject responsibility, service awareness, work skills, and technical platforms. Developed regions' governments, using "parallel" and "integrated" service models, have already pioneered management system efficiency competition in practice.

Combining the previous discussion on three types of resources, we can further study regional government competition from this perspective. Regional resources, i.e., urban resources, as mentioned in Chapter 3, can be divided into broad and narrow senses. Urban resources in the broad sense include industrial resources, livelihood resources, and infrastructure/public works resources; urban resources in the narrow sense refer to infrastructure/public works resources, including urban infrastructure hardware and software and even modern smart cities. Therefore, the urban economy in the broad sense includes industrial economy, livelihood economy, and urban economy mainly based on infrastructure construction; the urban economy in the narrow sense specifically refers to the investment, development, and construction of infrastructure. Thus, regional government competition also has the distinction between broad competition and narrow competition.

According to the "9-in-3 Competition Theory" or "Ram's Horn Competition Theory", regional government competition in the broad sense includes competition for region's operative resources, non-operative resources, and quasi-operative resources.

Competition in the livelihood economy field is mainly regional governments formulating and implementing relevant policies to provide non-operative resources, i.e., social public goods and public services, to achieve "basic bottom line, fairness and justice, effective improvement" of social security. The goal is to maintain regional social stability and create a good regional investment and development environment. In the "9-in-3 Competition Theory" system, regional governments' competition in the livelihood economy field is related to the third category, i.e., regional economic management efficiency competition.

Competition in the industrial economy field is mainly regional governments formulating and implementing policies related to operative resources, i.e., the three major industries, to play the role of "planning, guiding; supporting, regulating; supervising, managing". The

第三，管理体系效率竞争。区域政府的管理体系效率是其经济管理活力、速度、质量、效能的总体反映。它包括宏观效率、微观效率、组织效率、个人效率四类。就行政的合规性而言，区域政府在管理体系效率竞争中应遵循合法性标准、利益标准和质量标准；就行政的效率性而言，区域政府的管理应符合数量标准、时间标准、速度标准和预算标准。区域政府的管理体系效率竞争本质上是组织制度、主体责任、服务意识、工作技能和技术平台的竞争。发达区域的区域政府运用"并联式""一体化"的服务模式，已经在实践中开创了管理体系效率竞争之先河。

结合前文对三类资源的讨论，我们可以从这个角度进一步研究区域政府竞争。区域资源即城市资源，正如第三章所述，有广义与狭义之分。广义的城市资源包括产业资源、民生资源和基础设施/公共工程资源；狭义的城市资源就是指基础设施/公共工程资源，包括城市基础设施软硬件乃至现代化智能城市等。因此，广义的城市经济包括产业经济、民生经济和以基础设施建设为主体的城市经济；狭义的城市经济则专指基础设施的投资、开发与建设。由此，区域政府竞争也就有了广义竞争与狭义竞争之别。

按照"三类九要素竞争理论"或"羊角竞争理论"，广义的区域政府竞争包括对区域可经营性资源、非经营性资源和准经营性资源等的竞争。

在民生经济领域的竞争主要是区域政府通过制定和落实相关政策，提供非经营性资源即社会公共物品和公共服务，实现社会保障的"基本托底、公平公正、有效提升"。其目标是维护区域社会稳定，创造良好的区域投资发展环境。在"三类九要素竞争理论"体系中，区域政府在民生经济领域的竞争与第三类即区域经济管理效率竞争相关。

在产业经济领域的竞争主要是区域政府通过制定和落实与可经营性资源即三大产业相关的政策，发挥"规划、引导；扶持、调节；监督、管理"的作用。其目标是维护市场公开、公平、公正，促进产业经济协调发展，提高区域整体生产

goal is to maintain market openness, fairness, and justice, promote coordinated development of the industrial economy, and improve overall regional production efficiency. In the "9-in-3 Competition Theory" system, it is related to the first category, i.e., the level of regional economic development, and the second category, i.e., talent and technology support policies and fiscal and financial support policies of regional economic policy measures.

Competition in the narrow sense of regional economy is mainly regional governments' participation, allocation, and management of the urban economy. Regional governments should be able to both prevent problems of urban resource idleness and waste, low-quality and disorderly urban construction, and promote comprehensive and sustainable development of urban construction and socio-economy. In the "9-in-3 Competition Theory" system, it is related to the first category, i.e., the level of regional economic development, the second category, i.e., infrastructure investment policies of regional economic policy measures, and the third category, i.e., regional economic management efficiency.

According to the "9-in-3 Competition Theory", regional government competition in the broad sense is manifested as regional governments' competition for optimal allocation of three types of resources they can allocate through supporting policies, which is a competition in a large market system. It is specifically reflected in the competition of "9-in-3" such as the level of regional economic development, regional economic policy measures, and regional economic management efficiency. Its essence is the question of what policies regional governments adopt in regional resource allocation to enhance enterprise vitality in the industrial economy, create a good environment in the livelihood economy, and promote sustainable regional development in the urban economy. The strength of regional governments' allocation of three types of resources and policy measures in the "9-in-3" competition directly determines the fiscal revenue of the region during this period. Therefore, the essence of regional government competition in the broad sense is the competition of regional governments' objective functions in the fields of industrial development, urban construction, and social livelihood, i.e., the competition of regional fiscal revenue determination mechanisms.

According to the "9-in-3 Competition Theory", regional government competition in the narrow sense is mainly manifested as regional governments' competition for urban infrastructure investment, development, and construction, i.e., the competition of government supporting policies and resource optimization allocation in the urban infrastructure field. In the

"9-in-3" sequence, this is mainly reflected in optimizing regional fiscal support policies and playing the role of fiscal investment expenditure. The essence of how regional governments participate, what rules they follow, and what supporting policies they implement in the investment, development, and construction of urban infrastructure hardware and software and even modern smart cities is all reflected in the structure of regional governments' fiscal expenditure. Therefore, regional government competition in the narrow sense, i.e., urban

效率。其在"三类九要素竞争理论"体系中，与第一类即区域经济发展水平，以及第二类即区域经济政策措施的人才、科技扶持政策和财政、金融支持政策的竞争相关。

在狭义的区域经济领域的竞争主要是区域政府对城市经济的参与、调配和管理。区域政府应既能防范城市资源闲置浪费、城市建设低质无序的问题，又能促进城市建设和社会经济全面、可持续发展。其在"三类九要素竞争理论"体系中，与第一类即区域经济发展水平、第二类即区域经济政策措施的基础设施投资政策，以及第三类即区域经济管理效率相关。

根据"三类九要素竞争理论"，广义的区域政府竞争表现为区域政府通过配套政策，对自身可调配的三种资源的优化配置的竞争，是一个大市场体系的竞争。它具体体现在区域经济发展水平、区域经济政策措施、区域经济管理效率等"三类九要素"的竞争上。其实质是区域政府在区域资源调配中，对产业经济采取什么政策以增强企业活力，对民生经济采取什么政策以创造良好环境，对城市经济采取什么政策以推动区域可持续发展的问题。区域政府对三种资源的调配和在"三类九要素"竞争中政策措施的力度，直接决定这一时期区域的财政收入。因此，广义的区域政府竞争的实质就是区域政府在产业发展、城市建设、社会民生领域的目标函数的竞争，即区域财政收入决定机制的竞争。

根据"三类九要素竞争理论"，狭义的区域政府竞争主要表现为区域政府对城市基础设施投资、开发、建设的竞争，即政府在城市基础设施领域的配套政策，以及资源优化配置的竞争。在"三类九要素"序列里，这主要体现在对区域财政支持政策的优化和发挥财政投资性支出的作用上。区域政府对城市基础设施软硬件乃至现代化智能城市的投资、开发与建设，采取什么方式参与，遵循什么规则运作，配套什么政策推动，其实质都体现在区域政府的财政支出结构中。因

infrastructure competition, is also the competition of regional fiscal investment expenditure determination mechanisms.

In summary, regional government competition is specifically manifested as "9-in-3" competition. Its essence is regional governments' broad competition for effective allocation of three types of regional resources (at this time, government behavior focuses on the regional fiscal revenue determination mechanism), with its focus concentrated on urban economic competition, mainly based on investment, development, and construction of quasi-operative resources in the resource generation field, i.e., urban infrastructure (at this time, government behavior focuses on the structure of regional fiscal expenditure, mainly the proportion of fiscal investment expenditure). This is the core of the "9-in-3 Competition Theory".

## Section 4: Determination Mechanism of Regional Government Competitiveness: DRP Model

This section introduces the regional government competitiveness determination mechanism in mezzoeconomics, that is, the District Resource Planning/Optimization Allocation Model (DRP Model). Regional governments can reasonably allocate regional dispatchable resources and rationally adjust resource structures through this model, thereby improving the utilization efficiency of region's resources.

### I. Fiscal Surplus and "9-in-3" Determination Mechanism

Within a specific time and interval, when regional governments adjust the total amount of their fiscal expenditure ($FE$), they can also adjust its structure, that is, adjust the allocation proportion of fiscal expenditure in different aspects to obtain maximum benefits. It is known that regional government fiscal expenditure mainly includes three categories: first, consumption expenditure ($CE$), mainly used to enhance the region's environmental supporting facilities, management system supporting facilities, and policy supporting level, with its core influencing regional economic management efficiency; second, investment expenditure ($IE$), mainly used to enhance the region's infrastructure construction level, such as roads, bridges, power grids, etc., with its core influencing regional economic policy measures; third, transfer

此，狭义的区域政府竞争即城市基础设施的竞争，也就是区域财政投资性支出决定机制的竞争。

综上，区域政府竞争具体体现为"三类九要素"竞争，其实质是区域政府对区域三种资源有效调配的广义竞争（此时政府行为聚焦在区域财政收入决定机制上），其重点又集中在城市经济竞争上，它以对资源生成领域中的准经营性资源，即城市基础设施的投资、开发、建设为主体（此时政府行为聚焦在区域财政支出结构上，主要是财政投资性支出的占比）。这就是"三类九要素竞争理论"的核心所在。

## 第四节 区域政府竞争力决定机制：DRP 模型

本节对中观经济学区域政府竞争力决定机制，也即区域资源规划/优化配置模型（DRP 模型）进行介绍。[1][2] 区域政府可通过该模型合理分配区域能调度的资源，合理调整资源结构，从而提高区域资源的利用效率。

### 一、财政盈余与"三类九要素"的决定机制

在特定时间和特定区间内，区域政府在调节其财政支出（$FE$）的总量时，也可以同时调整其结构，即调整财政支出在不同方面的分配比例，以获得最大收益。已知区域政府的财政支出主要包括三类：一是消费性支出（$CE$），主要用于提升区域的环境配套、管理体系配套和政策配套水平，其核心是影响区域经济管理效率；二是投资性支出（$IE$），主要用于提升区域的基础设施建设水平，如

---

[1] 陈云贤：《市场竞争双重主体论——兼谈中观经济学的创立与发展》，北京大学出版社，2020，第 115–124 页。
[2] 陈云贤：《市场竞争双重主体论——兼谈中观经济学的创立与发展》，北京大学出版社，2020，第 61–65 页。

expenditure (*TE*), mainly used to enhance the region's support level for talent, science and technology, and fiscal and financial aspects, with its core also influencing regional economic policy measures. Therefore, regional government fiscal expenditure can be expressed by the following equation:

$$CE + IE + TE = FE \quad (4-1)$$

After introducing variable coefficients $\varphi_i$($i$= 1, 2, 3), we assume $Y_0$ represents the initial economic level, and assume the critical values of the factor-driven stage, investment-driven stage, and innovation-driven stage are $Y_1$、$Y_2$、$Y_3$ respectively, with $Y_1 < Y_2 < Y_3$. Then we have the following relationship:

$$Y = \varphi_1(Y_1, Y_0) \times CE + \varphi_2(Y_2, Y_0) \times IE + \varphi_3(Y_3, Y_0) \times TE + \text{Const1} \quad (4-2)$$

Here, $Y$ is the degree of market economy development, Const1 is other economic effects that cannot be influenced by fiscal expenditure.

Based on mezzoeconomics' explanation of quasi-operative resources, we use $\lambda$ ( $0 < \lambda < 1$ ) to represent the allocation proportion of quasi-operative resources in the public sector in society. It is jointly influenced by the degree of market economy development ($Y$), fiscal revenue and expenditure conditions (including fiscal budget $B$ and fiscal expenditure $FE$), and residents' cognition degree ( $\gamma$ ), that is:

$$\lambda = F(Y, B, FE, \gamma) \quad (4-3)$$

To further discuss the possible functional form of equation (4-3), let's first discuss the marginal effects of the above variables on $\lambda$.

Firstly, the degree of market economy development $Y$ is a variable greater than 0 and less than 1, representing the state of market economy development between highly underdeveloped and highly developed. The degree of market economy development will affect residents' disposable income level, which in turn will affect the amount of funds flowing into the quasi-operational resource field. If the degree of market economy development is high, then residents' disposable income level is high, at which time the private sector will have the ability and willingness to invest in quasi-operative resources, that is, the $\lambda$ value decreases, and the proportion of quasi-operative resources converting to operative resources increases. If the original $\lambda$ value is high, it means that there was originally less private sector fund supply in the quasi-operational resource market. Under the condition of unchanged total demand, the market will give new incoming funds a higher rate of return, thus accelerating the inflow of private sector funds. Therefore, referring to traditional economic theory, the growth rate of $\lambda$ is negatively correlated with $Y$. Assuming $a$ is a positive constant, we have:

$$\frac{\partial \lambda / \lambda}{\partial Y} = -a \qquad (4\text{–}4)$$

道路、桥梁、电网等，其核心是影响区域经济政策措施；三是转移性支出（$TE$），主要用于提升区域对人才、科技和财政、金融的支持水平，其核心也是影响区域经济政策措施。因此，区域政府财政支出可由下式表示：

$$CE + IE + TE = FE \qquad （4\text{–}1）$$

引入可变系数 $\varphi_i$（$i=1$，2，3）后，我们假定 $Y_0$ 代表期初的经济水平，假定要素驱动阶段、投资驱动阶段和创新驱动阶段的临界值分别为 $Y_1$、$Y_2$、$Y_3$，且有 $Y_1 < Y_2 < Y_3$。则又有如下关系：

$$Y = \varphi_1(Y_1, Y_0) \times CE + \varphi_2(Y_2, Y_0) \times IE + \varphi_3(Y_3, Y_0) \times TE + \text{Const1} \qquad （4\text{–}2）$$

式中，$Y$ 为市场经济发展程度，Const1 为无法由财政支出所影响的其他经济效应。

依据中观经济学关于准经营性资源的解释，我们用 $\lambda$（$0 < \lambda < 1$）来表示社会上准经营性资源在公共部门当中的配置比例，它受到市场经济发展程度（$Y$）、财政收支状况（包括财政预算 $B$ 和财政支出 $FE$）以及居民认知程度（$\gamma$）的共同影响，即：

$$\lambda = F(Y, B, FE, \gamma) \qquad （4\text{–}3）$$

为了进一步探讨式（4–3）的可能函数形式，我们先来讨论上述变量对 $\lambda$ 的边际影响。

首先，市场经济发展程度 $Y$ 是一个大于 0 小于 1 的变量，代表着市场经济发展程度在高度不发达和高度发达之间的状态。市场经济发展程度会影响居民可支配收入水平，而居民可支配收入水平又会影响流入准经营性资源领域的资金量。如果市场经济发展程度较高，则居民可支配收入水平较高，此时私人部门将有能力和意愿投资准经营性资源，即 $\lambda$ 值变低，准经营性资源转换为可经营性资源的比例变高。如果原有的 $\lambda$ 值较高，则意味着准经营性资源市场上原本的私人部门资金供给较少，在总需求不变的情况下，市场会给予新入资金更高的收益率，从而加速私人部门资金流入。因此，参考传统经济学理论，$\lambda$ 的增长率与 $Y$ 负相关，假设 $a$ 为正的常数，即有：

$$\frac{\partial \lambda / \lambda}{\partial Y} = -a \qquad （4\text{–}4）$$

Secondly, the government's input into quasi-operative resources will be affected by the government's fiscal revenue and expenditure conditions. If the government's fiscal budget $B$ is lower than its fiscal expenditure $FE$, then the government's fiscal funds are insufficient at this time, which will promote the conversion of quasi-operative resources to operative resources to reduce government expenditure; and because of insufficient fiscal funds, the government is willing to let the private sector obtain a higher rate of return, then the speed of private sector funds flowing into the quasi-operational resource field will also accelerate. In this case, the proportion of quasi-operative resources shifting to the private sector increases, and the $\lambda$ value decreases. Therefore, $\lambda$ is negatively correlated with the fiscal revenue and expenditure conditions, that is, the ratio of fiscal expenditure to fiscal budget ($FE/B$). Moreover, it needs to be considered that government fiscal expenditure is affected by the original $\lambda$ value level. If the original $\lambda$ value is high, that is, the proportion of quasi-operative resources funded by the public sector is high, it means that the government has higher fiscal expenditure. Therefore, the relationship between $\lambda$ and fiscal revenue and expenditure conditions can be expressed by equation (4-5), where $b$ is a positive constant:

$$\frac{\partial \lambda / \lambda}{\partial \left(\frac{FE}{B}\right)} = -b \tag{4-5}$$

Finally, the private sector's investment in quasi-operative resources is not only affected by the supply and demand of funds but also by the degree of residents' cognition. It's worth noting that the impact of residents' cognition degree on their willingness to invest funds is different at different economic stages: if the market economy development is at a backward stage, i.e., $Y < Y^*$ ($Y^*$ is the threshold value for a mature market economy, determined according to the standards of each country), then the higher the residents' cognition degree, the more residents can realize the driving value of infrastructure investment for economic development, and thus are more willing to invest funds in quasi-operative resources. At this time, $\lambda$ is negatively correlated with residents' cognition degree. If the market economy development is at a mature stage, i.e., $Y > Y^*$, then the higher the residents' cognition degree, the more residents can realize the negative impact of excessive infrastructure investment on sustainable environmental development. Thus, at the same rate of return level, residents are more willing to invest in other resources rather than quasi-operative resources. At this time, $\lambda$ is positively correlated with residents' cognition degree. Therefore, we add $\ln(Y/Y^*)$ as a correction coefficient for the above discussion. In addition, it needs to be considered that the original $\lambda$ value level has a significant impact on residents' cognition degree. If the market economy development stage is backward, then the higher the $\lambda$, the more it will enhance residents' preference for investing in quasi-operative resources; conversely, if the market economy development stage is mature, then the higher the $\lambda$, the more it will strengthen residents' desire to control infrastructure scale and be unwilling to invest in quasi-operative resources. Therefore, the relationship between

其次，政府对于准经营性资源的投入会受到政府的财政收支状况的影响。如果政府的财政预算 $B$ 低于其财政支出 $FE$，则政府此时财政资金不足，将推动准经营性资源向可经营性资源转换，以减少政府开支；且政府由于财政资金不足，愿意使私人部门获得更高的收益率，则私人部门资金流入准经营性资源领域的速度也会加速。在这种情况下，准经营性资源转向私人部门的比例升高，$\lambda$ 值变低。因此 $\lambda$ 与财政收支状况，即财政支出与财政预算的比值（$FE/B$）负相关。此外需要考虑的是，政府财政支出受到原有的 $\lambda$ 值水平的影响。如果原有的 $\lambda$ 值较高，即准经营性资源由公共部门出资的比例较高，则意味着政府具有更高的财政支出。因此，$\lambda$ 与财政收支状况的关系可用式（4-5）表示，其中 $b$ 为正常数：

$$\frac{\partial \lambda / \lambda}{\partial \left(\frac{FE}{B}\right)} = -b \quad (4-5)$$

最后，私人部门对准经营性资源的投入，不仅受到资金供求的影响，还受到居民认知程度的影响。值得注意的是，居民认知程度对于居民投入资金意愿的影响在不同经济阶段是不同的：如果市场经济发展处于落后阶段，即 $Y < Y^*$（$Y^*$ 为市场经济发展成熟的临界值，根据各国标准而定），则居民认知程度越高，居民越能意识到基础设施投资对于经济发展的带动价值，从而越愿意将资金投入准经营性资源，这时 $\lambda$ 与居民认知程度负相关；如果市场经济发展处于成熟阶段，即 $Y > Y^*$，则居民认知程度越高，居民越能意识到过度的基础设施投资对于环境的可持续发展具有负面影响，从而在同样的收益率水平下，居民更愿意投资其他资源而非准经营性资源，这时 $\lambda$ 与居民认知程度正相关。因此，我们加入 $\ln(Y/Y^*)$ 作为上述讨论的校正系数。另外需要考虑的是，原有的 $\lambda$ 值水平对居民认知程度有较大的影响。如果市场经济发展阶段落后，则此时 $\lambda$ 越高，越会增强居民投资准经营性资源的偏好；反之，如果市场经济发展阶段成熟，则 $\lambda$ 越高，越会加强居民控制基建规模的愿望，而不愿投资于准经营性资源。因此，$\lambda$ 与居民认知程

$\lambda$ and residents' cognition degree can be expressed by equation (4-6), where $c$ is a positive constant:

$$\frac{\partial \lambda / \lambda}{\partial \left[\gamma \ln\left(\frac{Y}{Y^*}\right)\right]} = -c \tag{4-6}$$

Based on the above analysis, we can establish a simple formula to express the relationship between the rate of change in the allocation proportion of quasi-operative resources in the public sector and the degree of market economy development ($Y$), fiscal revenue and expenditure conditions (including fiscal budget $B$ and fiscal expenditure $FE$), and residents' cognition degree ($\gamma$).

$$\frac{d\lambda}{\lambda} = -ad Y - bd\frac{FE}{B} - c\gamma \ln\left(\frac{Y}{Y^*}\right) d\gamma \tag{4-7}$$

Equation (4-7) expresses the dependence on different variables when quasi-operative resources are converted to operative resources and non-operative resources. It's worth noting that in extreme cases, i.e., when $\lambda$ is 0 (quasi-operative resources are completely converted to operative resources), the operation of quasi-operative resources will be completely unrelated to variables such as fiscal revenue and expenditure conditions and residents' cognition degree, that is, we cannot influence the nature of operative resources through variables such as fiscal revenue and expenditure conditions.

Equation (4-7) is a differential equation about $\lambda$, and solving it can obtain an explicit solution, as shown in equation (4-8). This explicit solution can help us understand the interaction of various variables more intuitively.

$$\lambda = e^{-\left(aY + b\frac{FE}{B}\right)} \left(\frac{Y}{Y^*}\right)^{-c\gamma} \tag{4-8}$$

Equation (4-8) gives the allocation proportion of quasi-operative resources in the public sector, which varies according to economic conditions in different periods. Now, we use the $\lambda$ multiplier to adjust equation (4-2) to obtain equation (4-9).

$$Y = \varphi_1(Y_1, Y_0) \times CE + \varphi_2(Y_2, Y_0) \times \frac{IE}{\lambda} + \varphi_3(Y_3, Y_0) \times TE + \text{Const1} \tag{4-9}$$

The government's fiscal income FInc (abbreviation for Fiscal Income) has the following relationship with tax revenue $\omega Y$ and fee income $\tau \text{CumP}(IE)$ obtained from infrastructure projects.

$$\text{FInc} = \tau \text{CumP}(IE) + \omega Y + \text{Const2} \tag{4-10}$$

Here, $\tau$ is the fee ratio, $\omega$ is the tax ratio, $\tau \text{CumP}(IE)$ is the fee income obtained by the government from infrastructure projects and is a function of *IE*, Const2 is other income.

Therefore, the fiscal surplus *FS* can be expressed by the following equation.

$$FS = \text{FInc} - FE = \tau \text{CumP}(IE) + \omega Y + \text{Const2} - FE \tag{4-11}$$

度的关系可用式（4-6）表示，其中 $c$ 为正常数：

$$\frac{\partial \lambda / \lambda}{\partial \left[ \gamma \ln \left( \frac{Y}{Y^*} \right) \right]} = -c \tag{4-6}$$

基于上述分析，我们可以建立一个简单的公式来表达准经营性资源在公共部门当中的配置比例的变化率与市场经济发展程度（$Y$）、财政收支状况（包括财政预算 $B$ 和财政支出 $FE$）及居民认知程度（$\gamma$）的关系。

$$\frac{\mathrm{d}\lambda}{\lambda} = -a\mathrm{d}Y - bd\frac{FE}{B} - c\gamma \ln\left(\frac{Y}{Y^*}\right)\mathrm{d}\gamma \tag{4-7}$$

式（4-7）表达了准经营性资源向可经营性资源和非经营性资源转换时对于不同变量的依赖性。值得注意的是，极端情况下，即 $\lambda$ 为 0（准经营性资源完全转换为可经营性资源）时，准经营性资源的运作将与财政收支状况、居民认知程度等变量完全无关，即我们不可能借助财政收支状况等变量影响可经营性资源的性质。

式（4-7）是关于 $\lambda$ 的微分方程，求解可得到一个显示解，如式（4-8）所示。这个显示解可以方便我们更加直观地理解各变量的相互作用。

$$\lambda = \mathrm{e}^{-\left(aY + b\frac{FE}{B}\right)} \left(\frac{Y}{Y^*}\right)^{-c\gamma} \tag{4-8}$$

式（4-8）给出了准经营性资源在公共部门中的配置比例，它是根据不同时期的经济状况而变化的。现在，我们用 $\lambda$ 乘子来调整式（4-2），得到式（4-9）。

$$Y = \varphi_1(Y_1, Y_0) \times CE + \varphi_2(Y_2, Y_0) \times \frac{IE}{\lambda} + \varphi_3(Y_3, Y_0) \times TE + \text{Const1} \tag{4-9}$$

政府的财政收入 FInc（Fiscal Income 的简称）与税收收入 $\omega Y$、基建项目中取得的收费收入 $\tau \text{CumP}(IE)$ 有如下关系。

$$\text{FInc} = \tau \text{CumP}(IE) + \omega Y + \text{Const2} \tag{4-10}$$

式中，$\tau$ 为收费比例，$\omega$ 为税收比例，$\tau \text{CumP}(IE)$ 为政府从基建项目中取得的收费收入，且为 $IE$ 的函数，Const2 为其他收入。

因此，财政盈余 $FS$ 可用下式表达。

$$FS = \text{FInc} - FE = \tau \text{CumP}(IE) + \omega Y + \text{Const2} - FE \tag{4-11}$$

Based on the above formulas, we can discuss the functional expression of the "9-in-3 Competition Theory".

First, the level of regional economic development (DEV) can be represented by the degree of regional market economy development ($Y$):

$$\text{DEV} = Y = \varphi_1(Y_1, Y_0) \times CE + \varphi_2(Y_2, Y_0) \times \frac{IE}{\lambda} + \varphi_3(Y_3, Y_0) \times TE + \text{Const1} \quad (4\text{-}12)$$

Second, regional economic management efficiency (EME) mainly refers to the supporting of regional government's policy system, environmental system, and management system, which is determined by the proportion of consumption expenditure in government fiscal revenue. Thus, we can define EME as:

$$\text{EME} = \omega \varphi_1(Y_1, Y_0) \times \frac{CE}{\text{FInc}} \quad (4\text{-}13)$$

Third, regional economic policy measures (POL) mainly refer to region's infrastructure construction, talent and technology level, fiscal and financial support level, which are determined by the proportion of investment expenditure and transfer expenditure in government fiscal revenue. Thus, we can define POL as:

$$\text{POL} = \omega \varphi_2(Y_2, Y_0) \times \frac{\frac{IE}{\lambda}}{\text{FInc}} + \omega \varphi_3(Y_3, Y_0) \times \frac{TE}{\text{FInc}} \quad (4\text{-}14)$$

## II. Comprehensive Measurement and Objective Function

In summary, in the short-term development stage of a region, the efficiency of regional resource allocation mainly depends on the following five measurement indicators: fiscal expenditure elasticity (ELA) and fiscal surplus (*FS*) in the total dimension, and regional economic development level (DEV), regional economic management efficiency (EME), and regional economic policy measures (POL) in the structural dimension. Regional governments mainly improve fiscal revenue for the current year by increasing the annual fiscal expenditure level and optimizing its structure. The main control variables are government fiscal expenditure (*FE*) and consumption expenditure (*CE*), investment expenditure (*IE*), and transfer expenditure (*TE*), which satisfy the relationship in equation (4-1).

The derived questions are: how to construct a comprehensive measurement indicator, i.e., regional resource allocation efficiency (SYN), based on the above five major measurement indicators? How to maximize this comprehensive measurement indicator (SYN) by adjusting the four major control variables (*FE, CE, IE, TE*)?

在以上公式的基础上，我们就可以讨论"三类九要素竞争理论"的函数表达。

第一，区域经济发展水平（DEV）可以用区域市场经济发展程度（$Y$）来表示：

$$\text{DEV} = Y = \varphi_1(Y_1, Y_0) \times CE + \varphi_2(Y_2, Y_0) \times \frac{IE}{\lambda} + \varphi_3(Y_3, Y_0) \times TE + \text{Const1} \quad (4\text{-}12)$$

第二，区域经济管理效率（EME）主要是指区域政府的政策体系、环境体系和管理体系的配套，由消费性支出在政府财政收入中的比重所决定，于是，我们可以将 EME 定义为：

$$\text{EME} = \omega\varphi_1(Y_1, Y_0) \times \frac{CE}{\text{FInc}} \quad (4\text{-}13)$$

第三，区域经济政策措施（POL）主要是指区域的基础设施建设，人才、科技水平，财政、金融支撑水平，由投资性支出和转移性支出在政府财政收入中的比重所决定，于是，我们可以将 POL 定义为：

$$\text{POL} = \omega\varphi_2(Y_2, Y_0) \times \frac{\frac{IE}{\lambda}}{\text{FInc}} + \omega\varphi_3(Y_3, Y_0) \times \frac{TE}{\text{FInc}} \quad (4\text{-}14)$$

## 二、综合测度和目标函数

综上所述，在区域的短期发展阶段，区域资源配置效率主要依赖于以下五个测度指标：总量维度上的财政支出弹性（ELA）和财政盈余（*FS*），结构维度上的区域经济发展水平（DEV）、区域经济管理效率（EME）和区域经济政策措施（POL）。区域政府主要通过提高年度财政支出水平，优化其结构来提高当年的财政收入，调控变量主要是政府财政支出（*FE*）和消费性支出（*CE*）、投资性支出（*IE*）及转移性支出（*TE*），它们之间满足式（4-1）的关系。

由此引申出的问题是：如何基于上述五大测度指标构造综合测度指标，即区域资源配置效率（SYN）？如何通过调整四大调控变量（*FE*、*CE*、*IE*、*TE*），使这个综合测度指标（SYN）最大化？

To solve these problems, the key is to find appropriate weights and functional forms to comprehensively reflect information from different dimensions through an overall indicator. We notice that regional resource allocation efficiency is reflected in two dimensions——total dimension and structural dimension.

The indicators in the total dimension consider the input end of the policy, focusing on measuring whether the policy can efficiently and sustainably exert effects; while the indicators in the structural dimension consider the output end of the policy, focusing on measuring whether the policy can bring actual economic efficiency. The two do not overlap in information, so the comprehensive measurement indicator of regional resource allocation efficiency is the weighted sum of the two:

$$\text{SYN} = \omega_1 Q(\text{ELA}, FS) + \omega_2 G(\text{DEV}, \text{EME}, \text{POL}) \tag{4-15}$$

Here, weights $\omega_1 + \omega_2 = 1$, $Q(\cdot)$ represents the function of the total dimension, $G(\cdot)$ represents the function of the structural dimension.

In specific cases, if we need to simplify model assumptions, we can also consider that the comprehensive measurement indicator only depends on the structural dimension, not on the total dimension. At this time, $\omega_1 = 0$, $\omega_2 = 1$. It's worth noting that fiscal expenditure elasticity ELA is not determined by the four major control variables, but by the current economic environment. This means that regional governments more often take it as an exogenous condition for discretionary decision-making. For the convenience of later discussion, we can propose the following simplified assumption and use ELA as the benchmark for allocating $\omega_1$ and $\omega_2$:

$$\text{SYN} = \left(\frac{\text{ELA}}{\text{ELA} + \overline{\text{ELA}}}\right) \times FS + \left(\frac{\overline{\text{ELA}}}{\text{ELA} + \overline{\text{ELA}}}\right) G(\text{DEV}, \text{EME}, \text{POL}) \tag{4-16}$$

Here, $\overline{\text{ELA}}$ is the average of ELA in historical time intervals.

The meaning of equation (4-16) is that under a rational discretionary principle, when fiscal expenditure elasticity is higher than the historical average level, regional governments should appropriately increase fiscal expenditure; when fiscal expenditure elasticity is lower than the historical average level, regional governments should retain fiscal surplus to maintain the sustainability of fiscal expenditure and prevent economic overheating.

As mentioned earlier, DEV is the joint result of EME and POL, which essentially also constitute the relationship between total and structure. For further intuitive discussion, we assume they are in a parallel relationship, that is:

$$G(\text{DEV}, \text{EME}, \text{POL}) = \text{DEV} \times (\omega_3 \text{EME} + \omega_4 \text{POL}) \quad (4-17)$$

Here, $\omega_3$ and $\omega_4$ represent the preference of the comprehensive measurement indicator for regional economic management efficiency and regional economic policy measures, and $\omega_3 + \omega_4 = 1$, depending on the decision-maker's preference for specific fields.

要解决以上问题，关键在于找到适当的权重和函数形式，通过一个总体性指标综合反映不同维度上的信息。我们注意到，区域资源配置效率体现为两个维度——总量维度与结构维度。

总量维度的指标考量的是政策的输入端，侧重于测度政策能否高效且持续地发挥效应；而结构维度的指标考量的是政策的输出端，侧重于测度政策能否带来实际的经济效率。两者在信息上不交叠，因此综合测度指标区域资源配置效率是两者的加权和：

$$\text{SYN} = \omega_1 Q(\text{ELA}, FS) + \omega_2 G(\text{DEV}, \text{EME}, \text{POL}) \quad （4-15）$$

式中，权重 $\omega_1 + \omega_2 = 1$，$Q(\cdot)$ 表示总量维度的函数，$G(\cdot)$ 表示结构维度的函数。

在特定的情况下，若需要简化模型假设，我们也可以认为综合测度指标仅依赖于结构维度，而不依赖于总量维度，此时 $\omega_1 = 0$，$\omega_2 = 1$。值得注意的是，财政支出弹性 ELA 并不由四大调控变量所决定，而是由当下的经济环境所决定。这意味着，区域政府更多是将其作为一个外生条件来进行相机抉择。为了方便以后的讨论，我们可以提出如下简化假设，并将 ELA 作为配置 $\omega_1$、$\omega_2$ 的基准：

$$\text{SYN} = \left(\frac{\text{ELA}}{\text{ELA} + \overline{\text{ELA}}}\right) \times FS + \left(\frac{\overline{\text{ELA}}}{\text{ELA} + \overline{\text{ELA}}}\right) G(\text{DEV}, \text{EME}, \text{POL}) （4-16）$$

式中，$\overline{\text{ELA}}$ 是历史各时间区间内 ELA 的均值。

式（4-16）的含义是，在一个理性的相机抉择原则之下，当财政支出弹性高于历史平均水平时，区域政府应当适当提高财政支出；当财政支出弹性低于历史平均水平时，区域政府应当保留财政盈余，以维持财政支出的可持续性并防止经济过热。

如前所述，DEV 是 EME 和 POL 的共同结果，它们实质上也构成了总量与结构的关系。为了进一步直观地讨论，我们假设两者是并行关系，即：

$$G(\text{DEV}, \text{EME}, \text{POL}) = \text{DEV} \times (\omega_3 \text{EME} + \omega_4 \text{POL}) \quad （4-17）$$

式中，$\omega_3$ 和 $\omega_4$ 代表综合测度指标对于区域经济管理效率和区域经济政策措施的偏好，且 $\omega_3 + \omega_4 = 1$，它依决策者对于具体领域的偏好而定。

If the decision-maker takes fiscal expenditure efficiency as the sole principle, we can use variable coefficients $\varphi_i$ to assign weights to $\omega_3$ and $\omega_4$, that is:

$$\omega_3 = \frac{\varphi_1}{\varphi_1 + \varphi_2 + \varphi_3}, \quad \omega_4 = \frac{\varphi_2 + \varphi_3}{\varphi_1 + \varphi_2 + \varphi_3} \tag{4-18}$$

Substituting equation (4-18) into equation (4-17), we can obtain:

$$G(\text{DEV}, \text{EME}, \text{POL}) = \text{DEV} \times \left( \frac{\varphi_1}{\varphi_1 + \varphi_2 + \varphi_3} \text{EME} + \frac{\varphi_2 + \varphi_3}{\varphi_1 + \varphi_2 + \varphi_3} \text{POL} \right) \tag{4-19}$$

In summary, we can obtain the expression of the comprehensive measurement indicator of regional resource allocation efficiency (SYN).

$$\begin{aligned} \text{SYN} = & \left( \frac{\text{ELA}}{\text{ELA} + \overline{\text{ELA}}} \right) \times \text{FS} + \left( \frac{\overline{\text{ELA}}}{\text{ELA} + \overline{\text{ELA}}} \right) \text{DEV} \times \\ & \left( \frac{\varphi_1}{\varphi_1 + \varphi_2 + \varphi_3} \text{EME} + \frac{\varphi_2 + \varphi_3}{\varphi_1 + \varphi_2 + \varphi_3} \text{POL} \right) \end{aligned} \tag{4-20}$$

Under the condition of satisfying budget constraints, regional governments maximize this comprehensive measurement indicator by adjusting the proportion of three types of fiscal expenditure. We define the DRP model as follows:

$$\max_{\{CE, IE, TE\}} \left( \frac{\text{ELA}}{\text{ELA} + \overline{\text{ELA}}} \right) \times \text{FS} +$$

$$\left( \frac{\overline{\text{ELA}}}{\text{ELA} + \overline{\text{ELA}}} \right) \text{DEV} \times \left( \frac{\varphi_1}{\varphi_1 + \varphi_2 + \varphi_3} \text{EME} + \frac{\varphi_2 + \varphi_3}{\varphi_1 + \varphi_2 + \varphi_3} \text{POL} \right) \tag{4-21}$$

$$\text{s.t.} \begin{cases} CE + IE + TE = FE \\ FS > 0 \\ \varphi_1 + \varphi_2 + \varphi_3 \neq 0 \end{cases}$$

This DRP model shows that regional governments can find the fiscal expenditure structure that gives the region the most competitive advantage by adjusting the three categories of fiscal expenditure, thereby optimizing the efficiency of regional resource allocation at a specific development stage.

## III. Government Performance Evaluation System

In short-term regional government competition, as shown in the DRP model above, the goal of regional governments is to optimize the fiscal expenditure structure and achieve optimal regional resource allocation efficiency. From a long-term perspective, government performance is not simply evaluated by phased economic development goals, but also includes

如果决策者以财政支出效率为唯一原则，则我们可以利用可变系数 $\varphi_i$ 来赋予 $\omega_3$ 和 $\omega_4$ 权重，即：

$$\omega_3 = \frac{\varphi_1}{\varphi_1 + \varphi_2 + \varphi_3}, \quad \omega_4 = \frac{\varphi_2 + \varphi_3}{\varphi_1 + \varphi_2 + \varphi_3} \quad (4-18)$$

将式（4-18）代入式（4-17），可得出：

$$G(\text{DEV}, \text{EME}, \text{POL}) = \text{DEV} \times \left( \frac{\varphi_1}{\varphi_1 + \varphi_2 + \varphi_3} \text{EME} + \frac{\varphi_2 + \varphi_3}{\varphi_1 + \varphi_2 + \varphi_3} \text{POL} \right) \quad (4-19)$$

综上，我们可以得到综合测度指标区域资源配置效率（SYN）的表达式。

$$\text{SYN} = \left( \frac{\text{ELA}}{\text{ELA} + \overline{\text{ELA}}} \right) \times FS + \left( \frac{\overline{\text{ELA}}}{\text{ELA} + \overline{\text{ELA}}} \right) \text{DEV} \times \\ \left( \frac{\varphi_1}{\varphi_1 + \varphi_2 + \varphi_3} \text{EME} + \frac{\varphi_2 + \varphi_3}{\varphi_1 + \varphi_2 + \varphi_3} \text{POL} \right) \quad (4-20)$$

在满足预算约束的条件下，区域政府通过调整三种财政支出的比例，使此综合测度指标最大化。我们定义 DRP 模型如下：

$$\max_{\{CE, IE, TE\}} \left( \frac{\text{ELA}}{\text{ELA} + \overline{\text{ELA}}} \right) \times FS + \\ \left( \frac{\overline{\text{ELA}}}{\text{ELA} + \overline{\text{ELA}}} \right) \text{DEV} \times \left( \frac{\varphi_1}{\varphi_1 + \varphi_2 + \varphi_3} \text{EME} + \frac{\varphi_2 + \varphi_3}{\varphi_1 + \varphi_2 + \varphi_3} \text{POL} \right) \quad (4-21) \\ \text{s.t.} \begin{cases} CE + IE + TE = FE \\ FS > 0 \\ \varphi_1 + \varphi_2 + \varphi_3 \neq 0 \end{cases}$$

这一 DRP 模型表明，区域政府通过调整三大类财政支出，能够找到使区域最具竞争优势的财政支出结构，从而使处于特定发展阶段的区域资源配置效率达到最优。

### 三、政府绩效评估体系

在短期的区域政府竞争中，如上述 DRP 模型所示，区域政府的目标在于实现财政支出结构的优化以及最优的区域资源配置效率。而从长期看，政府的绩效并

multiple dimensions such as urban economic construction and development. A reasonable performance evaluation system will help comprehensively assess the overall performance of a region, thereby identifying the shortcomings and advantages of different regions in the process of promoting industrial development, urban construction, and social livelihood security.

Referring to the structure and content of the "9-in-3 Competition Theory", we can set the following indicators and weights to construct a regional government performance evaluation system, as shown in Table 4-1.

Table 4–1  Regional Government Performance Evaluation System

| Category | Factor | No. | Indicator | Positive/Negative | Weight | |
|---|---|---|---|---|---|---|
| Regional Economic Development Level | Projects | 1 | Number of National Key Science and Technology Projects | + | 7 | 17 |
| | | 2 | Number of Social Investment Projects | + | 6 | |
| | | 3 | Number of Foreign Cooperation Projects | + | 4 | |
| | Industrial Chains | 4 | Degree of Completeness of Regional Resource Advantageous Industries | + | 6 | 13 |
| | | 5 | Degree of Cluster Development | + | 4 | |
| | | 6 | Status of Introduction and Development of High-tech Industries | + | 3 | |
| | Import-export | 7 | Proportion of Foreign Capital in Local Enterprises | + | 4 | 12 |
| | | 8 | Year-on-Year Growth Rate of Total Import and Export Trade | + | 5 | |
| | | 9 | Structure of Foreign Enterprise Investments | + | 3 | |
| Regional Economic Policy Measures | Infrastructure Investment Policies | 10 | Degree of Urban Intelligence | + | 5 | 15 |
| | | 11 | Convenience of Public Transportation | + | 3 | |
| | | 12 | Perfection of Basic Education Facilities | + | 3 | |
| | | 13 | Development Level and Coverage of Medical Facilities | + | 4 | |
| | Talent and Technology Support Policies | 14 | Local Employment Rate of Higher Education Graduates (including the number of high-end talents introduced) | + | 5 | 10 |
| | | 15 | Patent Index | + | 3 | |
| | | 16 | Proportion of R&D Expenditure by Enterprises | + | 2 | |
| | Fiscal and Financial Support Policies | 17 | Growth Rate of Circulating Market Value of Local Listed Companies | + | 4 | 9 |
| | | 18 | Degree of Financing Subsidies and Preferential Treatments for Small and Medium-sized Enterprises | + | 3 | |
| | | 19 | Degree of Industrial Structure Perfection | + | 2 | |

不是简单地以阶段性的经济发展目标为考核标准，它还包括了城市经济建设和发展等多个维度。一个合理的绩效考评体系将有利于综合评估区域的整体表现，从而发现不同区域在推动产业发展、城市建设、社会民生保障的过程中存在的不足及优势。

参考"三类九要素竞争理论"的结构和内容，我们可以设定下列指标和权重，构建区域政府绩效评估考核体系，如表4-1所示。

表4-1 区域政府绩效评估考核体系

| 类别 | 要素 | 序号 | 指标 | 正/负 | 权重 | |
|---|---|---|---|---|---|---|
| 区域经济发展水平 | 项目 | 1 | 国家重大科技项目数 | 正 | 7 | 17 |
| | | 2 | 社会投资项目数 | 正 | 6 | |
| | | 3 | 外资合作项目数 | 正 | 4 | |
| | 产业链 | 4 | 区域资源优势产业健全程度 | 正 | 6 | 13 |
| | | 5 | 产业集群发展程度 | 正 | 4 | |
| | | 6 | 高科技产业引进及发展状况 | 正 | 3 | |
| | 进出口 | 7 | 外资在本地企业投入占比 | 正 | 4 | 12 |
| | | 8 | 进出口贸易总额同比增速 | 正 | 5 | |
| | | 9 | 外资企业投资结构 | 正 | 3 | |
| 区域经济政策措施 | 基础设施投资政策 | 10 | 城市智能化程度 | 正 | 5 | 15 |
| | | 11 | 公共交通便捷程度 | 正 | 3 | |
| | | 12 | 基础教育设施完善程度 | 正 | 3 | |
| | | 13 | 医疗设施发展水平及覆盖度 | 正 | 4 | |
| | 人才、科技扶持政策 | 14 | 高等教育毕业生本地就业率（含高端人才引进数量） | 正 | 5 | 10 |
| | | 15 | 专利指数 | 正 | 3 | |
| | | 16 | 企业研发经费投入占比 | 正 | 2 | |
| | 财政、金融支持政策 | 17 | 本地上市公司流通市值增速 | 正 | 4 | 9 |
| | | 18 | 中小微企业融资补贴优惠程度 | 正 | 3 | |
| | | 19 | 产业结构完善程度 | 正 | 2 | |

| Category | Factor | No. | Indicator | Positive/Negative | Weight | |
|---|---|---|---|---|---|---|
| Regional Economic Management Efficiency | The Efficiency of Policy System | 20 | Social Welfare Security System | + | 4 | 8 |
| | | 21 | Level of Legal Education Penetration | + | 2 | |
| | | 22 | Satisfaction of Urban and Rural Residents with Their Housing | + | 2 | |
| | The Efficiency of nvironmental System | 23 | Residents' Happiness Index | + | 4 | 9 |
| | | 24 | Environmental Protection Index | + | 2 | |
| | | 25 | Frequency of Resident Complaints | − | 3 | |
| | The Efficiency of Management System | 26 | Satisfaction with Administrative Services for Residents | + | 3 | 7 |
| | | 27 | Complexity of Government Office Procedures | − | 3 | |
| | | 28 | Social Evaluation of Emergency Response | + | 1 | |

In actual evaluation, not all data may be complete and without anomalies, so we adopt the following methods to process the data.

If the current year's data is missing, we use the indicator for that region from the previous year or the same indicator for all regions in the current year as a reference. If the previous year's indicator for that region exists, we use it as a substitute; if it doesn't exist, we use the median of the same indicator for all regions in the current year as a substitute.

If an indicator is obviously abnormal, to prevent the data from causing significant disturbance to the regional performance evaluation, we can use the following method: if the indicator value is less than the median of historical data and outside two standard deviations from the median, we replace it with the median minus two standard deviations; if the indicator value is greater than the median of historical data and outside two standard deviations from the median, we replace it with the median plus two standard deviations.

To better use this regional government performance evaluation system, we can adopt basic scoring, quality scoring, and adjustment scoring to evaluate indicators. The total basic score is 50, the total quality score is 30, and the total adjustment score is 20.

Due to different economic development stages and levels in different regions, the evaluation target standards set for different regions can also vary. This difference can be compensated by the region's basic score, that is, by setting grades for target completion, we can obtain corresponding basic scores ($B_i$).

续表

| 类别 | 要素 | 序号 | 指标 | 正/负 | 权重 | |
|---|---|---|---|---|---|---|
| 区域经济管理效率 | 政策体系效率 | 20 | 社会福利保障制度 | 正 | 4 | 8 |
| | | 21 | 法治教育普及程度 | 正 | 2 | |
| | | 22 | 城乡居民居住满意度 | 正 | 2 | |
| | 环境体系效率 | 23 | 居民生活幸福指数 | 正 | 4 | 9 |
| | | 24 | 绿色环保指数 | 正 | 2 | |
| | | 25 | 居民投诉频次 | 负 | 3 | |
| | 管理体系效率 | 26 | 居民公务办事满意度 | 正 | 3 | 7 |
| | | 27 | 政府办公繁复程度 | 负 | 3 | |
| | | 28 | 紧急事态应对的社会评价 | 正 | 1 | |

资料来源：陈云贤：《市场竞争双重主体论——兼谈中观经济学的创立与发展》，北京大学出版社，2020，第120页。

实际评估时，不一定所有数据都完整并且无异常值，因此我们采用如下方式对数据进行处理。

若当年数据缺失，则以上一年该区域的指标或当年所有区域的相同指标作为参考。若该区域上一年指标存在，则以上一年指标代替；若该区域上一年指标不存在，则以当年所有区域相同指标的中位数代替。

若指标明显异常，为防止数据对区域绩效考核产生较大的扰动，我们可采用如下方法处理：若指标值小于历史数据的中位数，且在中位数的两倍标准差之外，则以中位数减去两倍标准差代替；若指标值大于历史数据的中位数，且在中位数的两倍标准差之外，则以中位数加上两倍标准差代替。

为了更好地使用这一区域政府绩效评估考核体系，我们可以采用基础评分、质量评分、调整评分对指标进行评价。其中基础评分总分为50，质量评分总分为30，调整评分总分为20。

由于不同区域所处的经济发展阶段和经济发展水平不同，所以不同区域设定的评估目标标准也可以有所区别。这种区别可以用区域的基础评分进行弥补，即通过设置目标完成情况的等级，我们可以得到相应的基础评分（$B_i$）。

For example, for a certain indicator, we can set the following four grades: none of the set targets are completed, obtaining a basic score of 20; some set targets are completed, obtaining a basic score of 30; all set targets are completed, obtaining a basic score of 40; targets are exceeded, obtaining a basic score of 50.

To measure quality scores, we introduce both positive and negative indicators, which can be used to calculate relative quality scores.

Positive indicator:

$$Q_i = \frac{x_i - x_{min}}{x_{max} - x_{min}} \times 30 \tag{4-22}$$

Negative indicator:

$$Q_i = \frac{x_{max} - x_i}{x_{max} - x_{min}} \times 30 \tag{4-23}$$

Here, $Q_i$ represents the quality score of the $i$-th indicator, $x_i$ represents the value of the $i$-th indicator, $x_{max}$ represents the maximum value of this indicator among all comparable regions, and $x_{min}$ represents the minimum value.

From equations (4-22) and (4-23), we can see that quality scores mainly measure the comparative advantage of this region in competition with other regions. In equation (4-22), the more the $i$-th indicator value exceeds the minimum value and approaches the maximum value, the higher its positive indicator score. The best case is when the $i$-th indicator value equals the maximum value, then the positive indicator score reaches the highest 30 points. Conversely, the worse the region's comparative advantage, i.e., the further the $i$-th indicator value is from the maximum value, the higher the negative indicator score. The worst case is when the $i$-th indicator value equals the minimum value, then the negative indicator score reaches the highest 30 points.

To measure adjustment scores, we similarly introduce both positive and negative indicators.

Positive indicator:

$$L_i = 20 \times I_{\{S_i > S_{med}\}} \tag{4-24}$$

Negative indicator:

$$L_i = 20 \times I_{\{S_i < S_{med}\}} \tag{4-25}$$

Here, $L_i$ represents the adjustment score of the $i$-th indicator, $S_i$ represents the value of the $i$-th indicator, $S_{med}$ represents the median of historical values of this indicator for this region (including the current period, same below). In the positive indicator formula, $I_{\{S_i > S_{\text{med}}\}}$ is an indicator function, taking value 1 when the current period indicator value exceeds the median of historical values of this indicator for this region, otherwise 0; in the negative indicator

举个例子，对于某个指标，我们可以设置如下四个等级：一个既定目标都未完成，获得基础评分 20；完成部分既定目标，获得基础评分 30；完成所有既定目标，获得基础评分 40；超额完成目标，获得基础评分 50。

为了衡量质量评分，我们引入正负两个指标，正负指标皆可用来计算相对的质量评分。

正指标：

$$Q_i = \frac{x_i - x_{\min}}{x_{\max} - x_{\min}} \times 30 \quad (4\text{-}22)$$

负指标：

$$Q_i = \frac{x_{\max} - x_i}{x_{\max} - x_{\min}} \times 30 \quad (4\text{-}23)$$

式中，$Q_i$ 表示第 $i$ 个指标的质量评分，$x_i$ 表示第 $i$ 个指标值，$x_{\max}$ 表示在所有可对比的区域中该指标值的最大值，$x_{\min}$ 则表示在所有可对比的区域中该指标值的最小值。

由式（4-22）和式（4-23）可知，质量评分衡量的主要是该区域在与其他区域竞争中的比较优势。式（4-22）中，第 $i$ 个指标值超过最小值越多，越接近最大值，则其正指标得分越高。最好的情况是第 $i$ 个指标值等于最大值，则正指标得分达到最高的 30 分。反之，区域比较优势越差，即第 $i$ 个指标值离最大值越远，则负指标得分越高。最差的情况是第 $i$ 个指标值等于最小值，则负指标得分达到最高的 30 分。

为了衡量调整评分，我们同样引入正负两个指标。

正指标：

$$L_i = 20 \times I_{\{S_i > S_{\text{med}}\}} \quad (4\text{-}24)$$

负指标：

$$L_i = 20 \times I_{\{S_i < S_{\text{med}}\}} \quad (4\text{-}25)$$

式中，$L_i$ 表示第 $i$ 个指标的调整评分，$S_i$ 表示第 $i$ 个指标值，$S_{\text{med}}$ 表示该区域该指标历史数值的中位数（计算时包含了本期，下同）。在正指标公式中，$I_{\{S_i > S_{\text{med}}\}}$ 为示性函数，当本期指标值超越该区域该指标历史数值的中位数时，它取值为 1，否则为 0；在负指标公式中，$I_{\{S_i < S_{\text{med}}\}}$ 为示性函数，当本期指标值低于该区域该指标历史数值的中位数时，它取值为 1，否则为 0。

formula, $I_{\{S_i<S_{med}\}}$ is an indicator function, taking value 1 when the current period indicator value is below the median of historical values of this indicator for this region, otherwise 0.

From equations (4-24) and (4-25), we can see that adjustment scores mainly measure the relative advantage of this region's current performance compared to its historical performance. In the positive indicator system, when the current period indicator value exceeds the median of historical values of this indicator for this region, the region obtains an adjustment score of 20 on this indicator; when the current period indicator value is below the median of historical values of this indicator for this region, the region does not obtain an adjustment score, i.e., the adjustment score is 0. The negative indicator is the opposite, if the current performance is poor, below the historical values of this indicator for this region, then the adjustment score is 20, otherwise 0. According to specific needs, we can choose positive or negative indicators to calculate adjustment scores.

In summary, we can obtain the score for indicator $i$:

$$V_i = B_i + Q_i + L_i \tag{4-26}$$

Therefore, to evaluate a certain factor, its score can be calculated using equation (4-27):

$$\text{Factor}_k = \sum_{i=1}^{n} \left[ V_i \times \left( \frac{\omega_i}{\sum_{j=1}^{n} \omega_j} \right) \right] \tag{4-27}$$

Here, $\text{Factor}_k$ represents the total score of the $k$-th factor, this factor includes $n$ indicators; $\omega_i$ represents the weight of the $i$-th indicator in the $k$-th factor.

Based on factor scores, we can finally obtain the total performance evaluation score for this region:

$$\text{Score}_p = \sum_{k=1}^{l} \left[ \text{Factor}_k \times \left( \frac{\omega_k}{\sum_{j=1}^{l} \omega_j} \right) \right] \tag{4-28}$$

Here, $\text{Score}_p$ represents the total performance evaluation score of the $p$-th region, this region has $l$ factors, $\omega_k$ represents the weight of the $k$-th factor in the $p$-th region.

This regional government performance evaluation system is similar to the "9-in-3" competition structure. From this, we can see that the level of regional economic development (projects, industrial chains, and import-export) is still the main competitive advantage of regions at the current stage, which is also the main reason for its relatively high overall weight.

As the level of urban construction and urban economic development gradually improves, residents' living standards will also continuously improve. Although at this time, the level of

由式（4-24）和式（4-25）可知，调整评分衡量的主要是该区域本期与历史表现的相对优势。在正指标体系中，当本期指标值超越了该区域该指标历史数值的中位数时，在该指标上，该区域获得的调整评分为20；当本期指标值低于该区域该指标历史数值的中位数时，在该指标上，该区域不获得调整评分，即调整评分为0。负指标与之相反，如果本期表现较差，低于该区域该指标历史数值，则调整评分为20，反之为0。根据具体需要，我们可选择正指标或负指标来计算调整评分。

综上，我们可以得到指标$i$的评分：

$$V_i = B_i + Q_i + L_i \tag{4-26}$$

因此，要评估某一要素，其评分可以用式（4-27）计算：

$$\text{Factor}_k = \sum_{i=1}^{n}\left[V_i \times \left(\frac{\omega_i}{\sum_{j=1}^{n}\omega_j}\right)\right] \tag{4-27}$$

式中，$\text{Factor}_k$表示第$k$个要素的总评分，此要素包含了$n$个指标；$\omega_i$表示第$k$个要素中的第$i$个指标的权重。

基于要素的评分，我们可以最终获得该区域的总绩效评估得分：

$$\text{Score}_p = \sum_{k=1}^{l}\left[\text{Factor}_k \times \left(\frac{\omega_k}{\sum_{j=1}^{l}\omega_j}\right)\right] \tag{4-28}$$

式中，$\text{Score}_p$表示第$p$个区域的总绩效评估得分，此区域内有$l$个要素，$\omega_k$表示第$p$个区域中第$k$个要素的权重。

这一区域政府绩效评估考核体系与"三类九要素"竞争结构相似，从中可以看到，区域经济发展水平（项目、产业链和进出口）仍然是现阶段区域的主要竞争优势所在，这也是其整体权重相对较高的主要原因。

随着城市建设水平和城市经济发展水平逐步提高，居民生活水平也会不断提高。虽然此时区域经济发展水平仍然是区域竞争优势的重要因素，但其他组成部分，如区域经济政策措施和区域经济管理效率，将逐渐在城市建设和经济发展中发挥更大的

regional economic development is still an important factor in regional competitive advantage, other components, such as regional economic policy measures and regional economic management efficiency, will gradually play a greater role in urban construction and economic development. The latter two will not only improve residents' life satisfaction but also further feed back into regional economic development, producing more far-reaching effects.

It's worth noting that in this regional government performance evaluation system, the weight settings can be appropriately adjusted according to the differences in development stages of different regions and the differences in regional resource advantages and development focus. Especially for researchers, this evaluation system is more flexible.

Comparing the DRP model and the regional government performance evaluation system, we can see: in the DRP model, we focus on studying regional resource allocation efficiency from the perspective of optimizing the phased fiscal expenditure structure of regional governments; while in the regional government performance evaluation system, we focus on studying from the perspective of regional governments promoting industrial development, urban construction, and social livelihood security, and construct a factor evaluation system starting from the most original indicators, progressing layer by layer, and finally concentrating on the evaluation of regional economic development level, regional economic policy measures, and regional economic management efficiency, forming an evaluation system centered on the "9-in-3" competition.

The DRP model and the regional government performance evaluation system complement each other, forming discussions on regional government competition and regional economic development from different angles, helping economic researchers recognize and understand regional government competition theory and the stages of regional economic development from different levels and perspectives.

作用。后两者不仅将提高居民的生活满意度，同时也将进一步反哺区域经济发展，产生更加深远的影响。

值得注意的是，在这一区域政府绩效评估考核体系中，根据不同区域所处发展阶段的差异以及区域资源优势、发展侧重点的差异，可以适当调整权重的设置。尤其对研究者而言，这一考核体系的灵活性更强。

对比 DRP 模型和区域政府绩效评估考核体系，我们可以看到：在 DRP 模型中，我们侧重从区域政府阶段性的财政支出结构优化出发，去研究区域资源配置效率；而在区域政府绩效评估考核体系中，我们侧重从区域政府推动产业发展、城市建设、社会民生保障的角度去进行研究，并从最原始的指标出发，构建要素评估体系，层层递进后，最终集中于对区域经济发展水平、区域经济政策措施、区域经济管理效率三方面的评估考核上，形成以"三类九要素"竞争为核心的评估体系。

DRP 模型与区域政府绩效评估考核体系两者相辅相成，形成对区域政府竞争和区域经济发展的不同角度的探讨，有助于经济学研究者从不同的层面和视角认识、理解区域政府竞争理论和区域经济发展的阶段性。

Chapter 5
# Four Stages Competitive Dynamic Characteristics of Regional Economic Growth

## Section 1: Growth Stage Dominated by Industrial Economic Competition and Cooperation

The growth stage dominated by industrial economic competition and cooperation refers to the development stage that mainly relies on factors and industrial economic competition and cooperation to drive economic growth. For regional governments, industrial economic competition and cooperation are mainly manifested in the competition and cooperation of regional industrial chain supporting, industrial cluster development degree, and regional industrial policies. The growth stage dominated by industrial economic competition and cooperation is the initial stage of regional economic growth, where factor-driven dominates, and this stage is mainly competition-oriented.

### I. Competition for Primary Resources

The essence of industrial economic competition is the competition for regional production factor allocation, which is a kind of allocation and competition for primary resources by regional governments. At this stage, primary resources mainly include land, labor, and capital. At this time, almost all enterprises or industries depend on the basic production factors of their region, and their competitive advantage is mainly reflected in whether they can supply products at lower prices.

第五章

# 区域经济增长四阶段竞争动态特征

## 第一节 由产业经济竞争与合作主导的增长阶段

由产业经济竞争与合作主导的增长阶段,是指主要依靠要素和产业经济竞争与合作驱动经济增长的发展阶段。对于区域政府来说,产业经济竞争与合作主要表现为区域产业链配套、产业集群发展程度和区域产业政策的竞争与合作。由产业经济竞争与合作主导的增长阶段是区域经济增长的初始阶段,要素驱动占据主导地位,此阶段以竞争导向为主。

### 一、对原生性资源的竞争

产业经济竞争的实质是区域生产要素配置的竞争,是区域政府对原生性资源的一种调配与争夺。在这一阶段,原生性资源主要包括土地、劳动力和资本等,此时,几乎所有企业或产业都依赖于本区域的基本生产要素,其竞争优势主要体现于能否以更低的价格供给产品。因此,在这一阶段,一个区域的经济增长就取决于该区域能否在原生性资源的获取上取得竞争优势,也即能否以更

Therefore, at this stage, a region's economic growth depends on whether the region can gain a competitive advantage in obtaining primary resources, that is, whether it can obtain these resources at lower costs. The products of enterprises in this region at this stage have not yet developed well in terms of technological content, functional varieties, and differentiation.

Among the main production factors needed for industrial economic competition at this stage, labor is relatively easy to obtain, while the production technology of enterprises in this region mainly depends on introduction from outside the region, or imitation of technology from foreign investors in the region. In other words, the higher product design level and technological level possessed by enterprises in this region are mostly provided by integrated operation factories built by foreign investors who choose this region as a production site, or learned by local manufacturing enterprises through semi-finished product processing. Therefore, the key primary resources needed for industrial economic competition at this stage are land and capital. As a result, the competition of regional governments is reflected in how to provide sufficient land and capital for industrial development, and of course, infrastructure such as roads, water, electricity, and communication is also very necessary.

In the initial stage of regional economic development, economic growth mainly relies on competition in the industrial economic field. The main competitive subjects in this field are enterprises, and almost all successful enterprises depend on the basic production factors of their region, such as labor, land, and capital. At this stage, enterprises in the region mainly have the following characteristics.

First, they compete entirely on price, can provide few products, and apply low levels of technology.

Second, they cannot create technology on their own and must rely on foreign enterprises to provide experience and technology.

Third, they rarely have direct contact with the final consumers of products, and most domestic and foreign market trade opportunities are in the hands of foreign agents.

Therefore, at this stage, regional governments should take effective measures to vigorously attract investment, carry out project competition, improve industrial chain supporting, form industrial clusters, encourage import and export trade, give play to the advantages of production factors, drive resource allocation, and continuously promote regional economic growth.

## II. Regional Industrial Policy Matching in the Growth Stage Dominated by Industrial Economic Competition and Cooperation

Regarding industrial policy issues, there is still widespread debate in academia, mainly

低的成本取得这些资源。而处于此阶段的本区域企业,其产品的技术含量、功能种类和差异化等尚未得到很好的发展。

在此阶段产业经济竞争所需的主要生产要素中,劳动力相对容易获取,本区域企业的生产技术则主要依赖区域外引进,或者是对在本区域投资的外商的技术进行模仿。也就是说,本区域企业拥有的较高的产品设计水平和技术水平,大多数或是由选择该区域作为生产网点的外商投资兴建的一体化作业工厂提供的,或是由本区域制造企业以半成品加工方式学习而来的。所以,此阶段产业经济竞争所需要的关键原生性资源是土地和资本。因此,区域政府的竞争就体现在怎样为产业发展提供充足的土地和资本,当然,公路、水、电、通信等基础设施也是非常必要的。

在区域经济发展的初始阶段,经济增长主要依靠产业经济领域的竞争带动,这一领域的主要竞争主体是企业,而几乎所有成功的企业都依赖于本区域的基本生产要素,如劳动力、土地、资本等。这一阶段,区域内的企业主要有如下特征。

一是完全以价格进行竞争,能够提供的产品不多,应用的技术层次也不高。

二是自身无法创造技术,必须依靠外来企业提供经验与技术。

三是很少能与产品的最终消费者进行直接接触,国内外市场的贸易机会大多掌握在外来代理商手中。

因此,在这一阶段,区域政府应该采取有效措施,大力招商引资,开展项目竞争,完善产业链配套,形成产业集群,鼓励进出口贸易,发挥生产要素优势,驱动资源配置,不断推动区域经济增长。

## 二、由产业经济竞争与合作主导的增长阶段的区域产业政策匹配

对于产业政策问题,学界尚存在广泛争论,争论主要集中于以下三点:一是

focusing on the following three points: first, whether industrial policies are needed; second, what kind of industrial policies are needed; third, what is the basic theory that can support industrial policies.

The viewpoints of mezzoeconomics on this are as follows.

First, the theoretical framework supporting industrial policies comes from the realistic demand for economic growth dominated by industrial economic competition and cooperation.

Second, realistic development requires regional governments to use industrial policies at three levels to overcome market failures. One is to overcome the defective failure of market mechanisms through planning and guidance; two is to overcome the blank failure of market mechanisms through support and regulation; three is to overcome the obstructive failure of market mechanisms through supervision and management.

Third, industrial policies do not only include industrial subsidies, and regional governments must abandon interventions that deviate from market rules. Industrial policies should be based on letting the market determine industrial resource allocation and better playing the role of government planning and guidance, support and regulation, and supervision and management. In the growth stage dominated by industrial economic competition and cooperation, regional government's fiscal expenditure will focus on fiscal transfer payment projects, and the role of regional governments will mainly be reflected in the competition of the first three elements in the "9-in-3 Competition Theory".

## III. Three Processes in the Growth Stage Dominated by Industrial Economic Competition and Cooperation

The growth stage dominated by industrial economic competition and cooperation is essentially the factor-driven stage of regional economic growth. The economic development during this period will generally go through three processes.

The first process is the development stage where regional economy depends on local resources. Initially, most economically developed regions were those with vast territories, rich natural resources, and abundant labor. The start of regional economic development and the short-term rise of industries all depend on the large-scale input of production factors and their extensive expansion.

However, from a long-term perspective, this factor-driven growth relying solely on local resources is unsustainable and is only a primary short-term expansion means. Therefore, the development mode relying on resources within the region will eventually turn to a

要不要产业政策；二是需要什么样的产业政策；三是能够支持产业政策的基础理论是什么。

中观经济学对此的观点如下所示。

第一，支持产业政策的理论框架来源于现实存在的由产业经济竞争与合作主导的经济增长的需求。

第二，现实的发展需要区域政府运用三个层面的产业政策来克服市场失灵。一是通过规划与引导，克服市场机制缺陷性失灵；二是通过扶持与调节，克服市场机制空白性失灵；三是通过监督与管理，克服市场机制障碍性失灵。

第三，产业政策不只包括产业补贴，区域政府必须摒弃脱离市场规则的干预行为。产业政策应该建立在让市场决定产业资源配置和更好地发挥政府规划引导、扶持调节和监督管理作用的基础上。在由产业经济竞争与合作主导的增长阶段，区域政府的财政支出将侧重在财政转移支付的项目上，区域政府的作用将主要体现在"三类九要素竞争理论"中第一类的三个要素的竞争上。

## 三、由产业经济竞争与合作主导的增长阶段的三个过程

由产业经济竞争与合作主导的增长阶段，本质上又是区域经济增长的要素驱动阶段。这一时期的经济发展大致会经历三个过程。

第一个过程是区域经济依赖本地资源的发展阶段。最初的经济发达区域多半都是地大物博、自然资源和劳动力丰富的区域。区域经济发展的起步和产业的短期崛起都依赖于生产要素的大量投入和对其规模的粗放式扩大。

但从长期来看，这种仅依靠本地资源的要素驱动式增长后继乏力，只是一种初级的短期扩张手段。因此，依赖区域内资源的发展模式终究会转向从区域外争夺资源的发展模式，这就是第二个过程，即区域全力开展招商引资、招才引智的

development mode of competing for resources from outside the region, which is the second process, namely the development stage where the region fully carries out investment attraction and talent introduction. At this time, the industrial development of the region depends not only on the competition for projects, improving industrial chain supporting, forming industrial clusters, expanding import and export trade, occupying domestic and foreign markets, but also more on the competition for scientific and technological talents and environmental supporting. At this stage, industrial parks, science and technology parks, industrial incubation parks, etc., emerge successively. These competitions will quickly push regional economic development into the next process.

In the third process, regional governments need to carry out competition in policy supporting and environmental optimization, which has an important impact on the effectiveness of investment attraction and talent introduction. Therefore, various regions need to compete in project policies, land policies, industrial subsidy policies, talent support policies, science and technology investment policies, guarantee interest subsidy policies, and even related policies for children's education and parents' medical care, to enhance the region's competitiveness for primary resources and promote sustainable regional economic growth.

As these three processes progress gradually, the importance of regional cooperation also becomes increasingly apparent. Late-developing regions can actively undertake industrial transfer from early-developing regions, and adjacent regions need to strengthen the coordination of industrial development to better realize the extension, completion, and strengthening of industrial chains in cross-regions spaces. In addition, how to avoid industrial homogenization between regions and reduce unnecessary vicious competition is also an important issue that needs coordination among regional governments. Therefore, as regional economy progressively unfolds in the growth stage dominated by industrial economic competition and cooperation, the level of competition continuously increases, and the importance of cooperation becomes increasingly evident.

# Section 2: Growth Stage Dominated by Urban Economic Competition and Cooperation

The growth stage dominated by urban economic competition and cooperation refers to the development stage that mainly relies on investment and urban economic competition

发展阶段。此时区域的产业发展就不仅依赖于争夺项目、完善产业链配套、形成产业集群、扩大进出口贸易、占领国内外市场等竞争，更依赖于科技人才和环境配套的竞争。在此过程，工业园区、科技园区、产业孵化园区等陆续涌现。这些竞争将很快推动区域经济发展进入下一个过程。

在第三个过程，区域政府要展开政策配套和环境优化的竞争，这对招商引资、招才引智的成效具有重要影响。因此，各区域需要在项目政策、土地政策、产业补贴政策、人才支撑政策、科技投资政策、担保贴息政策，甚至相关的子女就学、父母就医政策等方面展开竞争，以提升本区域对原生性资源的竞争能力，推动区域经济持续增长。

随着这三个过程的逐级推进，区域合作的重要性也不断显现。后发区域可以积极承接先发区域的产业转移，相邻区域之间需要加强产业发展的协同性，使产业链在跨区域空间里更好地实现延长、补齐和强化。另外，如何避免区域之间的产业同质化，减少不必要的恶性竞争也是区域政府之间需要协调的重要问题。因此，随着区域经济在由产业经济竞争与合作主导的增长阶段的递进式展开，竞争的层次不断提升，合作的重要性不断展现。

# 第二节 由城市经济竞争与合作主导的增长阶段

由城市经济竞争与合作主导的增长阶段，是指主要依靠投资和城市经济竞争与合作驱动经济增长的发展阶段。对于区域政府来说，城市经济竞争与合作主要

and cooperation to drive economic growth. For regional governments, urban economic competition and cooperation are mainly manifested in the development and construction of urban infrastructure hardware and software and even smart cities, as well as the competition and cooperation of supporting policies and measures. Urban economic competition and cooperation mainly occur in the second stage of regional economic growth, that is, when the investment-driven stage dominates. After entering this growth stage, regional development has broken through the limitations of economic growth driven by production factors and moved towards the process of investment-driven economic growth. At this time, regional governments have also shifted from focusing on competition for primary resources in the first stage to the development and competition for secondary resources. Similar to the first stage, this growth stage is still mainly competition-oriented, but the importance of cooperation is also continuously strengthened in the progressive development of this stage.

## I. The Process of Investment-driven Economic Growth Is the Development and Competition for Secondary Resources by Regional Governments

First, it needs to be pointed out that the investment-driven concept referred to in mezzoeconomics is investment in urban infrastructure, not fixed asset investment in a broad sense. Urban infrastructure includes: urban hardware infrastructure, namely six major engineering infrastructures such as urban energy supply systems, water supply and drainage systems, transportation systems, postal and telecommunications systems, environmental protection and sanitation systems, and defense and disaster prevention safety systems; urban software infrastructure, namely social infrastructures such as administrative management, culture and education, medical and health care, commercial services, finance and insurance, and social welfare; with the development of urban-rural integration, urban infrastructure also includes four major categories of infrastructure for rural production, living, ecological environment construction, and social development; along with the process of urban modernization, the development and construction of smart city projects have also become new content of urban infrastructure construction.

In fact, some countries falling into the low-level, low-standard "comparative advantage trap" is largely because regional governments have not been able to timely and effectively improve the supply level of urban hardware and software infrastructure, relying only on low-cost labor to participate in international industrial division, thus causing regional economic development to stagnate. Therefore, regional governments implementing a proactive foresighted leading strategy in the later stage of the industrial economy-dominated stage, that is, increasing efforts to improve urban infrastructure hardware and software and develop

表现为城市基础设施软硬件乃至智能城市开发建设，以及与之配套的政策措施的竞争与合作。城市经济竞争与合作主要是在区域经济增长的第二阶段，即投资驱动阶段占据主导地位。进入这一增长阶段后，区域发展已经突破了由生产要素驱动经济增长的局限，迈向由投资驱动经济增长的过程，此时，区域政府也从第一阶段中着重于对原生性资源的竞争转向对次生性资源的开发与争夺。与第一阶段相似的是，这一增长阶段仍以竞争导向为主，但合作的重要性也在此阶段的递进式发展中不断得到加强。

## 一、投资驱动经济增长的过程是区域政府对次生性资源的开发与争夺

首先需要指出的是，中观经济学所指的投资驱动，是城市基础设施的投资，而非广义上的固定资产投资。城市基础设施包括：城市硬件基础设施，即城市能源供应系统、供水排水系统、交通运输系统、邮电通信系统、环保环卫系统和防卫防灾安全系统等六大工程性基础设施；城市软件基础设施，即行政管理、文化教育、医疗卫生、商业服务、金融保险和社会福利等社会性基础设施；随着城乡一体化的发展，城市基础设施还包括乡村生产、生活、生态环境建设和社会发展四大类基础设施；伴随着城市现代化的进程，开发和建设智能城市系列工程也成为城市基础设施建设的新内容。

实际上，一些国家陷入低层次、低水平的"比较优势陷阱"，很大程度上就是因为区域政府没有能够适时有效地提升城市软硬件基础设施供应水平，仅依赖于低成本的劳动力参与国际产业分工，从而使区域经济发展停滞不前。因此，区域政府在产业经济主导阶段的后期实施有为的超前引领战略，即加大对城

smart cities, can both improve the regional economic investment environment and promote the region to break through the bottleneck of economic growth driven by production factors, turning towards investment-driven growth, and thus entering the growth stage dominated by urban economic competition and cooperation.

## II. Regional Governments Supporting Policies in the Growth Stage Dominated by Urban Economic Competition and Cooperation

In the growth stage dominated by urban economic competition and cooperation, regional governments play three roles: planning and layout, participation in construction, and orderly management.

Firstly, the planning and layout of urban economy involves three levels of regional resource allocation: the first level is the conceptual planning of regional economic development, which embodies the definition of the main economic and social functions of a region, with the goal of realizing innovative development, coordinated development, green development, open development and shared development towards a direction suitable for living, working, and touring; the second level is the urban-rural planning of regional economic development, which focuses on the layout, development, investment and construction of urban-rural integrated infrastructure hardware and software, which will directly affect the competitiveness of urban economy; the third level is the land planning of regional economic development, where regional governments should strictly distinguish different investment projects according to land use nature, formulate strict access systems, and construct a scientific and reasonable urban resource allocation pattern. The trinity of conceptual planning, urban-rural planning and land planning defines the policy scope of urban economic competition. Regional governments formulate detailed rules and play a role in urban economic strategic planning, implementation standards, project evaluation, market access, rule of law guarantee, etc., to promote urban economic development.

Secondly, in order to gain benefits from urban infrastructure investment and construction, regional governments will both reform the equity of existing stock assets and optimize the equity structure of incremental assets to comply with market competition rules. They will also use various financing methods through the capital market, as well as means such as charging rights and pricing rights, to implement capital operations of franchise rights through methods such as Design-Build-Operate (DBO), Build-Operate-Transfer (BOT), Build-Own-Operate (BOO), Build-Own-Operate-Transfer (BOOT), Build-Lease-Transfer (BLT), Build-Transfer-Operate (BTO), Transfer-Operate-Transfer (TOT), etc. Regional governments can

市基础设施软硬件的完善以及智能城市的开发力度,既能改善区域经济投资环境,又能促进区域突破以生产要素驱动经济增长的瓶颈,转向以投资驱动,从而进入由城市经济竞争与合作主导的增长阶段。

## 二、由城市经济竞争与合作主导的增长阶段的区域政府配套政策

在由城市经济竞争与合作主导的增长阶段,区域政府发挥着规划布局、参与建设、有序管理三重作用。

首先,城市经济的规划布局,涉及区域资源配置的三个层次:第一层次是区域经济发展的概念规划,它体现了一个区域的主要经济和社会功能的界定,其目标是使区域朝着宜居、宜业、宜游的方向,实现创新发展、协调发展、绿色发展、开放发展和共享发展;第二层次是区域经济发展的城乡规划,它侧重于对城乡一体化基础设施软硬件的布局、开发、投资与建设,这将直接影响城市经济的竞争力;第三层次是区域经济发展的土地规划,区域政府应严格按照用地性质,区分不同的投资项目,制定严格的准入制度,构建科学合理的城市资源配置格局。概念规划、城乡规划和土地规划三位一体,划定了城市经济竞争的政策范围,区域政府在城市经济的战略规划、实施标准、项目评估、市场准入、法治保障等方面制定细则,发挥作用,促进城市经济发展。

其次,区域政府为了在城市基础设施投资建设中获得收益,既会对原有的存量资产进行股权改造,又会对增量资产进行股权结构优化,使其符合市场竞争规则。同时,区域政府也会通过资本市场的各种融资方式,以及收费权、定价权等手段,运用设计—建设—经营(DBO)、建设—经营—移交(BOT)、建设—拥有—经营(BOO)、建设—拥有—经营—移交(BOOT)、建设—租赁—移交(BLT)、建设—移交—经营(BTO)、移交—经营—移交(TOT)等方式实施

also adopt different capital operation methods or cross-apply different capital operation methods according to the different characteristics and conditions of urban infrastructure projects, to further strengthen and expand urban infrastructure projects, thus enabling regional governments to overcome the constraints of capital bottlenecks, enhance the ability to invest, develop, operate and manage urban infrastructure, make it develop scientifically and sustainably, use limited regional finances to "leverage a thousand pounds with four ounces", and more effectively meet the growing demands of regional social public for public goods and public welfare undertakings. In the investment-driven stage, the intensity of regional government participation in urban economy, the scale and structure of fiscal investment expenditure and consumption expenditure, the degree of market openness and related policy measures will directly affect the regional economic growth situation.

Finally, orderly management is the guarantee for the efficient implementation of urban infrastructure construction. Just as there are different types of market failures, there are also three different types of government failures in countries or regions: the first type is "livelihood economy insufficient" government failure; the second type is "industrial policy missing" government failure; the third type is "urban construction blank" government failure. Among them, the third type of government failure is mainly manifested in the following aspects: first, policy measures to promote urban infrastructure construction are almost blank; second, the government neither participates as a competitive subject in urban construction nor plays the role of planning, supervising and regulating urban construction; third, the government participates in urban construction but does not follow market rules in the process of participation. These problems hinder the sustainable growth of regional economy in the investment-driven stage from another perspective. Only by strengthening orderly management can regional governments ensure the efficient implementation and upgrading of urban infrastructure construction.

## III. Dynamic Evolution of the Growth Stage Dominated by Urban Economic Competition and Cooperation

For regional governments, urban economic competition is primarily manifested in the competition for urban infrastructure investment, development, and construction, that is, the development and competition for secondary resources. In the early growth stage dominated by industrial economic competition and cooperation, workers' income levels are still relatively low, and consumption demand naturally focuses on basic goods such as food, clothing, housing, and transportation needed for survival. However, as economic development enters

特许经营权的资本运营。区域政府还可以根据城市基础设施项目的不同特点和条件，采取不同的资本运营方式，或交叉运用不同的资本运营方式，进一步把城市基础设施项目做强做大，从而使区域政府克服资金瓶颈的制约，提升城市基础设施投资、开发、运营、管理的能力，使其科学、可持续地发展，用有限的区域财政"四两拨千斤"，更加有效地满足区域社会民众日益增长的对公共物品和公益事业的需求。在投资驱动阶段，区域政府参与城市经济力度的大小，财政投资性支出和消费性支出的规模与结构，市场开放的程度及相关政策措施，都将直接影响区域的经济增长状况。

最后，有序管理是城市基础设施建设得以高效实施的保障。正如存在不同类型的市场失灵一样，国家或区域也存在三种不同类型的政府失灵：第一种是"民生经济不足型"政府失灵；第二种是"产业政策缺失型"政府失灵；第三种是"城市建设空白型"政府失灵。其中，第三种政府失灵集中表现在以下几个方面：一是推动城市基础设施建设的政策措施几乎空白；二是政府既没有作为城市建设的竞争主体参与其中，又没有发挥规划、监管、调节城市建设的作用；三是政府参与城市建设，但在参与过程中没有遵循市场规则。这些问题从另一个角度阻碍着区域经济在投资驱动阶段的可持续增长，区域政府只有加强有序管理，才能保障城市基础设施建设的高效实施、提档升级。

## 三、由城市经济竞争与合作主导的增长阶段的动态演进

对于区域政府来说，城市经济竞争首先表现为对城市基础设施投资、开发、建设的竞争，也即对次生性资源的开发与争夺。在由产业经济竞争与合作主导的增长阶段的早期，劳动者收入水平还比较低，消费需求自然集中在满足生存所需的衣食住行等基本商品上。但随着经济发展进入由产业经济竞争与合作主导的增长阶段的后期，随着工业化进程的推进，劳动者收入普遍提高，消费需求也随之

the later growth stage dominated by industrial economic competition and cooperation, with the advancement of industrialization, workers' incomes generally increase, and consumption demand upgrades accordingly. In particular, the demand for hardware and software urban infrastructure with higher demand elasticity will rapidly increase, including livable environments, convenient travel conditions, high-level educational facilities and medical facilities, advanced cultural and sports venues and other hardware infrastructure, as well as fair and just legal environments, well-functioning urban management systems and other software infrastructure.

At this stage, regional economic growth mainly relies on competition in the urban economic field, where the main competitive subjects are regional governments. They play three roles: planning and layout, participation in construction, and orderly management. That is, they not only need to do well in planning and layout but also follow market rules and play a role in macro guidance, effective regulation, and supervision management in investment, development, operation, and management in this field, achieving the trinity effect of government promotion, enterprise participation, and market operation through policy support. In this way, regional economic development enters the growth stage dominated by urban economic competition and cooperation.

In the growth stage dominated by urban economic competition and cooperation, low cost is still an important feature of the regional industrial economy. The economies of scale brought by the government's investment attraction "clustering" effect and the continuously improving industrial chain, under the guarantee of continuously improving urban hardware and software infrastructure, can still continuously enhance the competitive advantage of regional industries. However, at the same time, with the increase in costs of factors such as labor and land, the industrial economy also faces increasing competitive pressure. In addition, with the increase in regional income levels, there is also a demand for a wider variety of products and services. Providing these new products and services often requires new technologies and talents with professional skills. Therefore, it is crucial for regional governments to implement further foresighted leading strategies for the regional economy to smoothly enter the next stage of development.

# Section 3: Growth Stage Dominated by Innovative Economic Competition and Cooperation

The growth stage dominated by innovative economic competition and cooperation refers

升级，尤其是对那些需求弹性更高的软硬件城市基础设施的需求就会迅速增加，包括宜居的环境、便利的出行条件、高水平的教育配套和医疗设施、先进的文化和体育场馆等硬件基础设施，以及公平公正的法治环境、运转良好的城市管理体系等软件基础设施。

在此阶段，区域经济增长主要依靠城市经济领域的竞争带动，这一领域的主要竞争主体是区域政府，其发挥着规划布局、参与建设、有序管理的三重作用，即不但要做好规划布局，而且要遵循市场规则，还要在该领域的投资、开发、运营和管理中，发挥宏观引导、有效调节和监督管理的作用，通过政策配套，达到政府推动、企业参与、市场运作三位一体的效果。这样，区域经济发展就进入了由城市经济竞争与合作主导的增长阶段。

在由城市经济竞争与合作主导的增长阶段，低成本仍是区域产业经济的重要特征，政府招商引资"聚点"效应带来的规模经济和不断完善的产业链，在不断完善的城市软硬件基础设施的保障下，仍能够持续地提升本区域产业的竞争优势。但与此同时，随着劳动力、土地等要素成本的提高，产业经济也面临越来越大的竞争压力。另外，随着本区域收入水平的提高，区域内产生了对更多种类产品和服务的需求，提供这些新的产品和服务往往需要新的技术和掌握专业技术的人才，因此，对于本区域经济能否顺利地进入下一个发展阶段来说，区域政府能否实施进一步的超前引领至关重要。

## 第三节　由创新经济竞争与合作主导的增长阶段

由创新经济竞争与合作主导的增长阶段，是指主要依靠科技进步和创新经济

to the development stage that mainly relies on scientific and technological progress, as well as innovative economic competition and cooperation to drive economic growth. In the growth stage dominated by urban economic competition and cooperation, regions can reach middle-income levels. However, at this time, the industrial economy will encounter great resistance in continuing to break through to both ends of the value chain. Breaking through upwards will encounter technological blockades from developed countries, while breaking through downwards will also face suppression from global high-end brands. At this time, from the perspective of maximizing interests, industries themselves will avoid risks and be content with the status quo, which is also an important reason why many countries fall into the "middle-income trap". At this point, whether regional governments can play a foresighted leading role again is key to whether the regional economy can enter the growth stage dominated by innovative economic competition and cooperation. For regional governments, innovative economic competition and cooperation are mainly manifested in the competition of policy measures to promote concept innovation, technological innovation, organizational innovation, and institutional innovation. Similar to the previous two stages, competition still dominates at this stage, while the importance of cooperation is continuously reflected in the advancement of economic development stages.

## I. Concept Innovation of Regional Governments

Among the four types of innovation, regional government concept innovation is the focus of regional competition. As mentioned earlier, when regional economic development is in the factor-driven stage and investment-driven stage, economic growth mainly relies on competing for resources and costs, which can easily lead to problems such as excessive exploitation causing depletion of industrial and urban resources, low production efficiency, technological backwardness, talent loss, and intensification of social contradictions, necessitating rapid transformation. At this time, the development ideas, directions, and methods for the next stage of regional development are crucial, requiring advanced concepts to lead. Regional government concept innovation includes not only the overall grasp and regulation of regional resources, the positioning of future regional development strategies and comprehensive planning of development mode, but also solving problems such as development methods and development drivers in top-level design. After the factor-driven stage and investment-driven stage, regional governments should use concepts such as innovative development, coordinated development, green development, open development, and shared development to foresighted leading and promote sustainable regional economic development.

竞争与合作驱动经济增长的发展阶段。在由城市经济竞争与合作主导的增长阶段，区域已能够达到中等收入水平。但此时，产业经济继续向价值链两端突破会遇到极大阻力，向上突破会遇到发达国家的技术封锁，向下突破也会遇到全球高端品牌的打压。此时，从利益最大化的角度出发，产业自身就会规避风险、安于现状，这也是很多国家陷入"中等收入陷阱"的重要原因。此时，区域政府能否再次发挥超前引领作用是区域经济能否进入由创新经济竞争与合作主导的增长阶段的关键。对区域政府来说，创新经济竞争与合作主要表现为区域政府促进理念创新、技术创新、组织创新以及制度创新的政策措施的竞争。与前两个阶段相似的是，在这一阶段，竞争仍占据主导地位，而合作的重要性则是在经济发展阶段的推进中不断体现的。

## 一、区域政府理念创新

在四类创新中，区域政府理念创新是区域竞争的焦点。如前所述，在区域经济发展处于要素驱动阶段和投资驱动阶段时，经济增长以拼资源、拼成本为主，容易产生过分掠夺致使产业资源和城市资源枯竭、生产效率低下、技术滞后、人才流失、社会矛盾激化等问题，必须尽快转型。这时，区域下一阶段的发展思路、方向和方式就至关重要，需要先进理念来引领。区域政府的理念创新既包括对区域资源的整体把握和调控，对区域未来发展战略的定位和发展模式的全面规划，也包括在顶层设计上解决好发展方式和发展动力等问题。在要素驱动阶段和投资驱动阶段之后，区域政府应该用创新发展、协调发展、绿色发展、开放发展、共享发展等理念超前引领，推动区域经济可持续发展。

## II. Technological Innovation of Regional Governments

In the innovation-driven stage, regional government technological innovation is the winning point of regional competition. The driving effect of technological innovation on economic development is explosive, capable of promoting regional economy to make leaps from quantitative to qualitative changes, enabling breakthrough creation in the entire process and all factors of the economy, and optimizing resource allocation. At this stage, technological innovation is the core driving force, capable of spawning new products, new industries, new models, and new business forms. The integration of technological innovation with finance and industrial innovation will stimulate continuous innovation-driven power. Therefore, at this stage, technological innovation is the winning point of regional competition.

## III. Organizational Innovation of Regional Governments

In the innovation-driven stage, regional government organizational innovation is the key to regional competition. When economic development transitions from the factor-driven stage to the investment-driven stage, the main means of regional competition is to expand investment scale to stimulate economic growth. However, in the innovation-driven stage, the organizational innovation ability of regional governments becomes the key to regional competition. Regional governments should strengthen management standardization, enhance rapid response capabilities, stay close to the market, serve enterprises, develop network structures and matrix structures, reduce management levels, effectively improve management levels with higher efficiency and flexibility, promote stable and orderly economic development, and aid regional competition.

## IV. Institutional Innovation of Regional Governments

In the innovation-driven stage, regional government institutional innovation is an inevitable choice for regional competition. Institutional innovation is the fundamental guarantee for concept innovation, technological innovation, and organizational innovation, capable of promoting their integrated development. If regional economic development in

## 二、区域政府技术创新

在创新驱动阶段,区域政府技术创新是区域竞争的制胜点。技术创新对经济发展的驱动作用是爆发式的,能够推动区域经济产生从量变到质变的飞跃,使经济实现全过程、全要素的突破性创造,使资源得到优化配置。在此阶段,技术创新是核心驱动力,能够催生新产品、新产业、新模式、新业态。技术创新与金融、产业创新相融合,将激发持续的创新驱动力,因此在这一阶段,技术创新是区域竞争的制胜点。

## 三、区域政府组织创新

在创新驱动阶段,区域政府组织创新是区域竞争的关键。当经济发展从要素驱动阶段过渡到投资驱动阶段,区域竞争的主要手段是扩大投资规模,刺激经济增长。但在创新驱动阶段,区域政府的组织创新能力成为区域竞争的关键,区域政府应加强管理的规范性,强化快速反应能力,贴近市场,服务企业,发展网络结构和矩阵结构,减少管理层次,以更高的效率和灵活性有效提高管理水平,促进经济稳定、有序发展,助力区域竞争。

## 四、区域政府制度创新

在创新驱动阶段,区域政府制度创新是区域竞争的必然选择。制度创新是理念创新、技术创新和组织创新的根本保障,能够促进三者的融合发展。如果世界各国的区域经济发展都沿着要素驱动、投资驱动、创新驱动和财富驱动的阶段轨

all countries follows the stage trajectory of factor-driven, investment-driven, innovation-driven, and wealth-driven, then in the innovation-driven stage where the three major industries are developing rapidly, public environmental awareness is growing stronger, and new economic development mode and personal growth models are constantly emerging, regional governments not only need concept innovation, technological innovation, and organizational innovation, but more importantly, institutional innovation to ensure regional competitive advantages. Because in the innovation-driven stage, economic development shows flexible, rapid, and diverse characteristics. Only by matching institutions and policies with these characteristics can regional governments keep pace with the pulse of the innovation-driven era, lead the direction of economic development, and maintain lasting economic vitality. All-round, whole-process, and all-factor concept innovation, technological innovation, organizational innovation, and institutional innovation will be the inevitable choice for regional competition at this stage.

In summary, in the growth stage dominated by innovative economic competition and cooperation, regional governments should not only lead economic development with technological innovation, but also comprehensively and creatively deal with the harm that economic development brings to regional society. At this stage, regional governments need to scientifically carry out concept innovation, technological innovation, organizational innovation, and institutional innovation according to the actual operation of the economy. This will promote scientific and sustainable development of the regional economy, achieve gratifying results in the innovation-driven stage, that is, achieve growth based on improving "total factor productivity".

## Section 4: Growth Stage Dominated by Shared Economic Competition and Cooperation

The growth stage dominated by shared economy competition and cooperation refers to the development stage that mainly relies on the competition and cooperation of the shared economy to drive economic growth. For regional governments, after regional economic growth goes through different development stages dominated by industrial economy, urban economy, and innovative economy competition and cooperation, it enters the growth stage dominated by shared economy competition and cooperation. In this stage, the importance of cooperation significantly increases; it is no longer a supplement to competitive means but an effective strategy that parallels competition in promoting economic growth.

迹前行，那么，在三大产业发展日新月异、民众环境意识越来越强、新的经济发展模式和个人成长模式推陈出新的创新驱动阶段，区域政府就不仅需要理念创新、技术创新和组织创新，更需要制度创新来确保区域的竞争优势。因为在创新驱动阶段，经济发展呈现灵活、迅捷、多样的特点，区域政府只有使制度、政策与之相匹配，才能紧随创新驱动时代的脉搏，引领经济发展方向，保持经济的持久活力。全方位、全过程、全要素的理念创新、技术创新、组织创新和制度创新，将是这一阶段区域竞争的必然选择。

综上，在由创新经济竞争与合作主导的增长阶段，区域政府既要以技术创新引领经济发展，又要全面地、创造性地处置经济发展给区域社会带来的危害。在这一阶段，区域政府需要根据经济的实际运行状况，科学地开展理念创新、技术创新、组织创新和制度创新，这将促进区域经济科学、可持续发展，在创新驱动阶段取得可喜的成效，即实现基于提高"全要素生产率"的增长。

## 第四节　由共享经济竞争与合作主导的增长阶段

由共享经济竞争与合作主导的增长阶段，是指主要依靠共享经济的竞争与合作驱动经济增长的发展阶段。对于区域政府来说，区域经济增长经过由产业经济、城市经济和创新经济竞争与合作主导的不同发展阶段后，就进入由共享经济竞争与合作主导的增长阶段，在该阶段，合作的重要性明显提升，它不再是竞争手段的补充，而是与其并列的推动经济增长的有效战略。

# I. Characteristics of the Growth Stage Dominated by Shared Economic Competition and Cooperation

In this stage, regional economy will undergo a more profound transformation process: from relying on resources within the region to exploring resources outside the region and developing various international economic resources (such as space resources, deep-sea resources, polar resources, etc.), switching economic development mode; from simply allocating industrial resources through enterprise competition to regional governments competing with each other and participating in allocating urban resources and other new generative resources; from single market mechanisms playing a role to combining effective governments with efficient markets, constructing new investment engines and innovation engines for regional economic growth.

In this transformation process, competition between regions inevitably involves the issue of how to maintain the principles of fairness and justice in the economic governance system. On one hand, it is necessary to protect the economic interests of each region and the economic order between regions, and also to maintain and expand an open economic system; on the other hand, in the process of exploring new economic fields, regions need to formulate new norms to address new problems and face constantly emerging cross-regions new challenges, which objectively leads to a pattern of coexistence of competition and cooperation between regions. Therefore, in the fourth stage of regional economic growth, i.e., the wealth-driven stage, competition and cooperation will coexist.

At this stage, the regional industrial system has been upgraded to a modern industrial system with regional competitiveness.

First, traditional industries have completed transformation and upgrading, with the internet, big data, artificial intelligence deeply integrated with the real economy. Manufacturing has extended from processing and production links to research and development, design, branding, marketing, remanufacturing, and other links, achieving intelligent development.

Second, strategic emerging industries are continuously growing stronger. New generation information technology and biotechnology, new energy, new materials, high-end equipment, energy-saving and environmental protection equipment, 3D printing, intelligent robots, new energy vehicles, and other industries are booming, gradually forming new industrial clusters and industrial cluster belts with regional competitiveness.

Third, modern service industries are developing rapidly, with productive and lifestyle service industries such as finance, logistics, shipping, tourism, culture, and exhibitions transforming towards professional and high-quality service industries.

# 一、由共享经济竞争与合作主导的增长阶段的特点

在此阶段，区域经济将经历更为深刻的转化过程：从依赖本区域资源转向探索区域外、开发各类国际经济资源（如太空资源、深海资源、极地资源等），切换经济发展模式；从单纯通过企业竞争配置产业资源，到区域政府相互竞争，参与配置城市资源和其他新的生成性资源；从单一市场机制发挥作用，到有为政府与有效市场相结合，构建区域经济增长的投资新引擎和创新新引擎。

在这一转化过程中，区域间的竞争必然涉及如何维护经济治理体系的公平、公正原则的问题。一方面，既需要保护各区域的经济利益和区域间的经济秩序，也需要维持和扩大开放型经济体系；另一方面，各区域在开拓经济新领域的过程中，为应对新问题，需要制定新规范，还要面对不断产生的跨区域的新挑战，这在客观上会导致区域间竞争与合作共存的格局。因此，在区域经济增长的第四阶段，即财富驱动阶段，竞争与合作将共同主导经济增长。

在此阶段，区域产业体系已升级为具有区域竞争力的现代产业体系。

一是传统产业完成改造提升，互联网、大数据、人工智能和实体经济深度融合，制造业从加工生产环节向研发、设计、品牌、营销、再制造等环节延伸，实现智能化发展。

二是战略性新兴产业不断壮大，新一代信息技术和生物技术、新能源、新材料、高端装备、节能环保设备、3D打印、智能机器人、新能源汽车等产业蓬勃发展，逐渐形成具有区域竞争力的新兴产业集群和产业集群带。

三是现代服务业加快发展，金融、物流、航运、旅游、文化、会展等生产性、生活性服务业正向专业化、高品质化服务业转型。

The competition in regional industrial economies is driving the complementary advantages, close collaboration, and linked development of industries between regions.

At this stage, regional infrastructure has formed a functionally perfect network of interconnectivity within regions and smooth channels outside regions.

First, a modern comprehensive transportation system has been formed, with strong service capabilities of infrastructure such as ports, waterways, port railways, and highways focusing on major coastal ports, high efficiency in the use of airspace resources focusing on aviation hubs, and smooth comprehensive transportation channels based on highways, high-speed railways, and rapid railways.

Second, intelligent transportation systems focusing on the integrated application of information technologies such as the Internet of Things, cloud computing, and big data are increasingly improving.

Third, smart city infrastructure, urban software infrastructure, energy infrastructure, and water conservancy infrastructure in urban-rural integration are gradually improving.

The competition in regional urban economies is driving the interconnectivity, rational layout, and smooth connection of infrastructure between regions.

At this stage, regions have formed an open regional collaborative innovation community that gathers innovation resources through technological innovation.

On one hand, regional technology innovation highlands and important sources of emerging industries have gradually formed. The construction of technology innovation corridors, regional flow of innovative elements such as talent, capital, information, and technology, the construction of big data centers and innovation platforms, the development of technological innovation activities by universities, research groups, enterprises, etc., as well as the enhancement of basic innovation capabilities and the development of industry-university-research innovation alliances are continuously expanding and deepening.

On the other hand, various institutional and policy environments dedicated to enhancing the ability to transform scientific and technological achievements are being optimized. Regional innovation system and mechanism reforms, facilitation of regional cooperation in science and technology, academics, talent, projects, etc., transformation of scientific and technological achievements, technology transfer, cooperation in science and technology service industries, protection and application of intellectual property rights, as well as policies for the integration and innovation of science and technology, finance, and industry, and measures for the integration and innovation of science and technology, management, systems, and concepts are continuously deepening.

The competition in regional innovation economies is driving innovation cooperation, coordinated development, and integrated development between regions.

区域的产业经济竞争推动着区域间产业的优势互补、紧密协作和联动发展。

在此阶段，区域基础设施已形成区域内互联互通、区域外通道顺畅的功能完善的网络。

一是现代化的综合交通运输体系已形成，以沿海主要港口为重点的港口、航道、疏港铁路、公路等基础设施服务能力强，以航空枢纽为重点的空域资源利用效率高，以高速公路、高速铁路和快速铁路等为骨干的综合运输通道畅通。

二是以物联网、云计算、大数据等信息技术集成应用为重点的智能交通系统日趋完善。

三是智能城市基础设施、城市软件基础设施、城乡一体化中的能源基础设施和水利基础设施等逐渐完善。

区域的城市经济竞争推动着区域间基础设施的互联互通、布局合理和衔接顺畅。

在此阶段，区域通过技术创新，已形成集聚创新资源的开放型区域协同创新共同体。

一方面，区域技术创新高地和新兴产业重要策源地已逐渐形成，技术创新走廊的建设，人才、资本、信息、技术等创新要素的区域流动，大数据中心和创新平台的建设，高校、科研团体、企业等主导的技术创新活动的开展，以及创新基础能力的提升和产学研创新联盟的发展等，都在不断拓展和深化。

另一方面，致力于提升科技成果转化能力的各类制度和政策环境正在优化，区域创新体制机制改革，科技、学术、人才、项目等领域区域合作的便利化，科技成果转化、技术转让、科技服务业合作、知识产权保护和运用，以及科技、金融、产业融合创新政策，科技、管理、制度、理念融合创新举措等都在不断深化。

区域的创新经济竞争推动着区域间的创新合作、协同发展和融合发展。

## II. Four Basic Principles for Shared Products between Regional Governments

The competition-driven economic growth in regional economies objectively forms four types of shared products (or public goods) among people and society.

(1) Ideational Public Goods. For example, a re-understanding of the operation system of market mechanisms, where market competition exists not only in the competition among enterprises within the industrial economy but also in the competition among regional governments within the urban economy. A mature market economy should be a system integrating effective governments with efficient markets, etc.

(2) Material Public Goods. For example, the integration of informatization with industrialization, urbanization, agricultural modernization, and internationalization. Related infrastructure construction in software and hardware promotes improvements and enhancements in material conditions such as public transportation, educational resources, medical facilities, cultural facilities, energy, etc., within the region.

(3) Organizational Public Goods. For example, traditional urban construction often spreads out like a pancake, while modern urban construction requires a clustered layout. Therefore, when the framework of regional economic order transitions from the pancake spreading model to a clustered layout model, it achieves innovation and reform in organizational management.

(4) Institutional Public Goods. For example, institutional arrangements under the principles of "letting regions bring more development opportunities" and "letting the fruits of economic growth be widely shared", further improve labor, employment, and social security policies within the region, making their outcomes shareable.

From this, we can see that in the growth stage dominated by regional shared economic competition and cooperation, i.e., the wealth-driven stage, the basic principles that regional governments should follow include: first, reform-led and innovative development; second, comprehensive planning and coordinated development; third, ecological protection and green development; fourth, win-win cooperation and open development; fifth, benefiting livelihood and shared development. In summary, building a regional economic system that integrates competition and cooperation, is innovative, open, interactive, inclusive, and shared, will be the sustainable way of economic growth for this phase.

## 二、四种共享产品与区域政府间应遵循的基本原则

区域经济的竞争驱动或者说区域的竞争型经济增长，在客观上形成了人与社会的四种共享产品（或公共物品）。

（1）思想性公共物品。比如对市场机制运作体系的重新认识，即市场竞争不但存在于产业经济的企业竞争中，而且存在于城市经济的区域政府竞争中，成熟市场经济应该是有为政府与有效市场相融合的经济体系，等等。

（2）物质性公共物品。比如，信息化与工业化、城市化、农业现代化、国际化的结合，相关的软硬件基础设施建设推动了区域公共交通、教育资源、医疗设施、文化设施、能源等物质条件的改善与提升。

（3）组织性公共物品。比如，传统的城市建设如摊大饼，现代化的城市建设则要求组团式布局，因此，区域经济秩序的架构在从摊大饼模式走向组团式布局模式时，就实现了组织管理的改革创新。

（4）制度性公共物品。比如，在"让区域带来更多发展机遇""让经济增长成果普惠共享"等原则指导下的制度安排，使区域的劳动、就业和社会保障政策等进一步完善，其成果具有共享性。

由此可见，在区域由共享经济竞争与合作主导的增长阶段，即财富驱动阶段，区域政府间应遵循的基本原则是：第一，改革引领，创新发展；第二，统筹兼顾，协调发展；第三，保护生态，绿色发展；第四，合作共赢，开放发展；第五，惠及民生，共享发展。总之，构建竞争与合作相融合的创新型、开放型、联动型、包容型和共享型区域经济体系，将是这一阶段的可持续的经济增长方式。

# Chapter 6
# The Formation of Regional Economic Competition Gradient Structure and Gradient Equilibrium

## Section 1: Introduction to the Gradient Transference Model of Regional Economic

In the historical process of regional economic development worldwide, regional economic competition presents a gradient shift pattern across four stages. In Figure 6-1, A to I represent different regions, and 1 to 4 represent the four stages of regional economic development, namely: 1 is the growth stage dominated by industrial economic competition and cooperation, 2 is the growth stage dominated by urban economic competition and cooperation, 3 is the growth stage dominated by innovative economic competition and cooperation, and 4 is the growth stage dominated by shared economic competition and cooperation.

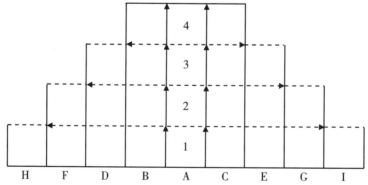

Figure 6–1 Gradient Transference Model of Regional Economic

第六章

# 区域经济竞争梯度结构与梯度均衡的形成

## 第一节 区域经济竞争梯度推移模型介绍

在世界各区域经济发展的历史进程中,区域经济竞争在四个阶段呈现出梯度推移的模式。在图6-1中,A至I表示不同的区域,1至4表示区域经济发展的四个阶段,即1是由产业经济竞争与合作主导的增长阶段,2是由城市经济竞争与合作主导的增长阶段,3是由创新经济竞争与合作主导的增长阶段,4是由共享经济竞争与合作主导的增长阶段。

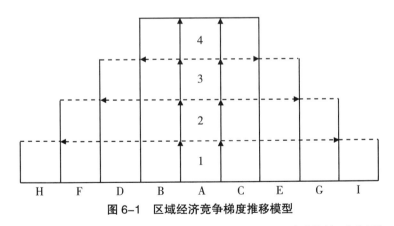

图 6-1 区域经济竞争梯度推移模型

资料来源:陈云贤:《市场竞争双重主体论——兼谈中观经济学的创立与发展》,北京大学出版社,2020,第152页。

The first stage is the growth stage dominated by industrial economic competition and cooperation. This stage belongs to the initial stage of regional economic development. At this stage, the technological level is low, capital accumulation is limited, and regions rely more on simple expansion in the quantity of production factors such as land, labor, and natural resources to form growth momentum. Therefore, it shows factor-driven characteristics, and its economic growth mode has fundamental and universal applicability. This is the first level of regional government competition. At this stage, the main way for regional governments to promote economic growth in their regions is to vigorously attract investment and provide sufficient land and labor for enterprise production, making their regions "Focus Point" for capital and labor, promoting industrial agglomeration and the formation of economies of scale. When the region has a relatively complete industrial chain supporting capability and the competitive advantage of industrial clusters becomes apparent, regional economic development begins to transition to the next stage.

The second stage is the growth stage dominated by urban economic competition and cooperation. This stage belongs to the expansion stage of regional economic development. This stage starts with large investments in urban hardware infrastructure, proceeds through large investments in urban software infrastructure and urban-rural integrated hardware and software infrastructure, and ends with the development and improvement of smart cities. Regional economic growth thus experiences one climax after another, showing investment-driven characteristics. The traces of government participation are evident in this economic growth mode, which is the second level of regional government competition. At this stage, the development of the industrial economy continuously raises the income level of residents in the region, and the demand for public goods with higher income elasticity in the region will rapidly expand. Therefore, to further attract and retain talent, regional governments not only need to greatly improve the supply level of hardware infrastructure but also need to improve the supply quality of software infrastructure, making the region not only able to attract domestic talent inflow but also become a "Focus Point" for international talent. At this time, regional economic development needs to upgrade to the next stage.

The third stage is the growth stage dominated by innovative economic competition and cooperation. This stage belongs to the high-quality development stage of regional economy. At this stage, technological innovation, as the dominant force, leads comprehensive innovation in concepts, organizations, and institutions, thus constantly updating the economic growth mode. The quality of economic development at this stage achieves all-round improvement, showing innovation-driven characteristics, pushing regional government economic competition towards high-end development. This is the third level of regional government competition. At this stage, regional governments should vigorously develop higher education to cultivate high-level

第一个阶段是由产业经济竞争与合作主导的增长阶段。这一阶段属于区域经济发展的初始阶段，在此阶段，技术水平较低，资本积累较少，区域更多是依靠土地、劳动力、自然资源等生产要素在数量上的简单扩张来形成增长动力，因此呈现出要素驱动的特征，其经济增长方式具有基础性和普及性，这是区域政府竞争的第一个层次。在此阶段，区域政府推动本区域经济增长的主要方式是大力招商引资，并为企业生产提供充足的土地和劳动力，使本区域成为资本和劳动力的"聚点"，促进产业集聚和规模经济的形成。当本区域拥有了较为完整的产业链配套能力，产业集群竞争优势得以显现时，区域经济发展就开始向下一个阶段过渡。

第二个阶段是由城市经济竞争与合作主导的增长阶段。这一阶段属于区域经济发展的扩张阶段，此阶段以城市硬件基础设施的大量投资为起点，以城市软件基础设施和城乡一体化的软硬件基础设施的大量投资为过程，以智能城市的开发和完善为终结。区域经济增长由此出现一个又一个高潮，因此呈现出投资驱动的特征，其经济增长方式中政府参与的痕迹明显，这是区域政府竞争的第二个层次。在此阶段，产业经济的发展使本区域居民收入水平不断提高，本区域对于具有更高收入弹性的公共物品的需求会迅速扩大。因此，区域政府为了进一步吸引人才、留住人才，不仅要大力提升硬件基础设施的供给水平，还要提高软件基础设施的供给质量，使本区域不但能够吸引国内人才流入，而且能够成为国际人才的"聚点"，此时，区域经济发展就要向下一个阶段升级。

第三个阶段是由创新经济竞争与合作主导的增长阶段。这一阶段属于区域经济高质量发展的阶段，在此阶段，技术创新作为主导力量，引领着理念、组织和制度的全面创新，从而使经济增长模式不断推陈出新。该阶段经济发展的质量获得全方位提升，呈现出创新驱动的特征，推动着区域政府经济竞争向高端化发展，这是区域政府竞争的第三个层次。在此阶段，区域政府应大力发展高等教育

talents for the region; provide effective incentives for R&D activities of enterprises, research institutes, etc.; increase efforts to introduce global R&D centers of multinational companies; actively cultivate regional innovation culture, and promote comprehensive innovation. Finally, make the region a "Focus Point" for scientific research talents and R&D activities, realizing the evolution of regional economic growth mode towards innovation-driven.

Eventually, regional economic development will move towards the fourth stage, namely the growth stage dominated by shared economic competition and cooperation. At this stage, regional economy will advance along the trajectory of "competition-dominated → coexistence of competition and cooperation → cooperation and win-win dominated", showing sharing-driven characteristics. At this time, the ideological, material, organizational, and institutional public goods formed in regional economic competition will become universally shared results of economic growth among regions, promoting the coordinated progress of regional economies and societies.

It is important to note that mezzoeconomics divides regional economic growth stages based on competitive advantage. Therefore, although the evolution of development stages seems to still depend on factor endowment upgrades, the key industries to be developed at each stage do not depend on comparative advantage. In fact, this book has repeatedly pointed out that, under the premise of factor mobility, a region's comparative advantage at a given time point is not absolute. The flow of capital between regions will cause dynamic changes in a region's factor endowments, and comparative advantage has been replaced by competitive advantage. Therefore, even in the factor-driven stage, capital-intensive and technology-intensive industries can be developed as long as such industries have sufficient market demand and the region can attract investment in these industries. What regional governments need to do is to implement appropriate foresighted leading strategies, formulate good development plans and industrial policies for their regions to make them "Focus Point" for various production factors.

Furthermore, the author believes that the relationship between each stage in the gradient transference model of regional economic under the mezzoeconomics framework is not a simple substitution of one stage for another, but rather entering a higher stage on the basis of a previous stage. For example, moving from the factor-driven stage to the investment-driven stage does not mean that factor inputs are no longer needed, but that the required factors need to be upgraded accordingly. Moving from the investment-driven stage to the innovation-driven stage does not mean that investment is no longer needed, but that under the new stage, economic growth is mainly driven by innovation, and factor inputs and investment methods also need to be upgraded accordingly. In Chapter 7, this book will use the development of the Shenzhen Special Economic Zone as an example to illustrate how regional governments should implement foresighted leading strategies at different growth stages.

事业，为本区域培养高层次人才；对企业、科研院所等的研发活动提供有效激励；加大力度引入跨国公司全球研发中心；积极培育本区域创新文化，推动全面创新。最终使本区域成为科研人才和研发活动的"聚点"，实现区域经济增长方式向创新驱动演变。

最终，区域经济发展竞争将迈向第四个阶段，即由共享经济竞争与合作主导的增长阶段。在此阶段，区域经济将沿着"竞争为主—竞争与合作共存—合作共赢为主"的轨迹前行，呈现出共享驱动的特征。此时，在区域经济竞争中形成的思想性、物质性、组织性和制度性公共物品，将成为区域间普惠共享的经济增长成果，推动各区域经济社会的协同进步。

这里，本书需要重点指出的是，中观经济学是基于竞争优势对区域经济增长阶段进行划分的。因此，尽管发展阶段的演进似乎仍依赖要素禀赋升级，但各个阶段所要重点发展的产业绝不依赖比较优势。实际上本书已多次指出，在要素可流动的前提下，区域在一个时点上的比较优势不是绝对的，资本在区域间的流动会导致某一区域要素禀赋发生动态变化，比较优势已被竞争优势所替代。因此，即使在要素驱动阶段，资本密集型和技术密集型的产业也不是不能够发展，只要这样的产业拥有足够的市场需求量，本区域能够吸引到这类产业的投资，就可以发展这类产业。而区域政府要做的，就是实施恰当的超前引领战略，制定好本区域的发展规划和产业政策，使本区域成为各类生产要素的"聚点"。

另外，笔者认为，中观经济学框架下的区域经济竞争梯度推移模型中各个阶段的关系不是简单的一个阶段对另一个阶段的替代，而是在一个阶段的基础上进入更高的阶段。举例来说，从要素驱动阶段进入投资驱动阶段，并不是说不需要要素的投入了，而是所需的要素需随之升级。从投资驱动阶段进入创新驱动阶段，并不是说不需要投资了，而是在新的阶段下，经济增长主要由创新驱动，要素的投入和投资方式也需随之升级。在第七章，本书将以深圳经济特区的发展为例，说明在不同增长阶段，区域政府应如何实施超前引领战略。

# Section 2: Four Supporting Economic Theories for the Gradient Transference Model of Regional Economic

Mezzoeconomics not only divides competitive economic growth into four stages but also clarifies four supporting economic theories corresponding to these four stages.

First, the industrial effect theory. In the growth stage dominated by industrial economic competition and cooperation, economic development in various regions is not synchronized in space. Often, some regions with internal factors and external conditions for industrial development develop first. The industries in these regions gradually agglomerate, the economy continues to grow, and they interact with regions lagging in industrial development, causing various production factors needed for industrial development to continuously concentrate from underdeveloped regions to developed regions, forming regional competitive advantages and industrial effects. Therefore, at this stage, for regional governments to stand out in competition, they should vigorously attract investment, introduce projects, improve industrial chains, encourage import and export, expand domestic and foreign markets, and improve supporting policies for planning and guiding, supporting and regulating, and supervising and managing the industrial economy.

Second, the urban expansion theory. In the growth stage dominated by urban economic competition and cooperation, the driving force of regional economic growth mainly comes from multi-level urban infrastructure input and urban-rural integration expansion, specifically including investment in core urban hardware and software infrastructure, construction of urban-rural integration infrastructure, and development and operation of smart cities. Regional governments in multi-level urban systems should follow the principle of "government promotion, enterprise participation, market operation" when investing in and constructing urban infrastructure to support policies. Only in this way can they promote the extension and expansion of urban functions, improve and optimize the regional economic development environment, build a perfect urban economic system, establish regional competitive advantages, and thus promote sustainable regional economic growth at this stage.

Third, the innovation-driven theory. In the growth stage dominated by innovative economic competition and cooperation, regions in the innovation-driven stage (generally economically developed regions) will see a series of innovative activities in aspects such as industrial sectors, products, technologies, production methods, and business marketing

## 第二节　区域经济竞争梯度推移模型的四种支持性经济学说

中观经济学不但划分了竞争型经济增长的四个阶段，还阐明了与这四个阶段相对应的四种支持性经济学说。①

第一，产业效应说。在由产业经济竞争与合作主导的增长阶段，各区域经济发展在空间上并不同步，往往是一些具备产业发展内在因素和外在条件的区域率先发展。这些区域的产业逐渐集聚、经济不断增长，并与产业发展滞后的区域相互影响，使产业发展需要的各种生产要素不断从不发达区域向发达区域集聚，形成区域竞争优势和产业效应。因此，在这一阶段，区域政府要在竞争中脱颖而出，就应大力招商引资、引进项目、完善产业链、鼓励进出口、拓展国内外市场，完善对产业经济的规划引导、扶持调节、监督管理等配套政策。

第二，城市扩展说。在由城市经济竞争与合作主导的增长阶段，区域经济增长的动力主要来自多层次的城市基础设施的投入和城乡一体化的扩展，具体包括核心城市软硬件基础设施的投资、城乡一体化基础设施的建设和智能城市的开发运作等。处于多层次城市系统中的各区域政府，对城市基础设施投资建设时，应遵循"政府推动、企业参与、市场运作"的原则来配套政策，唯有如此，才能推动城市功能的延伸、扩展，改善并优化区域经济发展环境，建设完善的城市经济系统，确立区域竞争优势，从而促进区域经济在此阶段实现可持续增长。

第三，创新驱动说。在由创新经济竞争与合作主导的增长阶段，处于创新驱动阶段的区域（一般都是经济较为发达的区域），其产业部门、产品、技术、生

---

① 陈云贤:《市场竞争双重主体论——兼谈中观经济学的创立与发展》，北京大学出版社，2020，第153-154页。

modes. Based on this, a series of innovative activities in organizational management methods, institutional policies and measures will also be extended. Over time, these innovations originating from economically developed regions will gradually be transmitted to economically backward regions. In regional economic competition at this stage, regional governments should timely and effectively promote the implementation of various policies and measures conducive to innovation, thereby promoting regional economic development and establishing regional economic advantages.

Fourth, the coordinated development theory. In the growth stage dominated by shared economic competition and cooperation, competition will cause industrial resources and urban resources to continuously concentrate towards economically developed regions. However, the growth of economically developed regions is naturally constrained by internal factors and external conditions at this stage. Therefore, various types of shared public goods will be formed between regions, ensuring the continuous progress of regional economies and societies. Therefore, at this stage, various economic policies and measures of regional governments should follow the trajectory of "competition → competition and cooperation → win-win cooperation" to promote coordinated development among regions.

## Section 3: Four Characteristics of the Gradient Transference Model of Regional Economic

Based on the above analysis, the gradient transference model of regional economic presented in Figure 6-1 has the following four characteristics.

First, regional economic competition was initially launched by economically developed regions that first promoted industrial economy, urban economy, and innovative economy development. As time passes and internal factors and external conditions of various regions change, regional economic competition gradually shifts horizontally from economically developed regions to economically backward regions. That is, it shifts horizontally from regions A, B, C to regions D, E, F, G, H, I in Figure 6-1.

Second, with the gradual improvement in the level of economic development and the continuous upgrading of economic growth stages, regional economic competition has progressively expanded from the industrial economy vertically into urban economy, innovation economy, and sharing economy sectors. This is akin to moving from stage 1 to stages 2, 3, and 4 in Figure 6-1.

产方式和商业营销模式等方面会出现一系列创新活动，以此为基础还会延伸出组织管理方式、制度政策措施等一系列创新活动。随着时间推移，这类源于经济发达区域的创新又会逐渐向经济落后区域传递。在这一阶段的区域经济竞争中，区域政府应及时、有效地推动实施各项有利于创新的政策措施，从而促进区域经济发展，建立区域经济优势。

第四，协同发展说。在由共享经济竞争与合作主导的增长阶段，竞争会使产业资源和城市资源向经济发达区域不断集中，但经济发达区域的增长天然地受到这一阶段区域内在因素和外在条件的制约，因此区域间会形成各类共享性的公共物品，从而保障各区域经济和社会的持续进步。因此在这一阶段，区域政府的各类经济政策和措施应沿着"竞争—竞争合作—合作共赢"的轨迹，促进各区域协同发展。

## 第三节 区域经济竞争梯度推移模型的四个特点

综合上述分析，图 6-1 所呈现的区域经济竞争梯度推移模型有以下四个特点。

一是区域经济竞争最早是由率先推动产业经济、城市经济、创新经济发展的经济发达区域启动的。随着时间的推移及各区域内在因素和外在条件的变化，区域经济竞争从经济发达区域逐渐向经济落后区域横向推移。即从图 6-1 中的 A、B、C 区域向 D、E、F、G、H、I 区域横向推移。

二是随着经济发展水平的逐渐提高和经济增长阶段的不断升级，区域经济竞争逐渐从产业经济纵向扩展至城市经济、创新经济、共享经济领域，即从图 6-1 中的阶段 1 向阶段 2、3、4 纵向推移。

三是在由产业经济、城市经济和创新经济竞争与合作主导的增长阶段，率先推出有效的政策措施的区域，其经济发展将具有领先优势。各区域政策措施的力度和效用差异，将使其在区域间梯度经济结构中居于不同的位置，图 6-1 中 A、B、C 区域即优于其他区域。

Third, in the growth stages dominated by industrial economy, urban economy, and innovative economy competition and cooperation, regions that first introduce effective policy measures will have a leading advantage in economic development. The differences in the strength and effectiveness of policy measures among regions will place them in different positions in the inter-regions gradient economic structure, with regions A, B, C in Figure 6-1 being superior to other regions.

Fourth, the upgrade of economic growth stages, from the growth stage dominated by industrial economic competition and cooperation, to the growth stage dominated by urban economic competition and cooperation, then to the growth stage dominated by innovative economic competition and cooperation, and finally to the growth stage dominated by shared economic competition and cooperation, is a long historical process. However, various public goods created jointly by human economic society will eventually drive the popularization of the shared economy and promote coordinated development of regional economies. Competition and cooperation interact and can jointly promote economic growth. Although there are differences in economic development among regions, the overall trend shows orderly horizontal shift and vertical coordinated development, ultimately making win-win cooperation the mainstream and forming a gradient equilibrium pattern.

# Section 4: Development Strategies for Livelihood Economy, Industrial Economy, and Urban Economy

## I. Safeguarding, Supporting, and Upgrading the Livelihood Economy

(i) Livelihood Economy and Regional Competitive Advantage

### 1. How to Understand the Livelihood Economy

"Livelihood" refers to people's lives. Improving livelihood has always been a key focus area of the country. Since the reform and opening-up, China's economic strength has significantly increased, and people's living standards have continuously improved accordingly. The report of the 19th National Congress of the Communist Party of China made a major judgment that "socialism with Chinese characteristics has entered a new era", pointing out that the main contradiction in our society has been transformed into "the contradiction between people's ever-growing needs for a better life and unbalanced and inadequate development". In the context of the new era, the areas involved in people's needs for a better life are more

四是经济增长阶段的升级,即从由产业经济竞争与合作主导的增长阶段,到由城市经济竞争与合作主导的增长阶段,再到由创新经济竞争与合作主导的增长阶段,最后到由共享经济竞争与合作主导的增长阶段,是个漫长的历史进程。但人类经济社会共同创造的各类公共物品,终将驱动共享经济的普及,促进区域间经济的协同发展。竞争与合作相互作用,可以共同推动经济增长,尽管各区域的经济发展存在差异,但整体呈现横向有序推移、纵向协同发展的趋势,最终使合作共赢成为主流,梯度均衡格局形成。

## 第四节 民生经济、产业经济与城市经济的发展战略

### 一、保障、托底、提升民生经济

#### (一)民生经济与区域竞争优势

**1. 怎样理解民生经济**

"民生"也就是人民的生活。改善民生,一直是国家重点关注的领域。自改革开放以来,我国经济实力显著增强,人民生活水平随之不断提高。党的十九大报告作出了"中国特色社会主义进入新时代"的重大判断,指出了我国社会主要矛盾已经转化为"人民日益增长的美好生活需要和不平衡不充分的发展之间的矛盾"。新时代背景下,人民美好生活需要所涉及的领域更加广泛,是一个可以促进人的

extensive, forming a large livelihood system that can promote the comprehensive development of people. Realizing people's yearning for a better life is the direction of efforts to guarantee, improve, and develop livelihood.

Under the traditional concept system, the livelihood economy is often seen as an aggregate of livelihood and economy, two independent concepts. The traditional concept system believes that developing the economy and improving livelihood are two parallel main lines of government work. Under this understanding, livelihood and economy are separated, and improving livelihood and developing the economy are contradictory. This understanding of the livelihood economy may lead to two extremes in practice: one is a one-sided understanding of "adhering to economic development as the center", emphasizing economic development while neglecting the improvement of livelihood, worrying that the government's improvement of livelihood will affect economic development; the other is blindly implementing livelihood projects detached from economic development, even turning livelihood projects into "image projects" or "achievement projects". Research by Luo Danglun and Gao Miaoyuan shows that there is indeed a negative correlation between economic development and livelihood expenditure, that is, local officials often neglect the improvement of livelihood while developing the economy. Chen Yunxian proposed the "livelihood economy insufficient" government failure, pointing out that this type of government treats the livelihood economy as a burden, neither providing a basic safety net nor effectively enhancing it, let alone considering the important role of fair and just livelihood foundations in creating a stable, harmonious, business-friendly, livable, workable, and tourist-friendly investment environment. This type of government failure is a "lack of knowledge" failure of the government.

Under the framework of mezzoeconomics, the livelihood economy is called "non-operative resources", emphasizing the non-operational attributes of this resource under current conditions. It mainly includes social welfare products and public goods in various regions, including economy (security), history, geography, image, spirit, ideas, emergency, safety, assistance, etc. Although it is "non-operative resources", the livelihood economy still belongs to urban resources in a broad sense. Regional governments need to provide guarantees and a safety net for the livelihood economy and take appropriate measures to enhance it, which is an important part of strengthening regional competitiveness. Therefore, under the mezzoeconomics framework, livelihood and economy are a unified body, no longer mutually exclusive. The development of the regional economy is inseparable from the enhancement of the livelihood economy, and the enhancement of the livelihood economy will also promote the improvement of regional competitiveness, thereby driving further growth of the regional economy.

全面发展的大民生体系。① 实现人民对美好生活的向往是保障民生、改善民生和发展民生的努力方向。

在传统的概念体系下，民生经济常被看作是民生和经济这两个相互独立概念的集合体。传统的概念体系认为发展经济与改善民生是政府工作两条并行的主线。② 在这种认知下，民生与经济是割裂的，改善民生与发展经济是矛盾的，对民生经济的这种理解可能引致实践中的两种极端：一是片面理解"坚持以经济发展为中心"，重视发展经济，忽视改善民生，担心政府改善民生会影响经济发展；二是脱离经济发展盲目实施民生工程，甚至把民生工程搞成"形象工程""政绩工程"。③ 罗党论和高妙嫒的研究表明，经济发展和民生支出确实存在负相关关系，也即地方官员在发展经济的同时往往忽视了民生的改善。陈云贤提出了"民生经济不足型"政府失灵，指出此类政府把民生经济当作一种负担，既没有基本托底，又没有有效提升，更没有考虑公平、公正的民生基础对营造稳定、和谐、宜商、宜居、宜业、宜游的投资环境的重要作用。此类政府失灵是政府"缺知型"的失灵。④

在中观经济学的框架下，民生经济被称为"非经营性资源"，强调的是这种资源在当前条件下所具有的不可经营的属性。它以各区域的社会公益产品、公共物品为主，包括经济（保障）、历史、地理、形象、精神、理念、应急、安全、救助等。尽管是"非经营性资源"，但民生经济仍属于广义的城市资源，区域政府需要对民生经济提供保障和托底，并采取适宜的措施予以提升，这是增强区域竞争力的重要一环。因此，中观经济学框架下的民生与经济是一个统一体，不再是互相排斥的，区域经济的发展离不开民生经济的提升，民生经济的提升也会促进区域竞争力的提升，从而推动区域经济的进一步增长。

---

① 郑功成：《习近平民生重要论述中的两个关键概念：从"物质文化需要"到"美好生活需要"》，《人民论坛·学术前沿》2018年第18期。
② 易宪容：《"两会"焦点：民生经济并行》，《中国经贸》2010年第4期。
③ 杜黎明：《中国民生经济发展及其承载的功能研究》，《华东经济管理》2012年第10期。
④ 陈云贤：《市场竞争双重主体论——兼谈中观经济学的创立与发展》，北京大学出版社，2020，第228页。

## 2. The Relationship between Livelihood Economy and Regional Competitive Advantage

As mentioned earlier, the improvement of the livelihood economy can enhance regional competitiveness and promote regional economic growth. Specifically, this effect is mainly reflected in expanding consumption, attracting investment, promoting the transformation of economic growth drivers, and driving high-quality development of the regional economy.

(1) Expanding consumption and attracting investment.

Government livelihood expenditure has the function of adjusting income distribution. Due to the diminishing marginal propensity to consume, a more equitable distribution of social wealth can increase the overall consumption rate of society, thereby providing momentum for improving the regional economic development environment. In addition, the improvement of the livelihood economy also means that residents can enjoy better pension and medical services. In a multi-period choice model, this will inevitably reduce consumers' worries about the future, further increasing their willingness to consume. The increase in consumption directly promotes the expansion of the total economy on one hand, and on the other hand, it also increases the investment multiplier of the region, enhancing the rate of return on capital, thereby strengthening the region's attractiveness to investment.

(2) Promoting the transformation of economic growth momentums.

The improvement of the livelihood economy enhances the material and cultural needs of residents in the region. On one hand, this drives consumption upgrading in the region, thereby promoting industrial upgrading; on the other hand, with the increase in disposable income and the improvement of social security levels, residents in the region have the ability to increase investment in human capital, thereby promoting the comprehensive development of people, improving regional labor productivity, and further promoting the transformation of regions' industries towards technology-oriented, environmentally friendly, and high value-added types. At the same time, the growth in the number of highly knowledgeable and skilled labor can also promote the improvement of innovation and entrepreneurship levels in the region, which can further enhance new drivers of economic growth in the region, providing new momentum for regional economic development.

(3) Driving high-quality development of the regional economy.

Improving the livelihood economy can not only expand the scale of consumption and investment but also promote the upgrading of consumption structure and industrial structure. It can be seen that improving the livelihood economy can expand and upgrade regional demand for material products, spiritual products, and ecological environmental products, which drives economic entities to make behavioral decisions centered on the real accumulation of material wealth, spiritual wealth, and ecological environmental wealth. The change in relative prices

### 2. 民生经济与区域竞争优势的关系

如前所述，民生经济的改善能够提升区域竞争力，推动区域经济增长，具体地说，这种效应主要表现在扩大消费、吸引投资，促进经济增长动力转换，推动区域经济高质量发展等方面。

（1）扩大消费、吸引投资。

政府的民生支出具有调节收入分配的职能，由于边际消费倾向递减，所以更加公平的社会财富分配能够提高社会整体的消费率，从而为区域经济发展环境的改善提供动力。另外，民生经济的改善也意味着居民能够享受到更好的养老和医疗服务，在多期选择模型中，这必将减少消费者的后顾之忧，进一步提高其消费意愿。消费的提升一方面直接促进了经济总量的扩大，另一方面也提高了本区域的投资乘数，使资本的收益率得到提升，从而增强本区域对投资的吸引力。

（2）促进经济增长动力转换。

民生经济的改善提升了本区域居民的物质文化需求水平，这一方面推动了本区域的消费升级，从而促进产业升级；另一方面，随着可支配收入的提高和社会保障水平的提升，本区域居民有能力加大在人力资本方面的投资，从而促进人的全面发展，提高区域劳动生产率，进而推动本区域产业向科技型、环境友好型、高附加值型转变。同时，高知识和高技能劳动力数量的增长也能够促进本区域创新创业水平的提高，这就可以进一步增强本区域经济增长的新动能，为区域经济发展提供新动力。

（3）推动区域经济高质量发展。

改善民生经济不但能够扩大消费和投资规模，而且能够促进消费结构和产业结构的升级。可见，改善民生经济能够扩大并升级区域对物质产品、精神产品、生态环境产品的需求，这驱使经济主体以物质财富、精神财富、生态环境财富的真实积累为中心做出行为决策。劳动力、资本和科技等生产要素之间相对价格的改变也以促进人的全方面发展为中心。这事实上是构筑了一道安全网，防止"高

among production factors such as labor, capital, and technology is also centered on promoting the all-round development of people. This, in fact, constructs a safety net to prevent the spread of traditional extensive economy characterized by "high input, high emissions, high pollution, and low efficiency", and guide economic development characterized by "high technology, low consumption, low emissions, and high efficiency", pushing regional economy onto the track of high-quality development.

## (ii) Strategic Measures for Regional Governments to Enhance the Livelihood Economy

### 1. Regional Governments are the Main Body for Developing the Livelihood Economy

Mezzoeconomics considers the livelihood economy as non-operative resources, with clear non-competitive and non-exclusive attributes of pure public goods. It is difficult for enterprises to implement effective allocation, so regional governments should fully and unequivocally assume responsibility to provide, allocate, manage, and develop such resources, and formulate supporting policies according to the principles of guarantee, providing a safety net, and enhancement. This is also why national finance, which takes from and uses for the people, should weaken its constructive fiscal function and strengthen its public (welfare) fiscal role.

In China, there are mainly three types of government institutions that coordinate, supervise, and manage such resources.

The first type is subdivided into five categories: first, relevant institutions of finance, audit, and establishment; second, relevant institutions of literature and history, counselors, and archives; third, relevant institutions of civil affairs, social security, and poverty alleviation; fourth, relevant institutions of women, children, disabled persons' federation, Red Cross, etc.; fifth, relevant institutions of ethnic affairs, religious affairs, and overseas Chinese affairs.

The second type is geological and meteorological related institutions.

The third type is subdivided into three categories: first, relevant institutions of emergency, safety, and civil air defense; second, relevant institutions of people's armed forces, public security, justice, and supervision; third, relevant institutions of fire fighting, armed police, border defense, coastal defense, and anti-smuggling.

Such coordination, supervision, and management institutions in various countries worldwide are similar in function but different in name, and the policy principles for allocating such resources are mainly "social security, basic safety net; fairness and justice, effective enhancement". This point is also very consistent in practice and understanding.

As China's economy enters a stage of high-quality development, the strengthening of

投入、高排放、高污染、低效益"的传统粗放型经济蔓延发展,引导"高科技、低消耗、低排放、高效益"的经济发展,推动区域经济进入高质量发展的轨道。

### (二)区域政府提升民生经济的战略举措

#### 1.区域政府是发展民生经济的主体

中观经济学认为,民生经济为非经营性资源,具有明确的非竞争性、非排他性这两种纯公共物品属性,企业难以对其实施有效配置,因此区域政府应责无旁贷地、全面地承担起责任,提供、调配、管理和发展此类资源,按照保障、托底、提升的原则去配套政策。这也就是取之于民、用之于民的国家财政要弱化其建设性财政职能、强化其公共(公益)性财政作用的缘故。[①]

在中国,政府协调、监督、管理此类资源的机构主要有三种。

第一种细分为五类:其一,财政、审计、编制相关机构;其二,文史、参事、档案相关机构;其三,民政、社保、扶贫相关机构;其四,妇女、儿童、残联、红十字会等相关机构;其五,民族、宗教、侨务相关机构。

第二种是地质、气象相关机构。

第三种细分为三类:其一,应急、安全、人防相关机构;其二,人民武装、公安、司法、监察相关机构;其三,消防、武警、边防、海防与打私相关机构。

世界各国的此类协调、监督、管理机构形同名异,且调配此类资源的政策原则主要都是"社会保障,基本托底;公平公正,有效提升"。这点在实践和认识上也很一致。

随着中国经济步入高质量发展阶段,经济实力的增强和社会财富的增长为民

---

[①] 陈云贤:《市场竞争双重主体论——兼谈中观经济学的创立与发展》,北京大学出版社,2020,第60页。

economic power and the growth of social wealth provide strong material guarantees for the development of the livelihood economy. Meanwhile, the enhancement of the livelihood economy is also an important driver for the sustainable and healthy development of the economy and society. The *Outline of the 14th Five-Year Plan for National Economic and Social Development of the People's Republic of China and the Long-Range Objectives Through the Year 2035* points out that we should "adhere to doing our best and acting within our capabilities, improve the basic public service system, strengthen the construction of inclusive, basic, and bottom-line livelihood, improve the social governance system of co-construction, co-governance, and sharing, formulate an action outline to promote common prosperity, consciously and actively narrow classification, urban-rural and income gaps, let development results benefit all people more and more fairly, and continuously enhance people's sense of gain, happiness, and security".

## 2. Reflections on Regional Governments Enhancing the Livelihood Economy

(1) Transforming the thinking on industrial development and livelihood decision-making.

In 2017, President Xi Jinping delivered a keynote speech titled *Jointly Shoulder Responsibility of Our Times, Promote Global Growth* at the opening ceremony of the World Economic Forum Annual Meeting 2017, pointing out: "China adheres to the development concept of people-centeredness, taking improving people's lives and enhancing people's well-being as the starting point and end point, seeking development momentum from the people, relying on the people to promote development, and making development benefit the people."

Therefore, the development of regional industrial economy and livelihood economy are by no means separate, but an organic unity. The development of industrial economy is for livelihood, and the development of livelihood economy also has a driving effect on industrial economy. Regional governments should take an overall view of the relationship between the two and scientifically formulate development policies.

First, they should focus on developing characteristic industries suitable for their region based on the realistic material needs of the social public, especially the broad middle and low-income groups, to prevent the phenomenon of blindly pursuing trendy industries regardless of regional development conditions, and avoid vicious competition among regions, redundant construction, and waste of economic resources.

Second, government livelihood decision-making should start from understanding livelihood needs, not from the government's presumed planning of livelihood needs; it should start from thinking what the people think and addressing what the people are anxious about, rather than organizing economic operations from the perspective of performance assessment and regional prosperity; it should take livelihood improvement, rather than economic scale expansion or fiscal revenue increase, as the starting point and end point of livelihood decision-making.

生经济发展提供了强大的物质保障,同时,民生经济的提升也是经济社会持续健康发展的重要推手。《中华人民共和国国民经济和社会发展第十四个五年规划和2035年远景目标纲要》指出,要"坚持尽力而为、量力而行,健全基本公共服务体系,加强普惠性、基础性、兜底性民生建设,完善共建共治共享的社会治理制度,制定促进共同富裕行动纲要,自觉主动缩小地区、城乡和收入差距,让发展成果更多更公平惠及全体人民,不断增强人民群众获得感、幸福感、安全感"。

**2. 区域政府提升民生经济的思考**

(1) 转变产业发展和民生决策思路。

2017年,国家主席习近平在世界经济论坛2017年年会开幕式上发表题为《共担时代责任 共促全球发展》的主旨演讲,指出:"中国秉持以人民为中心的发展思想,把改善人民生活、增进人民福祉作为出发点和落脚点,在人民中寻找发展动力、依靠人民推动发展、使发展造福人民。"

因此,区域产业经济的发展和民生经济的发展绝不是割裂的,而是一对有机统一体,产业经济的发展是为了民生,民生经济的发展也对产业经济有推动作用,区域政府应统筹看待二者的关系,科学制定发展政策。

第一,应依据社会民众,特别是广大中低收入者现实的物质需求重点发展适合本区域的特色产业,杜绝不顾区域发展条件,盲目追逐风口产业的现象,避免区域间的恶性竞争、重复建设、经济资源浪费等现象。

第二,政府民生决策应从摸清民生需求,而不是政府想当然的计划民生需求出发;要从想民众之所想、急民众之所急出发,而不是从政绩考核、区域繁荣出发组织经济运行;要把民生改善,而不是经济规模壮大、财政增收作为民生决策的出发点和落脚点。[①]

---

① 杜黎明:《中国民生经济发展及其承载的功能研究》,《华东经济管理》2012年第10期。

(2) Promoting the formation of resource generation and innovating public service provision methods.

Resource generation is not a product of planned settings, but things that already exist or appear due to objective needs as time progresses. It moves from static to dynamic until it possesses economic and productive characteristics. With the advancement of technology and the objective needs of the times, some non-operative resources can also be transformed into operative resources.

Therefore, for the livelihood economy, the government's main position in guaranteeing the supply of basic public services should be emphasized, while promoting the formation of resource generation, exploring the formation of operative resources in the livelihood economy field and accumulating experience, promoting the diversification of public service providers and provision methods.

For example, in service areas with prominent supply and demand contradictions such as child care and elderly care, social forces should be supported to expand the supply of inclusive and standardized services, ensuring that various institutions providing inclusive and standardized services enjoy equal preferential policies. Social forces should be encouraged to participate in public service supply through methods such as public-built private-operated, government purchase of services, and government and social capital cooperation. At the same time, around areas such as public education, employment and entrepreneurship, social insurance, medical and health care, social services, housing security, public culture and sports, preferential treatment and resettlement, services for disabled persons, etc., a standard system for basic public services should be established and improved, clarifying standards and establishing dynamic adjustment mechanisms, establishing access standards for social forces to participate in the livelihood economy, conducting periodic assessments of service providers, and implementing penalties such as fines, time-limited rectification, and cancellation of operating qualifications for providers who fail to meet standards.

(3) Accelerating the construction of livelihood finance.

Improve the guarantee mechanism of public finance, based on realistic livelihood needs, comprehensively considering factors such as government financial resources and the development stage of the region, do a good job in building inclusive, basic, and bottom-line livelihood finance, focus on major, urgent, and difficult livelihood issues, precisely exert efforts, and do a good job in basic social security for difficult groups at key time points. Adhere to taking the protection and improvement of people's livelihood as the starting point and end point for improving the level of fiscal public services, increase efforts to raise funds to support the development of livelihood undertakings, and effectively handle livelihood matters that concern the immediate interests of the masses.

（2）推动资源生成的形成，创新公共服务提供方式。

资源生成不是计划设定的产物，而是原已存在或随着时代进程的客观需要而出现的事物，它由静态进入动态，直至具备经济性和生产性。[①] 随着科技的进步和时代进程的客观需要，一些非经营性资源也可以转化为可经营性资源。

因此，对于民生经济来讲，应突出政府在基本公共服务供给保障中的主体地位，同时推动资源生成的形成，探索民生经济领域可经营性资源的形成和积累经验，促进公共服务提供主体多元化、提供方式多样化。

例如，在育幼、养老等供需矛盾突出的服务领域，应支持社会力量扩大对普惠性、规范性服务的供给，保障提供普惠性、规范性服务的各类机构平等享受优惠政策。鼓励社会力量通过公建民营、政府购买服务、政府和社会资本合作等方式参与公共服务供给。同时，应围绕公共教育、就业创业、社会保险、医疗卫生、社会服务、住房保障、公共文化体育、优抚安置、残疾人服务等领域，建立健全基本公共服务标准体系，明确标准并建立动态调整机制，建立社会力量参与民生经济的准入标准，对提供主体进行周期性考核，对无法达标的提供主体实施罚款、限期整改、取消经营资格等处罚。

（3）加快推进民生财政建设。

完善公共财政的保障机制，依据现实的民生需求，综合考虑政府财力、区域所处发展阶段等方面的因素，做好普惠性、基础性、兜底性民生财政建设，围绕民生大事急事难事，精准发力，做好关键时点困难人群的基本社会保障。坚持把保障和改善民生作为提高财政公共服务水平的出发点和落脚点，加大力度筹集财力支持民生事业发展，切实办好涉及群众切身利益的民生实事。

---

① 陈云贤：《市场竞争双重主体论——兼谈中观经济学的创立与发展》，北京大学出版社，2020，第56页。

The construction of livelihood finance should be promoted from three aspects.

First, improve the promotion mechanism conducive to more full and higher-quality employment, expand employment capacity, enhance employment quality, and alleviate structural employment contradictions.

Second, adhere to the basic synchronization of residents' income growth with economic growth, and the basic synchronization of labor remuneration increase with labor productivity increase, continuously increase the income of low-income groups, expand the middle-income group, and more actively promote common prosperity.

Third, adhere to the principle of providing protection to all who should be protected, according to the requirements of ensuring the bottom line, weaving a dense network, and building mechanisms, accelerate the improvement of a multi-level social security system that covers all people, coordinates urban and rural areas, is fair and unified, and sustainable.

## II. Guiding, Adjusting, and Warning the Industrial Economy

### (i) Government Departments Managing the Industrial Economy

Under the framework of mezzoeconomics, the industrial economy is referred to as "operative resources". Due to different economic, geographical, and natural conditions, each region generally chooses one industry from the three major industries as its leading industry. Of course, in the actual development process of regional economies in various countries, there are also successful cases where strong tertiary industries such as logistics, exhibitions, finance, tourism, intermediary services, and commercial retail have emerged in the process of developing primary or secondary industries. In traditional economics, the institutions corresponding to such resources, or institutions playing a main role in industrial economic development, are mainly enterprises.

In China, there are mainly three types of government departments coordinating, supervising, and managing such resources.

The first type is departments related to development and reform, statistics, and pricing.

The second type is further divided into four categories: first, departments related to finance, banking, taxation, and industry and commerce; second, departments related to industry, transportation, safety, energy, and tobacco; third, departments related to science and technology, information, specialized communications, and intellectual property; fourth, departments related to commerce, customs, maritime affairs, ports, postal services, quality inspection, foreign affairs, and tourism.

民生财政建设应从三个方面重点推进。

第一，健全有利于更充分更高质量就业的促进机制，扩大就业容量，提升就业质量，缓解结构性就业矛盾。

第二，坚持居民收入增长和经济增长基本同步、劳动报酬提高和劳动生产率提高基本同步，持续提高低收入群体收入，扩大中等收入群体，更加积极有为地促进共同富裕。

第三，坚持应保尽保原则，按照兜底线、织密网、建机制的要求，加快健全覆盖全民、统筹城乡、公平统一、可持续的多层次社会保障体系。

## 二、导向、调节、预警产业经济

### （一）管理产业经济的政府部门

在中观经济学的框架下，产业经济被称为"可经营性资源"。因为经济、地理和自然条件不同，所以各区域一般会选择三大产业中的某一产业作为主导产业。当然，在各国区域经济的现实发展进程中，也不乏在发展第一产业或第二产业的过程中产生强盛的物流业、会展业、金融业、旅游业、中介服务业和商贸零售业等第三产业的成功案例。传统经济学中对应此类资源的机构，或者说在产业经济发展中发挥主体作用的机构，主要是企业。

在中国，政府协调、监督、管理此类资源的部门主要有三种。

第一种是发展改革、统计、物价相关部门。

第二种又细分为四类：其一，财政、金融、税务、工商相关部门；其二，工业、交通、安全、能源、烟草相关部门；其三，科技、信息、专用通信、知识产权相关部门；其四，商务、海关、海事、口岸、邮政、质检、外事、旅游相关部门。

The third type is departments related to auditing, land supervision, and food and drug supervision and administration.

Government institutions coordinating, supervising, and managing such resources in various countries worldwide have their similarities and differences, but the policy principle for allocating such resources is mainly "revitalization", that is, guidance, regulation, and early warning. This point has already reached a consensus in theory.

The relevant policies, management levels, execution efficiency, etc. of the above-listed government departments will all have an impact on the development of the industrial economy. The following section will discuss the main measures for regional governments to develop the industrial economy from four aspects: regional government goal planning, regional government tax policies, regional government urban infrastructure supply levels, and regional government land policies.

## (ii) Regional Government Goal Planning and Industrial Economic Development

Since China's reform and opening-up, from the 12th to the 20th National Congress of the Communist Party of China, economic development goals have been formulated at each National Congress of the Communist Party of China, as shown in Table 6-1. The economic development goals set by the National Congress of the Communist Party of China are further detailed by policy documents such as five-year plans and medium and long-term development goal outlines, becoming publicly committed growth targets of the state. The national growth targets are decomposed through administrative levels to local governments at all levels, becoming publicly committed growth targets of local governments at all levels. Obviously, the goals set by local governments will not be lower than those set by the central government, resulting in the phenomenon of layer-by-layer increases. When announcing their goals, local governments will make clear plans and deployments for economic work, striving to achieve the goals. Therefore, a basic fact of China's economic growth is that local governments set regional development goals and work priorities based on important development goals and key directions, and then make efforts to fulfill government commitments.

第三种是审计、国土监察、食品药品监督管理相关部门。

世界各国政府协调、监督、管理此类资源的机构各有异同，但调配此类资源的政策原则主要是"搞活"，即导向、调节和预警。这点在理论上已经是共识。[①]

以上所列出的相关政府部门的相关政策、管理水平、执行效率等都会对产业经济的发展产生影响。下面本节从区域政府目标规划、区域政府税收政策、区域政府城市基础设施供给水平、区域政府土地政策四个方面探讨区域政府发展产业经济的主要措施。

## （二）区域政府目标规划与产业经济发展

中国改革开放以来，从党的十二大到党的二十大，历次中国共产党全国代表大会都制定了经济发展目标，具体见表6-1。中国共产党全国代表大会设定的经济发展目标会进一步由五年规划和中长期发展目标纲要等政策文件加以细化，并成为国家公开承诺的增长目标。国家的增长目标通过行政层级分解到各级地方政府，成为各级地方政府公开承诺的增长目标。显然，地方政府制定的目标不会低于中央政府制定的目标，于是出现了层层加码的现象。地方政府在公布目标的同时，会对经济工作进行明确规划和部署，力争实现目标。因此，中国经济增长的一个基本事实是，地方政府依据重要的发展目标和重点方向设定地区发展目标和工作重点，进而付出努力去完成政府承诺。

---

① 陈云贤：《市场竞争双重主体论——兼谈中观经济学的创立与发展》，北京大学出版社，2020，第58-59页。

Table 6-1　Economic Development Goals set by the National Congresses of the Communist Party of China from the 12th to the 20th CPC National Congress

| Congress | Year | Development Goals |
|---|---|---|
| 12th CPC National Congress | 1982 | From 1981 to the end of the 20th century, the overall goal for economic construction is: under the premise of continuously improving economic efficiency, strive to double the annual gross output value of the country's industry and agriculture, increasing it from 710 billion yuan in 1980 to around 2.8 trillion yuan by 2000, so that people's living standards reach a moderately prosperous level. The congress pointed out that to achieve the above goals, the first 10 years would mainly focus on laying a solid foundation, accumulating strength, and creating conditions; the next 10 years would enter a new period of economic revitalization |
| 13th CPC National Congress | 1987 | The 13th CPC National Congress, with a view to the overall situation of China's modernization construction, clarified the "three-step" strategic plan for economic construction: the first step is to double the Gross National Product (GNP) compared to 1980, solving the problem of food and clothing for the people; the second step is to double the GNP again by the end of the 20th century, bringing people's living standards to a moderately prosperous level; the third step is to reach the per capita GNP level of moderately developed countries by the middle of the 21st century, with people's lives being relatively affluent and the basic realization of modernization |
| 14th CPC National Congress | 1992 | The 14th CPC National Congress made a significant adjustment to the economic growth rate, deciding to adjust the 1990s' economic growth rate from the originally planned average annual growth of 6% of the GNP to 8% to 9%. The 14th CPC National Congress also made strategic deployments to accelerate economic development and proposed ten major tasks that must be achieved, which are crucial for the overall situation |
| 15th CPC National Congress | 1997 | The 15th CPC National Congress proposed the grand goal of our country's reform and opening up, and cross-century development of modernization construction, namely, to double the GNP compared to 2000 in the first decade of the 21st century, making people's moderately prosperous life more comfortable, and forming a relatively complete socialist market economy system; after another decade of effort, by the 100th anniversary of the founding of Communist Party of China, to further develop the national economy and improve various systems; by the middle of the century, at the 100th anniversary of the founding of People's Republic of China, to basically achieve modernization and build a strong, democratic, and civilized socialist country |
| 16th CPC National Congress | 2002 | On the basis of optimizing the structure and improving efficiency, the Gross Domestic Product (GDP) should aim to quadruple by 2020 compared to 2000, with a significant enhancement in comprehensive national strength and international competitiveness |
| 17th CPC National Congress | 2007 | On the basis of optimizing the structure, improving efficiency, reducing consumption, and protecting the environment, the per capita GDP should aim to quadruple by 2020 compared to 2000 |
| 18th CPC National Congress | 2012 | On the basis of significantly enhancing balanced, coordinated, and sustainable development, the GDP and per capita income of urban and rural residents should aim to double by 2020 compared to 2010 |
| 19th CPC National Congress | 2017 | No specific quantitative growth targets were set. However, it was clearly stated that China's economy has shifted from a phase of high-speed growth to a phase of high-quality development, and is currently in a critical period of transforming the mode of development, optimizing the economic structure, and converting the driving forces of growth. It must unswervingly take development as the top priority for the Communist Party of China's governance and rejuvenation of the country. By 2035, to basically achieve socialist modernization, and by mid-century, to build China into a great modern socialist country that is prosperous, strong, democratic, culturally advanced, harmonious, and beautiful |
| 20th CPC National Congress | 2022 | No specific quantitative growth targets were set. However, it was clearly stated that the overall strategic plan is to fully build a modern socialist country in two stages: from 2020 to 2035, to basically achieve socialist modernization; from 2035 to mid-century, to build China into a great and modern socialist country that is prosperous, strong, democratic, culturally advanced, harmonious, and beautiful |

表 6-1　从党的十二大到党的二十大，历次中国共产党全国代表大会制定的经济发展目标

| 会议 | 时间 | 发展目标 |
| --- | --- | --- |
| 党的十二大 | 1982年 | 从1981年到20世纪末，我国经济建设总的奋斗目标是：在不断提高经济效益的前提下，力争使全国工农业的年生产总值翻两番，即由1980年的7100亿元增加到2000年的2.8万亿元左右，使人民生活达到小康水平。大会指出，为实现上述目标，在部署上，前10年主要是打好基础，积蓄力量，创造条件；后10年要进入一个新的经济振兴时期 |
| 党的十三大 | 1987年 | 党的十三大着眼中国现代化建设全局，明确了我国经济建设的"三步走"战略部署：第一步，实现国民生产总值比1980年翻一番，解决人民的温饱问题；第二步，到20世纪末，使民生产总值再增长一倍，人民生活达到小康水平；第三步，到21世纪中叶，人均国民生产总值达到中等发达国家水平，人民生活比较富裕，基本实现现代化 |
| 党的十四大 | 1992年 | 党的十四大对经济发展速度作了大幅度的调整，决定将90年代我国经济的发展速度，由原定的国民生产总值平均每年增长6%调整为增长8%至9%。党的十四大还对加快经济发展作出了战略部署，提出了必须努力实现的十个方面关系全局的主要任务 |
| 党的十五大 | 1997年 | 党的十五大提出我国改革开放和现代化建设跨世纪发展的宏伟目标，即21世纪第一个十年实现国民生产总值比2000年翻一番，使人民的小康生活更加宽裕，形成比较完善的社会主义市场经济体制；再经过十年的努力，到建党100年时，使国民经济更加发展，各项制度更加完善；到世纪中叶新中国成立100年时，基本实现现代化，建成富强民主文明的社会主义国家 |
| 党的十六大 | 2002年 | 在优化结构和提高效益的基础上，国内生产总值到2020年力争比2000年翻两番，综合国力和国际竞争力明显增强 |
| 党的十七大 | 2007年 | 在优化结构、提高效益、降低消耗、保护环境的基础上，实现人均国内生产总值到2020年比2000年翻两番 |
| 党的十八大 | 2012年 | 在发展平衡性、协调性、可持续性明显增强基础上，实现国内生产总值和城乡居民人均收入比2010年翻一番 |
| 党的十九大 | 2017年 | 未提出量化增长目标。但明确指出：我国经济已由高速增长阶段转向高质量发展阶段，正处在转变发展方式、优化经济结构、转换增长动力的攻关期。必须坚定不移把发展作为党执政兴国的第一要务。到2035年基本实现社会主义现代化，到本世纪中叶把我国建成富强民主文明和谐美丽的社会主义现代化强国 |
| 党的二十大 | 2022年 | 未提出量化增长目标。但明确提出全面建成社会主义现代化强国，总的战略安排是分两步走：从2020年到2035年基本实现社会主义现代化；从2035年到本世纪中叶把我国建成富强民主文明和谐美丽的社会主义现代化强国 |

Existing literature has shown that the setting of government economic development goals creates economic growth pressure for regional governments, which has produced varying degrees of promoting effects on regional actual growth, total factor productivity, investment, land transfer, urbanization and even infrastructure construction. Regional governments exhibit significant horizontal competitive strategic interactions when setting economic development goals. Therefore, setting economic development goals and further formulating corresponding development plans and implementation schemes is also a manifestation of regional government competitive behavior, which promotes the development of regional industrial economy.

## (iii) Regional Government Tax Policies and Industrial Economic Development

Tax competition between regions mainly refers to attracting the inflow of valuable economic resources by reducing taxpayers' tax burden; public expenditure competition between regions is to compete for scarce economic resources through the provision of public goods and services. Because in reality, governments mainly use taxation to finance public expenditure, these two different types of competition will ultimately be reflected in the tax burden levels between regions. From a global perspective, tax competition between regions has long existed. In order to attract the factor resources needed in their regions, various regions implement tax reductions on the entry and even profitability of these factor resources in their regions. Some regions are even called "tax havens" due to extremely low tax rates.

Theoretically, the relationship between taxation and industrial economic development is relatively complex. The development of industrial economy requires the injection of factors such as capital, labor, and technology. According to public choice theory, taxation can be seen as the supply price of public goods.

From the perspective of the impact of specific taxes, at the micro-entity level: personal income tax and property tax affect households' actual income and wealth, thus affecting labor transfer and labor supply; corporate income tax and capital income tax also inversely affect entrepreneurs' actual income, thus affecting their investment decisions.

From the perspective of government macro-management: The actual tax burden of a region affects the region's total tax revenue, which in turn affects the public expenditure of regional governments in providing public goods. The level of public goods provision

已有文献表明，政府经济发展目标的设定形成了区域政府的经济增长压力，这对区域实际增长[①]、全要素生产率[②]、投资[③]、土地出让[④]、城镇化[⑤]乃至基础设施建设等方面产生了不同程度的促进作用，而区域政府在制定经济发展目标时存在显著的横向竞争性策略互动[⑥]。因此，设定经济发展目标并进一步制定相应的发展规划和实施方案也是区域政府竞争行为的一种体现，它推动了区域产业经济的发展。

### （三）区域政府税收政策与产业经济发展

区域间税收竞争主要指通过降低纳税人的税收负担来吸引有价值的经济资源的流入；区域间公共支出竞争则是以公共物品和服务供给来竞争稀缺经济资源。因为现实中政府主要是通过税收手段为公共支出筹资，所以这两种性质不同的竞争方式，最终都会在区域间的税负水平中得到反映。[⑦] 从全球范围看，区域间的税收竞争早已存在，各区域为了吸引本区域需要的要素资源，对这种要素资源的进入乃至在本区域的获利实施减税，一些区域甚至由于税率极低而被称为"避税天堂"。

从理论上说，税收和产业经济发展的关系比较复杂。产业经济的发展需要资本、劳动力、技术等要素的注入，依据公共选择理论，税收可被看作公共物品的供给价格。

从具体税种所产生的影响看，微观主体的角度：个人所得税和财产税会影响家庭的实际收入和财富，从而影响劳动力的转移和劳动供给；企业所得税和资本所得税也会反向影响企业家的实际收入，从而影响其投资决策。

政府宏观管理的角度：区域实际税负影响区域的总税收收入，进而影响区域

---

[①] 徐现祥、刘毓芸：《经济增长目标管理》，《经济研究》2017年第7期。

[②] 徐现祥、李书娟、王贤彬等：《中国经济增长目标的选择：以高质量发展终结"崩溃论"》，《世界经济》2018年第10期。

[③] 刘淑琳、王贤彬、黄亮雄：《经济增长目标驱动投资吗？——基于2001—2016年地级市样本的理论分析与实证检验》，《金融研究》2019年第8期。

[④] 胡深、吕冰洋：《经济增长目标与土地出让》，《财政研究》2019年第7期。

[⑤] 黄亮雄、王贤彬、刘淑琳：《经济增长目标与激进城镇化——来自夜间灯光数据的证据》，《世界经济》2021年第6期。

[⑥] 王贤彬、黄亮雄：《地方经济增长目标管理——一个三元框架的理论构建与实证检验》，《经济理论与经济管理》2019年第9期。

[⑦] 沈坤荣、付文林：《税收竞争、地区博弈及其增长绩效》，《经济研究》2006年第6期。

determines whether households and entrepreneurs will face external economies, thus affecting their location decisions.

It can be seen that for a region, high tax rates mean high prices for public goods, which undoubtedly increases the operating costs of the industrial economy, leading to the flow of industrial economy to low-tax regions. However, high tax rates also mean that the government can obtain more tax revenue, which provides the possibility of providing higher quality public goods. With the help of high-level public goods, the industrial economy can obtain higher external benefits, reduce operating costs, and thus accelerate development. Therefore, when regions engage in tax competition and adopt low tax burden policies, it seems to attract labor and capital inflows, but in the short term, local financial resources will decrease, public goods supply may decrease, leading to external diseconomies locally, which may in turn promote labor and capital outflows.

Tax competition between regions in China is considered to have officially begun with the tax-sharing system reform in 1994. Under the framework of the tax-sharing system, local governments were given relatively independent fiscal and administrative powers. To promote regional economic development, local governments used taxation as a means of competition. In a country like China where investment-driven economic growth is very typical, the goal of tax competition between local governments is to guide cross-region and cross-industry resource flows to influence investment direction and capital stock. This will greatly affect the process, intensity, and efficiency of industrial structure adjustment in the region.

Specifically, tax competition between regions in China mainly takes the following forms.

The first form is tax exemption. Tax exemption is the most direct means of tax competition among regions, but this exemption is characterized by local governments infringing on the unified tax authority of the central government. This form appeared from the beginning of the reform. After the tax-sharing system reform in 1994, as the central government took various measures to unify tax authority, tax exemption is no longer the main form of tax competition. However, there still exist forms of competition such as using preferential policies for development zones and free trade zones to provide tax exemptions, lowering industry entry barriers, and using special industry preferential policies for tax exemptions.

政府提供公共物品的公共支出，而公共物品的提供水平又决定了家庭和企业是否会面临外部经济，从而影响其区位决策。

可见，对一个区域来说，高税率意味着公共物品价格高，这无疑提升了产业经济的运行成本，导致产业经济向低税率区域流转；但高税率也意味着政府能够获取更多的税收，这为提供更高质量的公共物品提供了可能，在高水平公共物品的帮助下，产业经济能够获取更高的外部收益，降低运行成本，从而加快发展步伐。因此，区域之间进行税收竞争，竞相采取低税负政策，看似能够吸引劳动力和资本流入，但短期内地方财力会下降，公共物品供给可能下降，导致当地存在外部不经济的现象，这又可能促使劳动力和资本流出。①

中国各区域间的税收竞争被认为正式开始于1994年分税制改革，在分税制框架下，地方政府被赋予了相对独立的财权和事权，为了推动本区域经济发展，地方政府运用税收手段展开竞争。在中国这样一个投资拉动型经济增长非常典型的国家，地方政府间税收竞争的目标在于引导资源跨地区、跨行业流动，以影响投资方向和资本存量。这会在很大程度上对本区域产业结构调整的进程、力度与效率产生影响。②

具体地说，中国各区域间的税收竞争主要有以下几种形式。③④

第一种形式是税收减免。税收减免是各区域税收竞争的最直接手段，但这种减免是以地方政府侵犯中央政府统一税权为特征的。这种形式从改革之初就出现，1994年分税制改革之后，由于中央在税权统一上采取了种种措施，税收减免已不再是主要的税收竞争形式。但仍存在利用对开发区、自贸区等的优惠政策进行税收减免，降低行业准入门槛，利用特殊行业优惠政策进行税收减免等竞争形式。

---

① 李涛、黄纯纯、周业安：《税收、税收竞争与中国经济增长》，《世界经济》2011年第4期。
② 孔令池、高波、李言：《市场开放、地方财税竞争与产业结构调整——基于我国省级面板数据的实证研究》，《经济理论与经济管理》2017年第10期。
③ 杨志勇：《国内税收竞争理论：结合我国现实的分析》，《税务研究》2003年第6期。
④ 曾小林、陈俊宏：《我国地方政府非规范性税收竞争的策略形式及效应分析》，《中外企业家》2019年第5期。

The second form is fiscal support. Local governments support enterprises by injecting funds, but the level of support is actually linked to enterprise taxation, essentially a form of tax rebate. Specific forms include direct rebates of taxes and fees, low-price land supply, etc.

The third form is that local governments increase public expenditure in specific directions and reduce fees that should be charged through comprehensive supporting measures. Local governments use general tax revenue for specific investment projects and specific objects to improve infrastructure, which has the effect of attracting capital, but in fact reduces the disposable income of local governments for general public services.

In terms of the effects of tax competition, tax exemption and fiscal support can form an attraction effect on the industrial economy. However, if tax exemption and fiscal support policies are overused, it will form a race-to-the-bottom Bertrand-style competition in tax rates between regions, leading to tax rate differences being erased, bringing heavy fiscal burdens to regional governments, and ultimately harming the development of the industrial economy due to the difficulty in improving the quality of public goods supply. Therefore, regional governments should carefully implement tax competition measures. If regional governments want to attract industries that conform to their regional development strategies to form agglomeration effects, they can adopt corresponding tax exemption policies on the basis of effective coordination with surrounding regions. After forming agglomeration effects, these exemption policies can be timely withdrawn, allowing the region to enter a virtuous development track.

## (iv) Regional Government Urban Infrastructure Supply Level and Industrial Economic Development

Mezzoeconomics considers urban infrastructure as generative resources, referring to public works facilities that provide public services for social production and residents' lives. It is a public goods system used to ensure normal regional socio-economic activities and people's daily lives. Urban infrastructure can include three levels. The first level refers to the city's hardware and software infrastructure[①]; The second level refers to infrastructure invested

---

① Subsequently, we will provide a more detailed explanation of the classification of the city's hardware and software infrastructure.

and developed with the process of urban-rural integration; the third level refers to the series of smart city projects gradually developed and constructed with the process of urban-rural management modernization.

Urban infrastructure is an immovable resource of the city, defining the upper limit of

第二种形式是财政扶持。地方政府通过向企业注入资金对企业进行扶持，但扶持力度实际上与企业税收挂钩，实质是一种税收返还。其具体形式包括直接返还税费、低价供地等。

第三种形式是地方政府通过综合配套措施，增加特定方向的公共支出，并减少应该收取的费用。各地方政府将一般税收收入用于特定投资项目和特定对象进行基础设施改善，起到了吸引资本的作用，但事实上减少了地方政府用于一般公共服务的可支配收入。

从税收竞争的效果上看，税收减免和财政扶持能够对产业经济形成吸引效应，但如果税收减免和财政扶持政策被过度使用，就会形成区域间在税率上进行逐底的伯川德式竞争，从而导致税率差异被抹平，给区域政府带来沉重的财税负担，并最终由于公共物品供给质量难以提升而损害产业经济的发展。因此，区域政府应谨慎实施税收竞争措施，如果区域政府为了吸引符合本区域发展战略的产业以形成集聚效应，那么在与周边区域进行有效协调的基础上可以采取相应的税收减免政策，而在形成集聚效应后这种减免政策可以适时退出，从而使区域进入良性发展轨道。

### （四）区域政府城市基础设施供给水平与产业经济发展

中观经济学认为，城市基础设施属于生成性资源，指为社会生产和居民生活提供公共服务的公共工程设施，是用于保证区域社会经济活动和人们日常生活正常进行的公共物品系统。城市基础设施可包括三个层次，第一个层次指城市的软硬件基础设施①；第二个层次指随着城乡一体化的进程所投资与开发的基础设施；第三个层次指随着城乡管理现代化的进程，逐步开发和建设的智能城市系列工程等。

城市基础设施是城市不可移动的资源，它定义了区域对人口和产业的承载能

---

① 之后我们将对城市的软硬件基础设施的分类进行更为具体的阐述。

the region's carrying capacity for population and industry. In this sense, the supply scale and quality of urban infrastructure determine the development level of the regional industrial economy. With the advent of the high-quality development era, the supply quality of urban infrastructure is crucial to regional competitiveness, determining a region's industrial structure level and value chain position. High-tech urban infrastructure can support the development of high-tech industries, shaping the region's ability to attract talents, technology, capital, resources, and other factors by affecting the return on investment of industries, thereby influencing the industrial scale and quality of the region.

Facing fierce regional competition, regional governments should use the upgrade of urban infrastructure as a starting point to continuously enhance the region's ability to attract and support factors such as talent, technology, and capital.

First, in terms of infrastructure investment structure, they should widely absorb social capital and actively encourage social forces to participate in infrastructure construction.

Second, in terms of infrastructure operation and management, they can adopt sole proprietorship, share cooperation, state-owned private operation, and other methods, flexibly set property rights structures, and improve the level of infrastructure operation and management.

Third, efforts should be made to promote smart city construction, greatly enhance the technological level of infrastructure, and improve the region's carrying capacity for high-tech industries and high value-added industries.

Fourth, they should provide characteristic infrastructure that can adapt to the actual situation of the region, combining unique natural and historical conditions of the region. Regional governments should carefully design and plan urban infrastructure objectives, key implementation steps, and specific plans according to their development goals.

Finally, regional governments enhance regional competitiveness by strengthening urban infrastructure construction, attracting and carrying larger-scale and higher-quality industrial economies.

## (v) Regional Government Land Policies and Industrial Economic Development

Accompanying China's rapid economic growth is a rapid urbanization process. Factors such as talent, capital, and technology continue to concentrate in cities, constantly expanding their demand for urban land, thus making land factors an important bargaining chip for regional governments to promote regional economic growth, especially urban economic growth, in the early stages of economic development. With the gradual increase in the

力上限，从这个意义上讲，城市基础设施的供给规模和质量决定了区域产业经济的发展水平。随着高质量发展时代的来临，城市基础设施的供给质量对区域竞争力至关重要，它决定了一个区域的产业结构水平和价值链位置。高技术性城市基础设施能够支撑高新技术产业的发展，通过影响产业的投资回报率，塑造区域吸引人才、技术、资本、资源等要素的能力，从而影响区域的产业规模和产业素质。[①]

面对激烈的区域竞争，区域政府应以城市基础设施的提档升级为抓手，不断增强区域对人才、科技和资本等要素的吸引和支撑能力。

第一，在基础设施投资结构上，应广泛吸纳社会资本，积极鼓励社会力量参与基础设施建设。

第二，在基础设施运营管理方面，可采取独资经营、股份合作、国有民营等方式，灵活设置产权结构，提高基础设施运营管理水平。

第三，应努力推进智能城市建设力度，大力提升基础设施科技水平，提高区域对高新技术产业、高附加值产业的承载能力。

第四，应结合区域独特的自然和历史条件，提供能够适应本区域实际的有特色的基础设施。区域政府应根据其发展目标，精心设计和规划城市基础设施目标、重点实施步骤和具体方案。

最终，区域政府通过加强城市基础设施建设，吸引和承载更大规模和更高质量的产业经济，推动区域竞争力的提档升级。

## （五）区域政府土地政策与产业经济发展

与中国高速经济增长相伴而生的是迅速的城市化进程，人才、资本和科技等要素不断向城市集聚，不断扩大其对城市的土地需求，从而使土地要素成为区域

---

① 倪鹏飞：《中国城市竞争力与基础设施关系的实证研究》，《中国工业经济》2002年第5期。

marketization of land use, land transfer fees have become a major source of income for regional governments. Therefore, urban economic prosperity drives up land prices, thereby expanding government revenue, allowing the government to invest more funds in urban construction, which in turn further promotes the enhancement of urban competitiveness. It can be seen that how to scientifically and effectively develop and utilize land resources is an important means for regional governments to enhance urban competitiveness.

Figure 6-2 shows the land income situation of some cities in China from 2017 to 2021.

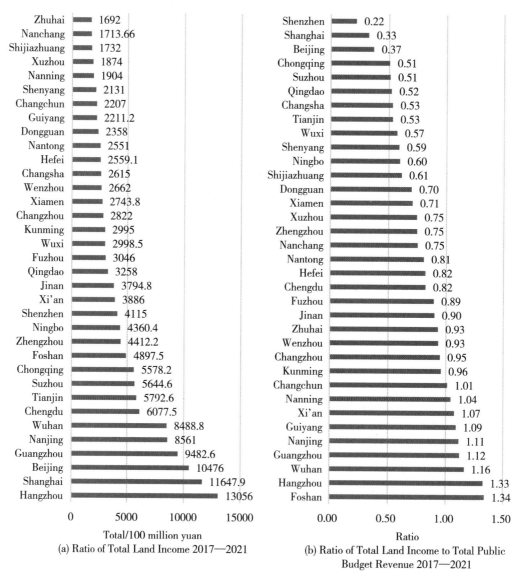

Figure 6-2　Land Income Situation of Some Cities in China from 2017 to 2021

政府在经济发展的初期阶段推动区域经济特别是城市经济增长的重要筹码。随着土地使用市场化程度的逐步提高，土地出让金已成为区域政府的一项主要收入来源。因此，城市经济繁荣推动土地价格提升，从而扩大政府收入，使政府有更多的资金投入城市建设，由此进一步推动城市竞争力的提升。可见，如何科学有效地开发和利用土地资源，是区域政府提升城市竞争力的重要手段。

我国部分城市2017—2021年土地收入情况见图6-2。

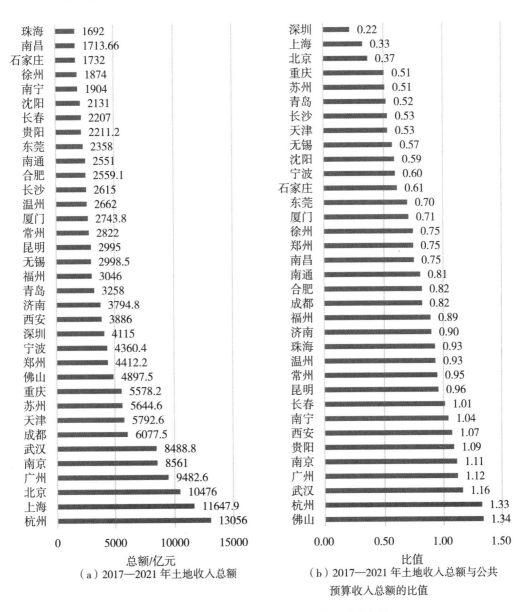

(a) 2017—2021年土地收入总额

(b) 2017—2021年土地收入总额与公共预算收入总额的比值

图6-2 我国部分城市2017—2021年土地收入情况

In contrast to the soaring land prices, regional governments have implemented land price preferential measures to attract industrial economies, forming a "race-to-the-bottom" land supply strategy that suppresses industrial land prices. However, as the economy and society enter a new stage of high-quality development, regional governments' strategies for using land to develop industrial economies have also changed. On one hand, industrial land in some regions has shown high premium phenomena, indicating that the prisoner's dilemma-style land competition among regional governments has eased; on the other hand, regions' land policies have been continuously refined, implementing land price preferential measures more targeted at key industries for regional development. For example, Shanghai, where land is extremely valuable, transferred industrial land to Tesla at a low price of about 1,200 yuan per square meter, thus supporting the development of Shanghai's new energy vehicle industry. These phenomena indicate that the trend of regional governments engaging in differentiated land-based investment attraction competition is becoming increasingly prominent.

The scale and price of land supply are important competitive means for regional governments, but from the perspective of coordinated regional development, regional governments should adopt scientific land competition strategies in combination with their actual situations.

First, economically developed regions should continue to adhere to and improve the marketization system of land transfer, implement an enterprise entry review system, actively attract high-tech enterprises to replace enterprises with backward production capacity, achieve "emptying the cage and changing birds", increase urban industrial added value, and enhance urban competitiveness.

Second, underdeveloped regions should actively expand non-land revenue and reduce fiscal revenue's dependence on land. At the same time, they should formulate industrial development strategies that fit their regional economic and social conditions based on their resource endowments and location advantages, guide the rational allocation of factor resources among industrial sectors, and then selectively undertake projects from developed regions.

Third, multi-dimensional competition between regional governments should be expanded to weaken the dependence on low-price land supply.

Fourth, when setting high thresholds and selectively introducing key industries, regional governments also need to avoid industrial restructuring problems caused by over-investment. They should grasp the inherent characteristics and development laws of industries to maximize the positive effects of differentiated land-based investment attraction.

与土地价格高涨相对的是，区域政府为了吸引产业经济，纷纷实施地价优惠措施，形成了压低工业用地价格的"寻底式"供地策略。① 然而，随着经济社会步入高质量发展新阶段，区域政府利用土地发展产业经济的策略也产生了变化。一方面，一些区域的工业用地出现了高溢价现象，表明区域政府囚徒困境式的土地竞争有所缓和；另一方面，各区域土地政策不断细化，更多地针对本区域重点发展的产业实施地价优惠措施。例如，寸土寸金的上海市将工业用地以约1200元／平方米的低价出让给了特斯拉公司，从而支持上海市新能源汽车产业的发展。这些现象表明，区域政府进行差别化以地引资竞争的态势正日趋凸显。

土地供给规模和供给价格是区域政府重要的竞争手段，但从区域协调发展的角度看，区域政府应结合本区域实际，采取科学的土地竞争策略。

第一，经济发达区域应继续坚持和完善土地市场化出让制度，对进入企业实施审查制度，积极吸引高新技术企业替代产能落后企业，实现"腾笼换鸟"，提高城市产业附加值，提升城市竞争力。

第二，欠发达区域应积极扩大土地外收入，降低财政收入的土地依赖性。同时结合本区域资源禀赋和区位优势制定符合本区域经济社会条件的产业发展战略，引导要素资源在产业部门间合理配置，进而可以有选择地承接来自发达区域的项目。

第三，应拓展区域政府间的多维竞争，削弱对低价供地的依赖程度。

第四，区域政府在设置高门槛，有选择地引入重点产业时，同样需要避免过度投资带来的产业重构问题，应把握好产业的自身特征和发展规律，最大限度地发挥差别化以地引资的正向效果。

---

① 杨其静、吴海军：《产能过剩、中央管制与地方政府反应》，《世界经济》2016年第11期。

## III. Allocating, Participating in, and Maintaining Order in Urban Economy

(i) Urban Economy and Regional Competitive Advantage

1. Definition of Urban Economy

After analyzing regional government competition in the livelihood economy (non-operative resources) and industrial economy (operative resources), we further discuss how regional governments compete in urban economic development. Under the framework of mezzoeconomics, urban resources are divided into broad and narrow senses. Urban resources in the broad sense include industrial resources, livelihood resources, and infrastructure/public works resources, while urban resources in the narrow sense include investment and construction of infrastructure hardware and software, as well as the development and operation of smart cities in the further modernization process. It is an important means for regional governments to promote economic development. The urban economy discussed here refers to urban resources in the narrow sense.

As mentioned earlier, urban infrastructure as a generative resource refers to public works facilities that provide public services for social production and residents' lives. It is a public goods system used to ensure normal regional socio-economic activities and people's daily lives, including the following three levels.

The first level is the city's hardware and software infrastructure.

Specifically, hardware infrastructure often refers to six major engineering infrastructure systems: first, energy supply system, including electricity, coal gas, natural gas, liquefied petroleum gas, and heating; second, water supply and drainage system, including water resource protection, waterworks, water supply network, drainage, and sewage treatment; third, transportation system, divided into external and internal transportation facilities, the former including aviation, railways, long-distance buses and highways, the latter including roads, bridges, tunnels, subways, light rail elevated lines, public transportation, taxis, parking lots, ferries, etc.; fourth, postal and telecommunication system, such as postal service, telegraph, fixed telephone, mobile phone, internet, radio and television, etc.; fifth, environmental protection and sanitation system, such as landscaping, garbage collection and treatment, pollution control, etc.; Sixth, defense and disaster prevention safety system, such as fire prevention, flood control, earthquake prevention, typhoon prevention, sand prevention, ground subsidence prevention, air defense, etc.

## 三、调配、参与、维序城市经济

### （一）城市经济与区域竞争优势

#### 1. 城市经济的界定

分析了区域政府在民生经济（非经营性资源）和产业经济（可经营性资源）中的竞争后，我们进一步对区域政府如何在城市经济的发展中展开竞争进行探讨。在中观经济学的框架下，城市资源有广义与狭义之分，广义的城市资源包括了产业资源、民生资源和基础设施/公共工程资源，而狭义的城市资源则包括基础设施硬件、软件的投资建设，以及更进一步的现代化进程中智能城市的开发和运作，它是区域政府推动经济发展的重要手段，这里所阐述的城市经济，是狭义的城市资源。

正如前面所述，作为生成性资源的城市基础设施指的是为社会生产和居民生活提供公共服务的公共工程设施，是用于保证区域社会经济活动和人们日常生活正常进行的公共物品系统，包括以下三个层次。

第一个层次为城市的软硬件基础设施。

具体来说，硬件基础设施多指六大系统工程性基础设施：第一，能源供应系统，包括电力、煤气、天然气、液化石油气和暖气等；第二，供水排水系统，包括水资源保护、自来水厂、供水管网、排水和污水处理；第三，交通运输系统，分为对外交通设施和对内交通设施，前者包括航空、铁路、长途汽车和高速公路，后者包括道路、桥梁、隧道、地铁、轻轨高架、公共交通、出租汽车、停车场、轮渡等；第四，邮电通信系统，如邮政、电报、固定电话、移动电话、互联网、广播电视等；第五，环保环卫系统，如园林绿化、垃圾收集与处理、污染治理等；第六，防卫防灾安全系统，如消防、防汛、防震、防台风、防风沙、防地面沉降、防空等。

Software infrastructure mainly refers to social infrastructure such as administrative management, culture and education, medical care, commercial services, finance and insurance, and social welfare.

The second level refers to four major categories of infrastructure that are included in urban infrastructure with the development of urban-rural integration: rural production infrastructure, rural living infrastructure, rural ecological environment construction, and rural social development infrastructure.

The third level refers to a series of smart city projects that are gradually developed and constructed with the modernization of urban-rural management, which are also the "new infrastructure" and the projects and facilities it use in the current stage.

## 2. How Urban Economy Affects Regional Competitiveness

Mezzoeconomics believes that enterprise competition mainly occurs in the industrial economy, while regional government competition mainly occurs in the urban economy, and this competition is mainly concentrated in the field of urban infrastructure construction. Its essence is the competition for various tangible or intangible resources in urban economic development, with the main purpose of optimizing urban resource allocation in the region, improving urban economic efficiency and investment return rate in the region. Regional governments mainly formulate supporting policies and measures around the leading advantages and sustainable development goals of the urban economy in their regions. Good urban infrastructure is a necessary material basis for enhancing the region's attractiveness and carrying capacity for resource factors. It influences the region's ability to attract various resource factors by affecting the return on investment of urban industries, thus having an important impact on the industrial scale and quality of the region.

(1) Urban Infrastructure Construction and Regional Competitiveness.

Let's first take the six major systems of hardware infrastructure as an example to explore how urban infrastructure construction affects regional competitiveness.

First, the energy supply system. With the expansion of urban scale, population growth, and industrial economic expansion, the support and guarantee of the energy supply system play a key role in the sustainable development of cities. Existing research shows that urban population density is one of the key indicators affecting urban energy consumption, and the increasingly apparent urban sprawl has led to a rapid rise in transportation energy

软件基础设施主要是指行政管理、文化教育、医疗卫生、商业服务、金融保险、社会福利等社会性基础设施。①

第二个层次指随着城乡一体化的发展，城市基础设施还包括乡村生产性基础设施、乡村生活性基础设施、乡村生态环境建设和乡村社会发展基础设施四大类。

第三个层次指随着城乡管理现代化的发展，城市基础设施还包括逐步开发和建设的智能城市系列工程等，也就是现阶段的"新基建"及其运用的项目设施。

**2. 城市经济怎样影响区域竞争力**

中观经济学认为，企业竞争主要发生在产业经济中，区域政府竞争主要发生在城市经济中，且这种竞争主要集中在城市基础设施建设领域，其实质是对城市经济发展中各种有形或无形资源的竞争，其目的主要在于优化本区域城市资源配置，提高本区域城市经济效率和投资回报率。区域政府主要围绕本区域城市经济的领先优势和可持续发展目标来配套政策措施。良好的城市基础设施是增强区域对资源要素的吸引力和承载能力的必要物质基础，它通过影响城市产业投资回报率，提升区域吸引各种资源要素的能力，对区域的产业规模和产业素质产生重要影响。②

（1）城市基础设施建设与区域竞争力。

首先我们以硬件基础设施的六大系统为例，探讨城市基础设施建设如何影响区域竞争力。

第一，能源供应系统。随着城市规模的扩大、人口的增长和产业经济的扩张，能源供应系统的支撑和保障对城市的可持续发展发挥着关键作用。已有研究表明，城市人口密度是影响城市能源消耗的关键指标之一，日益明显的城市蔓延导致交通能耗快速上升。程开明和徐扬③利用中国213个地级及以上城市面板数据所做的实证研究表明，城市蔓延对电力强度具有显著的正向影响。然而，在城市发展和用电增长的背景下，面对环境恶化和节能减排的压力，中国未来的电力

---

① 陈云贤：《市场竞争双重主体论——兼谈中观经济学的创立与发展》，北京大学出版社，2020，第57-58页。
② 倪鹏飞：《中国城市竞争力与基础设施关系的实证研究》，《中国工业经济》2002年第5期。
③ 程开明、徐扬：《城市蔓延对电力强度的影响——基于中国地级及以上城市面板数据的分析》，《城市问题》2019年第7期。

consumption. Cheng Kaiming and Xu Yang, using panel data from 213 prefecture-level and above cities in China, conducted an empirical study showing that urban sprawl has a significant positive impact on electricity intensity. However, against the background of urban development and electricity consumption growth, facing environmental degradation and pressure for energy conservation and emission reduction, China's future electricity intensity needs to be further reduced. Therefore, under the current tight constraints of the "dual carbon" goals, China's urban energy demand and supply structure are undergoing rapid changes. Regional governments should adapt to and even lead this change, which can not only reflect the level of comprehensive urban governance but also accumulate strength for enhancing regional competitiveness.

Second, the water supply and drainage system. The construction level of the water supply and drainage system is an important constraining factor for urban economic growth, especially for cities in northern China, where water supply capacity, quality, and price become prerequisites for industrial development and population agglomeration. The *Outline of the 14th Five-Year Plan for National Economic and Social Development of the People's Republic of China and the Long-Range Objectives Through the Year 2035* proposes to "adhere to water conservation priority, improve the water resource allocation system, construct backbone projects for water resource allocation, and strengthen the construction of key water sources and urban emergency backup water source projects". On the demand side, waste should be reduced, and on the supply side, infrastructure construction should be further strengthened. Enhancing urban water supply capacity is not only an important part of the overall planning system to accelerate urbanization but also has important significance for coordinating the dynamic relationship among living, production, and ecology, as well as maintaining sustainable economic and social development.

Third, the transportation system. The construction of the transportation system plays an important role in enhancing regional competitiveness. It can effectively expand urban space, provide necessary spatial conditions for urban development, allowing cities to spread in a leapfrog (enclave) manner, forming manufacturing clusters in far suburbs away from the central urban area. Some scholars have studied the impact of urban roads and public transportation on urban growth in the United States from 1980 to 2000, finding that a 10% increase in urban road stock would lead to a 2% increase in population and employment.

However, other studies have pointed out that infrastructure investment in underdeveloped areas may be inefficient, arguing that transportation facility investments in the United States tend to favor low-income, low-density areas, but these areas lack agglomeration effects, thus reducing the efficiency of infrastructure utilization. For China, with the rapid advancement of

强度需要进一步降低。① 因此，在当前"双碳"目标的紧约束下，中国的城市能源需求和供给结构正在发生快速转变。区域政府应适应乃至引领这种变革，这不仅可以体现城市综合治理水平，也可以为区域竞争力的提升积蓄力量。

第二，供水排水系统。供水排水系统的建设水平是城市经济增长的重要制约因素，尤其对中国北方城市而言，供水能力、供水质量和供水价格成为产业发展和人口集聚的先决条件。《中华人民共和国国民经济和社会发展第十四个五年规划和2035年远景目标纲要》提出，要"坚持节水优先，完善水资源配置体系，建设水资源配置骨干项目，加强重点水源和城市应急备用水源工程建设"，在需求层面应减少浪费，在供给层面应进一步加强基础设施建设。提升城市水供应能力不仅是加快城市化进程整体规划体系的重要组成部分，也对协调生活、生产、生态三者之间动态关系以及维护经济社会可持续发展具有重要意义。

第三，交通运输系统。交通运输系统的建设对区域竞争力的提升具有重要作用，它能够有效拉开城市空间，为城市发展提供必要的空间条件，使城市能够以蛙跳（飞地）方式蔓延，在远离中心城区的远郊形成制造业集聚区。② 有学者研究了美国1980—2000年城市道路和公共交通对城市增长的影响，发现城市道路存量增加10%，将导致人口和就业增加2%。③ 但也有研究指出，针对欠发达地区的基础设施投入可能是低效率的，认为美国交通设施投入偏向于低收入、低密度的地区，但这些地区缺乏集聚效应，从而会降低基础设施利用效率。④ 对中国来说，随着城市化进程的迅速推进，中国交通运输系统建设水平不断提高，这有效带动

---

① 林伯强、杜克锐：《理解中国能源强度的变化：一个综合的分解框架》，《世界经济》2014年第4期。

② 洪世键、张京祥：《交通基础设施与城市空间增长——基于城市经济学的视角》，《城市规划》2010年第5期。

③ Gilles Duranton and Matthew A. Turner, "Urban Growth and Transportation," *The Review of Economic Studies* 79, no.4 (2012): 1407-1440.

④ Edward L. Glaeser and Joshua D. Gottlieb, "The Economics of Place-Making Policies," *Brookings Papers on Economic Activity* 39, no.1 (2008): 155-239.

urbanization, the level of China's transportation system construction has been continuously improving, which has effectively driven the increase in surrounding land value and adjustment of industrial structure, playing a crucial role in the overall urban development process.

Fourth, the postal and telecommunications system. The construction of the postal and telecommunications system can effectively reduce transaction costs, lower enterprise operating costs, improve regional operational efficiency, thus having a positive promoting effect on regional economic growth. Some scholars have used telephone service prices, number of main telephone lines per 100 households, and fixed broadband speed to measure the construction status of the postal and telecommunications system, using panel data from OECD countries to examine the relationship between postal and telecommunications system construction and economic growth, finding that the construction of the postal and telecommunications system has a significant promoting effect on economic growth. In domestic Chinese research, Liu Shenglong and Hu Angang, Han Baoguo and Zhu Pingfang, Zheng Shilin et al., Zhang Xun and Wan Guanghua respectively used total postal and telecommunications business volume, broadband penetration rate, telephone penetration rate, and whether landline telephones can be obtained to measure the construction status of the postal and telecommunications system, confirming that the construction of the postal and telecommunications system has played a positive role in promoting economic growth, improving regional productivity, and improving income distribution. China launched the national smart city construction pilot and the "Broadband China" construction in 2012 and 2013 respectively, which are two important strategies for China to advance new infrastructure construction. Research has shown that national smart city construction can promote the improvement of the "quantity" and "quality" of green technology innovation through information support effects, scale agglomeration effects, and capital allocation effects. The "Broadband China" construction can significantly improve the level of urban internet development, thus driving the enhancement of urban innovation capabilities.

Fifth, the environmental protection and sanitation system. "Lucid waters and lush mountains are invaluable assets" is a scientific assertion put forward by Xi Jinping, then Secretary of the Zhejiang Provincial Party Committee, during his inspection in Yu Village, Anji County, Zhejiang Province in August 2005. Subsequently, Xi Jinping has reiterated the development concept of "Lucid waters and lush mountains are invaluable assets" on multiple occasions. On October 12, 2021, Xi Jinping emphasized in his video speech at Leaders' Summit of the 15th Meeting of the Conference of the Parties To the Convention on Biological Diversity: "Lucid waters and lush mountains are invaluable assets. A sound ecology and

了周边土地价值的提升与产业结构的调整[①],在城市整体发展过程中发挥着至关重要的作用[②]。

第四,邮电通信系统。邮电通信系统的建设能够有效降低交易成本,降低企业运行成本,提高区域运行效率,从而对区域经济增长产生正向促进作用。有学者分别以电话服务价格、每百户电话线主线数、固定宽带速度衡量邮电通信系统建设状况,运用经济合作与发展组织中国家的面板数据考察了邮电通信系统建设与经济增长的关系,发现邮电通信系统的建设对经济增长具有显著的促进作用。中国国内研究中,刘生龙和胡鞍钢,韩宝国和朱平芳,郑世林等,张勋和万广华分别以邮电业务总量、宽带渗透率、电话普及率、是否可取得座机电话衡量邮电通信系统的建设状况,证实邮电通信系统的建设在促进经济增长、提高区域生产率、改善收入分配等方面发挥了积极的作用。中国于 2012 年和 2013 年分别启动了国家智慧城市建设试点和"宽带中国"建设,这是中国推进新型基础设施建设的两项重要战略。有研究表明,国家智慧城市建设能够通过信息支撑效应、规模集聚效应和资金配置效应促进绿色技术创新"量"和"质"的提升。[③]"宽带中国"建设能够显著提高城市互联网发展水平,进而驱动城市创新能力的提升。[④]

第五,环保环卫系统。"绿水青山就是金山银山"是时任中国浙江省委书记的习近平于 2005 年 8 月在浙江省安吉县余村考察时提出的科学论断,之后,习近平在多个场合重申了要坚持"绿水青山就是金山银山"的发展理念。2021 年 10 月 12 日,习近平在《生物多样性公约》第十五次缔约方大会领导人峰会的视频讲话中强调:"绿水青山就是金山银山。良好生态环境既是自然财富,也是经

---

① 周耀东、张佳仪:《城市轨道交通经济效应实证研究:以北京市为例》,《城市问题》2013 年第 10 期。

② 孙钰、崔寅、冯延超:《城市公共交通基础设施的经济、社会与环境效益协调发展评价》,《经济与管理评论》2019 年第 6 期。

③ 宋德勇、李超、李项佑:《新型基础设施建设是否促进了绿色技术创新的"量质齐升"——来自国家智慧城市试点的证据》,《中国人口·资源与环境》2021 年第 11 期。

④ 冯苑、聂长飞、张东:《宽带基础设施建设对城市创新能力的影响》,《科学学研究》2021 年第 11 期。

environment is not just a natural asset, but also an economic asset, and it affects the potential and momentum of economic and social development. We need to speed up efforts to foster a green way of development and secure a win-win of economic growth and environmental protection, so as to build a homeland of coordinated advancement of economy and the environment."

Existing literature shows that there is an inverted "U" shaped relationship between economic growth and environmental pollution, that is, in the early stages of economic development, environmental pollution will worsen with economic growth, but when the economic level reaches a certain degree, economic growth will help alleviate environmental pollution. As China's economy and society enter a stage of high-quality development, people's attention to environmental quality is constantly increasing, and environmental quality has become a key factor in attracting high-quality investment and high-level talent, as well as an important dimension of regional competition.

Sixth, the defense and disaster prevention safety system. In China's rapid urbanization process, the occurrence of various disasters has brought enormous challenges to urban safety. These disasters not only include natural disasters such as drought, flood, wind, freeze, and sandstorms, but also safety hazards brought by disrepair of urban water, electricity, natural gas, and other pipeline networks. With the acceleration of the national digitalization process, network and data security have become new safety challenges in urban operations. Whether a city can effectively prevent safety risks and respond to safety challenges tests the city's comprehensive management capability and is also an important criterion for measuring urban competitiveness. In recent years, China has been continuously increasing the "high-tech" content in urban safety protection systems, and the defense and disaster prevention safety system has been continuously maintained and upgraded, safeguarding the smooth operation of cities.

So, how does software infrastructure affect urban competitiveness? In fact, we have already elaborated on the "comparative advantage trap" earlier. The fundamental reason why some economies fall into the "comparative advantage trap" is that they have not promoted the dynamic upgrade of comparative advantages, that is, they have not transformed the comparative advantage strategy into a competitive advantage strategy. In the stage of development relying on the comparative advantage strategy, factors such as labor, capital, and natural resources drive economic growth, promoting low-level industrialization in the region. However, in the stage of development relying on the competitive advantage strategy, regions need to rely on efficiency-driven, innovation-driven, and endogenous growth-driven approaches. At this time, regional governments need to increase efforts in constructing software infrastructure such as administrative management, culture and education, medical care, commercial services, finance and insurance, and social welfare, forming a relatively

济财富，关系经济社会发展潜力和后劲。我们要加快形成绿色发展方式，促进经济发展和环境保护双赢，构建经济与环境协同共进的地球家园。"

已有文献表明，经济增长与环境污染之间存在着倒"U"形关系，即在经济发展初期环境污染会随着经济增长而加重，而当经济水平达到一定程度后，经济增长将有利于缓解环境污染。[①] 随着中国经济社会进入高质量发展阶段，人们对环境质量的关注度不断提高，环境质量已成为吸引高质量投资和高水平人才的关键要素和区域竞争的重要维度。

第六，防卫防灾安全系统。在中国的高速城市化进程中，各种灾害的发生给城市安全带来了巨大挑战。这种灾害不仅包括旱、涝、风、冻、沙尘等自然灾害，也有城市水、电、天然气等管网失修带来的安全隐患。而随着国家数字化进程的加速，网络和数据安全已成为城市运行中新的安全挑战。城市能否有效预防安全风险和应对安全挑战考验着城市的综合管理能力，也是衡量区域竞争力的重要标准。近年来，中国正不断增加城市安全防护系统中的"高科技"含量，防卫防灾安全系统也随之不断得到维护和升级，为城市平稳运行保驾护航。

那么，软件基础设施又会怎样影响区域竞争力呢？实际上，前文中我们已经对"比较优势陷阱"进行过阐述，一些经济体陷入"比较优势陷阱"的根本原因是没能推动比较优势的动态升级，即没有将比较优势战略转化为竞争优势战略。在依靠比较优势战略发展的阶段，劳动力、资本、自然资源等要素驱动经济增长，推动区域实现低水平工业化。但在依靠竞争优势战略发展的阶段，区域则要依靠效率驱动、创新驱动、内生增长驱动。此时区域政府就要加大对行政管理、文化教育、医疗卫生、商业服务、金融保险、社会福利等软件基础设施的建设力

---

① 高挺、常启国、许海平：《中国经济增长与环境质量的关系研究——基于240个城市的双门槛效应检验》，《资源开发与市场》2018年第11期。

complete open innovation system and talent guarantee system, achieving the transformation of economic growth drivers, promoting regional economy to enter a high-quality development track, and thus crossing the "comparative advantage trap". Therefore, the construction of urban software infrastructure plays an important role in the high-quality development of regional economy and can further enhance regional competitiveness and the ability of sustainable regional economic growth.

(2) Development and Operation of Smart Cities and Regional Competitiveness.

The development and operation of smart cities is not simply about urban informatization, but about reshaping and remaking cities using smart technologies. It is a systematic project where new-generation technologies drive urban innovation and development, emphasizing the integration of technology, data, and business operations to coordinate the use of material resources, information resources, and intellectual resources for urban development. It promotes the innovative application of new-generation information technologies such as the Internet of Things, cloud computing, and big data, realizing their deep integration with urban economic and social development. Currently, China's economy has shifted from a high-speed growth stage to a high-quality development stage. The construction of new smart cities harbors enormous potential and space for innovative supply and expanded demand, conducive to promoting high-quality national economic development. Its role in enhancing regional competitiveness can be summarized in the following three points.

First, the construction of new smart cities helps improve the quality of new urbanization. The construction of new smart cities is an important nexus and breakthrough point for the simultaneous advancement of informatization, industrialization, and urbanization. New smart city construction plans cities with smart concepts, builds cities in smart ways, supports cities with smart industries, and governs cities with smart means, helping to promote the harmonious and efficient operation of various key urban and rural systems, thus improving the quality of new urbanization.

Second, the construction of new smart cities helps drive industrial transformation and upgrading. The emergence of smart industries such as big data, cloud computing, the Internet of Things, and artificial intelligence has brought enormous opportunities for urban development. At the same time, the accelerated advancement of new smart city construction has triggered a huge demand for new-generation smart technologies, providing broader space for the development of smart industries, forming a positive interactive effect. The institutional environment and ecosystem constructed by applying new-generation smart technologies are conducive to stimulating society-wide innovation vitality, better promoting the conversion of old and new economic drivers, and continuously enhancing economic innovation and competitiveness.

度，形成比较完善的开放创新系统和人才保障体系，实现经济增长动能转换，推动区域经济进入高质量发展轨道，从而跨越"比较优势陷阱"。因此，城市软件基础设施建设对区域经济高质量发展具有重要作用，能够进一步提升区域竞争力和区域经济可持续增长能力。

（2）智能城市的开发运作与区域竞争力。

智能城市的开发运作不是单纯的城市信息化，而是利用智慧技术对城市进行重塑和再造，是新一代技术倒逼城市创新和发展的系统工程，强调通过技术融合、数据融合、业务融合，统筹利用城市发展的物质资源、信息资源和智力资源，推动物联网、云计算、大数据等新一代信息技术创新应用，实现其与城市经济社会发展的深度融合。当前，中国经济已由高速增长阶段进入高质量发展阶段，新型智能城市建设蕴藏着创新供给和扩大需求的巨大潜力和空间，有利于推动国家经济高质量发展，它对区域竞争力的提升作用可概括为以下三点。[1]

第一，新型智能城市建设有助于提高新型城镇化质量。新型智能城市建设是信息化、工业化和城镇化同步推进的重要结合点和突破口。新型智能城市建设以智慧的理念规划城市，以智慧的方式建设城市，以智慧的产业支撑城市，以智慧的手段治理城市，有助于促进城乡各个关键系统和谐高效地运行，提高新型城镇化质量。

第二，新型智能城市建设有助于推动产业转型升级。大数据、云计算、物联网、人工智能等智慧产业的出现为城市发展带来了巨大的机遇，同时，新型智能城市建设的加速推进又引发对新一代智慧技术的巨大需求，为智慧产业发展提供了更广阔的空间，形成了良好的互动效应。而应用新一代智慧技术构建的制度环境和生态系统，有利于激发全社会创新活力，更好地推动经济新旧动能转换，不断增强经济创新力和竞争力。

---

[1] 陈海波：《以智慧城市建设助推高质量发展》，《智慧中国》2019年第5期。

Third, the construction of new smart cities helps improve management and service levels. With the acceleration of urban social transformation, traditional management and service modes are increasingly showing their limitations, making it urgent to improve urban governance levels. New smart cities, through the interconnection and interaction of things with things, things with people, and people with people, have broken through various information and data silos in cities. This is beneficial for realizing the collection, sharing, and utilization of various urban data, effectively leveraging the role of big data in "good governance, benefiting the people, and prospering businesses", better meeting the requirements of refined urban management and intelligent services.

(ii) Urban Economic Development Path from the Perspective of City Management

### 1. Management Institutions of Urban Economy

In the framework of mezzoeconomics, infrastructure/public works resources are called "quasi-operative resources". The level of hardware and software infrastructure directly affects a country or region's appearance, characteristics, tastes, functions, and roles. Improved hardware and software infrastructure will promote the development of various social and economic undertakings in countries and regions, and drive the optimization of urban spatial distribution patterns and structures.

In China, there are mainly five types of government institutions that coordinate, supervise, and manage quasi-operative resources: the first type is institutions related to state-owned assets and major projects; the second type is institutions related to land and resources, environmental protection, and urban-rural construction; the third type is institutions related to human resources and public resource transactions; the fourth type is institutions related to education, science and technology, culture, health, sports, press and publication, radio and television, research institutes, etc.; the fifth type is institutions related to agriculture, forestry, water conservancy, marine fisheries, etc.

For quasi-operative resources, i.e., (narrow sense) urban resources and urban economy, each region should determine whether to develop and allocate them as operative resources or operate and manage them as public welfare undertakings based on factors such as regional development direction, fiscal status, capital flow, enterprise demands, and the acceptance level and affordability of the society and public.

2. Transformation of Quasi-operative Resources and City Management

The so-called city management refers to the government, under market economy

第三，新型智能城市建设有助于提高管理服务水平。随着城市社会转型的加速，传统的管理服务模式日益显现出局限之处，提升城市治理水平已成当务之急。而新型智能城市通过物与物、物与人、人与人的互联互动，打通了城市的各类信息和数据孤岛，有利于实现对城市各类数据的采集、共享和利用，可有效发挥大数据在"善政、惠民、兴业"等方面的作用，更好地满足城市精细化管理与智能化服务的要求。

### （二）经营城市视角下的城市经济发展路径

#### 1. 城市经济的管理机构

在中观经济学框架下，基础设施/公共工程资源被称为"准经营性资源"。基础设施的软硬件水平，直接影响着一个国家或区域的外形、特征、品位、功能和作用。完善的软硬件基础设施将促进各国、各区域的社会、经济等各项事业发展，推动城市空间分布形态和结构的优化。

在中国，政府协调、监督、管理准经营性资源的机构主要有五种：第一种是国有资产、重大项目相关机构；第二种是国土资源、环境保护、城乡建设相关机构；第三种是人力资源、公共资源交易相关机构；第四种是教育、科技、文化、卫生、体育、新闻出版、广播影视、研究院所等相关机构；第五种是农业、林业、水利、海洋渔业等相关机构。

对于准经营性资源，也即（狭义的）城市资源、城市经济，各区域应根据区域发展方向、财政状况、资金流量、企业需求和社会民众的接受程度与承受力等因素，来确定其是按可经营性资源来开发调配，还是按公益性事业来运行管理。[①]

#### 2. 准经营性资源的转化与经营城市

所谓经营城市是指政府在市场经济条件下，按照经济规律，用资本化的手

---

① 陈云贤：《市场竞争双重主体论——兼谈中观经济学的创立与发展》，北京大学出版社，2020，第59-60页。

conditions, according to economic laws, using capitalized means, measures, and management methods to push operative projects in urban development towards the market and society, seeking benign development of urban construction and management. This is the essence of "city management", with its core being that regional governments, in various urban construction and development, through market-oriented, capitalized, and internationalized operations, not only solve the bottleneck constraint of severe capital shortage in the construction of modern large cities by governments at all levels, but also comprehensively improve urban management level, urban functions, urban environment, as well as urban carrying capacity, radiation capacity, and driving force, thereby comprehensively promoting the enhancement of regional competitiveness.

As mentioned earlier, urban resources in the narrow sense are quasi-operative resources. Among these quasi-operative resources, part can be transformed into operational urban resources, such as urban transportation, environmental protection, water supply, power supply, gas supply, non-compulsory education, science and technology, culture, health, sports matters, naming rights of major targets, and various industries; another part belongs to non-operational urban resources, i.e., other resources except the former category, which we usually call public welfare undertakings.

For the first category of urban resources, when managing the city, regional governments can, through capitalized means, measures, and management methods, hand them over to the market, to society, to various domestic and foreign investors to increase the supply scale and quality of infrastructure; for the latter category of urban resources, in areas that the market cannot reach, regional governments should unequivocally and comprehensively assume the responsibility for their construction, management, and development. This is why finance taken from and used for the people should weaken its constructive fiscal functions and strengthen its public (welfare) fiscal role.

It can be seen that city management——managing the city as a resource, is managing various operative projects in urban development as a resource. This specifically includes two levels of issues: one is determining the carriers for operating various operative resources; the other is raising funds needed for operating various operative resources. These two issues will be elaborated on below.

(1) Determining the carriers.

Apart from state-owned sole proprietorship, regional governments can usually also establish carriers for operating various operative resources through joint ventures, cooperation, joint-stock systems, or even state-owned private enterprises. When operating, these carriers

段、措施和管理方式将城市发展中的可经营性项目推向市场、推向社会，以求城市建设与管理的良性发展。这就是"经营城市"的精髓，其核心在于，区域政府在各城市建设发展中，借助于市场化、资本化和国际化的运作，既解决各级政府在现代化大城市建设中资金严重不足的瓶颈制约问题，又全面提升城市管理水平、城市功能、城市环境，以及城市承载力、辐射力、带动力，进而全面推动区域竞争力的提升。

如前所述，狭义的城市资源即准经营性资源，在这些准经营性资源中，一部分是可以转化为可经营性资源的城市资源，诸如城市交通、环保、供水、供电、供气、非义务性的教育、科技、文化、卫生、体育事项、主要标的冠名权以及各种产业等；另一部分是属于非经营性资源的城市资源，即除前类之外的其他资源，通常我们称之为公益性事业。

对于前一类城市资源，区域政府在经营城市时，可以通过资本化的手段、措施和管理方式，把它们交给市场，交给社会，交给国内外各类投资者以提高基础设施的供给规模和质量；对于后一类城市资源，在那些市场达不到的领域，区域政府应责无旁贷地、全面地承担起对其建设、管理、发展的责任，这也就是取之于民、用之于民的财政要弱化其建设性财政职能、强化其公共（公益性）财政作用的缘故。

可见，经营城市——把城市当作一种资源来管理，是把城市发展中的各种可经营性项目作为一种资源来管理。具体包括两个层次的问题：一是经营各种可经营性资源的载体的确定问题；二是经营各种可经营性资源所需资金的筹集问题。下面分别对这两个问题进行阐述。

（1）载体的确定问题。

除国有独资经营外，区域政府通常还可以通过合资、合作、股份制甚至国有民营等方式组建经营各种可经营性资源的载体。这些载体在经营时不但能根据市场需求、社会供给和国际经济发展的客观趋势进行有效投资，优化结构，促进经

can not only make effective investments, optimize structures, and promote steady economic and social development based on market demand, social supply, and objective trends of international economic development, but also effectively regulate and control based on market forecasts, prevent risks, and avoid major losses.

Therefore, in the process of changing urban development methods, i.e., regional governments managing cities, governments at all levels can implement property rights reform for the carriers of original urban operational projects——"stock assets", allowing them to form carriers adapted to the use of capital market means according to objective laws and requirements of market economic development. That is, through restructuring, using forms such as state-owned private enterprises, joint-stock systems, joint ventures, cooperation to introduce domestic and foreign investors to participate in or even independently operate, making them carriers of market-oriented urban operative resources.

For carriers of new urban operational projects——"incremental assets", regional governments can start from forms such as sole proprietorship, joint ventures, cooperation, or joint-stock systems to establish them, enabling them to lay a good carrier foundation and development conditions according to the market planning of city management. For those new urban operational projects, if due to temporary "shortage" of funds and investors, they are first funded by fiscal funds or government finance as a guarantee for bank loans, property rights reform can be carried out timely and effectively during their investment and construction process. Regional governments should promote the transformation of quasi-operative resources into operative resources through modern governance structure arrangements, thereby enhancing the supply level of urban infrastructure and strengthening urban economic vitality and competitiveness through broad participation of social forces.

(2) Raising required funds.

Regional governments can solve the problem of raising required funds through capital market financing methods, such as: ①issuing ordinary bonds, issuing convertible bonds; ②issuing stocks; ③setting up project funds or using domestic and foreign funds to invest in projects; ④project asset securitization; ⑤project mergers and acquisitions, bundled operations; ⑥leasing; ⑦mortgaging; ⑧exchanging; ⑨auctioning; etc. Regional governments can also attract investment and absorb foreign funds, private funds, or mixed enterprise group funds to build projects through project financing methods. Regional governments can also implement franchise financing using methods such as DBO, BOT, BOO, BOOT, BLT, BTO, TOT through means such as charging rights and pricing rights.

Various regional governments can adopt different financing methods or cross-apply different financing methods according to the characteristics and conditions of different urban operative resources.

济和社会的稳步发展，而且能根据对市场的预测进行有效调控，防范风险，避免重大损失。

因此，在城市发展方式变革，即区域政府经营城市的进程中，各级政府可对原有城市可经营性项目——"存量资产"的载体实行产权改造，让其按照客观规律和市场经济发展的要求，形成与运用资本市场手段相适应的载体，即通过改制，利用国有民营、股份制、合资、合作等形式引进国内外投资者参与乃至独立经营，使其成为市场化运作的城市可经营性资源的载体。

而对于新增城市可经营性项目——"增量资产"的载体，区域政府可一开始就从独资、合资、合作或股份制等形式入手组建，使其能够按照经营城市的市场规划奠定好载体基础和发展条件。对于那些新增的城市可经营性项目，如果由于资金与投资者一时"短缺"而先以财政资金或政府财政作为担保向银行贷款，从而获取资金组建，则可在其投资建设的过程中及时、有效地进行产权改造。区域政府应通过现代化的治理结构安排，推动准经营性资源向可经营性资源转化，从而通过社会力量的广泛参与，提高城市基础设施的供给水平，增强城市经济活力和竞争力。

（2）所需资金的筹集问题。

区域政府可以通过资本市场融资的方式解决所需资金的筹集问题，比如：①发行普通债券，发行可转换债券；②发行股票；③设立项目基金或借助于海内外的基金投资项目；④项目资产证券化；⑤项目并购组合，捆绑经营；⑥租赁；⑦抵押；⑧置换；⑨拍卖；等等。区域政府也可以通过项目融资的方式，招商引资，吸纳国外资金、民营资金或混合体企业集团资金来建设项目。区域政府还可以通过收费权、定价权等手段，运用DBO、BOT、BOO、BOOT、BLT、BTO、TOT等方式实施特许经营权融资。

各区域政府可根据不同的城市可经营性资源的特点和条件，采取不同的融资方式，或交叉运用不同的融资方式。

Taking urban sewage treatment projects as an example, regional governments can adopt the "3P" operation mode (of course, they can also use sole proprietorship operation mode), that is, the regional government's water supply company as a public company (Public) and one or more private companies (Private) form a partnership (Partner), using franchise methods such as BOT or TOT for the construction, operation, and management of urban sewage treatment plants and pipe networks. If the "3P" carrier and operation mode are appropriate, with low cost and high efficiency, regional governments can completely operate the entire city's sewage treatment project as a listed company in an appropriate period, issuing stocks for urban sewage treatment projects or public utility projects. This can not only improve the operation and management level of urban public utility projects but also use capital market means to issue stocks, further using the raised funds for environmental protection projects, strengthening and expanding urban environmental protection undertakings.

In this way, according to market-oriented and internationalized requirements, various regional governments use multi-level, multi-channel social direct financing means, combined with necessary indirect financing methods such as bank loans, and use the "leveraging" role of finance in urban construction and development to overcome capital bottleneck constraints in urban construction. Urban management levels can be improved, urban management can achieve scientific and sustainable development, and the limited finance of regional governments can truly be used as public finance for the increasing demands of the people for public welfare undertakings.

In summary, when regional governments convert quasi-operative resources into operative resources, their goal is to make the investment structure in urban infrastructure reasonable, the investment scale appropriate, and the investment efficiency improved. Their method is for regional governments to participate in the investment, development, operation, management, and competition of urban infrastructure together with other investors, following the openness, fairness, and competitiveness rules of the market economy. In developing countries, urban infrastructure investment plays a significant role in economic growth; in developed countries, urban infrastructure investment fluctuations are closely related to economic growth fluctuations. This has become an undeniable trend in the economic development of countries worldwide.

以城市污水治理项目为例，区域政府可以采取"3P"的运营方式（当然也可以用独资的运营方式），即区域政府的供水公司作为公共公司（Pubic）和一个或多个私人公司（Private）组建成合作伙伴（Partner），运用BOT或TOT等特许经营权方式进行城市污水处理厂和管网的建设、运营与管理。如果"3P"的载体、运营方式得当，成本低，效益高，则区域政府完全可以在适当的期间，把整个城市的污水治理项目作为一个上市公司来运作，发行城市污水治理项目或公用事业项目股票，这样既能够提升城市公用事业项目的经营管理水平，又可以借助于资本市场手段发行股票，把募集来的资金进一步用到环保项目上去，把城市环保事业做强做大。

这样，按照市场化、国际化的要求，各区域政府运用多层次、多渠道的社会直接融资手段，再结合必要的银行贷款等间接融资方式，并运用财政在城市建设和发展中"四两拨千斤"的作用，克服城市建设中的资金瓶颈制约，城市管理水平将能得到提升，城市管理也可以实现科学、可持续发展，区域政府的有限财政才能真正地作为公共财政用在人民群众日益增加的对公益性事业的需求上。[①]

综上，区域政府将准经营性资源转换为可经营性资源时，其目标是使城市基础设施领域的投资结构合理、投资规模适度、投资效益提升，其方式是区域政府与其他投资者一起参与城市基础设施的投资、开发、运营、管理和竞争，其遵循的是市场经济的公开性、公正性和竞争性规则。在发展中国家，城市基础设施投资在经济增长中具有重大的作用；在发达国家，城市基础设施投资波动与经济增长波动具有密切关系，这已经是世界各国经济发展中不可忽视的一种趋势。

---

① 陈云贤:《经营城市——把城市作为一种资源来管理》,《佛山科学技术学院学报(社会科学版)》2004年第3期。

# Section 5: Building New Engines for Economic Growth

The economic development of countries worldwide generally follows a path from factor-driven stage to investment-driven stage, innovation-driven stage, and then to wealth-driven stage. Many countries, especially those economies rich in natural resources such as minerals and agricultural products, have developed the economic growth mode driven by tangible factors such as land and labor to the extreme, showing unsustainability. Therefore, to achieve economic growth under these circumstances, it is necessary to construct new engines for economic growth. In the modern market system composed of "Effective Governments+Efficient Markets", launching new supply-side structural engines will fully leverage the role of enterprises in allocating industrial resources and governments in allocating urban resources in competition. These new supply-side structural engines, including new investment engines, new innovation engines, and new regulation engines that combine tangible and intangible factors, will play an important role in global economic governance and development.

## I. Building a New Global Investment Engines

Investment-driven growth depends on both the allocation and competition of supply-side products and industrial resources, and the competition performance of supply-side government in allocating urban resources and promoting infrastructure construction. It can bring capital growth to various regions, promote technological innovation and deepening development of market mechanisms, and increase employment opportunities, thus having long-term sustainability. To construct new global investment engines, we should adopt the following measures.

First, promote supply-side structural reform, which includes the following aspects.

(1) Promote new industrialization. The so-called new industrialization means adhering to driving industrialization with informatization and promoting informatization with industrialization. It is industrialization characterized by high technological content, good

economic benefits, low resource consumption, little environmental pollution, and full play of human resource advantages. Promoting new industrialization involves the following three aspects. One is to support and guide the transformation and upgrading of traditional industries.

## 第五节 构建经济增长新引擎

世界各国的经济发展基本遵循从要素驱动阶段到投资驱动阶段、创新驱动阶段，再到财富驱动阶段的路径。许多国家，尤其是那些矿产、农产品等自然资源丰富的经济体，已经将以土地、劳动力等有形要素驱动经济增长的方式，发展到了极致，并呈现出不可持续性。因此，要在这种情况下实现经济增长，需要构建经济增长新引擎。在由"有为政府＋有效市场"构成的现代市场体系中，发动供给侧结构性新引擎，将在竞争中充分发挥企业对产业资源、政府对城市资源的配置作用。这类供给侧结构性新引擎包括结合了有形与无形要素的投资新引擎、创新新引擎和规则新引擎，将对全球经济治理与发展起到重要作用。

### 一、构建全球投资新引擎

投资驱动型增长，既取决于供给侧产品和产业资源的配置与竞争状况，又取决于供给侧政府调配城市资源和推动基础设施建设的竞争表现。它能给各区域带来资本增长，促进技术革新和市场机制深化发展，并增加就业岗位，因而具有长期可持续性。为了构建全球投资新引擎，我们应采取如下措施。[①]

第一，推进供给侧结构性改革，这又包括以下几个方面。

（1）推动新型工业化。所谓新型工业化，就是坚持以信息化带动工业化，以工业化促进信息化，就是科技含量高、经济效益好、资源消耗低、环境污染少、人力资源优势得到充分发挥的工业化。推动新型工业化涉及以下三个方面。一是

---

① 陈云贤：《市场竞争双重主体论——兼谈中观经济学的创立与发展》，北京大学出版社，2020，第195-198页。

Two is to support and cultivate strategic emerging industries and high-tech industries. Three is that countries should leverage market competition to promote enterprise mergers and acquisitions, integration and reorganization, continuously eliminate old industries, advance the development of new industries, push industrialization to a higher level, and enhance the core competitiveness of enterprises.

(2) Accelerate agricultural modernization. Agricultural modernization refers to the process and means of transforming from traditional agriculture to modern agriculture. In this process, agriculture is increasingly armed with modern industry, modern science and technology, and modern economic management methods. Various regions should apply modern development concepts, combining agricultural development with ecological civilization construction, transforming backward traditional agriculture into ecological agriculture that conforms to the advanced productivity level of the contemporary world. Agricultural modernization can create a stable social environment for industrialization and urbanization, reduce social costs, and prosper regional economies.

Second, promote infrastructure investment and construction, which includes the following three aspects.

(1) Promote new urbanization. New urbanization is characterized by urban-rural integration, urban-rural unity, industrial interaction, conservation and intensiveness, ecological livability, and harmonious development. It is also urbanization where large, medium, and small cities, towns, and new rural communities develop in coordination and promote each other.

(2) Promote infrastructure modernization. Infrastructure modernization includes the modernization of energy, transportation, environmental protection, information, and agricultural water conservancy infrastructure. For example, promoting comprehensive urban transportation construction, building regional convenient transportation networks; accelerating the construction of sponge cities, enhancing urban disaster prevention and mitigation capabilities; promoting the treatment of urban black and odorous water bodies, reshaping urban water resource environmental quality; improving regional park and green space systems, sharing green urban life; constructing urban underground comprehensive pipe galleries, coordinating orderly and efficient operation of pipelines; strengthening urban water supply facility construction, improving water supply safety guarantee systems; orderly optimizing urban energy supply, vigorously promoting urban energy conservation and emission reduction;

enhancing the efficiency of garbage and sewage facilities, achieving resource conservation and recycling; etc. Investment in this area has large room for maneuver and potential, and can effectively promote regional economic growth.

(3) Promote smart city development and construction. Smart city is a system constructed by basic elements such as artificial intelligence, Internet of Things, and physical devices, promoting intelligent urban management. It specifically includes the intelligentization of

扶持、引导传统产业改造、提升。二是扶持、培植战略性新兴产业和高技术产业。三是各国应借助市场竞争，推动企业兼并收购、整合重组，不断淘汰旧工业，推进新型工业发展，将工业化推向更高水平，提升企业的核心竞争力。

（2）加快农业现代化。农业现代化指从传统农业向现代农业转化的过程和手段。在这一过程中，农业日益被现代化工业、现代化科学技术和现代化经济管理方法武装起来。各区域应运用现代化发展理念，将农业发展与生态文明建设结合起来，使落后的传统农业转化为符合当代世界先进生产力水平的生态农业。农业现代化能为工业化和城市化创造稳定的社会环境，降低社会成本，繁荣各区域经济。

第二，推进基础设施投资建设，这包括以下三个方面。

（1）推进新型城镇化。新型城镇化既是以城乡统筹、城乡一体、产业互动、节约集约、生态宜居、和谐发展为基础特征的城镇化，也是大中小城市、小城镇、新型农村社区协调发展、互促互进的城镇化。

（2）推进基础设施现代化。基础设施现代化包括能源、交通、环保、信息和农田水利等基础设施的现代化。比如促进城市综合交通建设，构筑区域便捷交通网络；加快推进海绵城市建设，增强城市防灾减灾能力；推进城市黑臭水体整治，重塑城市水资源环境品质；健全区域公园绿地体系，共享绿色城市生活；构建城市地下综合管廊，统筹管线有序高效运作；加强城市供水设施建设，健全供水安全保障体系；有序优化城市能源供给，大力促进城市节能减排；提升垃圾污水设施效能，实现资源节约循环利用；等等。这方面的投资回旋空间大、潜力足，能有效推动各区域经济增长。

（3）推进智能城市开发建设。智能城市是一个系统，它由人工智能、物联网和物理设备等基本要素建构，推动城市管理智能化，具体包括智能交通、智能电力、智能建筑、智能环保、智能安全等基础设施的智能化，智能医疗、智能教

infrastructure such as intelligent transportation, intelligent power, intelligent buildings, intelligent environmental protection, intelligent security, etc., the intelligentization of social life such as intelligent medical care, intelligent education, intelligent homes, etc., and the intelligentization of social production such as intelligent enterprises, intelligent banks, intelligent stores, etc. The smart city system can comprehensively enhance the modernization level of urban production, life, management, and operation, further opening up new economic growth points for various regions.

Third, increase investment in science and technology projects. For example, the Manufacturing USA, with an initial investment of $1 billion; the UK Knowledge Transfer Partnerships Program; Germany's Industry 4.0 strategy promoting intelligent manufacturing based on cyber-physical systems. These initiatives can integrate innovation resources of talents, enterprises, and social institutions, lead industrial R&D directions, and promote industrial upgrading and development. The investment of various regions in big data, cloud computing, Internet of Things, as well as in nanotechnology, biotechnology, information technology, and cognitive science, will promote the sustainable development of regional economies.

Fourth, enhance financial supporting capabilities. Various regions need both supporting policies to guide the financial industry to serve the real economy, and policy innovation to promote the integration of finance, technology, and industry. The new investment engine is inseparable from the reform, innovation, and development of the financial system.

## II. Building a New Global Innovation Engine

When regions enter the transition period of economic development modes, where the economic form develops from allocating industrial resources through enterprise competition to allocating urban resources through regional government competition, and the economic growth engine develops from a single market mechanism to a "Effective Governments + Efficient Markets" mechanism, these new situations in global economic development will inevitably lead to a series of new issues. For example, how to maintain the principles of fairness and justice in the global economic governance system, how to protect the interests of developing countries in the global economic order, how to maintain or enhance the openness of the economic system to resist protectionism, how to formulate norms to address challenges in new economic fields. To address these new issues, regional governments need to innovate and improve existing public mechanisms or public goods (including ideological public goods, material public goods, organizational public goods, and institutional public goods) that coordinate and govern the global economic order. To construct new global innovation engines,

育、智能家庭等社会生活的智能化，以及智能企业、智能银行、智能商店等社会生产的智能化。智能城市系统能全面提升城市生产、生活、管理、运行的现代化水平，进一步为各区域开拓新的经济增长点。

第三，加大科技项目投入。例如美国制造业创新网络计划，首期投入10亿美元；英国知识转移伙伴计划；基于信息物理系统推动智能制造的德国工业4.0战略。这些举措能整合人才、企业、社会机构的创新资源，引领产业研发方向，促进产业提升发展。各区域对大数据、云计算、物联网等的投入，以及对纳米技术、生物技术、信息技术和认知科学等的投入，将促进各区域经济的可持续发展。

第四，提升金融配套能力。各区域既需要配套政策，引领金融行业服务于实体经济，又需要通过政策创新，推进金融、科技、产业三者的融合。投资新引擎离不开金融体系的改革、创新和发展。

## 二、构建全球创新新引擎

当区域进入经济发展模式的转换时期，经济形式从通过企业竞争配置产业资源发展到通过区域政府竞争配置城市资源，经济增长引擎从单一的市场机制发展到"有为政府+有效市场"机制时，这些全球经济发展的新情况必然导致一系列新问题。比如如何维护全球经济治理体系的公平、公正原则，如何保护发展中国家在全球经济秩序中的利益，如何维持或提升经济体系的开放程度以抵制保护主义，如何制定规范以应对经济新领域的挑战。区域政府为了应对这些新问题，就需要对现存的协调、治理全球经济秩序的公共机制或公共物品（包括思想性公共物品、物质性公共物品、组织性公共物品和制度性公共物品），予以创新和完

regional governments should adopt the following measures.

First, promote the innovation of ideological public goods, i.e., concepts. Firstly, the market should be an efficient market. Some regions overly emphasize the competition of market elements and market organizations while neglecting the construction of the rule of law supervision system and the improvement of the market environment system and market infrastructure, all of which will deviate from the principles of openness, fairness, and justice in the market. Secondly, the government should be an effective government. Regional governments should not only implement planning, guidance, support, regulation, supervision, and management for the allocation of operative resources, i.e., industrial resources, but also provide a basic safety net for non-operative resources, i.e., livelihood resources, ensuring fairness, justice, and effective improvement. They should also regulate and participate in the competition for the allocation of quasi-operative resources, i.e., urban resources. Finally, the economic mode pursued by regions worldwide should be "Strong Effective Governments" + "Strong Efficient Markets", that is, in the large market economy system, allocating industrial resources through enterprise competition and allocating urban resources through government competition. Regional governments should play an important role in global economic growth.

Second, promote the innovation of material public goods, i.e., technology. The most typical path of current technological development is to promote infrastructure modernization through the integration of informatization with industrialization, urbanization, and agricultural modernization. Regional governments provide intelligent public transportation, urban management, education, medical care, culture, business, government affairs, environmental protection, energy, and security services to society by building smart cities that combine tangible and intangible elements, providing a safe, efficient, convenient, green, and harmonious development environment for social economy and people's livelihoods. This not only benefits the public but will also promote regions to accelerate industrial transformation, urban transformation, and international upgrading, thereby promoting regions' rise.

Third, promote the innovation of organizational public goods, i.e., management. In terms of organizational management, from a single city to a country and even the world, there are similarities. The traditional urban development structure (such as the "pancake" style) has led to the emergence of big city diseases. The development of modern cities requires scientifically planned group layout. The group-style urban development structure can effectively solve a series of problems brought by the traditional "pancake" style urban development structure. The organizational management of the world economic order, like cities, needs to reform from a "pancake" style to a group-style layout and continuously innovate and develop. However, this requires corresponding new rules and necessary infrastructure investment to form a reasonable

善。为了构建全球创新新引擎,区域政府应采取如下措施。[1]

第一,推进思想性公共物品即理念的创新。首先,市场应是有效市场。一些区域过分强调市场要素与市场组织的竞争,而忽视法治监管体系的建设、市场环境体系和市场基础设施的健全,这都将偏离公开、公平、公正的市场原则。其次,政府应是有为政府。各区域政府不仅应对可经营性资源即产业资源的配置实施规划、引导、扶持、调节、监督、管理,而且应对非经营性资源即民生资源基本托底,确保公平公正、有效提升,还应对准经营性资源即城市资源的配置进行调节并参与竞争。最后,世界各区域追求的经济模式应是"强式有为政府"+"强式有效市场",即在市场经济大系统中,通过企业竞争配置产业资源,通过政府竞争配置城市资源。各区域政府应在全球经济增长中发挥重要作用。

第二,推进物质性公共物品即技术的创新。当前科技发展的最典型路径是通过信息化与工业化、城镇化、农业现代化融合,促进基础设施现代化。区域政府通过建设结合了有形要素与无形要素的智能城市,向社会提供智能化的公共交通、城管、教育、医疗、文化、商务、政务、环保、能源和治安服务,为社会经济和民生事业提供安全、高效、便捷、绿色、和谐的发展环境。这不仅能造福民众,还将推动区域加快工业化转轨、城市化转型和国际化提升,进而促进区域的崛起。

第三,推进组织性公共物品即管理的创新。就组织管理而言,小到一座城市,大到一个国家乃至世界,都有相同之处。传统的城市发展架构(如"摊大饼"式),导致了大城市病的出现。现代城市的发展需要科学规划的组团式布局,组团式的城市发展架构能有效解决传统"摊大饼"式城市发展架构带来的系列问题。世界经济秩序的组织管理如城市一样,需要从"摊大饼"式向组团式布局改革并不断创新发展,但这需要有相应的新规则和必要的基础设施投

---

[1] 陈云贤:《市场竞争双重主体论——兼谈中观经济学的创立与发展》,北京大学出版社,2020,第199-200页。

layout and promote harmonious and sustainable world development.

Fourth, promote the innovation of institutional public goods, i.e., rules. The construction of regions is guided by a trinity planning system of conceptual planning, urban-rural planning, and land planning, forming specific guidelines that are both rigorous in system and finely divided in levels, such as strategic planning, layout positioning, standard setting, policy evaluation, and rule of law guarantee within this framework. Facing the current new situation, we need to innovate economic growth concepts and related institutional rules, promote structural reforms of fiscal and monetary policies in various regions, and maintain consistency and mutual support of economic development, labor, employment, and social policies. Only by attaching equal importance to demand management and supply-side reform, combining short-term policies with medium and long-term policies, advancing social and economic development along with environmental protection, and jointly discussing, building, and sharing the global economic governance pattern among various regions, can the global economy grow healthily and sustainably.

## III. Building a New Global Regulation Engine

Corresponding to the non-operative resources of various regions is the international public goods supply system, corresponding to the operative resources of various regions is the international industrial resource allocation system, and corresponding to the quasi-operative resources of various regions is the international urban resource allocation system. They each operate according to objectively existing rules. A perfect global economic governance system requires corresponding international rules, specifically as follows.

First, international security order rules——peace and stability. This has become a consensus among regions worldwide and is the basic guarantee of the international public goods supply system. Regions worldwide should work together to strengthen international security cooperation, uphold the purposes and principles of the *United Nations Charter*, maintain the basic norms of international relations, create a peaceful, stable, just, and reasonable international security order, and construct a healthy and orderly economic development environment.

Second, international economic competition rules——fairness and efficiency. These are the basic norms for enterprise competition in the industrial resource allocation system of regions worldwide. For example, the guiding principles of "promoting competition and improving the business environment" include strengthening the implementation of competition

资，才能形成合理布局，促进世界和谐、可持续发展。

第四，推进制度性公共物品即规则的创新。区域的建设有概念规划、城乡规划和土地规划这三位一体的规划系统作为引领，在这一框架下形成战略规划、布局定位、标准制定、政策评估、法治保障等既体系严谨又层次细分的具体方针。面对当前的新形势，我们需要创新经济增长理念和相关制度性规则，促进各区域财政、货币的结构性改革，保持经济发展、劳动、就业和社会政策的一致与相互配合。只有需求管理和供给侧改革并重，短期政策与中长期政策结合，社会经济发展与环境保护共进，各区域共商、共建、共享全球经济治理格局，全球经济才能健康、可持续地增长。

## 三、构建全球规则新引擎

与各区域非经营性资源相对应的是国际公共物品供给体系，与各区域可经营性资源相对应的是国际产业资源配置体系，与各区域准经营性资源相对应的是国际城市资源配置体系，它们各自遵循客观存在的规则运行。完善的全球经济治理体系需要相应的国际规则，具体如下。[①]

第一，国际安全秩序规则——和平、稳定。这已是世界各区域的共识，是国际公共物品供给体系的基本保障。世界各区域应共同努力，加强国际安全合作，捍卫《联合国宪章》的宗旨和原则，维护国际关系的基本准则，营造和平、稳定、公正、合理的国际安全秩序，构建健康有序的经济发展环境。

第二，国际经济竞争规则——公平、效率。这是世界各区域产业资源配置体系中企业竞争的基本准则。如"促进竞争并改善商业环境"指导原则，包括强化

---

① 陈云贤：《市场竞争双重主体论——兼谈中观经济学的创立与发展》，北京大学出版社，2020，第200-201页。

laws, reducing administrative and legal barriers to starting and expanding businesses, promoting fair market competition, implementing efficient bankruptcy procedures, reducing restrictive regulations that hinder competition, reducing additional regulatory compliance burdens, and effectively supervising regulatory policies, promoting the construction of the rule of law, improving judicial efficiency, combating corruption, etc. These are the fairness and efficiency rules that various regions should follow when guiding and regulating enterprise competitive behavior.

Third, international co-governance rules——cooperation and win-win. These are the basic norms that need to be followed in competition among regional governments in the urban resource allocation system. New urbanization, smart city development, and investment in the modernization of integrated facilities mainly comprising energy, transportation, environmental protection, information, and water conservancy will be new engines for economic growth in regions worldwide. They can bring effects such as capital expansion, employment increase, technological innovation, market deepening, sustainable economic growth, social benefit improvement, environmental improvement, and national strength enhancement. Due to the different urbanization processes, policy measures, and institutional arrangements in various regions, their investment-driven growth effects and competitiveness vary. However, competition among regional governments should be cooperative competition, should be sustainable development competition, should be competition that jointly enhances the global economic governance system and jointly innovates economic growth modes. Its basic principle should be win-win cooperation. Constructing an innovative, open, interconnected, and inclusive world economic system with win-win cooperation at its core will promote continuous innovation in growth modes, enhance global economic governance levels, and thus benefit various regions and the world.

落实竞争法律，减少开办企业和扩大经营的行政及法律障碍，促进公平的市场竞争，实施高效的破产程序，减少妨碍竞争的限制性规定，减少额外的监管合规负担，并对监管政策进行有效监督，推动法治化建设，提高司法效率，打击腐败，等等。这些都是各区域在引导、规范企业竞争行为时所要遵循的公平与效率规则。

第三，国际共同治理规则——合作、共赢。这是城市资源配置体系中区域政府间竞争所需要遵循的基本准则。新型城镇化，智能城市开发，以及对于以能源、交通、环保、信息和水利等为主体的集成设施现代化的投资，将是世界各区域经济增长的新引擎，能带来资本扩大、就业增加、技术革新、市场深化、经济可持续增长、社会收益提高、环境改善、国力提升等效果。由于各区域城市化进程、政策举措和制度安排不一，其投资驱动增长的效果与竞争力不一。但区域政府间的竞争应该是合作竞争，应该是可持续发展的竞争，应该是共同提升全球经济治理体系的竞争和共同创新经济增长方式的竞争。其基本原则应是合作共赢。构建以合作共赢为核心的创新型、开放型、联动型和包容型世界经济体系，将促进增长方式的持续创新，提升全球经济治理水平，进而造福于各区域，造福于世界。

# Chapter 7
# Practical Experience of Competitive Economic Growth in Shenzhen

## Section 1: Growth Stage Dominated by Industrial Economic Competition and Cooperation

In 1979, the first blast for land reclamation and port construction resounded in Shekou, Shenzhen, laying the foundation for China's first outward-oriented industrial park——China Merchants Shekou Industrial Zone. Since then, Shekou, with the courage to "dare to be the first in the world", became a pioneer in developing a market economy in China, witnessing over 40 years of the century-old China Merchants Group's journey alongside the country's reform and opening-up.

In April 1979, during the Central Working Conference of the Communist Party of China, when the leader of CPC Guangdong Provincial Committee mentioned leveraging Guangdong's advantages, comrade Deng Xiaoping first proposed the concept of "Special Zones". Following Deng Xiaoping's advocacy, the central government sent comrade Gu Mu with a working group to inspect Guangdong and Fujian to specifically discuss the issue of establishing special zones. Based on in-depth and detailed investigation and research, on July 15, 1979, the CPC Central Committee and the State Council approved and forwarded the reports from CPC Guangdong and Fujian provincial committees on implementing special policies and flexible measures in foreign economic activities. They decided to grant more autonomy to Guangdong and Fujian provinces in foreign economic activities to fully leverage the advantageous conditions of the two provinces, expand foreign trade, seize the current favorable opportunities, take the lead, and boost

# 第七章

# 深圳竞争型经济增长实践经验

## 第一节 由产业经济竞争与合作主导的增长阶段

1979年,深圳蛇口轰然响起填海建港的开山炮,奠基了中国第一个对外开放型工业园区——招商局蛇口工业区。自此,蛇口以"敢为天下先"的勇气,成为中国发展市场经济的先行者,见证了百年招商局与祖国改革开放同行的40余年时光。

1979年4月,在中共中央工作会议召开期间,当时广东省委负责人谈到要发挥广东的优势。邓小平同志首先提出"特区"的概念。根据邓小平同志的倡导,中央派谷牧同志带工作组赴广东、福建视察,具体商定办特区的问题。在深入细致的调查研究基础上,1979年7月15日,中共中央、国务院批转了广东、福建两省省委关于在对外经济活动中实行特殊政策和灵活措施的报告,决定对广东、福建两省的对外经济活动给予更多的自主权,以充分发挥两省的优越条件,扩大对外贸易,抓紧当前有利时机,先走一步,把经济尽快搞上去。同时决定,先在深圳、珠海两市划出部分地区试办出口特区,待取得经验后,再考虑在汕头、厦门设置特区。这一重大决策的实施,使广东、福建两省的对外经济活动迅速活跃起来。1980年5月16日,中共中央和国务院批准《广东、福建两省会议纪要》。"出口特区"被正式改名为"经济特区"。同年8月,第五届全国人大

the economy as quickly as possible. At the same time, it was decided to first demarcate parts of Shenzhen and Zhuhai cities to pilot export special zones, and consider setting up special zones in Shantou and Xiamen after gaining experience. The implementation of this major decision quickly invigorated the foreign economic activities of Guangdong and Fujian provinces. On May 16, 1980, the CPC Central Committee and the State Council approved the *Minutes of the Guangdong and Fujian Provinces Conference*. "Export Special Zones" were officially renamed "Special Economic Zones". In August of the same year, the 15th session of the Standing Committee of the Fifth National People's Congress reviewed and approved the establishment of special economic zones in Shenzhen, Zhuhai, Shantou, and Xiamen, and passed the *Regulations on Special Economic Zones in Guangdong Province*. This marked the official birth of China's special economic zones. However, at the beginning of construction, the Shenzhen Special Economic Zone (hereinafter referred to as Shenzhen) faced severe factor constraints. Therefore, how to gain an advantage in the development and competition of primary resources such as land and capital tested the Shenzhen government's ability to lead economic development.

## I. Constraints of Land and Capital Factors

After the establishment of the special economic zone, urban construction inevitably generated a huge demand for funds. Under these conditions, relying on the central government's policy support, Shenzhen attempted to exchange urban construction funds through land operations. Shenzhen began bold research and practice on the paid land use system from 1979. Starting from land leasing, it later developed into diversified forms of paid land use such as cooperative development and entrusted development, which to some extent guaranteed the supply of funds and land in the early stages of special economic zone construction. Shenzhen's innovative attempt had strong demonstrative significance.[①] It was

---

[①] The first agreement between Shenzhen and a business partner for real estate development was signed with Hong Kong's Mieli Group on December 31, 1979. To avoid conflict with old ideas and systems, the agreement was described as a "compensation trade method". The project was operated through cooperation: the Shenzhen side provided the land, while the investment party funded the construction of hotels or buildings. After completion, if there were profits, the money would first be returned to the investment party. Once the costs were repaid, the government would split the profits equally with the investment party. Therefore, the early paid use of land in Shenzhen did not take the form of direct land use rights transactions.

Shenzhen's successful practice that led to the introduction of documents including *Regulations on Special Economic Zones in Guangdong Province* issued in 1980, which clearly defined paid land use.①

---

① Article 12 of Chapter III of the *Regulations on Special Economic Zones in Guangdong Province*: "The land in the special zones is owned by the People's Republic of China. Land for business use shall be provided according to actual needs. The duration of land use, the amount of usage fees, and the methods of payment shall be given preferential treatment based on different industries and purposes, specific measures will be stipulated separately."

常委会第十五次会议审议批准在深圳、珠海、汕头、厦门设置经济特区,并通过了《广东省经济特区条例》。这标志着中国的经济特区正式诞生了。然而,建设伊始,深圳经济特区(以下简称深圳)面临严重的要素约束,因此,如何在土地和资本等原生性资源的开发和竞争中取得优势考验着深圳政府对经济发展的引领能力。

## 一、土地与资本要素约束

经济特区成立后,城市建设必然产生对资金的巨大需求。在这种条件下,依靠中央的政策支持,深圳试图通过对土地的经营换取城市建设资金。深圳从1979年就开始对土地有偿使用制度进行大胆的研究和实践。从土地出租开始,之后发展到合作开发、委托开发等多样化的土地有偿使用形式,这在一定程度上保障了经济特区建设初期的资金和土地供给。①深圳的这种创新性尝试具有很强的示范意义,正是深圳的成功实践,促成了包括1980年《广东省经济特区条例》等文件的出台,明确了土地有偿使用。②

---

① 深圳第一宗与客商合作经营房地产的协议书,于1979年12月31日与香港妙丽集团签订。为避免与旧观念、旧制度的冲突,协议书上用的是"补偿贸易方式"字样。项目是以合作的方式运行,深圳方出土地,投资方出钱建酒店或楼房,建成以后如能盈利,钱先还给投资方,还清成本后,盈利所得由政府与投资方五五分账。因此,深圳早期的土地有偿使用还不是以直接的土地使用权交易的形式进行的。

② 《广东省经济特区条例》第三章第十二条:"特区的土地为中华人民共和国所有。客商用地,按实际需要提供,其使用年限、使用费数额和缴纳办法,根据不同行业和用途,给予优惠,具体办法另行规定。"

From 1980 to 1987, although land in Shenzhen was still transferred through administrative allocation, it broke away from the traditional rigid method of indefinite free use without transfer rights, adopting practices of charging land use fees and using land as a condition for joint ventures and cooperation. This was a major start to fundamentally change the land management system. Nevertheless, since the initial transfer of land use rights was limited to between the Shenzhen government and land users, with only one allocation method available, and the use form still coexisting as free and paid, this fundraising function under the traditional administrative land allocation pattern increasingly failed to meet the enormous capital demands of the subsequent rapid urbanization process.

## II. Solutions by the Shenzhen Government

Under immense pressure, the Shenzhen government began to explore land system reform.

Based on thorough research on the topic "Whether land can be auctioned and how to advance land use system reform" and investigations in Hong Kong, in May 1987, the Shenzhen Municipal Party Committee Standing Committee discussed the *Shenzhen Special Economic Zone Land Management System Reform Plan* (hereinafter referred to as the Plan). The Plan decided to take the lead nationwide in piloting the reform of paid, fixed-term transfer and transferability of land use rights. After the Plan was passed by the Shenzhen Municipal Party Committee Standing Committee, a demonstration meeting for the reform plan was also convened, which greatly promoted the land use system reform in Shenzhen.

In September 1987, Shenzhen took the lead in implementing paid transfer of land use, transferring the use right of a piece of land over 5,000 square meters for a term of 50 years, marking the beginning of the reform of the state-owned land use system from unpaid, indefinite, and non-transferable to paid, fixed-term, and transferable. In November of the same year, the State Council designated Shenzhen, Shanghai, Tianjin, Guangzhou, Xiamen, and Fuzhou as pilot sites for land use system reform. In December of the same year, Shenzhen publicly auctioned the use right of a piece of state-owned land, which was the first public auction of land use rights since the founding of the People's Republic of China.

The *Amendment to the Constitution of the People's Republic of China* passed at the First

Session of the Seventh National People's Congress of the People's Republic of China on April 12, 1988, stipulated: "The right to use land may be transferred in accordance with the provisions of the law." This was a historic breakthrough and a fundamental change in China's land use system. In the same year, the *Decision on Amending the Land Administration Law of*

1980—1987年，深圳土地虽仍以行政划拨供应方式出让，但打破了传统的无偿无限期、不能转让的僵化方式，采取收取土地使用费和以土地作为合资合作的条件的做法。这是一个重大的从根本上改变土地管理制度的起始。尽管如此，由于初期的土地使用权流转仅限于深圳政府和土地使用者之间，提供方式也只有划拨一种，使用形式依然是无偿和有偿并存，故这种传统的行政划拨土地格局下的资金筹措功能越发不适应后来急剧的城市化进程对资金的巨大需求。

## 二、深圳政府的破解

深圳政府顶着巨大的压力，开始了土地制度改革探索。

在对"能否拍卖土地和如何推进土地使用制度改革"这一课题进行充分调研和赴港考察的基础上，1987年5月，深圳市委常委会讨论《深圳经济特区土地管理体制改革方案》（以下简称方案），方案决定在全国率先进行土地使用权有偿、有期出让和转让的试点改革。[①] 方案经深圳市委常委会通过后，还就此召开了改革方案论证会，这对深圳的土地使用制度改革推动很大。

1987年9月，深圳率先试行土地使用有偿出让，出让了一块5000多平方米土地的使用权，限期50年，拉开了国有土地使用制度从无偿、无限期、无流动变为有偿、有限期、可流动改革的序幕；同年11月，国务院确定在深圳、上海、天津、广州、厦门、福州进行土地使用制度改革试点；同年12月，深圳公开拍卖了一块国有土地的使用权，这是新中国成立后首次进行的土地使用权公开拍卖。

1988年4月12日第七届全国人民代表大会第一次会议通过的《中华人民共和国宪法修正案》规定："土地的使用权可以依照法律的规定转让。"这是一次历史性突破，是我国土地使用制度的根本性变革。同年，《关于修改〈中华人民共

---

① 付莹：《深圳经济特区土地有偿出让制度的历史沿革及其立法贡献》，《鲁东大学学报（哲学社会科学版）》2014年第4期。

*the People's Republic of China* clearly implemented the paid use system for state-owned land.

In 1990, the State Council issued the *Interim Regulations of the People's Republic of China Concerning the Assignment and Transfer of the Right to the Use of the State-owned Land in the Urban Areas*, establishing the system of assignment, transfer, and lease of state-owned land use rights in urban areas, which further laid the foundation and removed obstacles for the paid use of state-owned land.

The major changes made by Shenzhen to the land use system not only raised urgently needed construction funds for Shenzhen but also accelerated Shenzhen's supply of land as an important production factor. This not only accelerated Shenzhen's development speed in the early economic stage but also set an important example for the whole country. In this process, the Shenzhen government boldly promoted, the Guangdong provincial government fully supported, and the central government provided comprehensive guarantees, playing an extremely crucial role in institutional innovation, fully demonstrating the foresighted leading role of an effective governments in the factor-driven industrial economic competition stage, gaining Shenzhen a development head start and winning competitive advantages.

## III. Industrial Structure in the Early Stages of the Special Economic Zone

At the initial establishment of the special economic zone, various production factors depended on input from outside the region. Labor mainly relied on inflow from other regions in China, while capital mainly relied on foreign investment. From this perspective, factor endowment and comparative advantage theories cannot explain Shenzhen's economic growth. Figure 7-1 shows that in 1990, the output value of foreign-invested enterprises in Shenzhen's industrial sector accounted for nearly 70%, indicating that although capital was scarce at that time, the policy of attracting foreign investment could largely compensate for this deficiency in factor endowment.

Figure 7-2 shows the proportion of output value of the top ten industries with the highest output value in Shenzhen's industrial sector in 1990. It can be seen that although labor-intensive industries such as textile industry, and textile, garment, and apparel industry account for a high proportion, the largest share is taken by the computer, communication, and other electronic equipment manufacturing industry. Additionally, technology and capital-intensive industries such as general equipment manufacturing industry, electrical machinery and equipment manufacturing industry, and pharmaceutical manufacturing industry also account for a high proportion. It is evident that Shenzhen's development from the beginning was not driven by comparative advantage, but rather a manifestation of competitive advantage.

和国土地管理法〉的决定》明确实行国有土地有偿使用制度。

1990年,国务院出台《中华人民共和国城镇国有土地使用权出让和转让暂行条例》,确立了城镇国有土地使用权出让、转让、出租制度,为国有土地有偿使用进一步奠定了基础,清除了障碍。

深圳对土地使用制度所进行的重大变革,不仅为深圳筹集了急缺的建设资金,也加快了深圳对土地这种重要生产要素的供给。这不仅加快了深圳在经济起步期的发展速度,也为全国做出了重要示范。而在这一过程中,深圳政府大胆推动,广东省政府全力支持,中央政府给予全面保障,为制度创新发挥了极其关键的作用,充分体现了有为政府在要素驱动的产业经济竞争阶段的超前引领作用,为深圳获取了发展先机、赢得了竞争优势。

## 三、经济特区建立初期的产业结构

经济特区建立之初,各种生产要素都依赖区域外输入,劳动力主要依赖国内其他地区流入,资本则主要依赖外资,从这个角度看,要素禀赋和比较优势理论是不能解释深圳的经济增长的。图7-1展示出,1990年深圳工业部门中外商投资企业的产值占比接近70%,可见,尽管当时资本稀缺,但通过招商引资政策吸引外资,可以很大程度地弥补这一要素禀赋上的不足。

图7-2展示了1990年深圳工业部门中产值最高的十大工业行业的产值比例。可以看出,尽管劳动密集型的纺织业,纺织服装、服饰业等行业占比较高,但占比最大的是计算机、通信和其他电子设备制造业,另外,通用设备制造业、电气机械及器材制造业、医药制造业等技术和资本密集型行业的占比也很高。可见,深圳的发展从一开始就不是比较优势驱动的结果,而是竞争优势的体现。

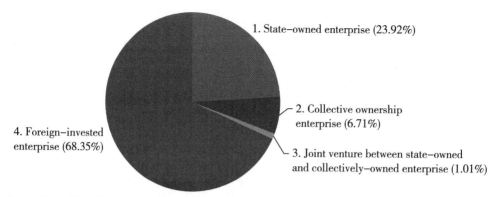

Figure 7-1　The Share of Output Value by Various Types of Ownership in Shenzhen's Industrial Sector in 1990

Data Source: *Shenzhen Statistical Yearbook* 1991(Because the data is rounded, the values in the figure do not add up to 1).

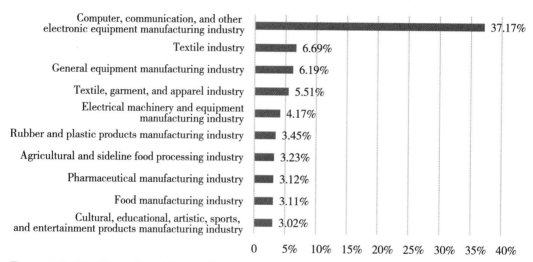

Figure 7-2　The Proportion of Output Value of the Top Ten Industries with the Highest Output Value in Shenzhen's Industrial Sector in 1990

Data Source: *Shenzhen Statistical Yearbook* 1991.

It can be seen from this that the development of a region is not driven by comparative advantage, because in the era of globalization where production factors can flow, the comparative advantage of a region has been greatly diluted. However, at the same time, the comparative disadvantages of a region can be compensated for in a short time using external factors. Therefore, if Shenzhen had only focused on developing those so-called "comparative advantage" industries, today's Shenzhen would not have high-tech enterprises like Huawei, ZTE, Tencent, etc., but would be more likely to fall into the "comparative advantage trap". Thus, regional governments should focus on enhancing the competitive advantage of their region, rather than only choosing to develop industries that conform to the region's comparative advantage.

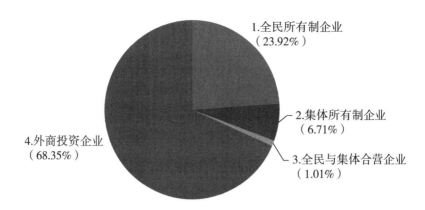

图 7-1 1990 年深圳工业部门中各类型所有制企业的产值比重

数据来源：1991 年《深圳统计年鉴》（因数据四舍五入，所以图中数值相加不为 1）。

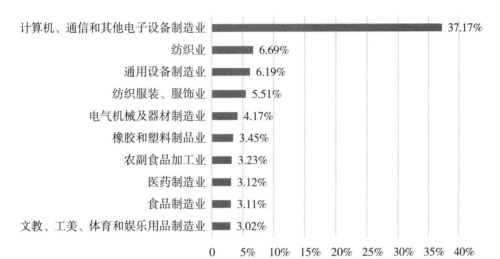

图 7-2 1990 年深圳工业部门中产值最高的十大工业行业的产值比例

数据来源：1991 年《深圳统计年鉴》。

由此可见，一个区域的发展不是由比较优势驱动的，因为在生产要素可流动的全球化时代，一个区域的比较优势已经被极大地冲淡，但与此同时，一个区域的比较劣势也能够在短时间内利用外部要素加以补足。因此，如果深圳仅专注于发展那些所谓的"比较优势"产业，那么今天的深圳就不可能拥有华为、中兴、腾讯等高科技企业，反而更有可能陷入"比较优势陷阱"。所以，区域政府应着力提升本区域的竞争优势，而不应只选择那些符合区域比较优势的产业来发展。

# Section 2: Growth Stage Dominated by Urban Economic Competition and Cooperation

With the reform of the system, the land factor constraint in Shenzhen's economic development was alleviated, talents and capital accelerated in accumulation, and the economy entered a stage of rapid growth. This was followed by an urgent demand for infrastructure. For example, in May 1980, when the Hong Kong-owned enterprise New Nanxin Dyeing Factory was built, it was planned to start production in August 1981. However, due to insufficient power supply, poor telecommunications, and uneven roads, only the main equipment was installed by August 1981, and production was delayed for several months, causing a negative impact. This reflected a contradiction: Shenzhen's almost blank infrastructure construction could not meet the demands of industrial development. Obviously, whether this contradiction could be effectively resolved depended on whether funds for infrastructure construction could be raised. To this end, the Shenzhen government boldly reformed, mainly using two methods to solve the funding problem for infrastructure construction: one was to obtain infrastructure construction loans from banks, and the other was to encourage social capital to participate in infrastructure construction.

## I. Loans for Infrastructure Construction

Shenzhen's infrastructure construction loans refer to banks providing loan support for Shenzhen's "seven connections and one leveling" and other infrastructure construction, and the Shenzhen government repaying within a certain period according to the loan agreement. This financing method for infrastructure construction, which is now very common, faced numerous difficulties at that time. Some representative opposing views included: infrastructure loans would extend the construction front, funds needed for infrastructure should be resolved through fiscal appropriations rather than credit methods, and there were difficulties in selecting loan targets and implementing debt. Facing multiple pressures, the Shenzhen government closely cooperated and fully communicated with various levels and types of banking institutions such as the People's Bank of China and China Construction Bank, receiving strong support from the banking industry in infrastructure construction, leading Shenzhen's economic development.

## 第二节　由城市经济竞争与合作主导的增长阶段

随着制度的改革，深圳经济发展中的土地要素约束得到缓解，人才、资本加速集聚，经济步入高速增长阶段，随之而来的是对基础设施的紧迫需求。例如，1980年5月，港商独资企业新南新印染厂兴建，计划1981年8月投产，但因电源不足、电信不通、公路不平，至1981年8月仅安装好主要的设备，拖延了几个月才投产，造成了不好的影响。[①] 这就体现了一种矛盾，即深圳几乎处于空白状态的基础设施建设无法满足产业发展需求。显然，这一矛盾能否得到有效解决，关键点在于能否筹集到基础设施的建设资金。为此，深圳政府大胆改革，主要通过两种办法破解了基础设施建设的资金难题：一是向银行进行基础设施建设贷款，二是鼓励社会资本参与基础设施建设。

### 一、基础设施建设贷款

深圳的基础设施建设贷款，就是银行对深圳"七通一平"等基础设施建设给予贷款支持，深圳政府再按贷款协议在一定期限内进行偿还。这种现在已经非常普遍的基础设施建设融资方式，在当时却面临着重重困难。几种比较有代表性的反对意见包括：基础设施贷款会拉长建设战线，基础设施所需资金应由财政拨款解决而不应采取信贷方式，贷款对象选择和债务落实存在困难等。[②] 面对重重压力，深圳政府与中国人民银行、中国建设银行等各级各类银行机构紧密协作，充分沟通，在基础设施建设上得到银行业的大力支持，引领了深圳的经济发展。

---

① 丘梁：《关于深圳经济特区基础设施贷款问题的探讨》，《广东金融研究》1983年第1期。
② 丘梁：《关于深圳经济特区基础设施贷款问题的探讨》，《广东金融研究》1983年第1期。

## II. Encouraging Social Capital Participation in Infrastructure Construction

Article 5, Chapter I of the *Regulations on Special Economic Zones in Guangdong Province* stipulates that "The land leveling project and public facilities such as water supply, drainage, power supply, roads, docks, communications, warehousing, etc. in the special zones shall be constructed by the Guangdong Province Special Economic Zone Management Committee. When necessary, foreign capital can also be absorbed to participate in the construction", which provides a legal basis for social capital to participate in infrastructure construction.

Shenzhen Shajiao B Thermal Power Plant (hereinafter referred to as Shajiao B Power Plant) is China's first thermal power plant built using the "Build-Operate-Transfer" (BOT) method. In fact, there were no formal legal provisions for the BOT method at that time, so the BOT method was not explicitly mentioned in the project contract, but the project was a typical BOT project. Party A (Shenzhen Special Economic Zone Power Development Company, the predecessor of Shenzhen Energy Group Co., Ltd.) and Party B [Hong Kong Hehe Power (China) Co., Ltd.[1]] jointly established Shajiao B Power Plant, which was a cooperative enterprise legal person with the sole purpose of developing the Shajiao B Power Plant project. The rights and obligations of both parties were defined as follows: during the cooperation period, Party A was responsible for helping Party B handle various procedures required for the construction project and for applying to relevant government departments for possible preferential policies. Apart from this, Party A did not need to invest any resources in the construction project, including funds, affairs, personnel, and technology. Party B was responsible for financing,

---

[1] Hong Kong Hehe Power (China) Co., Ltd. belongs to Hong Kong Hopewell Holdings Limited, which has actively participated in the infrastructure construction of the Guangdong–Hong Kong–Macao Greater Bay Area under the leadership of Gordon Wu. Apart from the Shajiao B Power Plant, Hopewell Holdings has also been involved in the construction of the Guangzhou–Shenzhen Expressway, the Guangzhou–Zhuhai section of the Beijing–Hong Kong–Macao Expressway, the Guangzhou Southeast West Ring Expressway, the Shunde road and bridge system engineering, the Humen Bridge, and other projects. Additionally, Hopewell Holdings has played a significant role in the planning and development of Shenzhen.

construction, and operation of the construction project. In terms of benefits, during the cooperation period, all benefits belonged to Party B, while Party A's benefits were limited to necessary management fees.

(1) Construction phase. In 1985, the construction of Shajiao B Power Plant officially began, with a construction period of 33 months. To ensure completion on schedule, reward and punishment measures were agreed upon. As a result, the general contractor completed the

## 二、鼓励社会资本参与基础设施建设

《广东省经济特区条例》第一章第五条规定"特区的土地平整工程和供水、排水、供电、道路、码头、通讯、仓储等各项公共设施,由广东省经济特区管理委员会负责兴建,必要时也可以吸收外资参与兴建",这使社会资本参与基础设施建设有法可依。

深圳沙角火力发电厂B厂(以下简称沙角B电厂)是中国首个以"建设—经营—转让",即BOT方式建造的火力发电厂。实际上,BOT方式在当时还没有正式的法律规定,因此在项目合同中并未在文字中体现BOT方式,但项目却是一个典型的BOT项目。甲方(深圳经济特区电力开发公司,深圳能源集团有限公司前身)与乙方[香港合和电力(中国)有限公司[①]]共同组建沙角B电厂,该公司为合作企业法人,其唯一目的是开发沙角B电厂项目。双方的权利与义务的界定方式为:在合作期间,甲方负责帮助乙方办理建设工程所需的各项手续,也负责向政府相关部门申请可能的优惠政策,除此之外,甲方无须对建设工程投入任何资源,包括资金、事务、人员和技术等。乙方负责建设工程的融资、建设和运营。在收益方面,合作期内,全部收益归乙方所有,甲方的收益仅限于提取必要的管理费。

(1)建设阶段。1985年,沙角B电厂正式开工建设,工期规定为33个月,为按期完工,约定了奖惩办法。结果,总承包商提前完成了建设任务,并因此赚取了提前竣工

---

① 香港合和电力(中国)有限公司隶属于香港合和实业有限公司,合和实业有限公司在胡应湘带领下,积极参与粤港澳大湾区基础设施建设,除沙角B电厂外,还参与建设了广深高速、京港澳高速广珠段、广州东南西环高速、顺德路桥系统工程、虎门大桥等项目。合和实业有限公司还深度参与了深圳的规划和开发。

construction task ahead of schedule and earned all the profits from early completion and power generation. Although this seemed to have lost some profits, given the extremely tight power supply in Guangdong at that time, being able to generate power ahead of schedule had great positive significance for promoting economic development in the region.

(2) Operation phase. Shajiao B Power Plant officially began operations in 1987. According to the cooperation agreement between the two parties, Party B would be responsible for the operation and management of Shajiao B Power Plant, and the operating profits would also belong to Party B.

## III. Development and Allocation of Secondary Resources in Shenzhen Metro Construction and Operation

As the urban economy continued to develop, Shenzhen's urban scale and population continuously expanded, and residents' income steadily increased, leading to increasingly strong demands for convenience in travel. Therefore, in December 2001, the Shenzhen Urban Planning Committee passed the metro construction plan and review opinions, proposing that by 2010, Shenzhen would invest 50.8 billion yuan to build an urban rail transit network consisting of 8 lines with a total length of 238.7 kilometers. However, metro construction is a very typical capital-intensive project. Even though Shenzhen's fiscal revenue was growing rapidly, there was still pressure on construction funds. Therefore, Shenzhen chose the "Build-Transfer" (BT) method for metro construction. Moreover, Shenzhen innovatively became the first among domestic cities to pay the appreciation of properties around the metro to the metro company as its operating income, making Shenzhen Metro Corporation one of the few profitable metro companies in China.

### 1. Innovative BT Method

The traditional BT method is: according to legal procedures, the project initiator (government or its authorized unit) selects an investor for the proposed infrastructure or public utility project. This investor is fully responsible for the project's financing and construction. After the project is completed and passes acceptance, the initiator buys back the project, realizing the transfer of the project. In rail transit construction projects in cities like Beijing

发电的全部利润。这虽然看似损失了一定的利润，但由于广东当时电力供应异常紧张，所以能够提前发电对促进该地区经济发展是有很大的积极意义的。

（2）运营阶段。1987年沙角B电厂正式投产。依据双方合作协议，乙方将负责沙角B电厂的运营管理，经营利润也归乙方所有。

## 三、深圳地铁建设和运营中对次生性资源的开发和配置

随着城市经济的不断发展，深圳城市规模和人口数量不断扩大，居民收入不断提高，对出行的便利性要求愈加强烈。因此，深圳市城市规划委员会于2001年12月通过了地铁建设方案和审议意见，提出到2010年，深圳将投资508亿元，建设8条线路共238.7千米城市轨道交通网络。[①]然而，地铁建设属于十分典型的资本密集型工程，即使深圳财政收入增长迅速，但仍存在建设资金压力。因此，深圳在地铁建设上选择了"建设—转让"（BT）方式。不仅如此，深圳还在国内各城市中首创性地将地铁周边物业升值收益付给地铁公司作为其经营收益，这也使深圳地铁公司成为国内为数不多的实现盈利的地铁公司之一。

### 1. 创新的BT方式

传统的BT方式是：依据法定程序，项目发起人（政府或其授权单位）选择拟建的基础设施或公用事业项目的投资人，该投资人对项目的融资、建设全权负责，项目建成且验收合格后，发起人对项目进行回购，也即实现项目的移交。在北京、南京等城市的轨道交通建设工程中，区域政府均应用过传统BT方式。

而在深圳地铁建设中，区域政府在传统BT方式基础上以工程建设目标控制为导向，实施了创新型的深圳地铁BT方式，其特色主要体现在：BT项目发

---

① 尤福永：《试论地铁资源的开发与利用——深圳地铁建设的启示》，《特区经济》2002年第8期。

financing with design and construction general contracting, and the flexibly set BT project buyback method and buyback time points. This innovative BT method achieved the following effects.

(1) Expanded the investment and financing channels for Shenzhen metro construction, solving short-term construction funding pressure;

(2) Solved the problem of whole life cycle management for BT project initiators;

(3) Favorable for BT project initiators to implement full-process control over progress and investment;

(4) Moderate control risks and control costs borne by BT project initiators;

(5) Reduced investment risks for BT project contractors.

Shenzhen metro construction's BT method achieved innovation in both theory and practice of the BT method, obtaining satisfactory results and providing reference significance for the development of domestic BT methods.

### 2. "Metro Operation + Benefit Return" Profit Model

From an input-output perspective, the output of urban rail transit construction and operation investment can be divided into four categories: metro lines, ancillary resources, appreciation of undistributed land along the lines, and appreciation of properties and distributed land along the lines. Currently, urban rail transit companies obtain the first two categories of output, while the latter two categories, which are several times larger than the first two, are either externalized or lost due to ineffective utilization. This is unfair to urban rail transit companies, governments, and taxpayers. If the benefits of the latter two externalized output categories are returned to urban rail transit companies, it would help them build a profit model. This profit model can be theoretically summarized as "Metro Operation + Benefit Return". In the operation of Shenzhen Metro, the regional government has made beneficial explorations into returning the third category of income to the metro company.

In August 2007, the Shenzhen government clarified: The land price income and development profits from properties above metro stations are to be used exclusively for rail transit construction and operation deficit compensation. In November 2008, the Shenzhen government decided: the development of properties above metro stations can be considered to be handled in a package manner by Shenzhen Metro, with all development profits used for metro construction and operation deficit compensation. In March 2012, the Shenzhen government clarified: land use rights obtained through capital contribution in kind have the same legal effect as those obtained through transfer. In February 2013, the Shenzhen government required reasonable definition of government responsibilities and enterprise

起人对工程建设的深度控制，承办人投融资和设计、施工总承包的一体化，以及灵活设置的 BT 工程回购方式和回购时间点。①这种创新型的 BT 方式实现了以下效果：

（1）拓展了深圳地铁建设的投融资渠道，解决了短期建设资金压力；

（2）解决了 BT 项目发起人全寿命周期管理的难题；

（3）有利于 BT 项目发起人对进度、投资的全过程实施控制；

（4）BT 项目发起人承担的控制风险和控制成本适中；

（5）降低了 BT 项目承办人的投资风险。

深圳地铁建设的 BT 方式在理论和实践上实现了对 BT 方式的创新，取得了满意的效果，对国内 BT 方式的发展具有借鉴意义。

**2. "地铁经营 + 效益返还" 盈利模式**

从投入产出角度看，城市轨道交通建设和运营投入的产出有四大类，分别为地铁线路、附属资源、沿线未出让土地的增值以及沿线物业、已出让土地的增值。目前，城市轨道交通公司获得的是前两类产出，后两类产出数倍于前两类产出，却被外部化了，或因未能有效利用而流失了。这对城市轨道交通公司、政府和纳税人都是不公平的。如果将后两类被外部化的产出效益返还给城市轨道交通公司，则有助于其构建盈利模式。这种盈利模式从理论上可概括为"地铁经营 + 效益返还"。②在深圳地铁的经营中，区域政府对返还地铁公司的第三类收益做出了有益探索。

2007 年 8 月，深圳政府明确：地铁上盖物业的地价收入和开发所得利润专款用于轨道交通建设和运营补亏；2008 年 11 月，深圳政府决定：上盖物业项目开发可考虑采取打包方式由深圳地铁统筹处理，其中上盖物业项目开发收益全部用于地铁建设及运营补亏；2012 年 3 月，深圳政府明确：以作价出

---

① 林茂德：《深圳地铁"建设-移交"（BT）模式创新和适应性分析》，《城市轨道交通研究》2012 年第 8 期。

② 张泓：《城市轨道交通企业盈利模式的探索与实践——以深圳地铁集团为例》，《城市轨道交通研究》2018 年第 5 期。

responsibilities, relevant government departments to provide policy support for Shenzhen's rail transit construction, fulfill supervisory duties, and decided to formulate land financing plans according to Shenzhen's rail transit construction needs, dynamically allocating land resources.

With the support of these policies, starting from 2008, Shenzhen Metro obtained development rights for multiple plots near metro lines through targeted bidding, auctioning, and listing, as well as land use rights contributed as capital by the Shenzhen government. The development profits were retained by Shenzhen Metro for repaying metro construction loans and compensating for operation deficits. This model greatly advanced the progress of Shenzhen's metro construction, effectively promoting infrastructure investment and construction through government foresighted leading in the growth stage dominated by urban economic competition and cooperation, facilitating sustained high-speed and high-quality regional economic growth.

It can be seen from this that Shenzhen raised funds from multiple sources for infrastructure construction, innovating development and daring to be the first. Under the government's foresighted leading, regional economic development took the lead in breaking through nationwide, further gaining a leading advantage, continuing to climb along the four stages gradient transference model of regional economic, setting a typical example for the development and construction of other regions across the country.

# Section 3: Growth Stage Dominated by Innovative Economic Competition and Cooperation

After 2000, Shenzhen's land resource supply became increasingly tight, labor costs gradually increased, and competitive pressure from other regions within China continued to grow. Faced with this situation, Shenzhen needed to transform its development mode, promote industrial upgrading, and continuously enhance regional competitiveness.

### I. The Special Zone Is No Longer Special

With the deepening of reform and opening-up, China's reform and opening-up policies had already expanded from regional experiments in special economic zones to replication and expansion in other regions. Market-oriented reform, opening up to the outside world, and aligning with international markets had become inherent requirements for economic

资方式取得的土地使用权，其法律效力等同于以出让方式取得的土地使用权；2013年2月，深圳政府要求合理界定政府责任与企业责任，相关政府部门要为深圳市轨道交通建设提供政策支持，履行监管职责，并决定根据深圳市轨道交通建设需求制订土地融资计划，动态配置土地资源。

在这些政策的支持下，从2008年开始，深圳地铁通过定向招拍挂以及深圳政府以土地使用权作价出资等方式取得了地铁线路附近多宗地块的开发权，开发收益留给深圳地铁，用于地铁建设贷款的还本付息和运营补亏。这种模式极大地推进了深圳地铁建设进度，以政府超前引领在由城市经济竞争与合作主导的增长阶段有效推动了基础设施的投资建设，促进了区域经济持续高速、高质量增长。

由此可见，深圳在基础设施建设方面多方筹措资金，创新发展、敢为人先，在政府的超前引领下，区域经济发展率先在全国突出重围，进一步获取了领先优势，沿着四阶段区域经济竞争梯度推移模型继续攀升，为全国其他区域的发展建设做出了典型示范。

## 第三节 由创新经济竞争与合作主导的增长阶段

2000年以后，深圳土地资源供给不断趋紧，劳动力成本逐步提高，来自国内其他区域的竞争压力不断加大。面对这种情况，深圳需要转变发展方式，推动产业升级，不断增强区域竞争力。

### 一、特区不特

随着改革开放的深入，中国的改革开放政策已经从经济特区的区域性试验向其他区域复制和扩展，市场化改革、对外开放、接轨国际市场，已经成为全国各

construction in all regions of the country. Especially under the framework of World Trade Organization rules, China's opening up could no longer be limited to a few special economic zones but should achieve more comprehensive openness. Against this background, the policy advantages of special economic zones had gradually been lost, and Shenzhen's economic growth rate also showed a decline after entering the new century. Some industries also showed signs of moving to the Yangtze River Delta and other regions. At this time, questions arose such as "the special zone is no longer special" and "who has abandoned Shenzhen". However, by this time, Shenzhen had already accumulated the strength for innovation-driven development and was about to embark on a far-reaching process of industrial transformation and upgrading.

According to the definition by American scholar Porter, industrial transformation and upgrading is a dynamic process, referring to the flow of production factors from sectors with low productivity levels or low productivity growth to sectors with high productivity levels or high productivity growth, as driven by changes in technology, market, and other developmental forces. This promotes the advancement and rationalization of industrial structure and enhances the quality and efficiency of economic and social development.

In fact, the concept of innovation-driven development was reflected in the establishment of the Shenzhen Special Economic Zone from the very beginning. In August 1980, the 15th session of the Standing Committee of the Fifth National People's Congress clearly stated: special economic zones adopt different systems and more open policies than the mainland, fully utilizing foreign funds and technology to develop industry, agriculture, animal husbandry, aquaculture, tourism, residential construction, high-tech research and manufacturing, and other industries. This was the first time that the central government had written records proposing that Shenzhen should develop high-tech research and manufacturing industry.

On July 30, 1985, Shenzhen established the country's first high-tech industrial park jointly operated by the Chinese Academy of Sciences and a city——the Shenzhen Science and Technology Industrial Park. The establishment of this park accelerated the landing and transformation of scientific and technological achievements in Shenzhen and actively explored the incubation of high-tech enterprises.

In the subsequent 1990s, to adapt to the wave of scientific and technical personnel starting businesses, the Shenzhen government introduced a series of policies and regulations to encourage scientific and technical personnel to establish enterprises and attract them to engage in R&D work in Shenzhen enterprises. Nationwide, Shenzhen was the earliest to form an urban cultural atmosphere that valued scientific and technological R&D and allowed scientific and technical personnel to become wealthy first. This series of policies and regulations included:

个区域经济建设的内在要求。尤其是在世界贸易组织规则框架下,中国的对外开放不能仅局限在几个经济特区,而应实现更加全面的开放。在这一背景下,经济特区在政策上的优势已经逐步丧失,深圳的经济增长速度也在进入新世纪后出现下降,一些产业也出现了向长三角和其他区域外移的迹象,此时出现了"特区不特""深圳被谁抛弃"的疑问。但是,此时的深圳已经积蓄了创新驱动发展的力量,并即将迎来一次意义深远的产业转型升级过程。

依据美国学者波特的定义,产业转型升级是一个动态的过程,这是指随着技术、市场等发展动力的变化,生产要素从低生产率水平或者低生产率增长的部门向高生产率水平或者高生产率增长的部门流动,进而推动产业结构的高级化和合理化,并提升经济社会发展的质量和效益。[①]

实际上,创新驱动发展的理念在深圳经济特区成立之初就有所体现。1980年8月,第五届全国人大常委会第十五次会议明确:经济特区采取与内地不同的体制和更加开放的政策,充分利用国外的资金和技术,发展工业、农业、畜牧业、养殖业、旅游业、住宅建筑业、高技术研究制造业和其他行业。这是中央有文字记载的第一次对深圳提出要发展高技术研究制造业。

1985年7月30日,深圳建立了国内第一个中国科学院与地市合办的高科技产业园区——深圳科技工业园,深圳科技工业园的建成加速了科技成果在深圳的落地转化,其对孵化高新技术企业也进行了积极探索。

在之后的20世纪90年代,为顺应当时科技人员下海创业的浪潮,深圳政府出台了一系列政策和法规,鼓励科技人员创办企业,吸引科技人员流入深圳企业从事研发工作。在全国,深圳最早形成了重视科技研发、让科技人员也能先富起

---

① 郭跃文、向晓梅等:《中国经济特区四十年工业化道路:从比较优势到竞争优势》,社会科学文献出版社,2020,第168页。

*Interim Provisions on Accelerating the Development of High-tech and Its Industries* (1991), *Provisions of the Shenzhen Municipal Committee of the Communist Party of China and Shenzhen Municipal People's Government on Promoting Economic Development Relying on Scientific and Technological Progress* (1991), *Interim Measures for Shenzhen Enterprises to Reward Technical Development Personnel* (1993), *Management Regulations for Private Science and Technology Enterprises in Shenzhen Special Economic Zone* (1993), *Management Measures for Intangible Asset Evaluation in Shenzhen Special Economic Zone* (1994), *Regulations on Protection of Enterprise Technical Secrets in Shenzhen Special Economic Zone* (1995), *Management Measures for Technology Achievement Investment in Shenzhen Special Economic Zone* (1998), and so on.

## II. Construction of an Innovative City

From the mid-1990s, Shenzhen's high-tech industry entered a golden age of development. The Shenzhen government also moved from initially promoting the transformation of scientific and technological achievements and encouraging scientific and technical personnel to start businesses, towards systematic design of science and technology industrial policies and overall innovation environment creation. Finally, in the first decade of the 21st century, it preliminarily constructed a mature regional high-tech industrial system. Some of the main measures and policies are shown in Table 7-1.

Table 7-1  Measures and Policies Supporting the Development of High-Tech Industries in Shenzhen

| Time | Measures and Policies | Main Content |
| --- | --- | --- |
| 1995 | *Decision of the Shenzhen Municipal Committee of the Communist Party of China and Shenzhen Municipal People's Government on Promoting Scientific and Technological Progress* | Established the strategic thought of "taking high-tech industries as the vanguard", and was the first in the country to specify the proportion of investment in three science and technology funds in written form |
| 1998 | *Several Provisions on Further Supporting the Development of High-Tech Industries* | Comprehensive improvement and standardization of the policies and measures adopted by the government to promote the development of high-tech industries. This was the first systematic industrial policy by a local government in China, triggering a fierce policy competition nationwide. In the history of China's high-tech industry development, this regulation was a significant milestone event |

来的城市文化氛围。这一系列政策和法规包括:《加快高新技术及其产业发展的暂行规定》(1991年),《中共深圳市委 深圳市人民政府关于依靠科技进步推动经济发展的规定》(1991年),《深圳市企业奖励技术开发人员暂行办法》(1993年),《深圳经济特区民办科技企业管理规定》(1993年),《深圳经济特区无形资产评估管理办法》(1994年),《深圳经济特区企业技术秘密保护条例》(1995年),《深圳经济特区技术成果入股管理办法》(1998年),等等。

## 二、创新型城市建设

从20世纪90年代中期开始,深圳高新技术产业进入了发展的黄金时代,深圳政府也从最初的促进科技成果转化、鼓励科技人员创业,走向了系统的科技产业政策设计,以及整体的创新环境打造,最终在21世纪前10年,初步构建了一个成熟的区域高新技术产业体系,一些主要的政策措施如表7-1所示。

表7-1 深圳支持高新技术产业发展的政策措施

| 时间 | 政策措施 | 主要内容 |
| --- | --- | --- |
| 1995年 | 《中共深圳市委 深圳市人民政府关于推动科学技术进步的决定》 | 明确"以高新技术产业为先导"的战略思想,在全国率先以文件形式,规定了科技三项经费投入比例 |
| 1998年 | 《关于进一步扶持高新技术产业发展的若干规定》 | 全面完善并规范了政府推动高新技术产业发展的政策措施,这是国内地方政府首个系统的科技产业政策,在全国引发了一波激烈的政策竞赛。在中国高新技术产业发展历史上,该规定是一个重要的节点事件 |

continued

| Time | Measures and Policies | Main Content |
|---|---|---|
| 1999 | Several Provisions on Further Supporting the Development of High-Tech Industries (Revised) | In response to the national policy competition, promoted the development of high-tech industries comprehensively from aspects such as fiscal input, venture capital, tax incentives, distribution incentives, intellectual property rights, land use, talent introduction, investment and financing systems, attracting foreign investment and returnees, and government rewards |
| 1999 | Hosting the First China Hi-Tech Fair | Provided a platform for the transaction of global high-tech achievements. Premier at the time Zhu Rongji attended the event and announced that this national-level exhibition would be permanently hosted in Shenzhen. In November 2023, the 25th China Hi-Tech Fair was successfully held in Shenzhen |
| 2000 | Establishment of Shenzhen International High-Tech Property Exchange | The first technology property exchange established in a company form in the country |
| 2001 | Regulations of Shenzhen Special Economic Zone on High-Tech Industry Park | Clarified fundamental issues such as the development goals of the high-tech industry park, qualification review for high-tech enterprises and projects entering the park |
| 2001 | Decision on Accelerating the Development of High-Tech Industries | Proposed strengthening leadership and coordination in industrial belt construction, setting reasonable tax sharing ratios, encouraging districts within the special zone to invest in developing high-tech zones within the industrial belt, and planning functional zones for project construction in Longgang Industrial Area |
| 2003 | Regulations of Shenzhen Special Economic Zone on Venture Capital | The first law on venture capital in the country, serving as a blueprint for the *Interim Measures for the Administration of Venture Capital Enterprises* jointly issued by the National Development and Reform Commission, Ministry of Science and Technology, and other ten ministries in 2005 |
| 2003 | Several Provisions of Shenzhen on Encouraging the Development of Technology Incubators | Arranged funds from the three science and technology funds and mobilized social resources to participate in the construction of incubators |
| 2004 | Decision of the Shenzhen Municipal Committee of the Communist Party of China and Shenzhen Municipal People's Government on Improving the Regional Innovation System and Promoting Sustainable and Rapid Development of High-Tech Industries | Document No. 1 of Shenzhen in 2004, systematically proposing the basic requirements and objectives for building a regional innovation system for the first time |
| 2004 | Operations of the SME Board of the Shenzhen Stock Exchange | Solved the exit issue for venture capital investments |
| 2006 | Decision of the Shenzhen Municipal Committee of the Communist Party of China and Shenzhen Municipal People's Government on Implementing an Independent Innovation Strategy and Building a National Innovative City | Officially proposed the basic framework for building a national innovative city. Document No. 1 of Shenzhen in 2006. In April 2006, the Shenzhen Science and Information Bureau and other departments formulated 16 supporting policy documents, forming a "1+N" policy system surrounding the independent innovation strategy from various aspects such as economy, science and technology, education, talent, intellectual property rights, law, customs, and business taxation |
| 2009 | Opening of the Growth Enterprise Market of the Shenzhen Stock Exchange | Provided a financing platform for start-up enterprises |

续表

| 时间 | 政策措施 | 主要内容 |
|---|---|---|
| 1999年 | 《关于进一步扶持高新技术产业发展的若干规定》（修订） | 作为对全国政策竞赛的回应，从财政投入、创业投资、税收优惠、分配激励、知识产权、土地使用、人才引进、投融资体系、吸引外资和归国留学生、政府奖励等方面全方位地促进高新技术产业发展 |
| 1999年 | 举办首届中国国际高新技术成果交易会 | 为全球高新技术成果交易提供平台，时任国务院总理朱镕基亲自出席，并宣布这一国家级展会永久驻在深圳。2023年11月，第二十五届中国国际高新技术成果交易会在深圳成功举办 |
| 2000年 | 成立深圳国际高新技术产权交易所 | 全国首家以公司制形式创建的技术产权交易所 |
| 2001年 | 《深圳经济特区高新技术产业园区条例》 | 明确高新技术产业园区的发展目标、高新技术企业和项目入区资格审查等园区发展中的许多根本性问题 |
| 2001年 | 《关于加快发展高新技术产业的决定》 | 提出加强对产业带建设的领导和协调，制定合理的税收分成比例，鼓励特区内各区到产业带投资开发建设高新技术片区，到龙岗大工业区规划功能区域投资兴建项目 |
| 2003年 | 《深圳经济特区创业投资条例》 | 全国首部关于创业投资的法规，为2005年国家发展改革委、科技部等10部委联合发布的《创业投资企业管理暂行办法》提供了蓝本 |
| 2003年 | 《深圳市鼓励科技企业孵化器发展的若干规定》 | 从科技三项经费中安排资金，并充分调动社会资源参与孵化器建设 |
| 2004年 | 《中共深圳市委 深圳市人民政府 关于完善区域创新体系 推动高新技术产业持续快速发展的决定》 | 深圳2004年的"1号文件"，第一次系统提出了建设区域创新体系的基本要求和目标 |
| 2004年 | 深圳证券交易所中小企业板块开始运作 | 解决了风险投资的投资出口问题 |
| 2006年 | 《中共深圳市委 深圳市人民政府 关于实施自主创新战略建设国家创新型城市的决定》 | 正式提出建设国家创新型城市的基本框架，深圳2006年的"1号文件"。2006年4月，深圳市科技信息局等部门制定了16个有关配套政策文件，从经济、科技、教育、人才、知识产权、法律、海关、工商税务等各方面，形成围绕自主创新战略的"1+N"政策体系 |
| 2009年 | 深圳证券交易所创业板开市 | 为初创企业提供了融资平台 |

## III. The "Focus Point" Effect of Daring to Be the First

As can be seen from Table 7-1, although facing the development trend of "the special zone is no longer special", the Shenzhen government still dared to take the lead and innovate. At the turn of the century, Shenzhen's scientific and technological resources, both in absolute and relative terms, could not take a leading position among domestic cities. However, through introducing a series of policy measures favorable to high-tech industry development, the Shenzhen government took the lead in making Shenzhen a "Focus Point" for the whole country, thereby rapidly driving the aggregation of industries, capital, talent, and technology, turning the original comparative disadvantage into a comparative advantage.

Figure 7-3 shows the full-time equivalent (person-years) of R&D personnel in industrial enterprises above designated size in Shenzhen, Guangdong, and the whole country for 2001, 2004, 2009, 2014, and 2019. The data shows that during these 19 years, the full-time equivalent (person-years) of R&D personnel in industrial enterprises above designated size in Shenzhen increased by 22.22 times, while the national figure only increased by 4.26 times. Therefore, if we estimate Shenzhen's 2019 data for full-time equivalent (person-years) of R&D

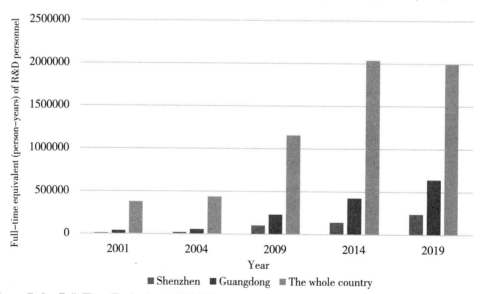

Figure 7-3 Full-Time Equivalent of R&D Personnel in Industrial Enterprises above Designated Size in Shenzhen, Guangdong, and the Whole Country for 2001, 2004, 2009, 2014, and 2019

Data Source: Calculated and organized based on data from the *Guangdong Statistical Yearbook* and *China Statistical Yearbook* over the years.

## 三、敢为人先的"聚点"效应

从表7-1可以看出,尽管面临"特区不特"的发展趋势,但深圳政府却仍敢为人先,勇于创新。在世纪之交,深圳科技资源不论在绝对量还是相对量上,都无法在国内城市中居于领先地位。但是,深圳政府却通过推出一系列有利于高科技产业发展的政策措施,率先使深圳成为全国的一个"聚点",从而迅速带动产业、资本、人才和技术的集聚,使原来的比较劣势变为比较优势。

图7-3给出了2001年、2004年、2009年、2014年和2019年深圳、广东和全国规模以上工业企业R&D人员全时当量(人年)的情况。数据显示,在这19年间,深圳市规模以上工业企业R&D人员全时当量(人年)增长了22.22倍,而全国则仅增长了4.26倍。因此,如果以全国增长速度来估算深圳2019年的规模以上工业企业R&D人员全时当量(人年)数据,则该指标仅为43808.8(人年),而实际数值比该估算值多194804.38(人年),平均每年高出10252.86(人年)。对于这一数据,我们可以理解为每年有10252.86(人年)的R&D人员全时当量从全国各地流入了深圳的规模以上工业企业。

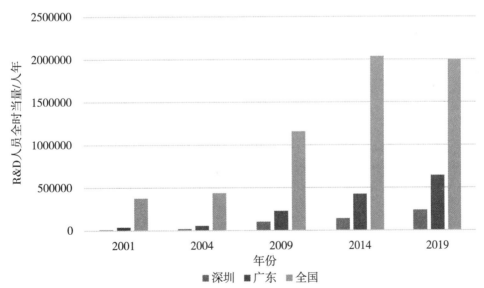

图7-3 2001年、2004年、2009年、2014年和2019年深圳、广东和全国规模以上工业企业R&D人员全时当量(人年)的情况

数据来源:根据历年《广东统计年鉴》《中国统计年鉴》相关数据整理计算。

personnel in industrial enterprises above designated size based on the national growth rate, this indicator would only be 43,808.8 (person-years), while the actual value is 194,804.38 (person-years) more than this estimate, averaging 10,252.86 (person-years) higher each year. We can interpret this data as meaning that each year, 10,252.86 (person-years) of full-time equivalent R&D personnel flowed into industrial enterprises above designated size in Shenzhen from all over the country.

Figure 7-4 illustrates the changes in R&D expenditures of industrial enterprises above designated size in Shenzhen, Guangdong, and the whole country in the years 2001, 2004, 2009, 2014, and 2019. Consistent with the growth trend of full-time equivalent of R&D personnel, Shenzhen's R&D expenditure increased by 39 times during these years, while Guangdong's increased by 23 times, and the national average increased by 22 times over the same period. It is evident that Shenzhen's growth rate in R&D expenditure is almost double the national average.

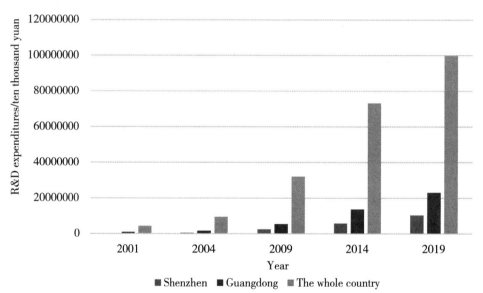

Figure 7–4 Changes in R&D Expenditures of Industrial Enterprises above Designated Dize in Shenzhen, Guangdong, and the Whole Country in the Years 2001, 2004, 2009, 2014, and 2019

Data Source: Calculated and organized based on data from the *Guangdong Statistical Yearbook* and *China Statistical Yearbook* over the years.

Figures 7-5 and 7-6 respectively show the changes in the proportion of full-time equivalent R&D personnel and R&D expenditures of industrial enterprises above designated size in Shenzhen compared to the corresponding figures for Guangdong and the whole country. These two charts reveal that the proportion relative to Guangdong experienced a rapid increase before 2010, with some years after 2010 showing a slight decline but maintaining a stable trend. On the other hand, the proportion relative to the national figures has consistently shown a growing trend. Particularly noteworthy is the significant increase in the number of full-time equivalent R&D personnel, indicating a continuously strengthening attraction of Shenzhen to scientific personnel and technological activities, and demonstrating an increasingly pronounced "Focus Point" effect.

图 7-4 给出了 2001 年、2004 年、2009 年、2014 年和 2019 年深圳、广东和全国规模以上工业企业 R&D 经费（万元）的变动情况。与 R&D 人员全时当量的增长趋势相一致，深圳在这些年份，R&D 经费投入增长了 39 倍，同期广东增长了 23 倍，全国增长了 22 倍。可见，深圳 R&D 经费的增长速度接近全国的 2 倍。

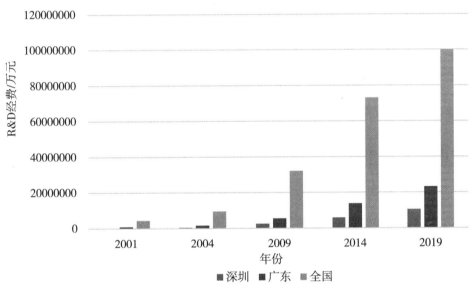

图 7-4　2001 年、2004 年、2009 年、2014 年和 2019 年深圳、广东和全国规模以上工业企业 R&D 经费（万元）的变动情况

数据来源：根据历年《广东统计年鉴》《中国统计年鉴》相关数据整理计算。

图 7-5 和图 7-6 则分别给出了深圳规模以上工业企业 R&D 人员全时当量和 R&D 经费占广东相应数据的比例和占全国相应数据的比例的变动情况。从这两幅图中可以看出，这两项指标的比例占广东的比例在 2010 年之前迅速提高，2010 年之后有的年份有所回落，但保持了平稳态势。而这两项指标占全国相应数据的比例则一直保持了增长态势。尤其是 R&D 人员全时当量的增幅更加显著，这表明深圳对科技人员和科技活动的吸引力不断增强，"聚点"效应不断显现。

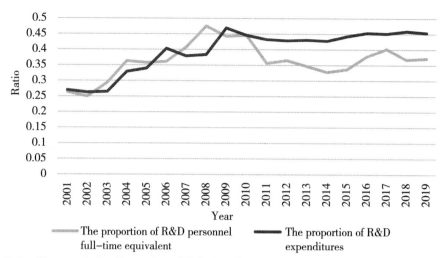

Figure 7-5   Changes in the Proportion of Full-time Equivalent R&D Personnel and R&D Expenditures of Industrial Enterprises above Designated Size in Shenzhen Compared to the Corresponding Figures for Guangdong from 2001 to 2019

Data Source: Calculated and organized based on data from the *Guangdong Statistical Yearbook* and *China Statistical Yearbook* over the years.

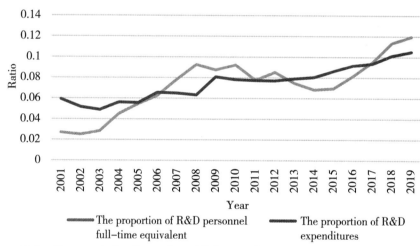

Figure 7-6   Changes in the Proportion of Full-time Equivalent R&D Personnel and R&D Expenditures of Industrial Enterprises above Designated Size in Shenzhen Compared to the Corresponding National Figures from 2001 to 2019

Data Source: Calculated and organized based on data from the *Guangdong Statistical Yearbook* and *China Statistical Yearbook* over the years.

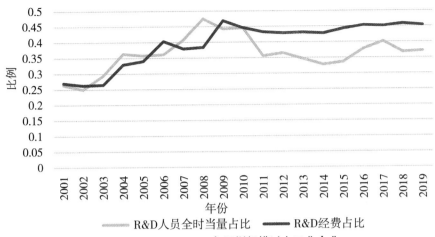

图 7-5 2001—2019 年深圳规模以上工业企业
R&D 人员全时当量和 R&D 经费占广东相应数据的比例变动情况

数据来源：根据历年《广东统计年鉴》《中国统计年鉴》相关数据整理计算。

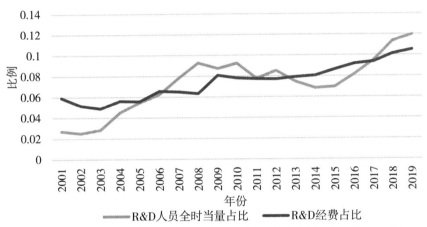

图 7-6 2001—2019 年深圳规模以上工业企业 R&D 人员全时当量和 R&D
经费占全国相应数据的比例变动情况

数据来源：根据历年《广东统计年鉴》《中国统计年鉴》相关数据整理计算。

## IV. Revisiting Shenzhen's Industrial Structure

From the previous sections, we have seen that Shenzhen had already well developed capital-intensive and technology-intensive industries such as computers, general equipment manufacturing, and pharmaceutical manufacturing in 1990. So how have these industries developed after 20 years, and do they have "self-generating capabilities"? Tables 7-2 and 7-3 show the output value, and import and export situation of Shenzhen's high-tech industries from 2010 to 2018, respectively. The data indicates that these capital-intensive and technology-intensive industries in Shenzhen have not only developed well but have also become pillar industries of Shenzhen, possessing strong competitive advantages.

Table 7-2  Output Value of Shenzhen's High-Tech Industries from 2010 to 2018

(unit: hundred million yuan)

| Year | Total Output Value of the High-tech Industries | Among | | | | |
|---|---|---|---|---|---|---|
| | | Electronic Information | New Energy and New Materials | Mechatronics and Optoelectronics | Biotechnology | Environmental Protection and Others |
| 2010 | 10176.19 | 8963.26 | 553.88 | 490.78 | 101.16 | 67.11 |
| 2011 | 11875.61 | 10451.08 | 650.9 | 574.62 | 119.88 | 79.13 |
| 2012 | 12931.82 | 11360.2 | 722.5 | 625.7 | 134.1 | 89.3 |
| 2013 | 14159.45 | 12442.42 | 789.66 | 682.88 | 147.78 | 96.71 |
| 2014 | 15560.07 | 13689.76 | 337.59 | 728.5 | 724.88 | 79.34 |
| 2015 | 17296.87 | 15269.85 | 782.69 | 790.70 | 358.93 | 94.70 |
| 2016 | 19222.06 | 17096.10 | 804.64 | 844.31 | 367.07 | 109.94 |
| 2017 | 21378.78 | 19110.44 | 840.0 | 921.40 | 376.36 | 130.59 |
| 2018 | 23871.71 | | | | | |

## 四、再看深圳的产业结构

通过前文,我们已经看到 1990 年时深圳就很好地发展了计算机、通用设备制造业、医药制造业等资本和技术密集型产业,那么 20 年后,这些产业发展得如何,是否具有"自生能力"呢?表 7-2 和表 7-3 分别给出了 2010—2018 年深圳高新技术产业产值和进出口情况,数据表明,深圳的这些资本和技术密集型产业不仅发展良好,还成为深圳的支柱产业,具有很强的竞争优势。

表 7-2  2010—2018 年深圳高新技术产业产值情况 (单位:亿元)

| 年份 | 高新技术产业总产值 | 其中 | | | | |
|---|---|---|---|---|---|---|
| | | 电子信息 | 新能源及新材料 | 光机电一体化 | 生物技术 | 环保及其他 |
| 2010 | 10176.19 | 8963.26 | 553.88 | 490.78 | 101.16 | 67.11 |
| 2011 | 11875.61 | 10451.08 | 650.9 | 574.62 | 119.88 | 79.13 |
| 2012 | 12931.82 | 11360.2 | 722.5 | 625.7 | 134.1 | 89.3 |
| 2013 | 14159.45 | 12442.42 | 789.66 | 682.88 | 147.78 | 96.71 |
| 2014 | 15560.07 | 13689.76 | 337.59 | 728.5 | 724.88 | 79.34 |
| 2015 | 17296.87 | 15269.85 | 782.69 | 790.70 | 358.93 | 94.70 |
| 2016 | 19222.06 | 17096.10 | 804.64 | 844.31 | 367.07 | 109.94 |
| 2017 | 21378.78 | 19110.44 | 840.0 | 921.40 | 376.36 | 130.59 |
| 2018 | 23871.71 | | | | | |

数据来源:白积洋:《"有为政府+有效市场":深圳高新技术产业发展 40 年》,《深圳社会科学》2019 年第 5 期。

Table 7-3  Import and Export Situation of Shenzhen's High-Tech Industries from 2010 to 2018

(Unit: Ten Thousand USD)

| Year | Total Import and Export Value of the City | Export Value of the City | Total Import and Export Value of the High-Tech Industries | The Proportion of Total Import and Export Value in the High-Tech Industries | Export Value of the High-Tech Industries | The Proportion of Export Value in the High-Tech Industries |
|---|---|---|---|---|---|---|
| 2010 | 34674930 | 20418355 | 19770075 | 57.02% | 10872668 | 53.25% |
| 2011 | 41409312 | 24551760 | 22416000 | 54.13% | 12480000 | 50.83% |
| 2012 | 46683020 | 27136163 | 25206532 | 54.00% | 14122000 | 52.04% |
| 2013 | 53747437 | 30570191 | 30784842 | 57.28% | 16900557 | 55.28% |
| 2014 | 48774049 | 28436157 | 24762288 | 50.77% | 13674080 | 48.09% |
| 2015 | 44245863 | 26403895 | 25424844 | 57.46% | 14033773 | 53.15% |
| 2016 | 39843893 | 23754674 | 22764476 | 57.13% | 12154291 | 51.17% |
| 2017 | 42399222 | 25061181 | 22081542 | 52.08% | 11855158 | 47.30% |
| 2018 | 43609541 | 23670555 | | | 12006326 | 50.72% |

Obviously, Shenzhen's industrial upgrading is difficult to explain using comparative advantage theory. Rodrik once stated that China's industrialization did not fully follow the principle of comparative advantage. He believed that China's export structure was relatively good, usually only appearing in countries with higher per capita GDP, attributing this to China's industrial policy not fully following the principle of comparative advantage. For a city that was a blank slate not long ago, Shenzhen's industrial upgrading cannot be explained by comparative advantage theory.

In the 30 years after the establishment of the Shenzhen Special Economic Zone, Shenzhen's industrial structure upgraded from labor-intensive "three-processing and one compensation" to capital-intensive and technology-intensive high-tech industries. Perhaps it can be said that Shenzhen had a comparative advantage in labor at the beginning of reform and opening-up, but in any case, it is difficult for us to confirm that Shenzhen had a comparative advantage in capital and technology. The fundamental reason why Shenzhen was able to successfully develop high-tech industries, achieve industrial upgrading, and innovation-driven development lies in the government's foresighted leading through a series of policy measures to promote high-tech industry development. This foresighted leading made Shenzhen a "Focus Point" for national high-tech industries, causing capital, talent, and technology to continuously flow in and accelerate agglomeration, thereby creating competitive advantages and achieving gradient upgrading of economic growth stages.

The key to Shenzhen's successful industrial upgrading is that many of Shenzhen government's policy measures were ahead of the national level, which is Shenzhen's leading advantage. This leading advantage strengthened the "Focus Point" effect. The agglomeration

表 7-3　2010—2018 年深圳高新技术产业进出口情况　　　（单位：万美元）

| 年份 | 全市进出口总额 | 全市出口额 | 高新技术产业进出口总额 | 高新技术产业进出口总额占比 | 高新技术产业出口额 | 高新技术产业出口额占比 |
| --- | --- | --- | --- | --- | --- | --- |
| 2010 | 34674930 | 20418355 | 19770075 | 57.02% | 10872668 | 53.25% |
| 2011 | 41409312 | 24551760 | 22416000 | 54.13% | 12480000 | 50.83% |
| 2012 | 46683020 | 27136163 | 25206532 | 54.00% | 14122000 | 52.04% |
| 2013 | 53747437 | 30570191 | 30784842 | 57.28% | 16900557 | 55.28% |
| 2014 | 48774049 | 28436157 | 24762288 | 50.77% | 13674080 | 48.09% |
| 2015 | 44245863 | 26403895 | 25424844 | 57.46% | 14033773 | 53.15% |
| 2016 | 39843893 | 23754674 | 22764476 | 57.13% | 12154291 | 51.17% |
| 2017 | 42399222 | 25061181 | 22081542 | 52.08% | 11855158 | 47.30% |
| 2018 | 43609541 | 23670555 |  |  | 12006326 | 50.72% |

数据来源：白积洋：《"有为政府＋有效市场"：深圳高新技术产业发展 40 年》，《深圳社会科学》2019 年第 5 期。

显然，深圳的产业升级难以用比较优势理论加以解释，罗德里克就曾表示中国的工业化没有完全遵循比较优势原则。他认为，中国的出口结构比较好，通常只在人均 GDP 较高的国家才会出现这样的出口结构，他将这归因于中国产业政策并未完全遵循比较优势原则。对于一个不久之前还是一张白纸的城市，深圳的产业升级无法用比较优势理论进行解释。

在深圳经济特区成立后的 30 年时间内，深圳的产业结构就由"三来一补"的劳动密集型升级到了资本和技术密集的高新技术型，也许可以说深圳在改革开放之初具备劳动力的比较优势，但无论如何，我们都难以证实深圳在资本和技术上具有比较优势。而深圳之所以能够成功地发展高新技术产业，实现产业升级、创新驱动发展，其根本原因还在于政府通过实施一系列促进高新技术产业发展的政策措施所进行的超前引领，这种超前引领使深圳成为全国高新技术产业的一个"聚点"，使资本、人才和技术不断涌入，加速集聚，从而创造了竞争优势，实现了经济增长阶段的梯度升级。

深圳之所以能够成功实现产业升级，其关键点在于深圳政府的诸多政策措施

of industries, on one hand, formed economies of scale, thus achieving a circulating cumulative endogenous growth momentum, and on the other hand, brought further demand for institutional innovation, pushing Shenzhen to continue exploring and breaking through in the business environment and hardware and software infrastructure. Therefore, the "Focus Point" effect brought by Shenzhen government's foresighted leading is the real reason why Shenzhen's industrial structure has been continuously upgraded and economic growth has maintained a high speed for a long time.

## Section 4: Growth Stage Dominated by Shared Economic Competition and Cooperation

After 2010, Shenzhen had entered the national and even global leading ranks in some industrial fields. To achieve further breakthroughs, it not only required Shenzhen's full investment but also needed Shenzhen government to integrate national and even global resources. At this time, Shenzhen had preliminarily entered the growth stage dominated by shared economy competition and cooperation. Below, this book takes Shenzhen's integration of resources inside and outside the region to develop higher education and enhance innovation capacity as an example to illustrate the government's foresighted leading strategy adopted by Shenzhen at this stage.

### I. A Path for Higher Education Development Combining Self-Reliance and Introduction of Cooperation

From a temporal perspective, shortly after the establishment of the Shenzhen Special Economic Zone, in January 1983, the Shenzhen Municipal Committee of the Communist Party of China and Municipal People's Government clearly proposed to the Guangdong Provincial Committee of the Communist Party of China and Provincial People's Government the idea of establishing a local university, which received attention and support from the Ministry of Education and Guangdong Province. In May 1983, with the approval of the State Council, the

Ministry of Education issued a document approving the establishment of Shenzhen University. However, after establishing Shenzhen University, Shenzhen did not boldly establish new universities on a large scale. In 1993, Shenzhen Polytechnic (later renamed Shenzhen Polytechnic University) was established, mainly to meet the talent demand of manufacturing industry development. This was related to Shenzhen's focus on economic development as the

都是领先于全国的，这是深圳的领先优势，这一领先优势加强了"聚点"效应，产业的集聚一方面形成了规模经济效应，从而实现了循环累积的内生增长动力，另一方面也带来了对制度创新的进一步的需求，推动着深圳继续在营商环境、软硬件基础设施上不断探索、不断突破。因此，深圳政府超前引领所带来的"聚点"效应才是深圳产业结构得以不断升级，经济增长得以长期保持高速的真正原因。

## 第四节　由共享经济竞争与合作主导的增长阶段

2010年以后，深圳在一些产业领域已经进入了全国甚至全球领先行列，要实现进一步的突破不仅需要深圳的全力投入，更需要深圳政府整合全国乃至全球资源。此时，深圳已经初步进入由共享经济竞争与合作经济主导的增长阶段。下面，本书以深圳整合区域内外资源发展高等教育、提升创新能力为例，来阐述深圳在这一阶段采取的政府超前引领策略。

### 一、自力更生与引进合作相结合的高等教育发展路径

从时间上看，深圳经济特区建立后不久，1983年1月，深圳市委、市政府向广东省委、省政府明确提出创办一所本地高校的构想，并获得了教育部和广东省的重视和支持。1983年5月，经国务院批准，教育部发文批准成立深圳大学。但是，建立深圳大学之后，深圳并没有再大刀阔斧地新建高校。1993年深圳职业技术学院（后改为深圳职业技术大学）成立，主要是为了满足制造业发展对人

primary task at that time, unable to spare more energy and funds to increase construction in the fields of science, education, culture, and health; it was also related to Shenzhen's rapid development after the establishment of the special economic zone and the beginning of a talent attracting effect nationwide.

As the degree of talent competition intensified across the country, Shenzhen also increased its efforts in higher education construction. In 2010, Southern University of Science and Technology officially started preparation, in 2017, Shenzhen Technology University started preparation, and according to the recently issued *Action Plan for Shenzhen to Build a Pilot Demonstration Area of Socialism with Chinese Characteristics (2019—2025)*, universities such as Shenzhen Normal University and Shenzhen Conservatory of Music will also be prepared.

In the development of higher education, Shenzhen was one of the earliest cities in China to adopt the approach of introducing universities and cooperative education.

On one hand, Shenzhen continuously introduced universities. In 2001, Shenzhen established Peking University Shenzhen Graduate School and Tsinghua Shenzhen International Graduate School, and the following year established Harbin Institute of Technology Shenzhen Graduate School. In the construction process of Shenzhen University Town, the Shenzhen government, as the main investor, carried out overall planning and clearly proposed to build Shenzhen University Town into an important base for regional industry-university-research cooperation to meet the needs of Shenzhen's economic and social development. During this stage, the Shenzhen government also successively cooperated with hundreds of enterprises and institutions such as Huawei and ZTE to jointly build research institutions, graduate practice bases, or carry out technological research and development cooperation. Therefore, the interaction between higher education and urban development in Shenzhen was significantly upgraded during this stage.

On the other hand, the efforts in cooperative education have been continuously increasing. Cooperative education is a new chapter opened on the basis of the university introduction model. Not only are the cooperation models diversified, including both Sino-foreign cooperative education and cooperative education with well-known domestic universities in different locations, but it has also broken through the original small scale of postgraduate education, obtaining independent enrollment codes to recruit undergraduate students. Many cooperative universities such as The Chinese University of Hong Kong (Shenzhen), Harbin

Institute of Technology (Shenzhen), and Shenzhen MSU-BIT University, as well as Sun Yat-sen University Shenzhen Campus, have been officially established and started enrollment with the approval of the Ministry of Education. According to published plans, Shenzhen will have more large-scale projects in Sino-foreign cooperative education in the future.

才的需求。这一方面和当时深圳把发展经济作为第一要务,还未能腾出更多的精力和经费加大科教文卫领域的建设有关;另一方面和深圳经济特区建立后迅速发展并开始对全国人才产生虹吸效应有关。①

随着全国各地对人才竞争的程度不断加剧,深圳也加大了对高等教育的建设力度。2010年南方科技大学正式筹建,2017年深圳技术大学筹建,且根据新近出台的《深圳市建设中国特色社会主义先行示范区的行动方案(2019—2025年)》,还将筹建深圳师范大学、深圳音乐学院等高校。

在高等教育事业的发展上,深圳是中国较早采取引进高校和合作办学方式的城市。

一方面,深圳不断引进高校。2001年,深圳创立了北京大学深圳研究生院和清华大学深圳国际研究生院,次年又创立了哈尔滨工业大学深圳研究生院。在深圳大学城的建设过程中,深圳政府作为主要投资方进行了总体规划,明确提出要将深圳大学城建设成为区域产学研合作的重要基地,以符合深圳经济社会发展的需求。这个阶段深圳政府也陆续与华为、中兴等几百个企事业单位合建研究机构、研究生实践基地或开展技术研发合作。因此,这个阶段深圳高等教育和城市发展的互动得到了明显升级。

另一方面,合作办学的力度也在不断加大。合作办学是在引进高校模式基础上开启的新篇章,不但合作模式多样化,既有中外合作办学,也有国内知名大学的异地合作办学,而且突破了原来研究生教育的小规模,获设独立招生代码招收本科生。香港中文大学(深圳)、哈尔滨工业大学(深圳)和深圳北理莫斯科大学等多所合作办学高校及中山大学深圳校区纷纷获教育部批准正式设立并招生。根据已公布的规划,深圳未来还将在中外合作办学方面有更多大规模的项目。②

---

① 陈先哲:《城市竞争阶段升级与高等教育发展战略转型:深圳案例》,《高等教育研究》2020年第9期。
② 陈先哲:《城市竞争阶段升级与高等教育发展战略转型:深圳案例》,《高等教育研究》2020年第9期。

## II. Strategies for Building a Comprehensive Innovation Ecosystem that Integrates Resources Inside and Outside the Region to Enhance Innovation Capability

Since the 18th National Congress of the Communist Party of China, Shenzhen has actively grasped the major opportunities brought by the new round of global scientific and technological innovation and industrial revolution, focusing on solving the "bottleneck" problem of weak original innovation capacity in the regional innovation system, and gradually improving the "tropical rainforest" comprehensive innovation ecosystem including the whole process of innovation "basic research + technological breakthroughs + achievement industrialization + science and technology finance"[①].

Since 2012, Shenzhen has grasped the major opportunities of the new round of technological revolution, actively constructing major scientific and technological innovation strategic platforms such as the Shenzhen-Hong Kong Science and Technology Innovation Cooperation Zone, major scientific and technological infrastructure such as Guangming Science City, and major industrial innovation development platforms in fields such as 5G, artificial intelligence, third-generation semiconductors, intelligent equipment, life health, and high-end medical diagnostic equipment, to introduce and gather high-end innovation resources for technology enterprises. From 2012 to 2018, the number of start-up enterprises in Shenzhen achieved six-digit year-on-year growth every year, exceeding 1.97 million by 2018. Figure 7-7 shows the number of new enterprises in Shenzhen from 1990 to 2018.

---

① Silicon Valley venture capitalists Victor Huang and Greg Horowitt co-authored the book *The Rainforest:The Secret to Building the Next Silicon Valley*. In it, they propose that innovation requires an ecosystem, which they liken to a tropical rainforest. The characteristics of a tropical rainforest are not just about competition for survival; there is also symbiosis, mutual aid, and inclusiveness. What Silicon Valley has built is precisely such a tropical rainforest ecosystem, which cleverly integrates the creativity of innovators, business acumen, scientific discoveries, investment capital, and other supporting factors. This encourages the sprouting of new ideas, ultimately fostering an ecosystem that continuously produces great innovations.

## 二、整合区域内外资源提升创新能力的综合创新生态系统建设方略

自党的十八大以来，深圳积极把握全球新一轮科技创新和产业革命带来的重大机遇，着力破解区域创新体系中原始创新能力薄弱的"瓶颈"问题，逐步完善包括"基础研究+技术攻关+成果产业化+科技金融"创新全过程的"热带雨林"综合创新生态系统[①]。

自2012年起，深圳把握新一轮科技革命的重大机遇，积极建设深港科技创新合作区等重大科技创新战略平台、光明科学城等重大科技基础设施，以及5G、人工智能、第三代半导体、智能装备、生命健康、高端医学诊疗器械等领域的重大产业创新发展平台，为科技企业创新引进、集聚高端创新资源。2012—2018年，深圳创业企业数量每年实现了6位数同比增长，到2018年已超过197万家，1990—2018年深圳新增企业数量见图7-7。

---

① 硅谷风险投资家维克多·黄和格雷格·霍洛维茨在其合著的《硅谷生态圈：创新的雨林法则》中提出，创新需要生态，他们将这个生态圈比喻为热带雨林，热带雨林的特征不只有生存竞争，还有共生、互助、包容。硅谷建立起的正是这样的热带雨林生态系统，从而使得创新创业者的创造力、商业智慧、科学发现、投资资金以及其他支持因素被巧妙地嵌在一起，鼓励其萌发新想法，最终源源不断地培养出一个能够不断产出伟大创新的生态圈。

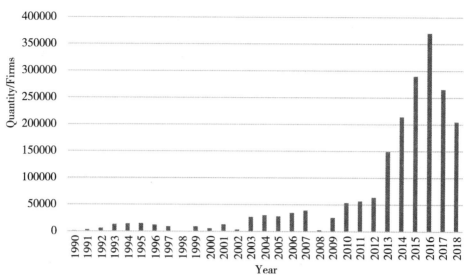

Figure 7-7　Number of New Enterprises in Shenzhen from 1990 to 2018
Data Source: Organized and calculated based on the *Shenzhen Statistical Yearbook* 2019.

In 2014, the Shenzhen National Independent Innovation Demonstration Zone was approved and established by the State Council, becoming the first national independent innovation demonstration zone approved for construction after the 18th National Congress of the Communist Party of China. The outbreak of China-US trade frictions made the Shenzhen government more aware of the importance of original innovation capacity for industrial chains and economic security. To this end, Shenzhen centered on building an international science and technology innovation center in the Guangdong-Hong Kong-Macao Greater Bay Area, deepening scientific and technological innovation system reform, constructing major innovation platforms, integrating into global innovation networks, gathering high-end technical talent resources, cultivating high-end research and development institutions, enhancing special zone technical standards, and constructing a policy chain oriented towards the entire innovation process, striving to improve original innovation capacity.

In 2017, the Shenzhen government signed a *Memorandum of Understanding on Hong Kong-Shenzhen Cooperation in Jointly Developing the Lok Ma Chau Loop* with the Hong Kong Special Administrative Region Government, cooperating to build the "Hong Kong-Shenzhen Innovation and Technology Park" in the Lok Ma Chau Loop area, promoting it to become a new high-end engine for scientific and technological innovation and a new strategic fulcrum and platform for Hong Kong-Shenzhen cooperation.

In terms of major scientific and technological infrastructure, in recent years, the planning and construction of major scientific and technological infrastructure clusters such as the China National GeneBank (Phase II) and Future Network Test Facility have been progressing in an orderly manner. In terms of major industrial innovation platforms, major scientific research institutions such as Peng Cheng Laboratory and the Third-Generation Semiconductor

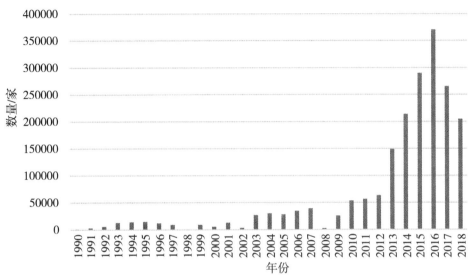

图 7-7　1990—2018 年深圳新增企业数量

数据来源：根据 2019 年《深圳统计年鉴》整理计算。

2014 年，深圳国家自主创新示范区经国务院批复设立，成为党的十八大后国家批准建设的首个国家自主创新示范区。中美经贸摩擦的爆发使深圳政府更加意识到原始创新能力对产业链与经济安全的重要性。为此，深圳以建设粤港澳大湾区国际科技创新中心为中心，深化科技创新体制改革，建设重大创新平台，融入全球创新网络，集聚高端技术人才资源，培育高端研发机构，提升特区技术标准，构建了面向创新全过程的政策链，努力提高原始创新能力。

2017 年，深圳政府与香港特别行政区政府签署《关于港深推进落马洲河套地区共同发展的合作备忘录》，在落马洲河套地区合作建设"港深创新及科技园"，推动其成为科技创新高端新引擎、深港合作新的战略支点与平台。

在重大科技基础设施上，近年来，深圳国家基因库（二期）、未来网络试验设施等重大科技基础设施群规划建设紧张有序推进。在重大产业创新平台上，鹏城实验室、第三代半导体技术创新中心等重大科研机构启动建设。到

Technology Innovation Center have started construction. By the end of 2017, Shenzhen had cumulatively built 41 provincial-level new R&D institutions; in 2017, 189 new innovation carriers such as national, provincial, and municipal key laboratories, engineering research centers, and enterprise technology centers were added, accumulating to 1,877; a cumulative total of 6 Nobel Prize scientist laboratories such as the Grubbs Institute and the Shuji Nakamura Laser Lighting Laboratory were established; more than 90 new "three-development" R&D institutions integrating scientific discovery, technological invention, and industry were cultivated, such as BGI Research, Kuang-Chi Institute of Advanced Technology, and Shenzhen Institutes of Advanced Technology; more than 100 Fortune 500 companies have invested or set up branches in Shenzhen, many of which have established R&D centers or regional operation centers in Shenzhen; Hong Kong universities have set up 72 scientific research institutions in Shenzhen, including 8 branches of national key laboratories, jointly training 9,211 talents, and transforming 269 achievements and technical services.

In addition to "bringing in", Shenzhen is also actively promoting innovation to "go out" and build a global innovation network. During the five years from 2014 to 2018, Shenzhen established 255 R&D institutions abroad and set up 7 overseas innovation centers in the United States, Israel, the United Kingdom, France, and other places.

Shenzhen proposed to implement seven major projects to construct a full-process innovation ecological chain of "basic research + technological breakthroughs + achievement industrialization + science and technology finance + talent support". Through the construction of major scientific and technological infrastructure clusters, new R&D institutions, and other carriers, as well as cooperation with global higher education institutions, Shenzhen is striving to transform from application research-driven to basic research-driven, meeting the demand for frontier knowledge after continuous iteration of enterprise application innovation.

These measures by Shenzhen have promoted the rapid development of its high-tech industries. In 2018, Shenzhen had over 14,000 high-tech enterprises, ranking second among Chinese cities, only behind Beijing (Figure 7-8). Among the 2022 Fortune 500 companies, Guangdong had 17 in total, with Shenzhen owning 10, including innovative enterprises such as Huawei Investment & Holding Co., Ltd.

2017年年底,深圳累计建成省级新型研发机构41家;2017年新增国家、省、市级重点实验室、工程研究中心、企业技术中心等创新载体189家,累计达1877家;累计组建格拉布斯研究院、中村修二激光照明实验室等6个诺贝尔奖科学家实验室;培育了华大研究院、光启高等理工研究院、中国科学院深圳先进技术研究院等90多家集科学发现、技术发明和产业于一体的"三发"新型研发机构;在深圳投资或开设分支机构的世界500强企业超过100家,其中不少跨国公司已在深圳设立研发中心或区域运营中心;香港高校在深圳设立科研机构72家,其中国家重点实验室分室8个,联合培养人才9211名,转化成果及技术服务269项。

除"引进来"以外,深圳同时积极推动创新"走出去",构建全球创新网络。2014—2018年5年期间,深圳在境外建立的研发机构达到255家,在美国、以色列、英国、法国等地成立7家海外创新中心。[①]

深圳提出实施七大工程,构建"基础研究+技术攻关+成果产业化+科技金融+人才支撑"全过程创新生态链。通过建设重大科技基础设施群、新型研发机构等载体,以及与全球高等教育机构合作办学,深圳努力从应用研究驱动向基础研究驱动转变,满足企业应用创新不断迭代后对前沿知识的需求。

深圳的这些举措推动其高新技术产业迅猛发展,2018年,深圳高新技术企业超过1.4万家,位居中国城市第二,仅次于北京(图7-8)。2022年世界500强企业中,广东共17家,深圳就拥有10家,包括华为投资控股有限公司等创新型企业。

---

① 郭跃文、向晓梅等:《中国经济特区四十年工业化道路:从比较优势到竞争优势》,社会科学文献出版社,2020,第285-286页。

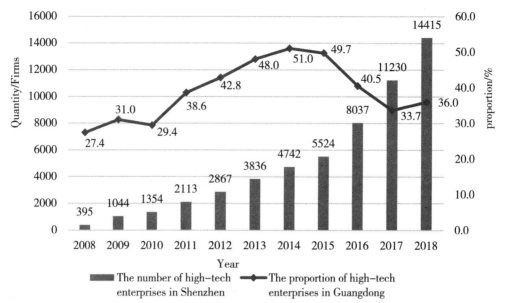

Figure 7-8　The Number of High-Tech Enterprises in Shenzhen and Its Proportion of High-Tech Enterprises in Guangdong from 2008 to 2018

Data Source: Website of Shenzhen Municipal Bureau of Science and Technology Innovation.

By the end of 2019, Shenzhen had 7 unicorn enterprises, accounting for about 47% of the total number of unicorn enterprises in Guangdong (Table 7-4). Most of Shenzhen's new format enterprises and high-tech enterprises have independent innovation products, with innovation capabilities in 4G and 5G technologies, metamaterials, gene sequencing, 3D display, graphene terahertz chips, flexible display, new energy vehicles, drones, and other industrial fields at the forefront of the world. They not only have the ability to lead China's industrial progress but are also leading global industrial development.

Table 7-4　Comparison of Unicorn Enterprises by Region (As of End 2019)

| Region | Number of Enterprises | Proportion /% | Valuation /USD billion | Valuation Proportion/% |
| --- | --- | --- | --- | --- |
| Global | 433 | 100 | 13350 | 100 |
| America | 236 | 54.5 | 7040 | 52.7 |
| China | 101 | 23.3 | 3900 | 29.2 |
| Guangdong, China | 15 | 3.5 | 495 | 3.7 |
| Shenzhen, Guangdong | 7 | 1.6 | 310 | 2.3 |

Data Source: CB Insights Global Unicorn Enterprise Database.

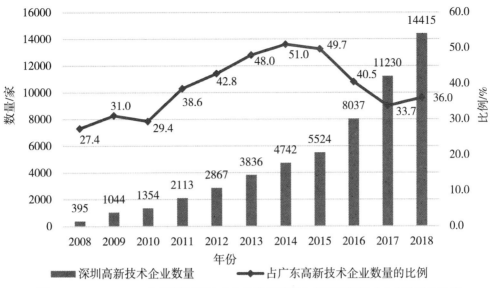

**图 7-8　2008—2018 年深圳高新技术企业数量及其占广东高新技术企业数量的比例**

数据来源：深圳市科技创新局网站。

到 2019 年年底，深圳共拥有 7 家独角兽企业，约占广东独角兽企业总数的 47%（表 7-4）。深圳新业态企业、高新技术企业大多拥有自主创新产品，在 4G 和 5G 技术、超材料、基因测序、3D 显示、石墨烯太赫兹芯片、柔性显示、新能源汽车、无人机等产业领域的创新能力位居世界前沿。不但具备引领中国产业前进的能力，而且也在引领着全球产业发展。[①]

**表 7-4　各区域独角兽企业数量比较（截至 2019 年年底）**

| 区域 | 数量/家 | 数量占比/% | 估值/亿美元 | 估值占比/% |
| --- | --- | --- | --- | --- |
| 全球 | 433 | 100 | 13350 | 100 |
| 美国 | 236 | 54.5 | 7040 | 52.7 |
| 中国 | 101 | 23.3 | 3900 | 29.2 |
| 中国广东 | 15 | 3.5 | 495 | 3.7 |
| 广东深圳 | 7 | 1.6 | 310 | 2.3 |

数据来源：CB Insights 全球独角兽企业数据库。

---

① 郭跃文、向晓梅等：《中国经济特区四十年工业化道路：从比较优势到竞争优势》，社会科学文献出版社，2020，第 289 页。

# Section 5: Cultivating Competitive Advantage Is the Fundamental Path to Promoting Regional Economic Growth

Shenzhen has entered a growth stage dominated by shared economic competition and cooperation, bearing the responsibility of breaking through key core technology links in the national industrial chain, breaking the technological blockade imposed by Western countries, and promoting the nation's industries to the forefront of the world. At this stage, the Shenzhen government must possess the ability to integrate resources from across the country and even globally. With an open and cooperative attitude, it should embrace the new mission bestowed by the new era, perform foresighted leading functions at a higher level, and provide new "Focus Points" for various elements.

## I. The Economic Growth Practices of Countries Worldwide Indicate the Existence of Dual-entity in Market Competition

Worldwide practices in economic growth indicate that there is dual-entity in market competition.

Firstly, both regional governments and enterprises are entities that allocate resources. Enterprises have a mechanism for allocating resources that can replace the way market resources are configured, allocating the resources they possess according to the principle of maximizing profit. Similarly, regional governments own certain public resources and use means such as planning guidance, fiscal budget expenditures, organizational management, and policy support to become the main bodies that allocate regional resources.

Secondly, both regional governments and enterprises aim for maximum benefit as their initial goal. Among them, as independent competitive entities, the primary behavioral objective function of regional governments is the fiscal revenue determination mechanism.

Thirdly, competition among regional governments and enterprises constitutes the dual driving forces of regional economic development. Enterprise competition is the original driving force for the development of the industrial economy, whereas competition among regional governments is the original driving force for the development of the regional economy.

Fourthly, both the behavior of regional governments and enterprises must abide by market rules. Enterprises allocate enterprise resources through continuous exploration of market laws

# 第五节　培育竞争优势是推动区域经济增长的根本路径

深圳已经进入了由共享经济竞争与合作主导的增长阶段，肩负着突破国家产业链关键核心技术环节，打破西方国家技术封锁，推动国家产业走向世界前沿的重任。在这一阶段，深圳政府必须具备整合全国乃至全球资源的能力，以开放合作的姿态迎接新时代赋予的新使命，在更高的层面上发挥超前引领职能，使深圳为各类要素提供新的"聚点"。

## 一、世界各国的经济增长实践表明市场竞争存在双重主体

世界各国的经济增长实践表明，市场竞争存在双重主体。

第一，区域政府与企业都是资源调配的主体。企业有一种可以和市场资源配置方式相互替代的资源配置机制，其对拥有的资源按照利润最大化原则进行调配。相似地，区域政府也拥有一定的公共资源，其运用规划引导、财政预算支出、组织管理和政策配套等手段，成为区域资源调配的主体。

第二，区域政府与企业都以利益最大化为初始目标。其中，区域政府作为独立的竞争主体，其主要行为目标函数是财政收入决定机制。

第三，区域政府竞争与企业竞争是区域经济发展的双驱动力。企业竞争是产业经济发展的原动力，区域政府竞争是区域经济发展的原动力。

第四，区域政府行为与企业行为都必须遵循市场规则。企业通过对市场规律的不断探索和对市场形势的准确判断来调配企业资源。区域政府对产业经济实施

and accurate judgment of market conditions. When implementing industrial policies for the industrial economy, acting as investors in the urban economy, and continuously improving the livelihood economy, regional governments also need to follow market rules to promote the socioeconomic development of the region to stay at the forefront among regions.

The relationship between "dual-entity" in market competition is reflected in the following two aspects.

### (i) Fields of Competition between Enterprises and Regional Governments

Enterprise competition takes place in the field of industrial economy. Regional governments can only be creators, coordinators, and supervisors of the environment for enterprise competition. They can only maintain a fair, just, and equitable competitive environment through policy, systems, and the environment, without the power to directly intervene in the microeconomic affairs of enterprises. The "9-in-3" competition among regional governments revolve around the conditions, environment, policies, and efficiency of supporting services for the survival of enterprise competition. Competition among regional governments is based on respecting enterprise competition but does not incorporate enterprise competition into the level of competition among regional governments. Therefore, in the modern market economic system, competition among regional governments refers to the competition in aspects such as attracting major projects to the region, improving the industrial chain, facilitating imports and exports, and providing supportive services in terms of talent, technology, funds, policy, environment, and efficiency, during the process of establishing and improving the modern market system.

Enterprises and regional governments together constitute the dual-entity of market competition. Enterprise competition is the foundation, and regional government competition relies on enterprise competition, guiding, promoting, coordinating, and supervising enterprise competition. They operate independently on different levels but are interrelated in a dual-loop system.

### (ii) The Core of Enterprise Competition and Regional Government Competition

It can be summarized that enterprise competition is the competition for optimal resource allocation under resource scarcity conditions in microeconomic operations. Its research focus is on the main economic variables in enterprise competition, namely the issues of price determination and price formation mechanisms. Its research content and its development have formed theories of supply, demand, equilibrium price, and consumer choice theory, perfect competition and imperfect competition market theory, as well as general equilibrium theory, welfare economics theory, game theory, market failure theory, and microeconomic policy theory.

产业政策、对城市经济担当投资角色和对民生经济不断改善提升时，也要遵循市场规则，这样才能促使该区域的经济社会发展不断走在区域间的前沿。

市场竞争"双重主体"的关系表现在以下两个方面。①

### （一）企业竞争与区域政府竞争的领域

企业竞争在产业经济领域展开，区域政府只能是企业竞争环境的营造者、协调者和监管者，只能从政策、制度和环境上维护公开、公平、公正的竞争环境，而没有权力对企业微观经济事务进行直接干预。区域政府间的"三类九要素"竞争，是围绕着企业竞争生存的条件、环境、政策和效率等配套服务而展开的。区域政府间的竞争以尊重企业竞争为前提，但不将企业竞争纳入区域政府间的竞争层面。因此，在现代市场经济体系中，区域政府竞争是指，在现代市场体系的健全和完善过程中，区域政府对区域内重大项目落地，产业链完善，进出口便利和人才、科技、资金、政策、环境、效率等的配套方面的竞争。

企业与区域政府共同构成市场竞争双重主体。企业竞争是基础，区域政府竞争以企业竞争为依托，并对企业竞争产生引导、促进、协调和监管作用，它们是在两个不同层面各自独立但又相互联系的双环运作体系。

### （二）企业竞争与区域政府竞争的核心

可以这样概括，企业的竞争是企业在微观经济运行中对资源稀缺条件下的资源优化配置的竞争，其研究焦点是企业竞争中的主要经济变量的问题，即价格决定和价格形成机制问题，其研究的内容及其展开形成了供给、需求、均衡价格理论，消费者选择理论，完全竞争与不完全竞争市场理论，以及一般均衡论、福利

---

① 陈云贤：《探寻中国改革之路：市场竞争双重主体论》，《经济学家》2020年第8期。

Regional government competition, on the other hand, is the competition for optimal resource allocation based on resource generation in mezzoeconomic operations. Its research focus is on the main economic variables affecting regional government competition, namely the issues of regional fiscal revenue determination and fiscal expenditure structure mechanisms. Its research content and its development have formed theories of resource generation, dual attributes of government, regional government competition, competitive economic growth, government foresighted leading, new engines of economic development, dual-entity of market competition, and the "dual-strong mechanism" of mature market economies.

Enterprises, regional governments, and the state as the subject of macroeconomic research together construct the competitive subject network in the modern market economic system.

In the modern market economy, there is not only enterprise competition from the microeconomic field, but also regional government competition from the mezzoeconomic field. They are the dual-entity of competition in the modern market economic system, jointly constituting the dual driving force for the development of the modern market economy, promoting sustainable development of regional economy.

Therefore, the core of enterprise competition is the issue of optimal resource allocation under resource scarcity conditions, while the core of regional government competition is the issue of optimal resource allocation based on resource generation.

## II. Three Laws of Regional Competition

In China and countries worldwide, the competition of the dual-entity of market competition——enterprises and regional governments——has become the dual driving force for a country to promote industrial development, urban construction, and social livelihood development. They present three laws in actual economic operations.

(i) The Law of The Phenomenon of 80/20 Agglomeration

From the analysis of economic theory and the process of economic development practice in China and countries worldwide, whether it is enterprise competition or regional government competition, the actual results present a gradient shift state and ultimately manifest the "80/20 rule" phenomenon. That is, if the two types of competitive subjects in their competition process, centered around their objective functions, can adopt various foresighted leading

经济学理论、博弈论、市场失灵理论和微观经济政策理论等。

而区域政府竞争是区域政府在中观经济运行中对资源生成基础上的资源优化配置的竞争,其研究焦点是影响区域政府竞争的主要经济变量的问题,即区域财政收入决定与财政支出结构机制问题,其研究的内容及其展开形成了资源生成理论、政府双重属性理论、区域政府竞争理论、竞争型经济增长理论、政府超前引领理论、经济发展新引擎理论、市场竞争双重主体理论和成熟市场经济"双强机制"理论等。

企业、区域政府与宏观经济研究的主体国家一道,共同构筑成现代市场经济体系中竞争主体脉络图。

现代市场经济中,不仅存在来自微观经济领域的企业竞争,而且存在来自中观经济领域的区域政府竞争。它们是现代市场经济体系中竞争的双重主体,共同构成现代市场经济发展的双驱动力,推动着区域经济的可持续发展。

因此,企业竞争的核心是在资源稀缺条件下的资源优化配置问题,区域政府竞争的核心是在资源生成基础上的资源优化配置问题。

## 二、区域竞争三大定律[①]

在中国乃至世界各国,市场竞争的双重主体——企业与区域政府的竞争,成为一国推动产业发展、城市建设和社会民生发展的双驱动力。它们在实际经济运行中呈现出三大定律。

### (一)二八效应集聚律

从经济学理论上的分析和中国乃至世界各国经济发展实践的进程看,不管是企业竞争还是区域政府竞争,其实际结果都呈现梯度推移状态,并最终表现

---

① 陈云贤:《探寻中国改革之路:市场竞争双重主体论》,《经济学家》2020年第8期。

measures, effectively promote innovation in concepts, technology, management, and systems for enterprises or regions, and achieve sustainable growth, they can ultimately stand out and become leaders in their industry or region. Those enterprises or regions that lag behind in foresighted leading and reform and innovation will be in a backward state.

At this time, in the gradient structure of economic development, the leading 20% of enterprises or regions will occupy about 80% of the market and about 80% of the benefits; while the 80% of downstream enterprises and 80% of lagging regions in the backward position may only occupy about 20% of the market and about 20% of the benefits. The "80/20 rule" phenomenon will be manifested in the results of enterprise competition or regional government competition. This law exhibits three major characteristics.

First, enterprise competition and regional government competition grow together. Microeconomics studies the issue of optimal resource allocation under resource scarcity conditions, where enterprises are the subjects of resource allocation; mezzoeconomics studies the issue of optimal resource allocation based on resource generation, where regional governments are the subjects of resource allocation (macroeconomics studies the issue of resource utilization under the premise of optimal resource allocation, where the state is the subject of resource utilization); enterprises and regional governments play different roles in the industrial economy and urban economy fields in the modern market economy's vertical and horizontal system, growing together in the competition system of the modern market economy.

Second, enterprise competition and regional government competition have different development trajectories. The operational trajectory of enterprise competition in the factor-driven stage, investment-driven stage, innovation-driven stage, and wealth-driven stage of economic development mainly presents as the evolution and struggle process of perfect competition, monopolistic competition, oligopolistic competition, and perfect monopoly competition. The trajectory of perfect competition among enterprises shows signs of "gradually weakening" in the progressive process of various stages of regional economic development. Regional government competition, on the other hand, initially manifests in the growth stage dominated by industrial economic competition and cooperation, then gradually enters the growth stage dominated by urban economic competition and cooperation, the growth stage dominated by innovative economic competition and cooperation, and the growth stage dominated by shared economic competition and cooperation. The scope of regional government competition and the role of its "9-in-3" competition show a trajectory of "gradually strengthening" in the progressive process of various stages of regional economic development.

Third, both enterprise competition and regional government competition ultimately lead to the "80/20 rule" phenomenon. In the process of economic development in China and countries worldwide, or under market economy conditions, firstly, regional economic

出"二八定律"现象,即两类竞争主体如果在其竞争进程中,围绕目标函数,能够采取各种超前引领措施,有效地推动企业或区域在理念、技术、管理和制度上创新,实现可持续增长,那么最终都能脱颖而出,成为此行业或此类区域的领头羊。而那些滞后于超前引领和改革创新的企业或区域,将会处于落后状态。

此时,在经济发展的梯度结构中,处于领先地位的20%的企业或区域,将占有80%左右的市场和80%左右的收益;而处于落后地位的80%中下游企业和80%滞后区域,将可能只占有20%左右的市场和20%左右的收益。"二八定律"现象将呈现在企业竞争或区域政府竞争的结果上。此定律表现出三大特征。

第一,企业竞争与区域政府竞争同生共长。微观经济研究资源稀缺条件下的资源优化配置问题,此时企业是资源调配主体;中观经济研究资源生成基础上的资源优化配置问题时,此时区域政府是资源调配主体(宏观经济研究资源优化配置前提下的资源利用问题时,此时国家是资源利用主体);企业和区域政府在现代市场经济纵横体系中,各自在产业经济和城市经济领域发挥着不同作用,在现代市场经济的竞争体系中同生共长。

第二,企业竞争与区域政府竞争的发展轨迹不同。企业竞争在经济发展的要素驱动阶段、投资驱动阶段、创新驱动阶段和财富驱动阶段的运行轨迹,主要呈现为企业完全竞争、垄断竞争、寡头垄断竞争和完全垄断竞争的演变与争夺过程,企业完全竞争的轨迹在区域经济发展各个阶段的递进过程中,呈现出"由强渐弱"的迹象。而区域政府竞争,一开始表现在由产业经济竞争与合作主导的增长阶段,而后逐渐地进入由城市经济竞争与合作主导的增长阶段、由创新经济竞争与合作主导的增长阶段和由共享经济竞争与合作主导的增长阶段,区域政府竞争的范围及其"三类九要素"竞争作用在区域经济发展各个阶段的递进过程中,呈现的是"由弱渐强"的轨迹。

第三,企业竞争与区域政府竞争最终都导致"二八定律"现象。在中国乃至世界各国经济的发展过程中,或者说在市场经济条件下,其一,区域经济发展首

development primarily manifests as competitive economic growth; secondly, regional economic growth shows a gradient development trend. Industrial chain agglomeration, urban agglomeration, and improvement of people's livelihood and welfare are mainly concentrated in the regions that develop first.

The Law of The Phenomenon of 80/20 Agglomeration manifests as the development of regional economies in China and the world, with the historical process of different economic development stages, driven by the dual wheels of enterprise competition and regional government competition, gradually showing the phenomenon of increasing concentration of industrial clusters, urban clusters, and people's livelihood and welfare in leading development regions or leading developed countries. The result of economic development in China and the world presents a gradient pattern. The Law of The Phenomenon of 80/20 Agglomeration is a version of the "80/20 rule" in the process of regional government competition.

### (ii) The Law of Gradient Change Equilibrium

The effect of The Law of Gradient Change Equilibrium manifests in three stages.

The first stage is when resource scarcity and resource generation are paired in the field of regional resource allocation, that is, resource scarcity is the prerequisite for enterprise competition, and resource generation is the prerequisite for regional government competition. When economic development extends from enterprise competition to regional government competition, from microeconomics to mezzoeconomics, from industrial resources to urban resources, and even gradually involves competition for space resources, deep-sea resources, and polar resources, the equilibrium of regional economic development worldwide will take a substantial step forward.

The second stage is when positive resources (primary resources and secondary resources) and negative resources (inverse resources) check and balance each other in the field of regional resource generation. The development of positive resource fields will bring new platforms for enterprise competition and regional government competition, boosting regional economic development and constantly creating new economic growth points for the region, while negative resources bring many drawbacks to regional economic growth or human social harmony. They check and balance each other, promoting balanced development of regional economies.

The third stage is when the goals of regional economic growth shift from singular to plural. This stage is also the process of regional economic operation evolving from the factor-driven stage and investment-driven stage to the innovation-driven stage and wealth-driven stage. At this time, the goals of economic growth are not only the balance of investment, consumption, and exports, but also the balance of industry, ecology, and people's livelihood, the balance of industrial development, urban construction, and social livelihood progress, as

先表现为竞争型的经济增长；其二，区域经济增长呈现出梯度发展趋势。产业链集聚、城市群集聚、民生福利提升等，都主要集中在先行发展的区域中。

二八效应集聚律，表现为中国和世界各区域经济的发展，随着不同经济发展阶段的历史进程，在企业竞争和区域政府竞争的双轮动力驱动下，正逐渐出现先行发展区域或先行发达国家的产业集群、城市集群和民生福利越来越集中的现象。中国乃至世界经济发展的结果呈现梯度格局。二八效应集聚律是"二八定律"在区域政府竞争过程中的一个翻版。

### （二）梯度变格均衡律

梯度变格均衡律的作用表现在三个阶段。

第一阶段，区域的资源配置领域出现资源稀缺与资源生成相配对的阶段，即资源稀缺是企业竞争的前提条件，资源生成是区域政府竞争的前提条件。当经济发展从企业竞争延伸到区域政府竞争，从微观经济延伸到中观经济，从产业资源延伸到城市资源，甚至逐步涉及太空资源、深海资源、极地资源竞争的时候，世界各区域经济发展的均衡性，将迈出实质性的一个步伐。

第二阶段，区域的资源生成领域出现正向性资源（原生性资源和次生性资源）与负向性资源（逆生性资源）相掣肘的阶段。正向性资源领域的开发将给企业竞争和区域政府竞争带来新的平台，助推区域经济发展，并不断创造出区域新的经济增长点，而负向性资源却给区域经济增长或人类社会和谐带来诸多弊端，它们相互掣肘，可以促使区域经济均衡性发展。

第三阶段，区域的经济增长目标由单一转向多元的阶段。此阶段也是区域在实际经济运行中从要素驱动阶段、投资驱动阶段向创新驱动阶段和财富驱动阶段演进的过程。此时经济增长的目标不仅是投资、消费和出口的均衡，还有产业、生态、民生事业的均衡，产业发展、城市建设、社会民生进步的均衡，以及一国

well as the comprehensive balance of livability, workability, and tourism in various regions of a country. The pursuit of diversified economic growth goals by regional governments and the formulation and implementation of effective supporting policy measures will promote balanced development of regional economies.

The Law of Gradient Change Equilibrium manifests both as the trend of balanced development of industrial development, urban construction, and social livelihood progress within a region, and as the trend of balanced development of industrial development, urban construction, and social livelihood progress between regions. The trend of balanced development of industrial development, urban construction, and social livelihood progress between regions manifests in practice as the equilibrium of gradient structure, or directly called gradient equilibrium, which is a topic that needs to be seriously studied and considered in the field of economics.

### (iii) The Law of Coordination of Competition and Cooperation

Since the trend of balanced development between regions (or countries) presents a gradient equilibrium state, The Law of Coordination of Competition and Cooperation, as an objective inevitable trend, is more manifested in three major synergies of inter-regional economic development.

First, policy synergy. Enterprise competition plays a regulatory role in industrial resources; regional government competition plays a regulatory role in urban resources and other generative resources; government participation in the competition of a specific project will be intervened by its carrier——state-owned enterprises or state-owned joint ventures or state-owned shareholding enterprises. Therefore, the issues of appropriate industrial policy and the application of competitive neutrality principles in enterprise competition, the series of policy support and measure promotion issues in regional government competition, and the policy synergy issues in the process of advancing new industrialization, new urbanization, smart city development, science and technology project investment, infrastructure modernization and agricultural modernization between regions (countries) become particularly important. The results of enterprise competition and regional government competition require policy synergy among various competitive subjects, which is an objective inevitable trend.

Second, innovation synergy. It is manifested in three aspects: one is that the breakthrough of major scientific and technological projects brings a series of problems such as large capital investment, long cycle, and high risk, requiring innovation synergy among various competitive subjects; two is that the breakthrough of new scientific and technological achievements requires comprehensive use of human wisdom, needing innovation synergy from various

各区域宜居、宜业、宜游的全面均衡。区域政府对经济增长多元化目标的追求，以及对有效的配套政策措施的制定和实施，将能促进区域经济均衡化发展。

梯度变格均衡律既表现为某一区域产业发展、城市建设和社会民生进步的均衡性趋势，又表现为区域间产业发展、城市建设和社会民生进步的均衡性趋势。区域间产业发展、城市建设和社会民生进步的均衡性趋势，在实践中呈现出来的是梯度结构的均衡性，或直接称为梯度均衡，它是需要我们在经济学领域认真研究思考的课题。

### （三）竞争合作协同律

既然区域间（或国家间）经济发展的均衡性趋势呈现梯度均衡状态，竞争合作协同律作为客观必然趋势就更多地表现在区域间经济发展的三大协同上。

其一，政策协同性。企业竞争对产业资源起调节作用；区域政府竞争对城市资源和其他生成性资源起调节作用；政府参与某一具体项目的竞争，将由其载体——国有企业或国有合资企业或国有股份企业介入其中。因此，企业竞争中的产业政策适度和竞争中性原则运用问题，区域政府竞争中的系列政策配套与措施推动问题，以及区域间（国家间）新型工业化、新型城镇化、智能城市开发、科技项目投入、基础设施现代化和农业现代化等推进过程中的政策协同性问题，就显得特别重要。企业竞争和区域政府竞争的结果要求各竞争主体的政策协同，这是一种客观必然趋势。

其二，创新协同性。它表现在三个方面，一是科技重大项目的突破带来资金投入大、周期长、风险大等系列问题，需要各竞争主体的创新协同；二是科技新成果的突破需要综合运用人类智慧，需要得到各竞争主体的创新协同；三是跨区域、跨领域的思想性、物质性、组织性和制度性公共物品的不断出现和形成，需要各竞争主体的创新协同。在中国乃至世界各区域经济发展模式转换和社会转型

competitive subjects; three is the continuous emergence and formation of cross-classification, cross-domain ideological, material, organizational, and institutional public goods, requiring innovation synergy among various competitive subjects. In the deepening stage of economic development mode transformation and social transformation in China and regions worldwide, inter-regional innovation synergy is also an objective inevitable trend.

Third, rule synergy. Inter-regional economic competition rules (fairness and efficiency), inter-regional co-governance rules (cooperation and win-win), inter-regional security order rules (peace and stability), etc., will also be objectively placed on the agenda of various competitive subjects as regional economic development stages deepen.

The Law of Coordination of Competition and Cooperation is essentially that in different stages of regional economic development, various competitive subjects, for common development goals, rely on various industrial, investment, innovation, and other platforms to gather talents, capital, information, technology, and other factors, to achieve synergy of competition policies, synergy of innovation-driven development, and synergy of competition rules, thereby breaking through competition barriers, effectively cooperating, and developing together. The Law of Coordination of Competition and Cooperation can promote economic co-growth and win-win cooperation between regions in China and the world, and this will become an objective inevitable trend.

At this point, it can be said that the success of China's reform and opening-up, as well as the theories explored in practice with Chinese characteristics, such as the division of the modern market economy's vertical and horizontal system, the need for mature and effective governments to foresighted leading, the existence of dual-entity in market competition, and the three laws of regional competition, not only explored the development direction for China's socialist market economy but also found an effective path for countries worldwide to solve the difficult problem of the relationship between government and market.

## III. Cultivating Competitive Advantage Is the Fundamental Path to Promoting Regional Economic Growth

From the economic development practices of China and countries around the world, to achieve rapid economic growth, a region must possess certain advantages. These advantages can only be competitive advantages jointly cultivated by enterprises and regional governments.

First, since the First Industrial Revolution, technological progress has become the fundamental driving force for regional economic growth. So what determines the pace of technological progress? Clearly, the overall competitive advantage consisting of factors such as a country's education level and talent reserve, the R&D investment and capabilities of

的深化阶段，区域间的创新协同也是客观必然趋势所在。

其三，规则协同性。区域间经济竞争规则（公平与效率）、区域间共同治理规则（合作与共赢）、区域间安全秩序规则（和平与稳定）等，也将随着区域经济发展阶段的深化客观地摆在各竞争主体的议事日程上。

竞争合作协同律，实质上就是在区域经济发展的不同阶段，各竞争主体为了共同的发展目标，依靠各种不同的产业、投资、创新等平台，汇聚人才、资本、信息、技术等要素，实现竞争政策的协同、创新驱动的协同和竞争规则的协同，从而突破竞争壁垒，有效合作，共同发展。竞争合作协同律可以促进中国和世界各区域间经济同生共长，合作共赢，并且这将成为一种客观必然趋势。

至此可以说，中国改革开放的成功，以及在实践中摸索出来的具有中国特色的现代市场经济纵横体系之分、成熟有为政府需要超前引领、市场竞争存在双重主体、区域竞争呈现三大定律等理论，不仅为中国特色社会主义市场经济探讨了发展方向，而且也为世界各国解决政府与市场关系的难题寻找到了有效路径。

## 三、培育竞争优势是推动区域经济增长的根本路径

从中国乃至世界各国的经济发展实践看，要实现经济快速增长，区域必须具备某种优势，而这种优势只能是由企业和区域政府共同培育出的竞争优势。

第一，自第一次工业革命以来，科技进步成为区域经济增长的根本推动力量。那么，科技进步的步伐又是由什么决定的呢？显然，一国的教育水平和人才储备，企业、高校和科研院所等研发主体的研发投入和研发能力，区域政府提供的软硬件基础设施等要素构成的整体竞争优势是推动区域科技进步的最终力量，进而也构成促进区域经济增长的根本力量。

enterprises, universities and research institutes, and the hardware and software infrastructure provided by regional governments is the ultimate force driving region's technological progress, and thus constitutes the fundamental force promoting regional economic growth.

Second, competitive advantage is the common dominant factor in different stages of regional economic development. In the four different stages of regional economic development——factor-driven stage, investment-driven stage, innovation-driven stage and wealth-driven stage, competitive advantage plays a leading role. Regions with competitive advantages can attract more production factors such as talent, capital and technology. The agglomeration of these production factors can also form economies of scale, further promoting regional economic development. This acquisition of production factors relies on the overall competitive advantage of a region, rather than the comparative advantage a region has in a particular industry.

Third, competitive advantage is the fundamental path for gradient transfer development and economic growth of regional economies. Only by continuously cultivating and forming new competitive advantages can regional economies achieve advancement from low development stages to high development stages. From the development of industrial economy to the rise of urban economy and then to the prosperity of innovative economy and shared economy, from the development of primary resources to the formation of secondary resources and then to the utilization of retrograde resources, competitive advantage has been playing a dominant role. It is a comprehensive competitive advantage formed by the coupling of enterprises and regional governments. Other regional advantages, including comparative advantage, can be seen as components of competitive advantage, but cannot replace competitive advantage.

第二,竞争优势是区域经济不同发展阶段的共同主导因素。在要素驱动阶段、投资驱动阶段、创新驱动阶段和财富驱动阶段这四个区域经济不同的发展阶段中,竞争优势都发挥着主导作用。具备竞争优势的区域能够吸引更多的人才、资本、技术等生产要素,这些生产要素的集聚还能够形成规模经济,进一步促进区域经济发展。这种生产要素的获取依靠的是一个区域的整体竞争优势,而不是一个区域在某一个产业上所具有的比较优势。

第三,竞争优势是区域经济梯度推移发展和经济增长的根本路径。只有不断地培育和形成新的竞争优势,区域经济才能够实现从低发展阶段向高发展阶段的攀升。从产业经济的发展到城市经济的兴起再到创新经济和共享经济的繁荣,从原生性资源的开发到次生性资源的形成再到逆生性资源的利用,都是竞争优势在发挥着主导作用,它是一种由企业和区域政府相互耦合所形成的综合性竞争优势,包括比较优势在内的其他区域优势都可看作竞争优势的一个组成部分,而不能替代竞争优势。

# 参考文献

## 中文参考文献

白积洋，2019."有为政府＋有效市场"：深圳高新技术产业发展40年[J].深圳社会科学（5）：13-30.

波特，2002.国家竞争优势[M].李明轩，邱如美，译.北京：华夏出版社.

陈德祥，2019.自我革命与保持党的先进性和纯洁性[J].马克思主义理论学科研究，5（1）：120-130.

陈健，郭冠清，2021.政府与市场：对中国改革开放后工业化过程的回顾[J].经济与管理评论，37（3）：20-30.

陈立敏，2006.波特与李嘉图的契合点：从国家竞争力角度对竞争优势理论和比较优势理论框架及核心概念的对比分析[J].南大商学评论（4）：70-80.

陈明华，刘玉鑫，刘文斐，等，2020.中国城市民生发展的区域差异测度、来源分解与形成机理[J].统计研究，37（5）：54-67.

陈瑞荣，1990.深圳特区土地出让状况综览与分析[J].特区经济（5）：52-53.

陈先哲，2020.城市竞争阶段升级与高等教育发展战略转型：深圳案例[J].高等教育研究，41（9）：25-31.

陈新明，刘丰榕，朱玉慧兰，2020."抢人大战"会推高城市房价吗？：基于"人才新政"的政策效应检验[J].管理现代化，40（3）：90-94.

陈新明，萧鸣政，张睿超，2020.城市"抢人大战"的政策特征、效力测度及优化建议[J].中国人力资源开发，37（5）：59-69.

陈云贤，2017.陈云贤：论政府超前引领[J].财经界（25）：29-33.

陈云贤，2019.中国特色社会主义市场经济：有为政府＋有效市场[J].经济研究，54（1）：4-19.

陈云贤，2020. 市场竞争双重主体论：兼谈中观经济学的创立与发展 [M]. 北京：北京大学出版社.

程开明，徐扬，2019. 城市蔓延对电力强度的影响：基于中国地级及以上城市面板数据的分析 [J]. 城市问题（7）：37-42.

程霖，张申，陈旭东，2020. 中国经济学的探索：一个历史考察 [J]. 经济研究，55（9）：4-24.

邓正来，1999.《中国书评》选集 [M]. 沈阳：辽宁大学出版社.

丁建军，2011，产业转移的新经济地理学解释 [J]. 中南财经政法大学学报（1）：102-107.

樊纲，1995."苏联范式"批判 [J]. 经济研究（10）：70-80.

樊纲，2019."发展悖论"与"发展要素"：发展经济学的基本原理与中国案例 [J]. 经济学动态（6）：148-151.

樊纲，2020."发展悖论"与发展经济学的"特征性问题" [J]. 管理世界，36（4）：34-39.

樊纲，2023. 比较优势与后发优势 [J]. 管理世界，39（2）：13-21.

范晨，2007. BT投融资模式在我国城市轨道交通建设中的应用研究 [D]. 北京：北京交通大学.

方兴起，2020. 基于历史唯物主义评价新结构经济学 [J]. 当代经济研究（6）：63-72.

费维照，胡宗兵，1998. 有限政府论：早期资产阶级的政府观念与政制设定 [J]. 政治学研究（1）：49-55.

冯苑，聂长飞，张东，2021. 宽带基础设施建设对城市创新能力的影响 [J]. 科学学研究，39（11）：2089-2100.

付才辉，2014. 发展战略的成本与收益：一个分析框架：对新结构经济学的目标、争议与拓展的探讨 [J]. 南方经济（1）：29-48.

付莹，2014. 深圳经济特区土地有偿出让制度的历史沿革及其立法贡献 [J]. 鲁东大学学报（哲学社会科学版），31（4）：67-71.

傅辉煌，2011."中国社会民生与经济增长"学术研讨会暨首都经济学家论坛主席团会议纪要 [J]. 经济学动态（8）：158.

傅勇，张晏，2007. 中国式分权与财政支出结构偏向：为增长而竞争的代价 [J]. 管理世界（3）：4-12.

高挺，常启国，许海平，2018. 中国经济增长与环境质量的关系研究：基于 240 个城市的双门槛效应检验 [J]. 资源开发与市场，34（11）：1505-1510.

耿强，2018. 从城市定位与竞争战略看"抢人大战" [J]. 人民论坛（15）：12-14.

郭熙保，张薇，2017. "比较优势陷阱"存在吗？：基于马尔科夫链模型多维动态分析方法 [J]. 贵州社会科学（2）：117-126.

郭跃文，向晓梅，等，2020. 中国经济特区四十年工业化道路：从比较优势到竞争优势 [M]. 北京：社会科学文献出版社．

韩宝国，朱平芳，2014. 宽带对中国经济增长影响的实证分析 [J]. 统计研究，31（10）：49-54.

何炼成，丁文峰，1997. 中国经济学向何处去 [J]. 经济学动态（7）：6-15.

何颖，2008. 中国政府机构改革 30 年回顾与反思 [J]. 中国行政管理（12）：21-27.

何自力，2014. 对"大市场、小政府"市场经济模式的反思：基于西方和拉美国家教训的研究 [J]. 政治经济学评论，5（1）：19-32.

洪世键，张京祥，2010. 交通基础设施与城市空间增长：基于城市经济学的视角 [J]. 城市规划，34（5）：29-34.

洪银兴，1997. 从比较优势到竞争优势：兼论国际贸易的比较利益理论的缺陷 [J]. 经济研究（6）：20-26.

胡晨光，程惠芳，俞斌，2011. "有为政府"与集聚经济圈的演进：一个基于长三角集聚经济圈的分析框架 [J]. 管理世界（2）：61-69.

胡凤英，1986. 浅谈中苏贸易的发展 [J]. 今日苏联东欧（3）：35-36.

胡深，吕冰洋，2019. 经济增长目标与土地出让 [J]. 财政研究（7）：46-59.

胡晓鹏，2015. 论市场经济的起源、功能与模式：兼论中国特色社会主义市场经济的本质 [J]. 社会科学（7）：48-59.

黄亮雄，王贤彬，刘淑琳，2021. 经济增长目标与激进城镇化：来自夜间灯光数据的证据 [J]. 世界经济，44（6）：97-122.

江小涓，1999. 理论、实践、借鉴与中国经济学的发展：以产业结构理论的研究为例 [J]. 中国社会科学（6）：4-18.

姜明安，2004. 建设"有限"与"有为"的政府 [J]. 法学家（1）：13-15.

蒋永甫，谢舜，2008. 有限政府、有为政府与有效政府：近代以来西方国家政府理念的演变 [J]. 学习与探索（5）：73-76.

孔令池，高波，李言，2017. 市场开放、地方财税竞争与产业结构调整：基于我国省级面板数据的实证研究 [J]. 经济理论与经济管理（10）：45-57.

库珀，2001. 协调博弈：互补性与宏观经济学 [M]. 张军，李池，译. 北京：中国人民大学出版社.

李建标，汪敏达，刘家琦，2010. 协调博弈实验研究概览 [J]. 首都经济贸易大学学报（2）：48-53.

李慷，黄辰，邓大胜，2021. 省级科技人才政策对科技人才集聚的影响分析 [J]. 调研世界（7）：41-47.

李书娟，徐现祥，2021. 目标引领增长 [J]. 经济学（季刊），21（5）：1571-1590.

李涛，黄纯纯，周业安，2011. 税收、税收竞争与中国经济增长 [J]. 世界经济，34（4）：22-41.

李艳，柳士昌，2018. 全球价值链背景下外资开放与产业升级：一个基于准自然实验的经验研究 [J]. 中国软科学（8）：165-174.

李燕萍，刘金璐，洪江鹏，等，2019. 我国改革开放 40 年来科技人才政策演变、趋势与展望：基于共词分析法 [J]. 科技进步与对策，36（10）：108-117.

梁琦，2004. 产业集聚的均衡性和稳定性 [J]. 世界经济（6）：11-17.

梁琦，2005. 空间经济学：过去、现在与未来：兼评《空间经济学：城市、区域与国际贸易》[J]. 经济学（季刊）（3）：1067-1086.

林伯强，杜克锐，2014. 理解中国能源强度的变化：一个综合的分解框架 [J]. 世界经济，37（4）：69-87.

林江，孙辉，黄亮雄，2011. 财政分权、晋升激励和地方政府义务教育供给 [J]. 财贸经济（1）：34-40.

林茂德，2012. 深圳地铁"建设－移交"（BT）模式创新和适应性分析 [J]. 城市轨道交通，15（8）：1-6.

林青，余熙，2018. 新结构经济学视角下经济增长与产业转型升级研究 [M]. 北京：中国水利水电出版社.

林毅夫，2002. 发展战略、自生能力和经济收敛 [J]. 经济学（季刊）（1）：269-300.

林毅夫，2011. 新结构经济学：重构发展经济学的框架 [J]. 经济学（季刊），10（1）：1-32.

林毅夫，2012. 新结构经济学：反思经济发展与政策的理论框架 [M]. 苏剑，译. 北京：北京大学出版社.

林毅夫，2017. 新结构经济学的理论基础和发展方向 [J]. 经济评论（3）：4-16.

林毅夫，2017. 产业政策与我国经济的发展：新结构经济学的视角 [J]. 复旦学报（社会科学版），59（2）：148-153.

林毅夫，2020. 如何做新结构经济学的研究 [J]. 上海大学学报（社会科学版），37（2）：1-18.

林毅夫，2020. 有为政府参与的中国市场发育之路 [J]. 广东社会科学（1）：5-7.

林毅夫，蔡昉，李周，1994. 对赶超战略的反思 [J]. 战略与管理（6）：1-12.

林毅夫，付才辉，2022. 比较优势与竞争优势：新结构经济学的视角 [J]. 经济研究，57（5）：23-33.

林毅夫，李永军，2003. 比较优势、竞争优势与发展中国家的经济发展 [J]. 管理世界（7）：21-28.

刘春林，田玲，2021. 人才政策"背书"能否促进企业创新 [J]. 中国工业经济（3）：156-173.

刘戒骄，2019. 竞争中性的理论脉络与实践逻辑 [J]. 中国工业经济（6）：5-21.

刘力群，1994. 重工倾斜政策的再认识：兼论赶超战略 [J]. 战略与管理，（6）：13-18.

刘尚希，2015. 流行的经济理论已不适应现实发展需要 [N]. 北京日报，04-20（17）.

刘生龙，胡鞍钢，2010. 基础设施的外部性在中国的检验：1988—2007[J]. 经济研究，45（3）：4-15.

刘淑琳，王贤彬，黄亮雄，2019. 经济增长目标驱动投资吗？：基于2001—2016年地级市样本的理论分析与实证检验 [J]. 金融研究（8）：1-19.

刘再起，王曼莉，2018. 全球价值链中的"比较优势陷阱"：基于整体网和国别面板数据的实证分析 [J]. 国际贸易问题（3）：100-112.

陆善勇，叶颖，2019. 中等收入陷阱、比较优势陷阱与综合优势战略 [J]. 经济学家（7）：15-22.

罗党论，高妙媛，2014. 经济发展、城市质量与民生支出 [J]. 当代经济管理，36（4）：54-62.

罗影，汪毅霖，2023. 全球化时代后发大国经济成长的比较优势、后发优势与竞争优势 [J]. 经济学家（5）：24-32.

马草原，朱玉飞，李廷瑞，2021. 地方政府竞争下的区域产业布局 [J]. 经济研究，56（2）：141-156.

毛丰付，郑芳，何慧竹，2019. "以房抢人"提高了城市创新能力吗 [J]. 财经科学（7）：108-121.

孟宪章，1991. 中苏贸易史资料 [M]. 北京：中国对外经济贸易出版社.

倪鹏飞，2002. 中国城市竞争力与基础设施关系的实证研究 [J]. 中国工业经济（5）：62-69.

裴长洪，2009. 共和国对外贸易60年 [M]. 北京：人民出版社.

钱乘旦，2007. 欧洲国家形态的阶段性发展：从封建到现代 [J]. 北京大学学报（哲学社会科学版）（2）：36-44.

钱穆，2012. 中国历代政治得失 [M]. 3版. 北京：生活·读书·新知三联书店.

钱颖一，2002. 理解现代经济学 [J]. 经济社会体制比较（2）：1-12.

丘梁，1983. 关于深圳经济特区基础设施贷款问题的探讨 [J]. 广东金融研究（1）：51-54.

瞿商，2008. 我国计划经济体制的绩效（1957—1978）：基于投入产出效益比较的分析 [J]. 中国经济史研究（1）：121-128.

沈坤荣，付文林，2006. 税收竞争、地区博弈及其增长绩效 [J]. 经济研究（6）：16-26.

石广生，2013. 中国对外经济贸易改革和发展史 [M]. 北京：人民出版社.

石佑启，2013. 论有限有为政府的法治维度及其实现路径 [J]. 南京社会科学（11）：92-99.

斯蒂格利茨，2005. 公共部门经济学：第3版 [M]. 郭庆旺，杨志勇，刘晓路，等译. 北京：中国人民大学出版社.

斯蒂格利茨，2009. 发展与发展政策 [M]. 纪沫，仝冰，海荣，译. 北京：中国金融出版社.

宋德勇，李超，李项佑，2021. 新型基础设施建设是否促进了绿色技术创新的"量质齐升"：来自国家智慧城市试点的证据 [J]. 中国人口·资源与环境，31（11）：155-164.

隋广军，郭南芸，2008. 东部发达城市产业转移的角色定位：广州证据 [J]. 改革（10）：46-52.

孙文浩，张益丰，2019. 城市抢"人"大战有利于地区新旧动能转换吗？[J]. 科学学研究，37（7）：1220-1230.

孙钰，崔寅，冯延超，2019. 城市公共交通基础设施的经济、社会与环境效益协调发展评价 [J]. 经济与管理评论，35（6）：122-135.

孙锐，2013. 国家人才战略规划绩效评估相关问题研究 [J]. 中国科技论坛（12）：92-96.

陶然，周巨泰，1996. 从比较优势到竞争优势：国际经济理论的新视角 [J]. 国际贸易问题（3）：29-34.

田国强，2016. 林毅夫、张维迎之争的对与错 [N]. 第一财经日报，11-23（A9）.

田国强，2016. 供给侧结构性改革的重点和难点：建立有效市场和维护服务型有限政府是关键 [J]. 人民论坛·学术前沿（14）：22-32.

王佃凯，2002. 比较优势陷阱与中国贸易战略选择 [J]. 经济评论（2）：28-31.

王家强，陈静，赵雪情，2016. 客观看待我国对外投资净收益逆差问题 [J]. 中国国情国力（2）：22-25.

王贤彬，黄亮雄，2019. 地方经济增长目标管理：一个三元框架的理论构建与实证检验 [J]. 经济理论与经济管理（9）：30-44.

王勇，华秀萍，2017. 详论新结构经济学中的"有为政府"的内涵：兼对田国强教授批评的回复 [J]. 经济评论（3）：17-30.

王勇，沈仲凯，2018. 禀赋结构、收入不平等与产业升级 [J]. 经济学（季刊），17（2）：801-824.

文贯中，2002. 市场机制、政府定位和法治：对市场失灵和政府失灵的匡正之法的回顾与展望 [J]. 经济社会体制比较（1）：1-11.

文宏，林仁镇，2020. 中国特色现代化治理体系构建的实践探索：基于新中国70年机构改革的考察 [J]. 社会科学战线（4）：190-198.

吴易风，1996. 两种"范式危机"论 [J]. 当代经济研究（2）：31-39.

徐雷，2011. 运输成本、土地价格与生产集聚区迁移 [J]. 科学决策（4）：47-58.

徐现祥，李书娟，王贤彬，等，2018. 中国经济增长目标的选择：以高质量发展终结"崩溃论" [J]. 世界经济，41（10）：3-25.

徐现祥，刘毓芸，2017. 经济增长目标管理 [J]. 经济研究，52（7）：18-33.

许涤新，吴承明，2003. 中国资本主义发展史 第一卷 中国资本主义的萌芽 [M]. 2版. 北京：人民出版社.

杨成钢，李海宾，2019. 人口迁移、住宅供需变化与区域经济发展：对当前国内城市"抢人大战"的经济学分析 [J]. 理论探讨（3）：93-98.

杨其静，吴海军，2016. 产能过剩、中央管制与地方政府反应 [J]. 世界经济，39（11）：126-146.

杨文爽，刘晓静，2018. 东北地区"比较优势陷阱"研究 [J]. 经济问题（4）：7-13.

杨志勇，2003. 国内税收竞争理论：结合我国现实的分析 [J]. 税务研究（6）：14-17.

姚洋，郑东雅，2008. 重工业与经济发展：计划经济时代再考察 [J]. 经济研究（4）：26-40.

易宪容，2010."两会"焦点：民生经济并行 [J]. 中国经贸（4）：14-17.

尤福永，2002. 试论地铁资源的开发与利用：深圳地铁建设的启示 [J]. 特区经济（8）：50-53.

于光远，1996. 中国理论经济学史 [M]. 郑州：河南人民出版社.

于源，苑德宇，2016."新常态"下补贴和人才对企业自主创新的影响 [J]. 技术经济与管理研究（9）：39-45.

余斌，2021. 新结构经济学批判 [J]. 当代经济研究（1）：67-75.

余永定，2013. 发展经济学的重构：评林毅夫《新结构经济学》[J]. 经济学（季刊），12（3）：1075-1078.

袁方成，2020. 城市人才政策转向的创新路径 [J]. 人民论坛（21）：73-75.

曾小林，陈俊宏，2019. 我国地方政府非规范性税收竞争的策略形式及效应分析 [J]. 中外企业家（5）：42-43.

张泓，2018. 城市轨道交通企业盈利模式的探索与实践：以深圳地铁集团为例 [J]. 城市轨道交通研究，21（5）：90-94.

张金昌，2001. 波特的国家竞争优势理论剖析 [J]. 中国工业经济（9）：53-58.

张军，2013."比较优势说"的拓展与局限：读林毅夫新著《新结构经济学》[J]. 经济学（季刊），12（3）：1087-1094.

张军，高远，傅勇，等，2007. 中国为什么拥有了良好的基础设施？[J]. 经济研究（3）：4-19.

张琦，2015. 公共物品理论的分歧与融合 [J]. 经济学动态（11）：147-158.

张树森，2006. BT 投融资建设模式 [M]. 北京：中央编译出版社.

张昕竹，2002. 中国基础设施产业的规制改革与发展 [M]. 北京：国家行政学院出版社.

张新宁，2021. 有效市场和有为政府有机结合：破解"市场失灵"的中国方案 [J]. 上海经济研究（1）：5-14.

张勋，万广华，2016. 中国的农村基础设施促进了包容性增长吗？[J]. 经济研究，51（10）：82-96.

张雅林，1999. 推进行政改革 建立有限政府 [J]. 中国行政管理（4）：41-44.

张媛，2018. 城市人才战略的提升路径 [J]. 人民论坛（19）：60-61.

赵全军，2021. "为人才而竞争"：理解地方政府行为的一个新视角 [J]. 中国行政管理（4）：40-45.

郑功成，2018. 习近平民生重要论述中的两个关键概念：从"物质文化需要"到"美好生活需要" [J]. 人民论坛·学术前沿（18）：64-74.

郑世林，周黎安，何维达，2014. 电信基础设施与中国经济增长 [J]. 经济研究，49（5）：77-90.

钟坚，2008. 深圳经济特区改革开放的历史进程与经验启示 [J]. 深圳大学学报（人文社会科学版），25（4）：17-23.

周黎安，2007. 中国地方官员的晋升锦标赛模式研究 [J]. 经济研究（7）：36-50.

周黎安，刘冲，厉行，等，2015. "层层加码"与官员激励 [J]. 世界经济文汇（1）：1-15.

周耀东，张佳仪，2013. 城市轨道交通经济效应实证研究：以北京市为例 [J]. 城市问题（10）：58-62.

朱富强，2017. 如何通过比较优势的转换来实现产业升级：评林毅夫的新结构经济学 [J]. 学术月刊，49（2）：64-79.

朱富强，2018. 如何认识有为政府的经济功能：理论基础和实践成效的检视 [J]. 学术研究（7）：87-96.

## 外文参考文献

AKERLOF G A, 1970. The market for "lemons": quality uncertainty and the market mechanism [J]. The quarterly journal of economics, 84（3）：488-500.

BALDWIN R E, KRUGMAN P R, 2001. Agglomeration, integration and tax harmonization [J]. European business review, 13（3）：18-19.

BRAKMAN S, GARRETSEN H, VAN MARREWIJK C, 2002. Locational competition and agglomeration: the role of government spending [J]. CESifo working papers, 22（9）.

CAMERER C F, 2003. Behavioral game theory: experiments in strategic interaction [M]. Princeton: Princeton University Press.

COATE S, LOURY G C, 1993. Will affirmative-action policies eliminate negative stereotypes? [J]. The American economic review, 83（5）：1220-1240.

COOPER R W, DEJONG D V, FORSYTHE R, et al., 1990. Selection criteria in coordination games: some experimental results [J]. The American economic review, 80（1）: 218-233.

COWLING K, MUELLER D C, 1978. The social costs of monopoly power revisited[J]. The economic journal, 91（363）: 721-725.

CRAWFORD V P, 1995. Adaptive dynamics in coordination games[J]. Econometrica, 63（1）: 103-143.

DATTA A, AGARWAL S, 2004. Telecommunications and economic growth: a panel data approach[J]. Applied economics, 36（15）: 1649-1654.

DIODATO D, NEFFKE F, O' CLERY N, 2018. Why do industries coagglomerate? How marshallian externalities differ by industry and have evolved over time [J]. Journal of urban economics, 106（0）: 1-26.

DIXIT A K, STIGLITZ J E, 1993. Monopolistic competition and optimum product diversity: reply[J].The American economic review, 83（1）: 302-304.

DURANTON G, TURNER M A, 2012. Urban growth and transportation[J]. The review of economic studies, 79（4）: 1407-1440.

FANG H, 2001. Social culture and economic performance[J]. The American economic review, 91（4）: 924-937.

FANG H, NORMAN P, 2006. Government-mandated discriminatory policies: theory and evidence[J]. International economic review, 47（2）, 361-389.

FUJITA M, 1988. A monopolistic competition model of spatial agglomeration: differentiated product approach [J]. Regional science & urban economics, 18（1）: 87-124.

FUJITA M, THISSE J-F, 2002. Economics of agglomeration: cities, industrial location, and regional growth[M]. New York: Cambridge University Press.

GLAESER E L, GOTTLIEB J D, 2008. The economics of place-making policies[J]. Brookings papers on economic activity, 39（1）: 155-253.

GOCE-DAKILA C, MIZOKAMI S, 2010. Core-periphery relations and urban transport infrastructure investment[J]. Journal of the EASTERN ASIA society for transportation studies（8）: 216-231.

GREENWALD B C, STIGLITZ J E, 1986. Externalities in economics with imperfect information and incomplete markets[J]. The quarterly journal of economics, 101（2）: 229-264.

GUDIPUDI R, FLUSCHNIK T, ROS A G C, et al., 2016. City density and $CO_2$ efficiency[J]. Energy policy, 91(4): 352-361.

HARBERGER A C, 1954. Monopoly and resource allocation[J]. The American economic review, 44(2): 77-87.

JENNY F, WEBER A-P, 1983. Aggregate welfare loss due to monopoly power in the French economy: some tentative estimates[J]. The journal of industrial economics, 32(2): 113-130.

JU J, LIN J Y, WANG Y, 2015. Endowment structures, industrial dynamics, and economic growth[J]. Journal of monetary economics, 76: 244-263.

KOUTROUMPIS P, 2019. The economic impact of broadband: evidence from OECD countries[J]. Technological forecasting and social change, 148(0): 119719.

KRUGMAN P R, 1979. Increasing returns, monopolistic competition and international trade[J]. Journal of international economics, 9(4): 469-479.

KRUGMAN P, 1991. Increasing returns and economic geography[J]. Journal of political economy, 99(3): 483-499.

LANASPA L F, PUEYO F, SANZ F, 2001. The public sector and core-periphery models [J]. Urban studies, 38(10): 1639-1649.

LI X, LIU C, WENG X, et al., 2019. Target setting in tournaments: theory and evidence from China[J]. The economic journal, 129(623): 2888-2915.

LIN J Y, 2009. Beyond keynesianism: the necessity of a globally coordinated solution[J]. Harvard international review, 31(2): 14-17.

MATSUYAMA K, 1991. Increasing returns, industrialization, and indeterminacy of equilibrium[J]. The quarterly journal of economics, 106(2): 617-650.

MEHTA J, STARMER C, SUGDEN R, 1994. The nature of salience: an experimental investigation of pure coordination games[J]. The American economic review, 84(3): 658-673.

MONTINOLA G, QIAN Y, WEINGAST B R, 1996. Federalism, Chinese style: the political basis for economic success in China[J]. World politics, 48(1): 50-81.

MUSGRAVE R A, 1959. The theory of public finance: a study in public economy[M]. New York: McGraw-Hill.

O'SULLIVAN A, STRANGE W C, 2018. The emergence of coagglomeration [J]. Journal of economic geography, 18（2）: 293-317.

POTER M E, 1990. The competitive advantage of nations[M] New York: The Free Press.

QIAN Y, ROLAND G, 1998. Federalism and the soft budget constraint[J]. The American economic review, 88（5）: 1143-1162.

REGE M, 2008. Why do people care about social status? [J]. Journal of economic behavior and organization, 66（2）, 233-242.

RÖLLER L-H, WAVERMAN L, 2001. Telecommunications infrastructure and economic development: a simultaneous approach[J]. The American economic review, 91（4）: 909-923.

SAMUELSON P A, 1954. The pure theory of public expenditure[J]. The review of economics and statistics, 36（4）: 387-389.

SAMUELSON P A, 1983. Thünen at two hundred[J]. Journal of Economic Literature, 21（4）: 1468-1488.

SCHELLING T C, 1960. The strategy of conflict[M]. Cambridge: Harvard University Press.

SHLEIFER A, VISHNY R W, 1998. The grabbing hand: government pathologies and their cures[M]. Cambridge: Harvard University Press.

SPENCE A M, 1973. Job market signaling[J]. The quarterly journal of economics, 87（3）: 355-374.

SPENCE A M, 1974. Market signaling: information transfer in hiring and related screening processes[M]. Cambridge: Harvard University Press.

STIGLITZ J E, WEISS A, 1981. Credit rationing in markets with imperfect information[J].The American economic review, 71（3）: 393-410.

STIGLITZ J E, 1989. Markets, market failures and development[J]. The American economic review, 79（2）: 197-203.

WHITING S H, 2000. Power and wealth in rural China: the political economy of institutional change[M]. New York: Cambridge University Press.

# Afterword

From Adam Smith's *The Theory of Moral Sentiments*, which reveals that the behavior of individuals living in society is constrained by the invisible hand of the unity of opposites between self-interest and sympathy, we can derive four management modes for society's regulation of individuals: strengthening self-interest, strengthening sympathy, respecting self-interest while considering sympathy, and advocating sympathy while considering self-interest. From Adam Smith's *The Wealth of Nations*, which reveals that the behavior of enterprises living in the market is constrained by the invisible hand of the unity of opposites between selfishness and altruism, we can derive four management modes for governments' regulation of enterprises: strengthening selfishness, strengthening altruism, respecting selfishness while considering altruism, and advocating altruism while considering selfishness. Mezzoeconomics reveals that the behavior of regional governments is constrained by the invisible hand of the unity of opposites between quasi-micro attributes (profit-seeking/competitiveness) and quasi-macro attributes (coordination/cooperation), which can also derive four management modes for countries' regulation of regional governments: strengthening competitiveness, strengthening cooperation, focusing on competitiveness while considering cooperation, and focusing on cooperation while considering competitiveness. While acknowledging the comparative advantage theory's advocacy for full utilization of natural resource endowments and the competitive advantage theory's advocacy for promoting innovation in micro-enterprises, this book advocates that in exploring the sources and paths of economic growth, a region should highly value the role of regional governments as market entities in the mezzoeconomic field. This role, in conjunction with the market entity behavior of enterprises in the microeconomic field, forms a correlation effect that jointly promotes sustainable and high-quality development of a region's economy.

From conception to outline to final draft, this book took over three years to complete,

# 后记

　　从亚当·斯密《道德情操论》揭示出的生存在社会中的个人的行为受到自我心与同理心这一对立统一看不见的手所约束，可推导出社会对个体的规制管理具有基于强化自我心、强化同理心、尊重自我心为主兼顾同理心、倡导同理心为主兼顾自我心的四种管理模式。从亚当·斯密《国富论》揭示出的生存在市场中的企业的行为受到利己性与利他性这一对立统一看不见的手所制约，可推导出政府对企业的规制管理具有基于强化利己性、强化利他性、尊重利己性为主兼顾利他性、倡导利他性为主兼顾利己性的四种管理模式。中观经济学揭示出区域政府行为受准微观属性（逐利性/竞争性）与准宏观属性（协调性/合作性）这一对立统一看不见的手所制约，由此也可推导出世界各国对区域政府的规制管理也有基于强化竞争性、强化合作性、以竞争性为主兼顾合作性、以合作性为主兼顾竞争性的四种管理模式。本书在认同比较优势理论提倡的对自然资源禀赋应充分利用和竞争优势理论提倡的应对微观企业的创新进行推动外，倡导一个区域在对经济增长源泉的挖掘和路径探讨中，应高度重视区域政府在中观经济领域的市场主体作用，它与微观经济领域的企业市场主体行为形成关联效应，共同推动着一个区域经济的可持续、高质量发展。

　　本书从立论到撰写大纲再到定稿，历时三年多，其中修改不少于六次。陈

with no less than six revisions. Professor Chen Yunxian is the pioneer of mezzoeconomics, and the competitive advantage theory described in this book originates from Professor Chen's systematic summary of years of practical work experience and deep thinking on regional competitiveness and economic growth issues within the framework of mezzoeconomics. Professor Chen designed the overall approach, writing outline, and logical structure of this book, and wrote the core theoretical parts. Professor Xu Lei has studied mezzoeconomics for many years and undertook the main writing work of the book, including the introduction and comparison of related theories, as well as providing data and case support for theoretical exposition.

Mezzoeconomics is a theoretical economics discipline that has been recently established and is still in the process of development and evolution. Some theoretical logic also needs further empirical or theoretical model verification and support. We sincerely seek advice from fellow economists. We are grateful for the great new era and the process of national reform and opening-up, which has given us opportunities to explore and learn. We also thank editors at Peking University Press, for their tireless efforts in editing, proofreading, typesetting, and other aspects of the manuscript, which ensured the high-quality publication of this book.

November 5, 2024

云贤教授是中观经济学的开创者,本书所阐述的竞争优势理论源自陈云贤教授对多年实践工作经验的系统总结,以及在中观经济学框架下对世界各国区域竞争力和经济增长问题的深度思考。陈云贤教授设计了本书的整体思路、写作提纲和逻辑脉络,并撰写了本书的核心理论部分。徐雷教授对中观经济学研习多年,承担了本书的主要撰写工作,包括对相关理论的介绍与比较,以及为理论阐述提供数据和案例支撑等工作。

中观经济学是一门创立不久且正处于发展演进过程的理论经济学,一些理论逻辑也需要实证或理论模型的进一步验证支撑,我们诚心地请教于各经济学同人。我们要感谢伟大的新时代,国家改革开放的进程给了我们摸爬滚打、不断探索的机会。我们也感谢北京大学出版社的编辑老师,他们在书稿的编审、校对、排版等方面付出了不懈的努力,保证了本书的高质量出版。

2024 年 11 月 5 日